Frantic Panoramas

Frantic Panoramas

American Literature
and Mass Culture, 1870–1920

Nancy Bentley

PENN

University of Pennsylvania Press
Philadelphia

Copyright © 2009 University of Pennsylvania Press

All rights reserved. Except for brief quotations used for purposes of review or scholarly citation, none of this book may be reproduced in any form by any means without written permission from the publisher.

Published by
University of Pennsylvania Press
Philadelphia, Pennsylvania 19104-4112

Printed in the United States of America on acid-free paper

10 9 8 7 6 5 4 3 2 1

Library of Congress Cataloging-in-Publication Data

Bentley, Nancy, 1961–
  Frantic panoramas : American literature and mass culture, 1870–1920 / Nancy Bentley.
    p.   cm.
  Includes bibliographical references and index.
  ISBN 978-0-8122-4174-7 (alk. paper)
  1. American literature—20th century—History and criticism.   2. American literature—19th century—History and criticism.   3. Popular literature—United States—History and criticism.   4. Popular culture and literature—United States—History.   5. Popular culture in literature.   6. Popular culture—United States—History—19th century.   7. Popular culture—United States—History—20th century.   I. Title.
PS228.P67B46   2009
810.9'355—dc22

2009001005

Contents

Introduction: The Analytic Instinct and the Art of the Crash 1

1 Literature and the Museum Idea 22

2 Realism and the Gordian Knot of Aesthetics and Politics 69

3 Women and the Realism of Desire 109

4 Celebrity Warriors, Impossible Diplomats, and the Native Public Sphere 151

5 Black Bohemia and the African American Novel 188

6 Wharton, Mass Travel, and the "Possible Crash" 218

7 Neurological Modernity and American Social Thought 247

Conclusion: Literary Analysis and the Perception of Incongruities 288

Notes 303

Index 349

Acknowledgments 363

Introduction
The Analytic Instinct and the Art of the Crash

On a September day in 1896, more than forty thousand people traveled by chartered railcars to a site fifteen miles north of Waco, Texas, where they prepared to watch a novel form of entertainment: the head-on collision of two locomotive trains. A sign in the newly built depot informed the visitors they had arrived in Crush, Texas, a name that managed to pay tribute to both the spectacular event and the man who had dreamed it up, William George Crush. This was not the first train wreck staged for spectators; William Crush was inspired by a similar event in Ohio earlier in the year, and there had been other planned collisions before that. What newspapers called "the Crash at Crush" belonged to a species of public entertainment that was immediately popular though necessarily rare. But it was a spectacle that quickly was becoming commonplace in the emergent medium of film; by 1905 train and motorcar crashes were already a regular feature in cinematic shorts. Films like *Asleep at the Switch* (1910), *The Railroad Smash-Up* (1904), and *How It Feels to Be Run Over* (1900) brought the mediated experience of observing a high-speed collision to an even larger mass audience, while offering a proximity to the crash that was closer than any eyewitness in Texas or Ohio.[1]

The enduring popularity of cinematic crashes shows that mechanical destruction and kinetic shocks do not necessarily belong outside the sphere of culture, the domain of aesthetic expression and convention. But in 1896, the leading arts authorities no doubt would have objected to including the Texas train crash in the realm of culture, regardless of its drawing power with audiences or its compatibility with film. For some four decades, artists and intellectuals in the United States had been busy building up a very different map of the terrain of culture, organized around an impressive constellation of new metropolitan museums, concert halls, and scholarly institutions. Not long after Crush staged his spectacle in Texas, a number of leading figures in the arts established what would become the American Academy of Arts and Letters. For these founders, a national academy—modeled after the Académie française—would supply the visibility and prestige due the nation's highest artists and institution builders, and they borrowed this Old World form to stake a claim for parity with European nations in matters cultural.[2] For all its appeal, William Crush's brainchild possessed none of the criteria for culture that these authorities were intent on enshrining in civil and even state structures.

But what exactly was the spectacle of a train wreck if not culture? Authorities could not count a railway crash as a species of art, but they knew a rival when they saw one. "The Crash at Crush" was an intensified sensory event that had been deliberately set outside the quotidian realities of everyday life. It excited and moved an audience gathered expressly to see it. To stage the event, Crush had borrowed and developed protocols necessary for constructing a distinct kind of visual and aural experience, protocols that would be cultivated further through the formal resources of film.[3] At the time it was hard to name or classify this order of event. But the genre of staged wrecks was clearly inspired by what William Dean Howells, the first academy president, had dubbed the "spectacular muse," a modern goddess who reigned over a bewildering new landscape of commercial forms and productions, from the visual innovations of advertising to the new sorts of kinetic experience available in amusement parks and urban subcultures. Several decades later, intellectuals would eventually settle on a compromise term for this domain: mass culture.[4] Observers at the time, however, were at a loss and tended to cite older, smaller-scale forms of amusements like the carnival or to invoke the names of publicity titans—P. T. Barnum or Buffalo Bill Cody—in their attempts to find compass points for this seemingly unbounded world.

The close proximity of these "frantic panoramas" to the territories of traditional art was unnerving, and yet the differences seemed all but unaccountable.[5] Like a concert or an art exhibit, the train wreck in Texas drew an eager audience, but the scale of that audience far exceeded what anyone was accustomed to seeing in museums or performance halls. Publicists had expected twenty thousand spectators to make the trip to see the spectacle in Texas, and when twice as many people tried to crowd onto the charter trains, the more adventurous—or more desperate—had to ride on top of the railcars. Authorities thought of culture as something necessarily rooted, as the distinct forms of human cultivation that are an outgrowth of sustained local habitation and continuities of time. But the event in Crush,

Texas, invented its own place and time in the uninhabited space of an empty valley. The train depot, restaurant, bandstands, carnival midway, and two telegraph offices of this nominal town were erected only for what transpired on a single September day. The locale was then abandoned as quickly as it was constructed.[6]

Just as culture was rooted, it was also created and transmitted through forms, the inherited genres, conventions, and story patterns that were the necessary basis for creativity. But the Texas crash was centered on the thrill of watching forms implode. At the moment of impact, familiar shapes and functional forms were violently extinguished in a sudden hail of wreckage, enacting literally what Henry James described as the tendency in modernity toward "collapse of all the forms."[7] To critics, moreover, the events and genres of this new field of culture seemed designed for nothing but the pursuit of sheer sensation. The train wreck in Texas had neither narrative development nor even any human protagonist—at least not until three spectators were killed when the boilers of both locomotives exploded simultaneously and created a force far beyond what engineers had anticipated. The fatalities then fit the mass culture version of tragedy: the "accident" narrative, a genre already developing a set of enduring conventions and a new species of observing subject—the "mass subject," in Michael Warner's formulation—primed to see and read about destructive mechanical accidents and large-scale disasters.[8]

Profit alone was the governing force behind these kinds of spectacular productions. In its fealty to the profit motive, mass culture opened an expressive space freed not just from the tastes of aristocrats and wealthy patrons but also from the judgment of informed critics still attached to evaluating culture through established criteria of beauty. After Crush's successful Texas venture, an entrepreneur who came to be known as "Head-On" Joe Connolly began to accrue a fortune by staging live collisions before crowds that sometimes reached 150,000, making him among the first of many connoisseurs of kinetic wreckage who would succeed in making large amounts of money, especially in Hollywood, from refining the art of the crash.[9] The Texas crash also demonstrated the ease with which mass culture products could create spin-off commodities in other media. Scott Joplin wrote a march, "Great Crush Collision," to capitalize on the fame already in circulation, and an Edison film, *The Railroad Smash-Up*, was directly inspired by the Texas spectacle.[10]

The alarm felt by cultural authorities in the face of mass culture has been well documented. When the American Academy declared its opposition to the "tyranny of novelty," it was a backhanded tribute to the power already wielded by commercial culture.[11] And yet historians' portrait of the "great divide" between high art and mass culture in this period has often obscured as much as it has revealed.[12] It is true—and highly consequential—that the advent of mass culture created starkly different aesthetic forms and styles; giving attention to the distinct aesthetics of mass culture is one of the aims of this book. But it is a mistake to assume that artists at the highest levels were unmoved by the novel sensory experiences and iconic events that drew mass audiences. For leading artists and intellectuals, evocations of vertigo, speed, and collective shock began to supply creative structures and informing energies for use in even the most refined or cerebral of their works.

Even members of the American Academy of Arts and Letters drew on these mass materials. Howells shaped the plots of his novels around events such as rail and trolley accidents and the public chaos of apartment house fires. Although Henry James was distressed by "the collapse of all the forms" in modernity, his own stories and even his sentences seemed to explode the formal conventions of his genre and inject what he called the "imagination of disaster" into the thoughts and haunts of the transatlantic affluent classes.[13] Edith Wharton (nominated in 1908 but not elected to the academy until 1930) made the sensation of anticipating the "possible crash" of a train or car into a dominant motif in her novels.[14] It is not too much to say that Henry Adams, after producing multiple volumes of narrative history, became obsessed with the idea of a destructive historical velocity, a physical force that outstripped any narrative form and one that would finally leave his "historical neck broken by the sudden irruption of forces totally new."[15] William James wrote often of physical feelings of "ontological wonder-sickness" that characterized modern life. As unnerving as he sometimes seemed to find those uprooted sensory symptoms, however, James also represented creative breakthroughs in his thinking in similar sensorial terms—as the result of "speeding with the train to Buffalo," for instance, or of looking up at a workman "on the dizzy edge of a sky-scaling iron construction," a sight, he wrote, that "brought me to my senses very suddenly."[16] W. E. B. DuBois (spurned by the academy until 1944, when he was seventy-six) turned to disaster fables to transform standard modes of sociological analysis, imagining sensory reactions to scenarios such as a comet striking Manhattan or comparing the historical "movement" of the world to a "rushing express."[17] Devoted as they were to matching the highest cultural achievements of Europe, these writers were still drawn to the unique kinds of sensorial consciousness emerging in modern commercial culture and explored overtly in a film like *How It Feels to Be Run Over*.

What is the significance of these momentary convergences between otherwise opposed domains? I take this question as a governing critical lens for understanding the high literary culture that emerged in the United States at the turn of the century and its self-appointed task of analyzing mass culture. In response to the scholarship that emphasized a definitive divide between literary culture and mass culture, a number of scholars have stressed aesthetic continuities that unite these disparate domains, finding unintended similarities between the prose of Henry James and the "consuming vision" of the urban shopper, for instance, or between the Kantian "laws of beauty" in Howells's fiction and the "aesthetic equipment of the slum."[18] While this second wave of scholarship has produced far-reaching insight—much of which I have drawn upon in this study—it tends to erase crucial differences in the social location of cultural production and thus to elide what I will argue is the era's most important structural development: the uneven, conflicted intersection of the bourgeois public sphere with the emergent publics (such as cinema, consumer cultures, and mass publications) made possible through mass-mediated communication and industry. In order to highlight this *intersection* of different locations, it is important to resist the move to place mass culture and high culture on a single plane. Both are products of the same modern conditions, to be sure, but so is every object or process from this same period if we take up too distant an analytic vantage point. I approach this encounter between literary culture and mass culture not as a symptom of modernity but as a modern event—and not simply a *literary* event (the category theorized by scholars such as Hans Robert Jauss and Pascale Casanova) but an event in social history that inaugurates a "postliterary" era when literary culture could no longer presume to be the implicit model of the public sphere and the central arena for negotiating norms of public reason.[19]

Jürgen Habermas famously diagnosed this event as the "disintegration of the public sphere in the world of letters." His compelling historical study describes the "collapse" of the literary public sphere in this moment, a breakdown that occurred when the dialectic joining private reading and public discussion was severed by a new culture industry based in forms of mass communication. Because Habermas models public discourse after a reading public (the bourgeois public sphere that emerged in eighteenth-century Europe), for him the postliterary communication and association fostered by mass media cannot be truly public—intersubjective, reflexive, critical, and at least partially autonomous from private economic interests. With the advent of mass culture, Habermas argues, "the web of public communication unraveled into acts of individuated reception" within consumer culture, on one hand, and more privatized, estranging avant-garde literary production, on the other.[20] Subsequent scholars have argued that it is possible to accept Habermas's history of a transformation in the public sphere while still contending that other types of circulation—no longer modeled after a reading public—might offer conditions for public reason and reflexivity.[21] But scholars on all sides of the debate agree that whether communicative modes cultivated in sites like cinema and the mass press can count as genuinely public, they are qualitatively different from the modes of circulation and reception that characterize literary culture.

The encounter between literary culture and postliterary publicity is the story at the heart of *Frantic Panoramas*. The effort by U.S. literary authors to come to grips with a new order of mass culture publicity, I argue, was not simply a matter of patrician recoil or an attempt at social control. Nor was it merely a strategy for converting mass culture material into the formal innovations of modernism. Instead, the literary analysis of mass culture expression, experience, and conditions was an attempt to understand the fate of literary expression in its relation to public communication and reason—critical issues that have continued to intrigue and vex cultural critics throughout the twentieth century and into our own postmodern moment. What is needed is a way to understand how and why writers found critical resources in the transformations wrought by mass culture, even as they posed tough-minded questions about changes in cultural perception and expressivity that they could not wish away. Pursuing the question of convergence, then, requires close attention to the separate institutions, aims, and genealogies that created markedly distinct spheres.

To pursue the history of this postliterary encounter, this study follows a method of cultural close reading that offers sustained, comparative analyses of high art and mass forms in immediate conjunction with one another. Henry James's fiction, I argue, can be read next to the kinetic experience available at amusement parks and the bravado style of lithograph posters. I analyze the writing of Howells alongside the dime museum, burlesque theater, and how-to manuals for getting rich. The rise of the African American novel achieved through the work of Charles Chesnutt, Paul Laurence Dunbar, and Pauline Hopkins is understood through analysis of "Black Bohemia," the generative urban culture of black musicals, dance, and celebrity performers like Aida Overton Walker and Leo Gowongo. Kate Chopin's fiction, I argue, can be illuminated by innovations in the design of department stores, innovations that are both a stimulation for and a record of desublimated female desire. I analyze the writing of Native American intellectuals such as Arthur Parker, Charles Eastman, and Gertrude Bonnin in tandem with the international fame of Wild West performers and the celebrity charisma of Geronimo.

Broadening my critical framework, I include literary analyses of some of the global economic transformations that created the commercial matrix for mass culture forms. Edith Wharton's polished fiction is reinterpreted in light of the new exhilarations and hazards produced in mass transportation and the "Americanization" of culture around the globe. I read the social thinkers Henry Adams, W. E. B. DuBois, William James, and John Dewey as writers who grapple with the disorder and energies erupting from mass print, technology, and consumer capitalism, as those energies transformed a literary model of the human subject. Finally, I examine Henry James's cultural criticism alongside the generative effects of astonishment, disjuncture, and involuntary memory solicited in the early "cinema of attractions." Hostility and friction are evident in all of these encounters, but this friction, I argue, is also formative: although literary culture secured its autonomy as a separate sphere in this moment, high culture only became high through its hostile intimacy with the low. What Howells called "the flair of theatrical facts" became in turn a source of critical illumination, as writers drew upon the incongruities of mass culture to help fashion a new kind of literary analysis equal to the age.[22]

A larger historical irony lies behind the confrontation between mass culture and high art in this moment. In fulfilling the charge to create an "academic institution of unquestioned origin and standard," the founders of the American Academy were convinced that the United States could finally make a secure claim to world-class achievements in the arts.[23] The academy itself did not always reward the most talented or innovative American artists and critics, but its appearance as an official institution is an accurate enough index of the fact that this former colonial stepchild was making good on its ambitions to match the great powers of Europe in culture as well as commerce.[24] And yet, at the very moment the United States caught up to European nations in high culture, the global game was changing in a profound way. Arjun Appadurai describes this change as a deep structural shift, gaining momentum throughout the twentieth century, through which mass culture helped invent a new social role for the human imagination. For Appadurai, the advent of mass culture marked an epochal transition by which institutions of religion, art, and the state lost their effective monopoly over social imaginaries and personal imagining.[25]

The picture of global culture that emerges from the work of Appadurai and others is as paradoxical as it is provocative. As modern world systems have made societies of almost every kind increasingly bureaucratic and rationalized, the result has not been "the disenchantment of the world" predicted by Max Weber but something closer to the opposite: a startling expansion of the role of the imagination in everyday life. In Appadurai's terms, "The image, the imagined, the imaginary—these are all terms that direct us to something critical and new in global processes: the imagination as a social practice." There is nothing new, of course, in the idea that social norms are animated and sustained by myth, ritual, and expressive art, or that those norms can be altered or even overturned by the same energies of cultural imagining. In that sense the imagination has always been a social practice. But the history of global modernization, Appadurai argues, produces a decisive break with earlier epochs when it was only forceful leaders—the charismatic individuals who fostered "great revolutions, cargo cults, and messianic movements"—who could inject a new social vision into ordinary lives and thus reorder the traditional patterns of imagination informing everyday life.[26] In contrast with earlier eras, however, modern technology and its expressive offshoot, mass culture, have made it possible for currents of imagination to bypass the dictates of tradition and charismatic leaders alike. Increasingly, ordinary individuals select for themselves the stories, images, and sonic rhythms that most stimulate their memory and desire, choosing from the materials of a mass-mediated imaginary that is more or less detached from the tastes of higher authorities and very often indifferent to national boundaries. That it is global capitalism that supplants traditional authorities as the agent of transmission and distribution, of course, may fatally compromise any idea that this shift represents an advance. But for Appadurai and others, these changes allow for at least the possibility that cultural subjects—not just individuals but groups, and not just producers but far-flung consumers—can "annex the global into their own practices of the modern."[27]

Appadurai's theory is an especially provocative hypothesis for students of literature, suggesting as it does that the stuff of art—concrete stories and images, resonant scripts and roles, imagined worlds—have become more important after global modernization, not less. And yet the same history of modernization introduces new uncertainty about the literary as a distinct domain; after the advent of mass culture and the transformations wrought by modern empire and trade, it becomes far more difficult to give literature and the arts pride of place as a laboratory of the human imagination. If Appadurai is correct, the imagination has become more socially significant precisely for having "broken out of the special expressive spaces of art, myth, and ritual" through routes opened up by mass media, migration, and global commerce.[28] Although many aspects of this historical argument are debatable, it presents an intriguing if surprising concurrence with Habermas's history of the origins of a postliterary era.

Against this uneven and still uncertain historical backdrop, I focus in this study on the intersection of two large transnational currents—the institutionalization of high culture and the inauguration of a mass-mediated imaginary—as the most illuminating context for understanding U.S. literary culture of this era, a context that approaches a self-consciously national project through far-reaching transnational developments. Viewed in this context, the literary object begins to look like an unstable compound molecule: literacy and print, mediated images, and everyday acts of imagining were becoming more powerful than ever before, even as the meaning and fate of literature as an institution were becoming more volatile and open to question.

From one perspective, Appadurai's account adds up to a hard luck story for the U.S. cultural elite of this era. At the moment that American artists finally earn a place alongside those of Europe, the foundation of their success was already eroding fast. The American Academy's assumption that "purity of expression" and refinement of perception were the true measures of cultural achievement was being abandoned—not just by the mass public but eventually by artists themselves. High modernism would soon arrive on the scene to reabsorb the more unruly energies of modernity for the domain of elite art and, in the process, generate a new mythology of the heroic dissenting artist. The intellectuals and artists who preceded the more self-conscious movement we call modernism, then, have often been portrayed as belonging to a becalmed historical moment, a "genteel" generation (few adjectives are as damning) that was too bound by conformity to heed the seismic changes remaking the world around them. The artistic virtues that seemed the most valuable and forward-looking to this generation—polished form and skillful execution, an ability to meet the highest standards inherited from European traditions—were viewed as the most backward. Nor have these American advocates of culture been portrayed as simply out of step. In the eyes of more suspicious critics, their efforts at fostering hierarchies of taste and building new institutions of high culture in this period were veiled ways of exercising social control. Fighting the "tyranny of novelty" was its own decorous form of tyranny, a way of turning high culture to the work of social discipline.[29]

There is much in the historical record to support this picture of an alarmed elite for whom high culture was a refuge and an indirect source of class power. But this line of interpretation is also marred by significant blind spots. Clearly turn-of-the-century artists and intellectuals distrusted mass culture, sometimes reflexively, and the social class that profited most from modernization was also drawn to anachronistic or seemingly "antimodern" cultural styles.[30] But the more open and incisive thinkers, I contend, confronted this antagonist with real intellectual curiosity, looking closely at a strange external landscape of mass forms that still seemed to have the uncanny ability to shape human subjectivity from within. And competition also produces kinship: as I demonstrate in the chapters that follow, American artists and intellectuals learned from and, indeed, even imitated elements of the rival mass culture they also subjected to sharp critical analysis. The critical habits and techniques that seemed most under threat, I will argue, are in fact the *product* of an emergent postliterary moment in which artists and intellectuals were required to rethink the relation of literature and public discourse. Understanding their artistic production and critical thought thus depends on recognizing the context of mass culture not just as a source of friction but also as a spur to insight and high creativity. Reading from this perspective changes the backstory regarding the place of high literary culture in a larger global history: what from one angle looks like a piece of bad luck for U.S. ambitions can be seen from another as a fortuitous conjunction, a moment in which sharpened techniques of literary analysis met a brave new world of commercial culture. I situate literary culture not at the end of a declining Victorian regime but at the beginning of the analytic exploration of sensory consciousness that has generated much of the critical theory of our time.

As Henry James saw it, an "analytic instinct" had become the "supreme" aesthetic value of the age.[31] This is a key insight that requires careful unpacking. Attachment to analysis, I will argue, implants a certain contradiction in the turn-of-the-century effort to make high culture serve the ends of national elevation. Advocates looked to art for civic uplift and even social redemption—or, by another name, social control. They were convinced that building up the best cultural institutions would produce a more unified nation: an "America of art." But this national project produced dissonant results that most scholars have overlooked. For many Americans, the push for high culture threatened to drain art of its spiritual qualities and seemed to foster habits of critical penetration they often found unnerving. Even educated viewers and readers frequently found the "analytic school" unpleasant or distressing—too cerebral, too unsparing, too close to what is performed in a medical dissection. Indeed, one reviewer complained that Howells's fiction serves up "Boston under the scalpel," and Thomas Eakins's paintings of surgeons operating on unconscious patients struck many as a grotesque confirmation of the worst tendencies in modern art.[32] Artists and critics were after more than simply entrenching the cultural sovereignty of a genteel tradition, and their aims and ambitions provoked resistance in more than one quarter.

The larger significance of this new taste for analytic art, however, lies with its indirect and often elusive effects. To anyone who read his work, James's own "analytic instinct" was obvious; it quickly became notorious. But he was only the most overt of the writers devoted to creating art that could offer, in James's words, "a more analytic consideration of appearances."[33] Howells liked to advertise American literary realism as "democracy in literature," but even scholars who debate his achievement have too quickly accepted the label at face value, echoing the idea that his fiction was designed to foster a cohesive citizenry by representing a "common" world of everyday life that should be of interest to all. In truth, however, Howells's way of articulating the common—in terms of the typical, the probable, and other sociological regularities—was also a function of the "analytic instinct" applied to the art of the novel. The operations of mental selection necessary to grasp meaningful types and socially illuminating plots were not democratic operations; this species of analytic mentality was far from common, as Howells knew all too well. Pleasure in the art of the scalpel was an acquired taste; it required readerly training and a kind of reflective mentality far more likely to appeal to the men and women of the new professional classes than to a broad democratic citizenry. As Phillip Barrish has argued about realist fiction, moreover, it is likely that no small part of the appeal of embracing advanced culture was the social distinction one could claim by possessing restricted tastes.[34] The aesthetic sensibilities most responsive to the new institutions of high culture can be seen as counterparts to the new kinds of mental operations and reflexive thinking emerging in a competitive industrialized society where science and technology were ascendant powers.[35]

Leading artists and intellectuals, then, shared a marked if sometimes uneasy attraction to the powers of secular, analytic reason. In the realm of culture, that power was perhaps most visible in the new institution of the metropolitan museum, a secular temple for modernity that replaced the cathedral as the leading institution for housing authentic artifacts and expert authority. As historian Steven Conn notes, the list of museums founded during this period is "staggering"; major institutions appeared in virtually every large American city and many midsize ones as well.[36] Drawing on both historical evidence and textual analysis, I show that advocates sought to give American letters and philosophy the new civic glamour enjoyed by the modern museum. But this effort was at odds with its own aspirations to represent (in both senses) the collective life of the nation. For, in contrast with the largely secular tendencies of the new analytic culture, what Americans shared most in matters of culture was an affinity for religion and, increasingly, a taste for the experiences available through mass media and entertainment. (In fact, Gregory Jackson has shown how innovators were bringing these two currents, evangelical religion and mass culture, into new forms of conjunction at just this moment.)[37] As a result, the analytic habits prized by leading critics and artists engendered precisely the kind of social static that great art, literary expertise, and elevated culture were supposed to transcend.

Writers found different ways to suppress this indwelling tension—though some (like Mark Twain and Charles Chesnutt) preferred to finesse or exploit it and others (like DuBois) to politicize it. Howells, for one, attempted to make fiction an instrument of cultural pedagogy that would turn the popularity of the novel to the work of cultivating higher tastes in a broad national public. But at a moment when publishers had succeeded in making the novel into what James called a mass "article of commerce" and a thing of "easy manufacture," Howells's pedagogical project had to push back against the very novelistic pleasures that were drawing huge numbers of new readers to the genre.[38] How does one inculcate a taste for secular reason, for analytic dissection and the pleasures of critical detachment and reflection? For Howells in particular, mass culture seemed a nemesis, a rival for the work of shaping the sensibilities of a national public. Heedless of any objectives other than profit (for producers) and sentiment or sensation (for consumers), the new terrain of mass culture appeared able to seduce even cultivated people into seeking out experiences that in Howells's view afforded no contemplative thought or directed purpose. And yet, precisely because he looked to an art form to foster a more analytic sensibility, Howells's pedagogical project was built on the implicit understanding that rationality is embedded in one's sensory life, that it is conjoined at some level with unreflective, bodily experience—an understanding, in other words, that reason is not wholly the other of mass culture's sensation seeking. James's conceit of an "analytic instinct," a mental operation akin to a bodily reflex, carried the same unspoken understanding.

In this and other ways, high culture's confrontation with mass culture put new pressure on reigning assumptions about reason. By examining how and why high literary culture invested new value in the analytic, this study shares an interest with a body of recent scholarship on the "cultivation of detachment" in nineteenth-century Anglo-American art and criticism.[39] Motivated in part by a desire to challenge anti-Enlightenment critiques of liberal thought they consider too sweeping, these scholars reexamine the forms of rationality—from scientific objectivity and political disinterestedness to cosmopolitanism—that nineteenth-century artists and thinkers championed for the ends of art. Literary scholars, they urge, are obliged to be more discriminating about the nineteenth-century romance with reason, to pose questions and parse differences. When writers such as Matthew Arnold and George Eliot sought to valorize habits of critical distance, were they showing an unwitting allegiance with the more pernicious Enlightenment legacies of instrumental reason and social surveillance? Or were they instead cultivating practices that might be capable of loosening the tight bonds between modern knowledge and modern power? When political writers like Frederick Douglass and DuBois appealed to the principle of universalism, could their use of this Enlightenment ideal break with the history of racial oppression underwritten by the texts of the Enlightenment? This book confirms scholars' contention that "modern practices of detachment" became a governing preoccupation and an inspiration for art in this period.[40] And I share a desire to refrain from deciding in advance whether the "analytic instinct" that animated American high culture was necessarily disciplinary or emancipatory. In their faith in and fondness for analysis, these nineteenth-century literary authorities are our critical ancestors, whether or not we wish to claim the kinship. Rather than impose a sharp, qualitative difference on the nature of their critical practices, we can assume that their investment in analytic thought (whatever their distinct methods and archives) had the same potential for discovering insight—or falling into error and distortion—as our own.

As a working premise of this study, then, I take up analytic art as both a historical object and as genuine critical practice, an aesthetic body of thought that is not wholly different in kind than the critical operations I undertake to interpret it. Where I depart from other scholars, however, is in their tendency to see these writers' cultivation of "detachment" as part of a more or less unified cultural project—as constituting a liberal public sphere, for instance, or a transnational cosmopolitan community. In the cultural field I examine, the cosmopolitan values and habits of critical analysis never operate in uniform ways—nor even in the same critical spaces. This becomes especially clear when we widen the purview of high literary culture and consider not just the literary establishment that had acquired new civic prestige for American letters but also adjacent cultural projects that drew on the same energies of critical thought but remained invisible or excluded from the arts establishment.

The intellectuals who founded the American Negro Academy, for instance, were as committed as anyone in the period to the idea that high art and critical thought were to be prized. But they also knew that the white "cultured classes" were largely hostile to their goals and had excluded African Americans from most museums and concert halls. Native American intellectuals in this era originated literary traditions in English that are the foundation for the Native Renaissance of the 1960s and 1970s. Yet their efforts to articulate what Arthur Parker called an indigenous "thought world" proved all but impossible to disentangle from the mass culture publicity that was the conflicted foundation of Native public address. Indeed, close examination shows that it was the iconic fame of a celebrity like Geronimo or the glamour of Bill Cody's "show Indians"—far more than the writings of members of the Society for the American Indian—that brought Native expressive cultures within the purview of a collective "America of art." These fissures in the terrain of high culture in the United States make it a good deal harder to rely on governing liberal tenets when trying to understand literary culture, for a shared dedication to reflective thought did not produce commensurate spaces of public reason or aesthetic expression. To pursue the implications of this issue, I examine four cultural projects from this era—literary realism, African American belletristic letters, Native American scholarly production, and American pragmatism—all of which share an attraction to the powers of secular, analytic reason but which together display markedly uneven, syncopated, or broken connections between aesthetic reflection and liberal ideas of public reason.

These fractures might well cast doubt on aesthetic culture as a coherent category. What authorities touted as a single human capacity—the capacity for aesthetic feeling and judgment—can begin to look like the distinct sensibilities of separate classes or populations, an epiphenomenon of the social rather than a phenomenon of the aesthetic. Pierre Bourdieu has developed the most powerful theoretical account of aesthetic feeling as a social "taste for necessity"—as a responsiveness to cultural styles and objects that seems spontaneous and freely embraced but that is at bottom an index of one's deepest structures of socialization, the habitus rooted in class location.[41] In surveying institutions of culture in the turn-of-the-century United States, it is easy to surmise that social divisions are the real basis for cultural distinctions. When Antonin Dvorak, appointed in 1892 to direct the new National Conservatory of Music, proposed that "negro melodies of America" could be the foundation for the future of American symphonic music, most in the U.S. music world viewed the idea as the "absurd" error of an outsider, a European "negrophile" unable to grasp his basic category mistake. Even among those who were persuaded by the idea, moreover, Dvorak's prospect represented the absorption of a folk expression—a "spontaneous musical utterance" from out of "the canebrake and the cotton field"—into what would continue to be white institutions.[42] Reasoning in this way made it possible for white classical music authorities to recognize the powerful appeal of black "folksongs" while still remaining certain that African Americans themselves were "not inherently musical" and retaining their ignorance of or indifference to accomplished choral groups such as the Samuel Coleridge-Taylor Society of Washington, D.C.[43]

Yet even though the divisions in American expressive culture from this era reveal that cultural institutions were wedded to social hierarchies, a closer examination ultimately points to a different relation between the aesthetic and the social than the one-directional relation theorized by Bourdieu. Despite the analytic habits shared widely among literary intellectuals, a divided society produced divided literary publics. But the artists and intellectuals in these disparate social worlds also shared a formative experience: a cautious, conflicted encounter with mass culture as a powerful force field that seemed able to unravel socialized identities at the deep level of sensory experience and thus to unsettle inherited structures of feeling and perceiving. The internalized social position Bourdieu calls the habitus was precisely the structure of subjectivity most in question. For better or worse, inside the dizzying spaces of mass culture an individual's specific social location no longer seemed to strictly dictate experience or perception, even as traits of specific bodies—the defiant postures of white men, the angular grace of cakewalk dancers, the prowess of the Indian warrior—were among the fragments of sensory subjectivity reproduced in these mimetic zones and newly represented before spectators of both sexes and all class strata.[44]

The effects of this commercial mimesis were never certain. The potential for unsettling socialized tastes and perceptions is by no means proof that mass culture operated at cross-purposes with the reigning social restrictions and ideological norms; indeed, in an era of Jim Crow oppression and the aftermath of the Indian wars, the most profitable mass productions were often the most racist. But even the traffic in racist expressive objects belonged to the larger repertoire of pleasurable shocks that had the capacity to loosen inherited dispositions. If we assume with Bourdieu that the social habitus governs aesthetic taste, then, we will fail to account for the incoherence that mass culture was capable of introducing into the cultural field. Howells was dismayed, for instance, that middle-class men and women were just as eager as the uncultivated to see the theatrical troupes in which actresses dressed and performed as men. Mass markets catered to an appetite for departing from habitual roles and perceptions, and thereby fostered an uneven cultural topography with gaps and folds in aesthetic tastes and experiences that did not match hierarchies of class and race. The legalized racism of segregation could coexist with white Americans' admiration and even aspirational imitation of black expressive styles, just as state dispossession of Native peoples could go hand in hand with public stardom for notorious chiefs like Sitting Bull and mass fascination with Indian performances of "authentic" feats of battlefield riding and shooting.

Little wonder, then, that the energies of mass culture provoked the interest and alarm of cultural critics across a fractured society. Intellectuals operating in disparate critical spaces, from elite universities and literary journals to a Lakota reservation, together produced a shared examination of what historian James Livingston has called the "cultural revolution" at the end of the century, the tipping-point moment when consumer culture finally became an "unstable isotope" disrupting long-established ways of understanding selfhood and the social order. For Livingston this revolution enacted a shift in the way culture ratified authority, a transition from Atlantic ideologies of republican virtue to new sites of self-discovery in what William James called the "worldly wilderness" of industrial-commercial culture.[45] Although Livingston tends to elide differences in these unruly territories, the literary intellectuals of this period uncovered conflicting dimensions of mass culture; the commercial location of the "low" could have very different implications for white women or Native Americans than it did for European immigrants or male Ivy League professors. But literary intellectuals from all quarters, I argue, converged in a shared discovery: reflecting on sensory modes of mass modernity could change the very idea of rational reflection.

When Maxim Gorky described the experience of watching Lumière's famous cinematograph *The Arrival of a Train*, shown at a fair in 1896, he underscored the feeling of sensory invasion and bodily threat: "It speeds right at you—watch out! It seems as though it will plunge into the darkness in which you sit, turning you into a ripped sack full of lacerated flesh and splintered bones." Gorky's response was double, a mix of astonishment and dismay. Like many intellectuals, Gorky was uneasy at his own susceptibility to this startling form of entertainment and felt disdain at the idea of its mass appeal. However vivid the images, what is on the screen, he stressed, is "but a train of shadows." Anticipating a line of interpretation that would be developed further by critics on the left, Gorky argued that the stimulation and visual excess of film are really an index of the empty distractions crowding the spaces of modern industrial life. "Before you life is surging" on the screen, but it is "a life deprived of words and shorn of the living spectrum of colours—the grey, the soundless, the bleak and dismal life." Similarly, when he visited Coney Island in 1906, Gorky saw crowds caught in "slavery to a varied boredom," enchained by "an amazement in which there is neither transport nor joy."[46] External distractions seemed to correspond with a depletion of the mental life of the modern subject.

For all his disapproval, of course, Gorky found real significance in sites like film and modern amusement parks. Even if mass culture was regrettable or degraded, this low sphere still had a high critical value: it was a site for theorizing a broader aesthetics of distraction that was saturating everyday life, in the world of work as well as leisure. These expressive sites thus offered the analyst a privileged glimpse into the social enervation and restrictions of human freedom that were the real ends of modernization. For a thinker like Theodor Adorno, mass culture would remain the illuminating antithesis of the domain of high art, which was the only aesthetic domain capable of recollecting through its "halo of uniqueness" the lost unity in which human poiesis is merged with a larger absolute. In this view, the culture industry represents the victory of capital's encroachment into the furthest reaches of human imagining, a victory that can be resisted only by the most strenuous efforts of artistic genius.[47]

Like a latter-day doctrine of original sin, the possibility that commercial culture represents the total victory of capitalist interests is not easily countered, especially as it is articulated in Adorno's powerful critique. The possibility that we are the peasants of capital perhaps cannot ever be banished.[48] But among the intellectuals who explored commercial culture as a site of knowledge, the conclusions extracted by thinkers like Gorky and

Adorno represent only one strain of thought. For others, mass culture and commercial conditions were also a catalyst for returning anew to what Georg Simmel called "the sensory foundation of mental life" as a field in which to speculate on the possibilities that might emerge from the very changes wrought by modern capitalism. The profound changes to what Stephen Kern has described as "the culture of time and space" during this period—changes brought about by both technology and expressive culture—did not always look like they were leading to the depletion of a richer or more integrated kind of existence, or at least not to depletion alone.[49] Gorky understood his own sensations as a filmgoer in terms of cultural reification, but other writers would have approached the experience in the theater ("It speeds right at you—watch out!") not as an empty distraction but as a telling mental event, a distinct kind of imagining that realizes the idea of "flesh" or of a train as a form of sensory consciousness and thus as a witness to the startling truth that thoughts and things do not inhabit different ontological orders.

Uncovering the coextensive ontology of the mind and the world became the unorthodox goal of the American pragmatists. The disciplinary tools of philosophy and science, these thinkers believed, could turn analytic thought against the very disciplinary divide that sequestered the operations of the mind from the materiality of bodies and things. More startling yet, they came to argue that the "meeting of Mind and Reality," as John Dewey put it, occurs as much in activities of commercial "Trade" as in those of art, language, and thought.[50] By turning from the truths of logic to the matrix of experience, pragmatists sought out the dynamic speeds and "altered equilibriums" of a commercial society as the potential source of new ideals and social norms. Opposition to mass culture from pragmatists like William James, then, came from an unexpected direction. James worried that the "excessive novel-reading and theatre-going" encouraged by mass producers were making Americans too much like remote spectators who only looked on the world from a distance—it was making them, in other words, too much *like* traditional philosophers, observers blind to the interanimating processes by which mental activities and forms of worldly matter were forever mutually re-creating reality.[51]

But what if the energies of mass print and spectacle could be harnessed for new forms of thinking, infused into new modes of writing? For Walter Benjamin, the invention of cinema supplied a new and necessary aesthetic form in which "perception in the form of shocks was established as a formal principle," a formal principle, moreover, that Benjamin could adopt in turn for his own critical writing.⁵² Similarly, when social scientists like Henry Adams and W. E. B. DuBois found the protocols of their disciplines too limited for an analysis of modern life, they forged new kinds of writing, genres that permitted shock, velocity, and the somatic apprehension of force to become the formal means of generating insight. Brought together in composite forms, the incongruity of high and low materials might reopen topics such as lynching, nationalism, and Whig historicism that had hardened into closed sociological objects or historical dogma. DuBois and Adams, I argue, create literary analyses that owe as much to the "worldly wilderness" of mass culture as they do to established genres of literary fiction and autobiography.

Efforts to fashion disciplinary styles of thought into new mass genres, however, were distinctly less successful. Howells's attempt to have his brand of realist fiction supplant romance, for instance, did not prevail (although the writer he championed as the "greatest romancer," Mark Twain, did find ways to fashion "theatrical facts" into analytic narrative forms while still reaching a broad audience).⁵³ Similarly, John Dewey's early experiment in adapting techniques of the press for philosophy, a projected publication called *Thought News*, never got off the ground. Far more lasting, however, were the transformations effected *within* modes of critical thought and analytic art by intimate encounters with commercial culture, especially when the disorientations—both conceptual and somatic—deliberately cultivated by mass forms seemed to offer glimpses of new collectivities and ideals. In contemplating a mass reading audience in the millions (or the "fast-arriving billion"), Henry James recognized with no little dismay that a literary public of this scale would necessarily change the meaning of literature itself. In his essay "The Question of the Opportunities," he points to the fact that the literary criteria of "vitality and distinction" had become unfixed, and the very task of evaluating the worth of writing would be profoundly changed, since "all this depends on what we take it into our head to *call* literature." Yet James is also able to recognize an exhilarating prospect ("the drama and bliss when not the misery") inherent in the same enormity of scale that caused him such discomfort. For the very massiveness of the enterprise held the possibility of "new light struck out by the material itself." James seems to surprise even himself by his willingness to wager on commercial culture as a site of opportunity: "It is impossible not to entertain with patience and curiosity the presumption that life so colossal must break into expression at points of proportionate frequency. These places, these moments will be the chances."⁵⁴

Seen in retrospect, what James describes as "the question of the opportunities" may be said to mark a transitional moment when the bourgeois public sphere intersected with another order of publicness, an order consisting of what theorist Miriam Hansen has described as "industrial-commercial forms of publicity." Quite clearly, this commercial order does not even pretend to inhabit a location above the marketplace, but, by the same token, production and circulation in this domain are "no longer predicated on the exclusionary hierarchies of literary culture." Hansen describes a moment in which the turbulent conjunction of these publics creates spaces in which experience may be ordered either from above—by standards from high culture or social relations favored by the interests of capital—or from below—by the needs, desires, and mobile dispositions of experiencing subjects themselves, situated in different social locations. The fact that templates for giving shape to thought and feeling might come from either above or below is precisely the point. Whereas for Habermas the ascendance of mass culture can only signify the decline and disintegration of critical public discourse, Hansen sees the intersection of commercial and literary publics—enacted through modes of exploitation, alliance, and mutual borrowing—as a way that competing forms of collective social experience yielded possibilities for a "politics of relationality."[55] The hopefulness of such a prospect does not lie in a naïve or programmatic conviction that would equate mass culture consumption with political populism. Rather, the utopian dimension lies in the critical edge inherent in the idea of a public— inherent even in competing publics, in contest with one another but also thereby in relation—that offers structural conditions for possibilities of collective self-determination and world building.

William James gestured toward a similar notion of public possibilities when he argued that "altered equilibriums and redistributions diversify our opportunities and chances for new ideals."[56] The dynamic changes James calls "redistributions" presume different social worlds in conflict or disequilibrium—but they also presume a potential value inherent in those very differences. Protective of its autonomy and hard-won prestige, high literary culture attempted to sustain an institutional distance from both low pleasures of the masses and the "grope of wealth" of the rich, although efforts at disavowing Gilded Age materialism were compromised by institutionalizing projects that relied on the wealth of the new industrialists.[57] As much as this distance made literary culture insular, however, it also formed a structural distance across which habits of contemplative appreciation could be refashioned into new forms of critical thought, strains of analytic reflection alert to what the resulting frictions and contingencies might apprehend or create for the future. The high literary culture of this period is thus one in which "the rush of physical joy" of riding in a motorcar can count for Edith Wharton as the material for a novel of manners and where the dread of a "possible crash" can emerge as a literary trope that reverberates across fractured social spaces.[58] It is a culture in which Henry James, a mobile, "restless analyst," is compelled to study the "sword-swallowing" conspicuousness of the commercialized New York cityscape, and he does so with a style that could aspire to match the prowess of a Wild West performer, wrestling the unruly modern world with thought that styles itself as "great loops thrown out by the lasso of observation from the wonder-working motor-car."[59]

Chapter 1
Literature and the Museum Idea

William Dean Howells, in an 1888 editorial column for *Harper's Magazine*, noted that four prestigious American periodicals—*The Century*, *Scribner's*, the *Atlantic Monthly*, and his own *Harper's*—had all simultaneously published new stories by Henry James. "The effect," Howells writes, "was like an artist's exhibition." This "accidental massing" of James's fiction, in other words, reminded Howells of a unique kind of public place, the museum or exhibit gallery: "one turned from one masterpiece to another," viewing "a high perfection" on display in each one. Howells's trope, comparing published fiction to a museum exhibit, was not in itself unusual. A century earlier, for instance, a New York City serial that included fiction and poetry appeared under the title *Weekly Museum* (1788–1817). But the assumptions that motivate Howells's trope in the 1880s differ sharply from those that had informed the title of the earlier serial. The New York weekly was a "museum" because it collected for the reader heterogeneous materials of general interest, advertising itself as a "repository" or "assemblage of whatever can interest the mind." By 1888, however, the figure of the museum no longer connotes eclecticism but rather a consistency of "high perfection," aesthetic purity rather than diversity.[1] Howells's use of the museum trope, moreover, bespeaks a new kind of cultural authority also absent from the earlier era. By invoking the museum, he claims for fiction the imprimatur of a defining modern institution whose authority is based first and last on the importance of disciplined representation, the specialized exhibition of images and objects. Howells's analogy draws on the currency of what his contemporary George Brown Goode, director of the Smithsonian, called the modern "museum idea."[2]

As Goode's phrase suggests, in the later nineteenth century the museum is not just an institution or site but a resonant, organizing idea with a profound influence on cultural perception itself. The "museum idea" is also a literary idea: an ability to distill the values of high cultural authority and distinction makes the museum an important topos in the pages of fiction. Henry James opens the first scene of his novel *The American* (1877) in a room in the Louvre, one of innumerable gallery scenes in his novels. Henry Adams's novel *Esther* (1884) aggressively recasts New York's Cathedral of Saint John into a secular gallery for viewing religious art as treasures of humanist culture. Edith Wharton in *The Age of Innocence* (1920) locates a crucial meeting between lovers in front of a glassed-in collection of antiquities in the New York Metropolitan Museum of Art. The museum's importance as a symbolic site also makes it a setting for some of the most penetrating critiques of dominant cultural values. Jane Addams makes the art galleries of Europe her site for challenging the social sensibilities of affluent Americans. W. E. B. DuBois includes in his masterwork *The Souls of Black Folk* (1903) a race fable played out in a New York concert hall, and he uses the Chicago Institute of Art as a setting in his novel *Dark Princess* (1928).

What is even more significant than these works' museum settings is the fact that they address a reader who shares, or should aspire to share, the savvy of the novels' cosmopolitan characters. Unlike most of the fiction that preceded them, such works expect of their readers the same subtle discriminations of observation, the specialized tastes, and the acts of trained attention required of visitors to metropolitan museums. The museumgoer's habits of perception, moreover, are presumed by these writers to be indispensable for understanding the wider world. When the narrator of one of James's novels says that the characters form a "little gallery" (one woman is a "pastel under glass"), when he calls the country villa where they gather a "museum," James supplies an index to a much broader field of cognition.[3] The museum idea is a transportable belief that the world is most legible whenever the right kind of observer confronts and understands selected objects—within the walls of the museum or without. Thus Venice can be for James a "vast museum," complete with crowds passing through imaginary turnstiles and gondoliers and beggars who serve as custodians and ushers while "they are even themselves to a certain extent the objects of exhibition."[4]

Bridging institutions and cognition, the museum idea is fundamental to understanding literary production in the later nineteenth-century United States. Literature in this period succeeds as never before in claiming autonomy—fiction writing becomes a recognizable profession, literary pursuit earns the dignity of a national academy, and the history of American letters secures its place as a worthy object of study in the university.[5] Yet that very autonomy is symptomatic of a new integration of cultural, political, and social domains. The museum is the secular temple at the center of an American society in which the arts are at once more independent and more closely integrated into mechanisms of civic governance. For this reason the era's most consequential literary development—the emergence of a sphere of high literary culture—can be described as occurring under the sign of the modern museum, as witnessed by the fealty paid to the museum in the plots and tropes of the literature itself.

It is more than a casual analogy, then, to describe an editor like Howells as undertaking the new work of a literary curator. As the leading advocate of realism, Howells helps establish a new understanding of fiction in which selected works emerge not only as extraordinary art objects but also as artifacts of a special *order* of representation, an order which, like a museum exhibit, claims access to knowledge unavailable in other forms of display. Only with this distinctive literary sphere in place could Howells greet brand-new magazine stories like James's as the equivalent of the works of old masters—instant "masterpieces." But Howells's responsibility as a leading man of letters, as he saw it, was not only to publish and disseminate masterpieces of fiction but to counter the degenerative effects of a vast machinery of "shows and semblances" appearing everywhere in the American landscape. "Love of the marvellous," Howells laments, had produced a species of fiction on par with the circus and burlesque theater. Conceding that even a cultivated person might enjoy "the trapeze" in occasional "moments of barbarism," Howells is nevertheless adamant that circus-like attractions of unreal spectacle and melodrama, when absorbed into fiction, produce a literature of distortion. He writes, "In a world which loves the spectacular drama and the practically bloodless sports of the modern amphitheatre," novelists too often fall into the "service of sensation." Like "burlesque and negro minstrelsy," such literature will inevitably "misrepresent life."[6]

The mark of worthy fiction, in contrast, is precisely its aspiration to "represent life"—the same goal pursued, through their respective professional methods, by museums of ethnology, natural history, and fine art. Howells enlists for fiction his era's supreme confidence in the power of expert representations. Realism has cultivated an audience of serious readers who "require of a novelist . . . a sort of scientific decorum. He can no longer expect to be received on the ground of entertainment only." Howells claimed his friend Mark Twain for the campaign to cultivate American fiction, but it was Henry James who represented the "finished workmanship" and "dispassionate analysis" that were central to the highest realism. Only fiction like James's, possessing the kind of mastery on view in museum exhibitions, will be able to adequately "represent life."[7]

In truth, this fundamental opposition between real and unreal representation was itself a false conception, though a powerful one. Howells's lament that the "cheap effects" of mass entertainment too easily infected literature belies his anxious awareness of the frequent traffic between high and low arts, between realist artistry and commercial artifice.[8] To be sure, the rise of an autonomous high culture in this period is a momentous fact; high art's authoritative claims on beauty are of a piece with science's claims on empirical truth, a second passage to the real. But the very autonomy of high culture—art's self-defining, self-justifying value—forms itself by negotiating its proximity to those promiscuous materials, at a moment when a profound transformation of communication systems multiplied the sources, sites, and the very kinds of publicness emerging in American life. From the first, high culture carries an acute and formative interest in what it opposes: the dime novels and nickelodeons, the sprouting commercial posters and veiled peep shows, the acres of newsprint and the unreal worlds of amusement parks. The untethered, protean commercial signs and images of that sector had come to constitute a reality-shaping force of enormous magnitude. With this awareness, the disciplined institutions of high culture retain a complex tie—a mix of antagonism and envy, even imitation—to the unruly world of commercial entertainment they oppose.

The museum itself may be the institution that expresses most vividly the vexed kinship between high culture and its mass culture antagonists. Lurking just outside the preeminence of the great metropolitan museum was the popular dime museum, devoted to precisely the pleasures of eclectic spectacle that so distressed Howells. P. T. Barnum's establishment, the American Museum, had revealed an enormous public appetite for factitious visual images and for sheer performance brio in a society that was then still officially suspicious of the theatrical. Launching the venture in New York during the 1840s, Barnum made the most of this ambivalence by introducing his curiosities under the auspices of the museum and calling his performance hall a museum lecture room. The institution of the museum was capable of serving as something of a facade in those mid-century decades, allowing audiences to dodge any of the potentially troubling associations of commercial theater. All museums have a more or less suppressed theatricality, a latent sensationalism; Barnum's genius was to make the museum's surface disavowal into the very means for staging sensational commercial entertainment. The tactic is reflected in Barnum's *Struggles and Triumphs* (1869), an autobiography that became the most widely read book in the later nineteenth century after the Bible. Despite proudly acknowledging the kinds of "constantly diversified" exhibits in his "great Lecture Room" (from "industrious fleas, automatons, jugglers, ventriloquists, living statuary, tableaux, gypsies, Albinoes, fat boys, giants, dwarves" to "mechanical figures, fancy glass-blowing, knitting machines and other triumphs in the mechanical arts [and] American Indians"), Barnum still claimed the august national museums of Europe as his counterparts and rivals: "I frequently compared the annual number of visitors with the number officially reported as visiting (free of charge), the British Museum in London," Barnum boasts, "and my list was invariably the larger."[9]

By the 1880s, with the establishment of metropolitan museums in most leading American cities, the institution of the museum had finally rid itself of what Henry James called the open "Barnum associations and revelations."[10] But even in this later era the museum was not a pristine, autonomous space, a "classifying house" that merely ordered and preserved authentic specimens of art and nature.[11] It remained linked, in invisible but structurally important ways, to the more unruly world of commercial exhibition it opposed. The same animal-collecting agencies that supplied Barnum with animal attractions for his circus, for instance, also provided natural history museums with specimens for their scientific displays. There were even direct transfers between circus and museum: when one of Barnum's most famous elephants died in the middle of a tour, museum taxidermists rushed to transform the gigantic corpse into what eventually became one of the prized attractions of New York's American Museum of Natural History. The plate glass for that museum's exhibitions was supplied by one of the trustees, Theodore Roosevelt Sr., whose company manufactured the large glass sheets behind which the ornate displays of department store goods were staged for urban crowds. In many of their strategies of architectural design, crowd control, and exhibition, museums shared the techniques and even the selfsame materials of the world of amusement parks, fairs, and commercial spectacles.[12] These sub-rosa exchanges with mass cultural forms, together with a critical opposition to it, gave museum displays of this period their particular texture, authority, and appeal.

That the quiet prestige of the museum was in some sense indebted to the "blaring" commercial exhibitions it opposed is an instructive example of a larger social phenomenon. Recognizing the strands of dependence and rivalry that connected high and low domains complicates the story of cultural hegemony that has governed much recent literary history. Ties between high and low spheres were in the first instance economic. It is true that the large-scale transformation Alan Trachtenberg memorably called "the incorporation of America" allowed the propertied classes to consolidate their cultural authority along with their economic might. By sponsoring institutions like museums, industrialists and professionals were able to associate corporate capitalism with enduring traditions of Western art and learning and to position themselves as the "rightful inheritors of the mantle of European high culture and civilization."[13] But critical attention to capitalist consolidation has led many scholars to overlook a crucial counterdevelopment: the identical forces of economic incorporation also produced a greater diversity of media and a remarkable range of unanticipated opportunities for public association—in short, incorporation did not mean public homogenization. Paul Starr documents the way consolidated routes of transportation and unprecedented profit margins made possible "a growing profusion of publications," including foreign-language dailies (ranging from Russian, Slovenian, and Yiddish to Japanese, Chinese, and Arabic), magazines for African American, Jewish, and Asian readerships, and socialist, anarchist, and populist journals.[14] At the same time, new forms of mass culture permitted disparate social groups to enter zones of shared perception and sensory experience, further reordering inherited patterns of cultural reception. Robert Rydell and Rob Kroes argue that sites such as amusement parks and Wild West shows succeeded in bringing heterogeneous populations across "an important threshold toward a new cultural experience where consumerism and leisure became hallmarks of a new national identity," temporarily occupying if not usurping the space of national representation that had been claimed by the educated elite.[15]

Capitalization and consolidated networks of communication, in other words, actually instigated competition for the sphere of public representation, a sphere that was being dramatically expanded and diversified. Plate glass and turnstiles, cheap print and continental railroad lines were the common infrastructure for these rival formations of high art and mass culture. But the ties binding the two went beyond the economic. Commercial culture did not just challenge the preeminence of literary culture, it also helped *create* it—helped shape the self-understanding of a literary public as the source of a shared critical consciousness whose office it was to bring analytic thought and discriminating judgment to a crowded, disordered sphere of culture. When a critic castigated the typical American newspaper as "print published by a literary Barnum" ("certain to give us flippancy for wit," "bombast for eloquence," and "prolific of all kinds of sensational headings"), the denunciation demonstrates the way a new domain of higher expression relied on the materials of mass culture for both the terms and the substance of its critical distinctions.[16]

Retrospectively, Henry James acknowledged this generative relation when he pointed to an extensive "Barnum background" of large-scale circus acts and Broadway spectacles as among the "earliest aesthetic seeds" of his creative consciousness. In a remarkable chapter from his memoir *A Small Boy and Others* (1913), James recalls his still vivid responses to the acrobat shows and staged chariot races, to the sights of Barnum's "halls of humbug," with their "bottled mermaids, 'bearded ladies,' and chill dioramas," and to the popular stage dramas with the "creak of carpentry" audible in their more ambitious scenic effects—all thrilling stops in the excursions of his New York childhood. James seems by turns amused and dismayed by the fact that "sordidities and poverties" of vulgar entertainments could have produced in him such deep stirrings, "from the total impression of which things we somehow plucked the flower of the ideal." Although he conveys with considerable wit his adult knowledge of the "meanness" of what he once took for glamour, James is still at pains to stress that the "crude scenic appeal" of such spectacles could engender the highest kind of critical and aesthetic sensibility. It was in such places, he writes, that the young James "got his first glimpse of that possibility of a 'free play of mind' over a subject which was to throw him with force at a later stage of culture, into the critical arms of Matthew Arnold"—a high distinction born of low theatrics.[17]

Even the supreme "majesty" of Europe and European art turns out to be something James first experiences as an American spectacle. James's memory of Niblo's and Franconi's gardens, and "circuses under tents on vacant lots," leads directly to his recollection of visits to the nearby Crystal Palace, a New York re-creation of the London exhibition hall, where "showy sculpture" in "profuse exhibition" produce for him the effect of Europe and "big European Art" before he ever travels in a European country. It is here, then, that European art is first experienced through American artifice: "I remember being very tired and cold and hungry there . . . though concomitantly conscious that I was somehow in Europe, since everything about me had been 'brought over.' . . . If this was Europe then Europe was beautiful indeed." A gaudy American showplace literally stages for the young James the idea of Europe and conjures a future self who will be shaped by the continent he has not visited except in infancy: "The Crystal Palace was vast and various and dense, which was what Europe was going to be; it was a deep-down jungle of impressions that were somehow challenges."[18]

Against the contention that high and low spheres were inherently at odds, here James discovers a kinship, an essential relation binding their distinct identities. These low entertainments, James claims, were "a brave beginning for a consciousness that was to be nothing if not mixed, and a curiosity that was to be nothing if not restless."[19] James's ambivalent recollection—surprised but intrigued at realizing that these sensory pleasures could be a matrix for critical distinctions—captures the dual tendencies toward exchange and disavowal that were a controlling influence on literary production. In the new institutions of literary culture, as in the metropolitan museum, the imperative to "represent life" was never simply a matter of mimesis, of rendering a close transcription of social reality. At a deep and formative level, realist fiction and cultural criticism enacted a mimetic rivalry with other compelling cultural systems. In assessing this writing, James's account of the birth of his cultural consciousness in the halls of Barnum supplies an index to a critical history of high literary culture. Three related topics stand out as key concerns. First, the memoir invokes in detail a landscape of early mass cultural forms, a site for James in which diffuse pleasures and feelings stir closer calibrations of aesthetic judgment. A second topic, then, is the aesthetic consciousness born in a dialectical relation to that mass landscape: out of low theatrics emerges a power of discernment that will become identified with spaces of refuge and reflection such as the writer's study, the metropolitan museum, and the high art object itself. James's memoir identifies a third concern, finally, in his recollection of a phantom "Europe," where Europe is an idea or effect that precedes the place itself. This notional Europe is the geography that orients American high culture and U.S. transnational ties and territorial expansions. A powerful spur for a mixed transatlantic traffic in culture and capital, a record of racial valances that go largely unspoken and unchallenged, America's projected fantasy of Europe exerts a controlling force during the country's debut as, in W. E. B. DuBois's words, a "vast economic empire."[20] In mass spectacle, in cultural distinction, and in the force and racial charge of Europe, James's tale contains a grammar for articulating the history and possible meanings of high literary culture and its others.

At issue in these topics, I will be arguing, is the question of what Richard Brodhead calls the "appropriative mind." Brodhead argues persuasively that institutions of high culture fostered an "imagination of acquisition," habits of perception that conditioned affluent audiences to regard European histories and exotic or quaint geographies as symbolic possessions, as spaces and traditions they could claim vicariously through certain kinds of travel and reading experiences.[21] But Brodhead and others have often overlooked the fact that mass culture, too, generated forms of imaginative appropriation, methods for situating oneself in a world in which the lived contours of time and space were being reordered perpetually through technology and mass mediation and exploited in the "joy machines" of mass entertainment.[22] The competition between these rival cultures reflects not just their shared reliance on a set of new conditions but also their parallel—and sometimes overlapping—operations for ordering experience in a world of dizzying material changes. The worldliness of the high literary imagination cannot be understood apart from the kinds of imaginary possession and self-projection that characterized its mass culture rival.

Literature for the Billion

In Edith Wharton's novel *The House of Mirth* (1905), Lawrence Selden disparages the New York elite for staging their social life in the "glare of publicity," the high visibility of the mass circulation press and showy public appearances. Selden is not particularly bothered by wasted wealth or class snobbery in these circles. Rather, he is critical of the "ideals of a world where conspicuousness passed for distinction," where sheer public visibility counts for more than sensibility and where fame eclipses character.[23] In opposing "conspicuousness" to "distinction," Selden names a pair of key terms that define one of the abiding obsessions of the northeastern literary establishment in its uneasy alliance with the economically driven host culture of the later nineteenth century.

Both "conspicuousness" and "distinction" describe prominence or social recognition, but placed in opposition to one another they mark two divergent sources of that recognition. For the new class of literate professionals like the urbane lawyer Selden, "distinction" had become a complex, almost circular idea. To be a man or woman of distinction no longer meant one possessed a secure claim to membership in the leading propertied class, as it would have meant to the antebellum gentry. In the increasingly dynamic, competitive culture of postbellum America, the superiority of true distinction became a more elusive quality. Neither birth nor wealth alone could secure it; as Selden's note of disdain for the wealthy elite suggests, one could be rich and wellborn but still found wanting. Instead, distinction is now rooted in inward qualities of mind and perception. To possess real distinction is to be able to *make* distinctions, to discern aesthetic richness from commercial blandness, to value achievements of mind over merely material advances.[24] Selden has a striking name for men and women of distinction: they are citizens of a "republic of the spirit." Membership in this invisible nation depends on immaterial traits of refined seeing and understanding. "There are sign-posts" to this "country," Selden explains, but "one has to know how to read them."[25]

The attributes of true distinction, then, cannot be universally recognized or read; conspicuousness, in contrast, is what we cannot help reading. Like advertising and celebrity and other creations of modern publicity, conspicuousness supplies its own self-interpreting signs. Whereas distinction resides in exceptional discernment, conspicuousness is the insistent, iconic visibility that precludes any need for discernment. Hence the urgency felt by cultivated people like Selden for a semantic opposition between the two terms, for conspicuousness threatens to make distinction irrelevant, even obsolete. Cultural leaders believed that the "glare of publicity" present everywhere in the new commercial society was a direct threat to the softer, private illumination of the best aesthetic and moral judgment.

Language, though inherited, is alive to historical change. The splitting of related words into disparate concepts, or the blending of unique terms into a new and unified meaning, can signal reordered social possibilities and conditions. A deep shift of this kind may be behind the need to articulate a starker difference between notions of conspicuousness and distinction in the later nineteenth-century English lexicon. It is in this period that cities become centers of not only an enormously enlarged sphere of commerce but also of an unprecedented production of communication, the commerce of signs: words and photographs, faces and trademarks, visual styles and commercial rituals, all following paths of profit rather than the reasoning of deliberative politics or educated opinion. Under these conditions—conditions most obvious in the mass circulation press, in rapidly rising book sales, in the visual landscape of cities dominated by commercial display and advertising—an earlier cohesive idea of rationality is strained to the breaking point. The Enlightenment ideal of the rational presumed a perfect compatibility between human reason and human progress; an advance in one would secure an advance in the other. But the material changes wrought by rational modernization appear able to dwarf the power of personal reason and judgment. What was previously imagined as a sphere of shared, public reason, if only as a realizable ideal, is now viewed as a world divided between the indiscriminate fame conferred by public display and individual powers of reasoned discrimination. Enlightenment as an ideal illumination gives way to a self-generated rivalry: conspicuousness at war with distinction, the glare of signs against the lights of discernment.[26]

Although the writers who describe this stark opposition were rendering a profound cultural experience, there are good reasons to see the matter in rather different, less polarized terms. The belief that enlightened perception—the subtle capacities of aesthetic judgment, taste, and distinction—had become uniquely imperiled actually helped *create* what was thought to be under threat: a new canon of specialized judgments and closely calibrated forms of cultural perception. The critic and educator Charles Eliot Norton lamented that "no one knows how to think anymore" and laid the blame on the public appetite for popular magazines. His 1888 essay in the *New Princeton Review*, "The Intellectual Life of America," is a representative indictment of the popular publications that were "largely addressed to a horde of readers who seek in them not only the news of the day, but the gratification of a vicious taste for strong sensations; who enjoy the coarse stimulants of personalities and scandal, and have no appetite for any sort of proper intellectual nourishment."[27] Yet Norton's judgment issued from a new critical establishment that owed its increased authority in no small part to its place *within* that expanding sphere of print and image, as a metatopical space for adjudicating what had become a fantastically expanded sphere of communications.

To read the literary elite of the period is to realize that the scope and scale of popular writing—"literature for the billion," as James puts it—irrevocably changes the measurement of literary achievement. At one extreme, the sheer volume of printed matter in this period appears to foretell an extinction of the literary. In an essay from his *Literature and Life* (1902), Howells invents an interlocutor who wryly praises magazines and Sunday supplements by way of warning the editor against his foolish predilection for "intellectual" books: "If you don't amuse your readers, you don't keep them; practically, you cease to exist."[28] Beginning with a sharp rise at midcentury, magazine sales soon swelled exponentially. When Congress in 1885 reduced second-class postal rates to one cent per pound, magazines became a far cheaper venue for marketing than advertising circulars. Between 1885 and 1900, the number of periodicals that could boast of a readership of 100,000 rose from 21 to 85 titles, a fourfold increase; that number almost doubled again (reaching 159) by 1905. Newspapers, which had been steadily growing since the antebellum era, matched these phenomenal increases, and the number of dailies rose from 574 to 2,226 between 1870 and 1900.[29]

Norton's complaint that the floodtide of print had somehow washed away the ability to think is perhaps more accurately an admission of his own feelings of submersion, for certainly such numbers meant that far more readers than before were spending more time with the printed word—just not with the words of Norton and his peers. They were reading instead such works as the working-girl novels of Laura Jean Libbey, who pushed her sales past sixteen million books with titles like *Only a Mechanic's Daughter, Madcap Laddie,* and *Plot and Passion.* They were buying the books of Sylvanus T. Cobb, who parlayed his newspaper writing for the New York *Ledger* (2,305 pieces in all) into a career as the producer of over 122 novels. Reform fiction of all kinds—temperance novels, potboilers about urban degeneration, divorce novels, and labor stories—continued to prompt Americans to buy and consume books as reading became a more widespread form of mass social engagement. It was a form of religious engagement as well: religious novels like the best sellers from the minister Harold Bell Wright were often adapted for tent-show plays, where the millions inspired at the revivals could buy the book after the show.[30]

Mass-produced fiction, in other words, had not lowered readers' tastes so much as turned popular tastes to the work of creating new readers in unprecedented numbers. For Jürgen Habermas, the creation of a mass market for cultural goods like literature increased sales and profits by eliminating any need for the kind of reading he calls "accomplished appropriation," reading that has the "cumulative" effect of developing the reader's critical facility. Though it is true that mass fiction and newspapers reduced the "entrance requirements" for access, the new diversity of forms and publics made possible by cheap production costs and the spread of reading habits also produced their own kinds of readerly "facility."[31] The remarkable diversity of the popular press, for instance, allowed immigrants to read publications in their own language, something that became possible for many only *after* they become foreigners in the United States—not just because American literacy rates were higher but also because many European states prohibited any publication in the vernacular languages spoken by peasants.[32]

Although men of letters like Norton were far from becoming extinct, the explosion in print and in book buying did produce a new readership for whom elite authors were largely outsiders. Hence the writers' recorded sense of exile from what James called a "commonschooled and newspapered democracy."³³ The new consumption had reordered the map of literate America and elite authors existed on its margins, unread luminaries if not unknown names. The genre of the urban exposé, begun in the antebellum period by George Lippard and E. Z. C. Judson, flourished expansively in the post–Civil War era, and books like Edward Crapsey's *The Nether Side of New York* (1872), J. G. Grant's *The Evils of San Francisco* (1884), and George Stevens's *Chicago: Wicked City* (1896) disclosed to the new readers a fictional underworld that now reached as far as the West Coast. The revelation of these unfamiliar urban underworlds in fiction mirrored the unforeseen massing of the new population of readers who consumed them, and if the readers were less menacing than the urban underworld, they were hardly less mysterious, at least to the literary establishment. Where had they come from? Unbidden by literary gatekeepers, this new nation of readers seemed to materialize from nowhere.

They hadn't, of course. Technology, impersonal and largely invisible, played a foundational role. The introduction of linotype machines in 1885 and new printing presses of lightning speed enlarged production capacity beyond what anyone had foreseen. Print was not only voluminous but remarkably cheap. As newsprint (derived from wood pulp rather than rags) became the dominant material for newspapers and magazines, the cost of paper dropped by nearly 80 percent. Advertising revenues increased sharply beginning in the 1870s and soon rose to cover more than 50 percent of the income for dailies and periodicals. As a result, newspapers and paperbacks were suddenly everyday purchases for a population with steeply rising rates of literacy. The completion of national transportation routes ensured that readers were amassed not through localized bookselling alone but increasingly through the long reach of advertising campaigns, transcontinental distribution, and improved transatlantic trade.³⁴ These developments meant that the local place where readers bought and read their books mattered little; members of a sewing circle in Oregon Territory, stockyard supervisors in Chicago, and domestics in south Florida hotels might all spy the same ad or book cover and be enlisted into the readership for a given dime novel. The importance of location was displaced, as it were, from the site of the reader to the setting of the book. The shift may be one of the reasons historical romances fared especially well in the new mass market, as their exotic fictional settings—the Jerusalem of Jesus' day in Lew Wallace's *Ben Hur*, the Renaissance Italy of Francis Marion Crawford's novels—became a common ground for millions living in disparate places.

In this unbinding of people from the determinants of local place, mass fiction and journalism made vivid one of the signal developments of modernity. By making physical place less consequential, mass publishing illuminates a transformation that Anthony Giddens describes as "a 'lifting out' of social relations from local contexts of interaction and their restructuring across time and space."[35] As a mass form, the historical romance in vogue in the later nineteenth century exemplifies this new mediation of social relations: the genre presents a specificity of fictional locale that is the inverse of the dispersed location of its vast and scattered audience. The reader's freedom to traverse time is likewise a sign of these modern conditions. Despite the return in *Ben Hur* to the zero degree of Christian history, the life of Jesus, Wallace's best seller reflects a decidedly secular appropriation of time, a paperback tourism that made the Jerusalem of Jesus merely one site alongside Rider Haggard's fantastic African jungles in *King Solomon's Mines* (1887) and the medieval England of Charles Major's *When Knighthood Was in Flower* (1898).

Self-declared realists like Howells saw the huge popularity of historical romance as a troubling flight from modern life. But the genre is in fact a harbinger of an intensified modernity, an early rehearsal of habits of mind increasingly cut loose from more immediate proximities of place and time. The backward gaze of historical fiction, in other words, exemplifies the way technology and modern markets were rapidly encroaching on the authority of the local, the here and now of the congregation, the municipal bank, and the rural county calendar.[36] Like the stereographs that came to saturate homes of almost all class strata (the industry produced more than seven hundred million images), historical fiction placed a vast inventory of the world in the hands of ordinary readers who became as adept at traversing imagined space as the readers of James's and Wharton's international novels of manners.

Popular Spectacle and the Space of the Study

For cultural leaders, these results of modernization seemed starkly opposed to their idea of modern progress. Whereas realist writers saw themselves painting in the lines of social history, inscribing causal continuities and logical probabilities, mass fiction seemed riveted by mere sensation, an infantile regression. In Howells's words, a "spectacular muse" was the deity of the age.[37] The phrase resonates with one of his most interesting meditations on the fate of literature, an essay titled "At a Dime Museum" (1902). A distillation of the worst impulses of an emerging mass culture, the dime museum for Howells exposes the imperative to amuse that was pulling down all cultural expression to "the level of show business." As Howells knows, tact and humor are required in any critique of popular culture; to fulminate is to risk being cornered as a prig and thus to forfeit the grounds of sophistication that are the critic's only cultural advantage. To sidestep that trap, Howells invents an urbane "friend" who, in a campy tribute to "cheaper amusements of the metropolis," relates to the editor the knowing pleasures he found at an afternoon's visit to a dime museum, a jaunt during an idle hour "between two appointments."[38]

A report from the cultural wilds, the friend's account details the crowded collection of "clever" (194) things on display at the popular establishment, from "two gloomy apes" (195) to contortionists "of Spanish-American extraction" (197). Howells's readers, however, are implicitly asked to find a sharper cleverness in the friend's account itself. Delivered from the comfort of an easy chair in the editor's study, an intimate space into which the reader has gained privileged entry ("finding room for his elbow on the corner of my table he knocked off some books for review" [194]), the friend's story conveys the second-order enjoyment of recognizing both the charm and the naïveté of "popular taste" (201). All of the friend's avowals of delight are thus subtly—and instructively—disingenuous. His reported pleasure is real but always double: the discerning reader must hear two notes, the stated report and its damning overtones. To know, for instance, that his description of the "unflagging energy" (196) of the toiling actors in a museum theatrical is not a piece of praise but a superior smile is the reader's reward for finding herself at home with a Howells essay rather than at a dime museum.

The subtle pleasures from Howells's structure of layered discriminations become especially complex when the friend is able to mock—and thereby simultaneously affirm—his sense of his own superior sensibilities at viewing an exhibit of Australian aborigines.

On a platform at the end of the hall was an Australian family a good deal gloomier, than the apes, . . . staring down the room with varying expressions all verging upon melancholy madness, and who gave me such a pang of compassion as I have seldom got from the tragedy of the two-dollar theatres. They allowed me to come quite close up to them, and to feed my pity upon their wild dejection in exile without stint. I couldn't enter into conversation with them, and express my regret at finding them so far from their native boomerangs and kangaroos and pinetree grubs, but I know they felt my sympathy, it was so evident. I didn't see their performance, and

I don't know that they had any. They may simply have been there ethnologically, but this was a good object, and the sight of their spiritual misery was alone worth the price of admission. (195)

Exposing the coarseness of the racist exhibit, the passage is still primarily a striking extension of Howells's analysis of taste. The speaker's mockery of his own feelings of compassion, in other words, is Howells's sign that taste is likely to be a surer moral index than raw sentiment, which supplies moral gratification on the cheap.

Virtuosity can be tactical, an inoculation. Howells's demonstrated mastery of taste in this essay clears the way for his cultural criticism. The fictional "friend" and alter ego (who, as Howells's creation, displays the editor's own urbanity as author) becomes the figure to pose the strongest—because most knowing—challenge to the critic's concerns about mass culture: "Isn't all art one?" he asks. "How can you say that any art is higher than the others?" If spectacles like contortionists give ephemeral pleasure at appropriately low prices, the friend argues, what is the harm? "Why is it nobler to contort the mind than to contort the body?" (198). In the persona of this cultivated friend, Howells acknowledges multiple levels of pleasure—especially the pleasures of irony—available at a low site like a dime museum. But Howells also sees, quite correctly I would argue, that commercial culture will alter if not displace the status of the literary. He therefore grasps what his alter ego fails to see. To equate all arts as merely different branches of entertainment is to risk delivering up literature to the "spectacular muse" of a commercial age. In its witty tour of a dime museum, the essay is Howells's brief against the distortions of a commercial culture attuned only to the principles of "show business"—to the allure of novelty and the freakish (the contortionist), the power of ignorant wishes (a fortune-teller) or fraud (a perpetual motion machine), the appeal of indiscriminate display and visual shock (a curio hall). Howells's protest essay is at once a recognition of cultural commodification and a display of a new species of literate wit, namely, Howells's own cultural fluency and polyglot taste that can take up the myriad pleasures of mass culture and go them one better. He thus anticipates the strategies of the postmodern artists who, dropping protest, build intricate layers of literate discrimination out of the acknowledged power and disparate forms of mass culture.

In "At a Dime Museum," then, mass forms represent not an obstacle but in fact an occasion for an exhilarating performance of literary sensibility. For discriminating readers, Howells's multivalent tones and nimble reversals trump the sensational productions of show business, and reflection on the new, often pleasurable forms of commercial publicness becomes a generative source of an analytic sensibility. Alongside this literate display of fluency, however, is the essay's indirect acknowledgment of certain generative capacities in mass culture, capacities that can be said to outstrip the "intellectual character" (201) of the literary. Unwittingly, Howells in this way identifies a certain limitation to literary writing. This limitation comes into view in a mock defense of the circus, when Howells's imaginary friend admits only one complaint about that form of mass entertainment, namely the "superfluity" of the circus's three rings: "Fancy reading three novels simultaneously, and listening at the same time to a lecture and a sermon, which could represent the two platforms between the rings" (200). The absurdity of the conceit pits mass culture excess against literary profundity. Literature wins, of course. But the image also recognizes a circumscribed quality of the literary. The high fiction Howells has in mind works by focusing the reader's full attention through a single object, the text in hand. Reading of this sort requires the elimination of competing stimuli. Relative silence, bodily stillness, and physical comfort are its necessary if not sufficient conditions. Literary reading favors an individual mental concentration that acquires imaginative leverage by excluding other somatic and social realities. In contrast to this monopoly on the reader's attention, however, mass forms like the circus and the dime museum seek to multiply objects and stimuli. In their very excess such sites open out to multiple zones of experience and feeling, zones to which the high cultural novel has no access. By itself, the blunt sensation of spectacle may be literature's opposite number. Yet the simultaneous visual, aural, and kinetic stimulation of a modern three-ring circus suggests an aesthetic heterogeneity in mass culture that is as much a counterpart of the literary as it is a rival.

If Howells harbors any sense of a rival complexity from this quarter of popular culture, his essay downplays it. But his decision to focus most of the essay on the dime museum may betray a more defensive posture than Howells means to show. By making the dime museum his representative site, Howells chose a venue of popular culture that by 1902 would have been seen as rather outdated, even quaint. Already on the scene and flourishing were other forms in thrall to the muse of spectacle that promised a wider, more aggressive cultural reach. The subculture of the urban dance hall, the enveloping world of the amusement park, the planned mayhem of deliberately staged train wrecks—these and other forms of entertainment convey the complex power of popular spectacle in the late nineteenth century, and scholars have shown how the affective experiences available at these commercial sites were innovations in feeling that responded to the social and material technologies from which they spring.[39] Howells's mock fantasy of reading three novels simultaneously is a piece of satire, to be sure, but the image may harbor a wish that high literature had the ability to match the multiplicity of physical and mental experiences newly available at the sites of mass culture.

The dime museum offered its pleasures under a single roof, producing an "intimacy" among the visitors that Howells's interlocutor wryly likens to "a domestic circle" (197). In contrast to the dime museum's homeliness, Coney Island amusement parks like Steeplechase and Luna Park captured the scope and complexity of the modern city. During the 1870s and 1880s, the smaller (and seedier) carnivals and Atlantic seaside resorts of the immediate postwar years grew into the amusement parks that became the unofficial capitals of America's emergent mass culture. By the century's end, millions passed annually through the turnstiles of these enclosed but extensive worlds, make-believe cities with their own fantastic architecture and playful transport and trade. While they evoked the size and heterogeneity of a real city, amusement parks also recast the most daunting elements of modern urban life. The density and speed of industrial cities, their outsized scale and purposeful chaos, were refashioned as the ingredients of mass entertainment.

A Coney Island hotel in the shape of an enormous elephant could tame through sheer whimsy the increasingly massive size of urban buildings. Rides and attractions turned the hazards of industrialism into kinetic pleasures that millions were eager to purchase with their industry wages. Patrons who rode the Leap Frog Railway at Luna Park, for instance, rushed along in small, open-air railcars that appeared certain to crash into other oncoming cars until the tracks prevented the collision at the last second. Disasters and large-scale accidents, all too frequently emblazoned in newspaper headlines, became their own live theatrical spectacles at the parks. One production at Dreamland, "Fighting the Flames," involved a cast of four thousand characters, while at other parks visitors saw re-creations of famous disasters, from the "Fall of Pompeii," complete with a simulated eruption of Mount Vesuvius, to the notorious floods of Johnstown and Galveston. Any and all park spaces were a potential stage. Why limit the services of the ocean to providing waves for bathers when it could also serve to present the reenactment of a famous shipwreck? Why not build a raised platform over the man-made lagoon at the foot of the Shoot-the-Chute as the site for a three-ring circus, complete with equestrian acrobatics and cakewalk competitions on a stage suspended in midair?[40]

Although visitors felt they had entered "another world," amusement parks offered not an escape from modernity but rather a temporary mastery of modern experience made possible by a canny multiplication of the visual and kinetic stimulations of urban settings. The human crowds at amusement parks were themselves an exciting attraction. By the time the new parks were in full swing in the 1890s, over two hundred thousand people were descending daily on each of the leading parks. Whereas the audiences for such mass phenomena as the newspaper, the best seller, and later the radio remained invisible and disembodied, amusement parks allowed mass consumers to see themselves gathered as a visible social body, one that resembled a leisure class, at least for a day. Historians have shown how the parks helped erode older injunctions to defer pleasure and behave decorously, opening the way for large cultural transformations in twentieth-century mores. But most critical interpretations have tended to narrow the significance of such transformations, measuring the impact only in terms of the conformist behavior of mass consumers. In his classic study of Coney Island, for instance, John Kasson concludes that "beneath the air of liberation, its pressures were profoundly conformist, its means fundamentally manipulative." If parks offered social release, they did so only to inculcate standardized habits of consumption that were dictated from above.[41] While this verdict seems accurate enough when measured by the corporate homogeneity of a site like Disney World, there is no obvious reason to interpret the experience available at amusement parks in terms of consumerism alone. If we recognize early amusement parks as laboratories for a controlled exploration of the malleable culture of modern time and space, these sites are portals into deeper transformations that subtend consumer culture.[42]

It was these deeper transformations that stood out most starkly for literary observers of modern mass culture. The park's larger-than-life dimensions, its massing of populations, its offer of unbounded and frenetic activity—these features closely match the traits that literary critics most condemned in popular literature. Henry James remarked often on the "colossal" and "deafening" daily production of fiction and journalism, and was both repelled and intrigued by the "mere mass and bulk" of the new print industry and a mass reading public that "grows and grows each year." In James's mind the print world, no less than the amusement park, flaunted extremes of scale and mass volume as ends in themselves, tributes to the bourgeois household.⁴⁹ To the discerning reader, these interior details certify the value of dedicated reading by way of an implicit contrast: the knowing taste that created Archer's study is distinguished from the merely good taste of his genteel family and social circle. The study is thus a place for the active interplay of thought and feeling—for literary openness—as opposed to a repetition of inherited forms.

That the space of the study functions to showcase literary meaning through a kind of formal narrative relief is even clearer in a Howells novel, *The Minister's Charge* (1886). The Reverend Sewell, a literary man, accidentally encourages the poetic ambitions of a farmhand, the untutored (and largely untalented) Lemuel Barker. Sewell is at a loss when Barker unexpectedly turns up on his Boston doorstep one day, but he invites the young man into his study in an attempt to show kindness: "Come upstairs with me into my study, and I will show you a picture of Agassiz."

> He led the way out of the reception-room, and tripped lightly in his slippered feet up the steps against which Barker knocked the toes of his clumsy boots. He was not large, nor naturally loutish, but the heaviness of the country was in every touch and movement. He dropped the photograph twice in his endeavor to hold it between his stiff thumb and finger.⁵⁰

Whereas Howells's "Editor's Study" and Lowell's *My Study Window* invite readers into a shared textual space for a meeting of the minds, here the invitation to enter a study serves inversely to expose Barker's incomprehension. The very "heaviness" of his footfalls on the stairs bespeaks an inherent friction, a cultural resistance or drag that all but stops him in his tracks and foretells his inability to grasp (even to hold on to) the cultural touchstones collected in Sewell's study.

> [Sewell] went on pointing out the different objects in the quiet room, and he took down several books from the shelves that covered the whole wall, and showed them to Barker, who, however, made no effort to look at them for himself, and did not say anything about them. He did what Sewell bade him to do in admiring this thing or that; but if he had been an Indian he could not have regarded them with a greater reticence. (17)

The analogy with a silent "Indian" is hardly casual; Barker's stoic unresponsiveness is paradoxically expressive of deep cultural difference. Like a photographer's darkroom, Sewell's study brings into focus the absence of literary sensibility that will define Barker's life and defeat his poetic aspirations.

Here and elsewhere, Howells's realism makes personal qualities of taste and perception serve as the surest index to social realities.

Conceived in this way, the literary is defined less through books or authors than through distinctions in taste and cognition, differentials that identify literary meaning with a species of interiority. So conceived, the literary is also the opposite of the poetics of spectacle—invisible rather than visual, private rather than publicized, subtle and cumulative rather than blaring. In contrast to the self-display of a Barnum performer, the author's study signified a self-effacement characteristic of refined creation (critic Thomas Sargeant Perry identified Turgenev as a "realist in the sense of hiding himself" while he practiced "painstaking accuracy").[51] But while the topos of the author's study suggests the chaste work of the mind, it also locates a quiet glamour that is never directly claimed but everywhere implied: the disavowed glamour we call authority. And in modernity, where there is glamour, there is likely to be iconic display—in other words, spectacle. A predictable paradox follows: the author's private study in this period became a site of concentrated interest for tourists and celebrity seekers as well as literary devotees. Newspaper and magazine pieces like the British journalist Edmund Yates's *Celebrities at Home* series in the 1870s and 1880s often illustrated the "literary workshop" of famous American authors with lavish photographs and reverent captions. In similar books with titles such as *Authors at Home* (1889), *American Authors and Their Homes* (1901), and *Authors of Our Day in Their Homes* (1902), the standard photograph accompanying each featured author presented the man (or in one or two cases, the woman) seated and at work in his "library," "den," or "loft."[52] As James notes of his protagonist in "The Private Life" (1892), an author's fame might come from the unobserved act of writing in a darkened room, but for any writer who achieved public acclaim, that room was also a spectacle in its own right, at least for the author willing to give the public an "inside" glimpse. For dead authors, of course, the private study often became an iconic shrine—a frozen scene with carefully placed desk, inkwell and pens, a pair of folded spectacles—whether or not they had wished for that particular tribute.

Precisely the seclusion of the study could be put on display. The privacy of the private study could have an almost irresistible mass appeal. But what, then, of the authorial privacy that made the study a symbolic site of the literary to begin with? In one respect, public tours and magazine photos of writing rooms altogether missed the point that the setting of the study identifies literary meaning with interior sensibility and a refuge from mass exposure and kinetic stimuli. Only reading and writing offer entry to the literary; buying magazine photo spreads, seeking out interviews with famous writers, or visiting an author's home—seeking, in other words, what James called "the person of the author"—is at best a mistake, at worst a violation.[53] In another respect, however, the mass marketing of the author's study revealed an important truth: the association of literariness with privacy (interiority, refuge, singular perception) was itself mediated. The intimacy of the literary was established and circulated in print, not kept untainted in a preserve of individual sensibility. The figure of the study was a site of realist publicity, an aggressive advertisement for a new oppositional understanding of literature.

James frequently satirized as a kind of excited voyeurism the popular interest in seeing the inside of the author's study. In his story "The Death of the Lion," a journalist eager to market an "intimate" view of a literary celebrity is gleeful at gaining an entrance to the writer's study.

I was shown into the drawing-room, but there must be more to see—his study, his literary sanctum, the little things he has about, or other domestic objects or features. He wouldn't be lying down on his study table? There's a great interest always felt in the scene of an author's labours. Sometimes we're favoured with very delightful peeps. Dora Forbes showed me all his table-drawers, and almost jammed my hand into one into which I made a dash![54]

As this passage suggests, few authors could match James in skewering what he deemed the wrong kind of readerly enthusiasm, an eagerness to know (profitable) details about the personal life of an author. (The desire to reach a hand into "private drawers" of the writer's desk is one of his favorite—and most suggestive—images, appearing several times in his authors' tales and reviews.) It is not too much to say that James was obsessed with what he called "the pestilent modern fashion of publicity."[55] Moreover, for James the corrosive power of publicity was most evident when it invaded high literary values and institutions, the domain he believed should be antithetical to the "prodigious machinery" of mass forms.[56] Interviews, advertisements, book tours, and publisher's photographs, in James's view, all fed a desire to consume the privacy of the author as a mass-produced object while pretending to offer readers a view of the secluded life where the literary is born.

The culprit for James was a mass print industry that distorted literary meaning into celebrity spectacle. As he wrote in a notebook entry, the "devouring publicity" generated by modern media threatened the "extinction of all sense between public and private."[57] For James nothing illustrated this threat as vividly as the press's transformation of an author's study into a popular spectacle, a stage for the entertainment ("delightful peeps") of strangers. And yet, strikingly, no other author publicized the study—returned to portray it repeated times, in myriad ways—as frequently as James, and virtually all of James's many tales of "literary life" feature an author's study as a charged narrative site. There is an irony, then, in this obsessive return to the space of the study; James is hardly free from the temptation to make a literary spectacle out of a writer's workroom. At the same time, however, James's obsession with "devouring publicity" is also the source of exceptional insight about this aspect of modernity. For all his satire, James in his fiction undertakes a profound exploration of the way authorial privacy—the source of high literary expression—might not be able to exist apart from the mass pressures arrayed against it. For James, complex relations tied modern literary creativity to modern mass publicity.

The defining connections here are subtle but consequential. Certainly James believed with figures like Norton that serious engagement with literature was impossible without some shelter from the onslaught of modern conditions (the "false voice of commerce and cant").[58] Like those others, James associated that shelter with the intimate space of the author's study. In "The Right Real Thing" (1899), for instance, a biographer undertakes his nightly research on his subject in that famous author's study. Ashton Doyne's private study, the biographer believes, still holds the "personal presence" of the now dead author. So forceful is this "presence" for him (and so "personal" the space of the study) that the biographer awaits these hours of work in the study "very much as one of a pair of lovers might wait for the hour of their appointment."[59] With a characteristic irony, James confirms the value of authorial privacy by dramatizing the way an outsider—here a biographer—tries to acquire intimate knowledge about an artist by physically entering his study. When the biographer sees (or believes he sees) Doyne's own ghost blocking his entry to the study, the phantasm is both a rebuke to the intrusive biographer as well as James's confirmation of the symbolic importance of the private study.

Clearly, James is the source of the prohibition, the author-ghost who means to warn away the too-personal reader. For the literary authorities, to insist on the privacy of the author's study is to defend the autonomy of art, especially the art of the novel. Located a reflective distance from the complex social world it depicts, the novel requires impartial vision and aesthetic independence—"the beauty that comes from truth alone," as Howells wrote—in order to qualify as high art. Like a room dedicated to the work of writing, the worthy novel can serve no other purpose than the illumination created from the art of fiction—not social advocacy, not market success, not the attention of people of fashion, and certainly not the courting of mass publicity. But while the author's study represents authorial privacy and autonomy, in the unfolding of his plots the Jamesian study is above all the place of an exciting *violation* of privacy. That is, his stories always feature a pivotal intrusion or interruption in the space of the study, an intrusion that serves to entice readers with the promise of deep literary knowledge rather more than warn them away with stern threats. The intrusions are sometimes comic ("Death of a Lion," "The Altar of the Dead," "The Figure in the Carpet"), sometimes insidious ("The Aspern Papers," "The Lesson of the Master," "John Delavoy"), and often both. Like the biographer in "The Right Real Thing," the central characters in these stories are possessed of an overweening desire to enter into a study or a locked desk drawer where they are convinced they will find hidden knowledge. Even as that desire is condemned, however, the prohibition itself seems to signal the preeminent truth of the defining secret, usually hinted to be sexual or marital. In James's tales, the pursuit of literary meaning is the pursuit of prohibited meaning. The sense of hidden or privileged knowledge—a secret and the desire to know it—becomes the very sensibility James explores in his sustained treatment of "literary life."

Taken together, these stories show that the pursuit of a secret is for James a literary matter, the very substance of this fiction. In "The Aspern Papers," perhaps the best known of these tales, the narrator attempts to acquire a poet's private papers, convinced that they hold a suppressed secret about the artist's life. He is convinced, too, that it is a romantic or sexual secret. But James makes sure that his readers are far from being certain on either count—is the narrator's theory of Jeffrey Aspern's sexual secret really a reflection of the narrator's own intense desire to possess and publish the papers? That puzzle opens out into another: is the desire to possess the private papers the reader's sign of the narrator's *own* sexual secret, his impossible desire for the dead poet himself? This is the ambiguously sexual secret James embeds in his own tale. To read James's story is necessarily to want to know this secret; readers are allowed no superior position from which to avoid a "personal" wish to know that is disarmingly like that of the voyeuristic narrator. In "The Aspern Papers," the desire to know is a state of mind more complex than the "mania for publicity" linked with mass culture even as it is marked as inseparable from that culture.[60] The prospect of what

James calls the "extinction of all sense between private and public," however worrying, is also generative. The threat itself is the origin of a new aesthetic "sense," a consciousness generated out of the very erosion of clear demarcations between desire and knowledge, and between privacy and print. The instability (yet continued importance) of this boundary becomes the very ground of the literary; readers of James must possess this new sense to be able to follow the intricacies and ambiguities of the fiction. Indeed, to read James is to cultivate this sense, a sublime "perception of incongruities" that sharpens as it plays across the uncertain boundaries of private and public.[61]

Following Eve Sedgwick's lead, scholars have linked this narrative structure to the question of James's own sexuality and the cultural prohibitions on homosexual intimacy that kept it largely veiled.[62] This biographical explanation is compelling—no less so for the way it fulfills James's fictional warning (or is it a teasing invitation?) that scholars are wont to find literary meaning in sexual biography. But the fact that James himself anticipates this critical linkage shows that he already recognized the sexual energies bound up with the drive toward public exposure in mass culture. The reality of those energies—the *realism* of diffuse public feelings of excitement, speculation, and mediated intimacy circulating in mass print—become the *literary* energies that animate James's own aesthetics of secrecy and publicity. To be sure, realists like James remained opposed to the "irreflective and uncritical" drive to expose and display that they saw in mass culture.[63] But James in particular came to see the modern "insurmountable desire to *know*" as a profoundly reflective state of mind that springs from the conditions it opposes, a state at once personal to the reader (to *his* reader) and distinctly public—public in that it creates a new kind of collective reading experience out of a shared desire to know the literary.[64] Rooted in the same conditions, literary meaning is not opposed to mass culture but is rather meaning that relies on the commercial public for its work of "eternal distinction-making."[65]

Although James's style and thematic obsessions are among the most distinct literary artifacts of the age, they are created out of the same conditions of public communications that created mass culture. James's own study was a "refuge," but in composing and publishing his writers' tales he helps make the author's study a distinct "place of exhibition" (as he dubs it in "The Lesson of the Master"), a realist site at which private sensibility becomes a spectacle for others' eyes. James's fiction is nothing short of an exhibition of the impulse to expose—to "snap at the bait of publicity"—on display through the literary forms those impulses engender, and "collected in such store as to stock, as to launch, a museum" ("The Papers"). For James, the display of these intricacies of cultural perception is as much a "thrill" as any mass spectacle, for it offers readers who desire it the public intimacy of a shared adventure of discovering what literature would or could turn out to be in a new world of publicity.[66]

Europe, Race, and Travel

The literary autonomy championed by literary intellectuals is founded on a contradiction. Identified as it is with individual thought and expression, the domain of literature is open to any qualified author. Racial caste, sex, and social standing are all extraneous to the creative literary consciousness. But the same literary autonomy depends on constrained patterns of mobility. A lack of access to education is one obvious restriction; for whole categories of Americans, the distance to a requisite education is almost always too far to traverse. Less obviously, high literary expression—to qualify as such—must also be informed by an implicit geographical map, by specific routes of travel and their terminal cities. One needn't have traveled those routes in person, but literary understanding must embrace what one observer called "travel-improved taste."[67] The contours of the literary in this period follow specific links between travel and writing, connections that trace possible avenues for change even as they mark entrenched lines of racial and imperial power.

Even before appearing in print, Charles Chesnutt recognized the prestige he could claim through the autonomy of the literary. "Shut up in my study," he records in his journal, "without the companionship of one congenial mind, I can enjoy the society of the greatest wits and scholars of England, can revel in the genius of her poets and statesmen, and by a slight effort of the imagination, find myself in the company of the greatest men of earth." Here the space of the study identifies a peculiarly social solitude, a species of belonging that is cognitive and therefore unconstrained by time or place. Unconstrained, too, by color: for Chesnutt, an African American living in the post-Reconstruction South, the space of the study also means a temporary release from the stigma attached to blackness. But this literary privacy is emphatically not a retreat or withdrawal. Chesnutt's journal illustrates instead the way his study is also a point of departure. "I will go to the Metropolis," he writes, and the generality of the phrase is apt: high literary aspiration in this moment is a simultaneous ambition for the literal and cultural mobility of a metropolitan life. Part of Chesnutt's literary sensibility is his recognition of the continuity between authorship and the self-projection realized in travel: "I worked hard, worried Susie [Chesnutt's wife] into a positive dislike for me, reading so much, [then] packed my valises, and the following week took the train for Washington[,] N. Y. etc."[68] The national recognition Chesnutt would receive through his published short stories and novels proved his ambitions were warranted. Yet even the fulfillment of Chesnutt's desire for travel and authorship confirmed channels of national and global restriction. The pursuit of high authorship would eventually leave Chesnutt stranded outside national literary institutions, just as it would prompt W. E. B. DuBois to choose exile in Africa.

Patterns of travel encourage national feeling while separating cultural strata. Just as immigrants share rites of arrival and inspection, the oceanic travel of the new professional classes in this era consolidates a distinct cultural identity for those Americans who depart from the same U.S. ports where immigrants come ashore. Transatlantic crossings, more than any other travel route, come to define a zone of shared experience for the American elite. "A voyage across the Atlantic is today such a common undertaking that most travellers make as brief preparation for it as if they were going by train from New York to Chicago," the poet Edmund Clarence Stedman wrote.[69] A leisure voyage to Europe was not common, of course; it was still a luxury open to a relatively small number of Americans of means. But as an idea and a cultural symbol, the transatlantic travel of affluent Americans also articulated a wider national significance. It represented an accreditation for American artists and thinkers (James Russell Lowell wrote that Howells's stay in Venice was "the University in which he has fairly earned the degree of Master"); it signified an American claim on a notion of transnational "civilization" in an age of empire; and it was a sign of the arrival of the United States as a global economic power.[70]

Circuits of transatlantic travel also form the literal field of production for high literary art. The work of writing travel sketches, literary translations, and reviews of foreign books is the standard apprenticeship for the high literary career, and writers dispatch manuscripts from European cities to publishers in Boston, New York, and Chicago. The travel impressions Howells wrote in Italy and sent to the *Atlantic* and the *Boston Advertiser*, for instance, became the material for his first books, *Venetian Life* (1866) and *Italian Journeys* (1869). James's travel writings for E. L. Godkin's *The Nation* in 1870–71 were collected in his *Transatlantic Sketches* (1875), the first of several travel volumes James would produce in his career. Constance Fenimore Woolson, Henry Adams, John DeForest, Edith Wharton, and John Hay all made transatlantic travel integral to the shape and substance of their works. Howells's first novel, *Their Wedding Journey* (1871), was fashioned explicitly as an extension of his travel writing, a "form of fiction" he describes as "half-story, half-travel sketch." His protagonists, Basil and Isabel March, return from Europe to embark upon a tour of the diverse scenes of American life. They undertake this venture, the reader is told, as "very conscious people," and it is clear that their consciousness, their manner of seeing and feeling, is informed by their recollected "passages of European travel."[71]

"Very conscious people": the word "conscious" acquires a particular semantic density in the high literary writing of this period. As Howells's plot suggests, the valence attached to the word is inseparable from Europe as symbol and cultural site. When James defined the novelist as a historian of consciousness, he was sure that the deepest source for such a history was the "thicker civility" of Europe. The American, he asserts, "*must* deal, more or less, even if by implication, with Europe."[72] But exactly what was the substance of this travel-enriched "consciousness"? There are clues in the grammar of James's formulations. "Consciousness" has a history (recorded in novels) and an ancestral home (Europe) but, as the abstract noun suggests, consciousness can be conceived as something transpersonal or transcendent with the capacity to rise above the determination of any particular origins. In this sense, the idea of "fine consciousness" is the heir of the Enlightenment belief that human understanding, if developed and intensified, can free itself from partisan interest and local blindness. Following the "trained judgment of the wisest and the best," one *Dial* writer insisted, "leads us towards, though never quite to, a rounded perfection of mind and soul."[73]

Matthew Arnold, of course, was the most famous proponent of this secular perfectionism. *Culture and Anarchy* (1869) was a text of enormous influence in American literary circles, and Arnold's own 1883 transatlantic journey, for a lecture tour through a series of major American cities, made his ideas available to an even broader U.S. audience. The wide acceptance of Arnold's ideas among educated Americans suggests something of the eagerness in this moment for thought and expression more expansive than the era's nationalist pieties and commercial values. From another perspective, the appeal of a perfected "mind and soul" is the appeal of a fantasy, a desire for an impossible wholeness or omniscience. But the force of the notion is also recognizable in the wariness—sometimes it was hostility—with which many in the United States greeted the cultural dictates of the new transatlantic consciousness. Walt Whitman spoke for the wary when he dissented from the new authority of an Arnoldian "delicacy, refinement, elegance, prettiness, propriety, criticism, analysis: all of them things which threaten to overwhelm us."[74] For Whitman it was not mass sensation but a narrow sensibility of refined "analysis" that threatened to submerge other modes of aesthetic understanding. The consciousness advocated in high culture was not simply the "general humane spirit" of the human race, to use Arnold's phrase, but a particular framework of thought—particular, and therefore partial, for all its cosmopolitan expansiveness. Forgetting its own particularity is the risk for transatlantic consciousness.

Jane Addams analyzes this risk in her book *Twenty Years at Hull-House* (1910). In the chapter "The Snare of Preparation," the writer and urban reformer looks back to her own transatlantic travel in the 1880s (Henry James was a fellow passenger on one crossing).[75] It was a time, Addams remembers, when American daughters (unlike their mothers' generation) "crossed the seas in search of culture."[76] But not long after her arrival, the "pursuit of cultivation" (71) begins to seem blinkered and insular. Addams visits a London slum and sees a large massing of the poor gathered to receive cheap vegetables, "clutching forward for food which was already unfit to eat" (68). For Addams the shock of the experience creates a stark shift in perception. The ideal of a cultivated consciousness suddenly appears not as a universal subjectivity but rather a particular "attitude" that springs from distinct class conditions. The young American woman travels across Europe unable to make a "real connection to the life around her" and is "only at ease when in the familiar receptive attitude afforded by the art gallery and the opera house" (72). Intellectual acuity now reappears as a hardened and diminished object. The young American's "trained and developed powers" of perception, Addams sardonically writes, found use only "as she sat 'being cultivated'" in concert halls or museums, spaces that are merely "sublimated and romanticized" classrooms (72).

Yet importantly, Addams's own realization about "the feverish search after culture" was a revelation ratified through art.

It was doubtless in such moods [of "moral revulsion"] that I founded my admiration for Albrecht Dürer, taking his wonderful pictures, however, in the most unorthodox manner, merely as human documents. I was chiefly appealed to by his unwillingness to lend himself to a smooth and cultivated view of life, by his determination to record its frustrations and even the hideous forms which darken the day for our human imagination and to ignore no human complications. (75)

What does it mean when a gallery of Dürer's pictures confirms Addams's conviction that art galleries can cultivate insularity? Rather than exposing a lapse in logic, Addams's "unorthodox" reflections redefine the relation between art and consciousness. In the wake of a perceptual shock, Addams finds that Dürer's lines and shades express her specific experience in London, experience she now conceives in terms of "hideous forms" capable of breaking open a too-insular understanding of human conditions. Addams's critique actually confirms the "eternal distinction-making" function of high art, even as the distinction she finds expressed in Dürer permanently alters her way of seeing and defining what art actually is.

Addams freely acknowledges she has appropriated Dürer, taking his centuries-old masterpieces as artifacts or forms that distill her own crisis of consciousness. But this act of what Brodhead would call imaginative "acquisition" or possession goes hand in hand with a deliberate *dis*owning of a prescribed program of narrow cultivation, now seen as a likely "snare" that might well limit her ability to recognize darker tracts of experience and social perplexities. Appropriation in this sense is markedly reflexive, a means by which Addams turns from aesthetic artifacts to questions of social and material conditions, then returns yet again to recognize an image of her own reordered consciousness in this set of "human documents." Cultivation here has come to mean an ability to see incongruities in social experience as a means of transforming consciousness, with the art gallery as a site of relay between aesthetic reflection and worldly conditions.

It is therefore significant that when Addams later ponders artifacts of modern city life, her thinking exhibits the same sort of reflexivity. The attraction among city populations to popular amusements like "looping the loop" ("amid shrieks of simulated terror") or "dancing in disorderly saloon halls," Addams theorizes, are not forms of regressive or infantile sensation-seeking but rather a "natural reaction to a day spent in noisy factories and in trolley cars whirling through the distracting streets." Mass amusements, in other words, might be another mode of appropriation, a means of giving pleasurable or uncanny form to everyday shocks and disorienting conditions. Like Dürer's pictures, mass amusements can be grasped as artifacts or "human documents" that permit one to reflect on the dynamic relations between cultural consciousness and social conditions.[77]

The best fiction in the transatlantic mode achieves a similar reflexivity of critical insight. The visit to a European art gallery forms a pivotal site for the formation of consciousness in a transnational context. One of James's favorite shorthand phrases, "'doing' a gallery," conveys through its telegraphic brevity something of the way European museum-going is assumed to be in the background of any serious cultural analysis, part of the infrastructure of high consciousness.[78] While a cosmopolitan sensibility is a ground for meaning in this context, a close examination shows that the "acquisitive mind" that issues from the work of "doing a gallery" is neither uniform nor predictable.

The opening scene in James's early novel *The American* (1877) offers a glimpse into this transatlantic frame, for the novel's protagonist is presented to the reader through his own attempt to take on the Louvre in Paris. Sitting before a painting on a large circular divan, Christopher Newman experiences "profound enjoyment"—not, however, an enjoyment of the famous painting but a relief in his relaxed bodily "posture."

The gentleman in question had taken serene possession of its softest spot, and, with his head thrown back and his legs outstretched, was staring at Murillo's beautiful moon-borne Madonna in profound enjoyment of his posture. He had removed his hat, and flung down beside him a little red guidebook and an opera-glass.[79]

Newman's tour of Louvre paintings ("he had looked at all the pictures to which an asterisk was affixed in those formidable pages of fine print in his Bädeker") has left him with an "aesthetic headache" (515). His first real pleasure is this languid extension of his physical frame on the divan. Newman's lack of responsiveness to the art is thus made to correspond to the prominence given his body, and the reader quickly recognizes that Newman is not a museum patron but the novel's equivalent of a museum specimen, an object exhibited for the close scrutiny of a literary observer.

The largest significance of the gallery, then, is not as a setting for realist characters but as the ground for the consciousness of realist readers. James's text brings to the surface what is usually subtextual: that understanding national meaning depends on extranational sites such as the Louvre. The museum gallery is a second transnational home for a reader who possesses the requisite trained sight: "An observer with anything of an eye for national types would have had no difficulty in determining the local origin of this [gentleman], . . . a powerful specimen of an American."

He had a very well-formed head, with a shapely, symmetrical balance of the frontal and the occipital development, and a good deal of straight, rather dry brown hair.

His complexion was brown, and his nose had a bold, well-marked arch. His eye was of a clear, cold gray, and save for a rather abundant mustache he was clean-shaved. He had the flat jaw and sinewy neck which are frequent in the American type; but the traces of national origin are a matter of expression even more than of feature, and it was in this respect that our friend's countenance was supremely eloquent. (516)

The superabundance of visual detail here, characteristic of realist writing, establishes what the narrator calls "the conditions of his identity" as an American "specimen" (516). Sympathetic but superior, the "eye" of the presumed reader who has the acuity to appreciate great European paintings also has the experience to discern national "types." These two kinds of visual objects, the artwork and the human type, are aesthetically distinct (the narrator emphasizes that the sprawled Newman "is by no means sitting for his portrait" [517]). Nevertheless, museum-trained sight is a key faculty for the realist "observer" and reading the national type presumes an international museum tutelage.

Whitman's warning against the tyranny of elegance makes itself felt here. Certainly in *The American*, Newman is marked out as less knowing than the cosmopolitan "observer" who is invited to take Newman's measure against the backdrop of the Louvre. The observing consciousness is expansive, reflective; the national "specimen" a more inert representative object. The fact that the cosmopolitan observer—the narrator and by extension the reader—is the more knowing subject in this pair is clearly significant; as critics such as Amy Kaplan and June Howard have argued, in much American realism and naturalism the subject who inhabits the position of the observer tends to enjoy (or at least aspire to) social power that is denied to the objects of literary vision.[80] Even a millionaire can become a restricted object, the social inferior of a canny reader. What this critical paradigm overlooks, however, is the fact that sites like the art gallery can foster oscillations between the positions of observer and object, allowing for reflexive shifts in perspective between an observing mind and the feeling body as an analytic route toward examining *connections* between consciousness and conditions. In a surprising yet telling private letter, the thoroughly urbane James identified his own Americanness through a self-reflective moment in a Venice gallery, "a certain glorious room at the Ducal Palace, where Paolo Veronese revels on the ceilings and Tintoret rages on the walls": "I feel as if I might sit there forever (as I sat there a long time this morning) and only feel more and more my inexorable Yankeehood."[81]

Of course, there are Yankees and Yankees. The transatlantic context sometimes functions for American authors as a species of disavowal, a means of distinguishing the self from the felt strictures of national identity—even the identity of the transatlantic American traveler. Such is James's aim in *Italian Hours* when, evoking an image of a "huge Anglo-Saxon wave" flooding through Berne and into Italy (fifty thousand "accommodated spectators" with a "season-ticket" to the Alps), he throws into relief the singular Henry James, a figure apart in Lucerne, satisfied to sit, unhurried, "in the immense new Hotel National and read the *New York Times* on a blue satin divan."[82] But as much as this may be a tactic of self-exemption, it is also an act of self-objectification, the construction of a slightly self-mocking "Henry James" who, like his own Christopher Newman, is seated on a divan and subjected to the reader's vision as a specimen—in this case, an example of what Alistair MacIntyre calls "the consuming aesthete."[83]

Aesthetic disavowal in such instances is the other side of critical vision. Picturing American travelers as "trooping barbarians" may be snobbery or self-exemption, but it may also be a flippant instance of what is elsewhere a more careful analysis of the American as a "commercial person" (the label James gives Christopher Newman's subspecies of American), now recognized as a subject who could not be cordoned off from the conditions of transatlantic aesthetic consciousness itself. Edith Wharton's most sustained transatlantic novel, *The Custom of the Country* (1913), makes the critique of the "commercial person" unmistakable—and darkly comic. Wharton uses the cross-cultural perspective to embody brilliantly the destructive capacity of the energies of American capitalism. Her protagonist, Undine Spragg, is a rich American divorcée who blazes a path of ruin through Europe. With a "business-like intentness on gaining her end," Undine sees absolutely everything as a form of commodity in one vast open market, whether it is pearls, paintings, or husbands.[84] In Undine, Wharton shows the instrumentalist nature of a market society as wondrously corrosive. Undine possesses a cultural Midas touch under which every custom, human relation, and aesthetic creation is converted to brittle gold and thus destroyed.

The very extravagance of Undine's portrait as a "commercial person," however, hints at a degree of unease. Here and elsewhere, Wharton is at pains to sort the transatlantic sheep from the goats—that is, to separate those who travel for culture from those who travel for profit (the "buccaneers," as Wharton labels them). But the distinction is hard to maintain. Captains of industry and connoisseurs of art literally traveled in the same transatlantic circles, and the most famous art collectors, such as Henry Clay

Frick and Andrew Carnegie, were also the most famous "commercial persons" of the age. American travelers were, in a sense, the human objects in a larger field of transatlantic commerce and communication. Cyrus Field laid the first transatlantic cable in 1866, making possible the almost instantaneous exchange of stock prices and securities, diplomatic communications, and syndicated news, and this rapid electronic exchange made possible a new transnational economy that underwrote the leisure travel on land and sea.[85] Although travelers to Europe frequently conceived their journey as a "return" to a premodern way of life (illustrated in stories such as James's 1875 story "The Passionate Pilgrim"), even the search for a cultural inheritance was never outside this new circuit of economic development.

How, then, to distinguish travel from transatlantic trafficking? In moments of the sharpest self-awareness, literary works of the period reflect the knowledge that high consciousness itself can be subject to the instrumentalities and forms of the "blaring" commercial world it seeks to transcend. In many stories and novels, the transatlantic context seems suddenly to stand exposed as little more than a debased trade route, an economic circuit in which art and aesthetic feeling become no different than brokered goods. In Wharton's novella *The Touchstone* (1900), for instance, artistic consciousness is made to undergo the starkest commodification. The private letters of a famous expatriate novelist, Margaret Aubyn, fall prey to an "alchemistic process" that transforms these literary inscriptions into an economic object of transatlantic theft and sale—they become, variously, a "check," a "bribe," a "weapon," and a collection of "stolen goods." Wharton holds out the hope for a countermagic: the "inexhaustible alchemy" of human love may be able to redeem the sale. Yet even these "luxuries" of human feeling (they are drawn from a "funded passion") bear the imprint of the commodity form they try to overcome.[86]

In James's fiction, this self-reflexive question about aesthetic consciousness intensifies in tone and reach over the course of his career. His Gilbert Osmond in *Portrait of a Lady* (1881) is only one of James's many connoisseurs whose appreciation of art and beauty—including, in Osmond's case, his wife—is inseparable from a desire for ownership. Any real distinction between beauty and property has collapsed. In *Portrait of a Lady* this erosion is a clear sign of Osmond's amorality, but by the time of his late novel *The Golden Bowl* (1904), James removes any such moral delimitation. The American millionaire Adam Verver makes London his headquarters for a campaign to collect the greatest European art treasures—not for personal property but for the national prestige of an American Museum.

But, like the snake that swallows its own tail, Verver's ambitions for "a museum of museums" makes aesthetic history a self-consuming institution and the great museums of Europe akin to warehouses poised for a monopoly takeover by a commercial empire.[87]

Transatlantic fiction also finds commercial traffic in what is supposed to be the intimate sphere of marriage and home. By the rules of the genre, American novels depicting European settings are compelled to contemplate prospects of international marriage, and narratives of cross-cultural marriages—most often involving American women wedding European men—become a notable subgenre. Journalists take up the theme, too; stories of American heiresses abroad are a favorite of the mass press. But in high realist novels, the specter of a flourishing industry in transatlantic fortune hunting is less entertaining than it is internally corrosive. In fiction by writers such as Woolson, Wharton, and James, the cross-cultural marriage provides a lens through which the novel's traditional subject matter, the social and affective material of middle-class life, is seen at least momentarily to be penetrated to the core by the values of a market culture—its habits of display, its idolizing of quantity and novelty, its supreme principle of property. Testing these forces, James's novels and stories of transatlantic marriage such as "The Siege of London" (1882) and "Lady Barberina" (1883) put pressure on every kind of domestic sentiment, however genuine or duplicitous, to discover its degree of infiltration by the modern marketplace. After Wharton's *The Custom of the Country* (1913) and James's *The Wings of the Dove* (1902) and *The Golden Bowl* (1904), the Anglo-American novel's traditional reliance on a separation of private family feeling and public systems like the market will no longer pretend to hold. As Bill Brown has argued, James's late novels begin to revise the portrait of the "commercial person" by trying to understand a human subjectivity that *relies* on modern powers of objectification to experience intimacy and to know the world.[88]

The cross-cultural marriage in James's "Lady Barberina" uncovers another crucial aspect of the matter of travel. "Intermarrying" between Americans and Britons is "quite fair play," one observer declares, because "they were all one race after all."[89] The felt need to articulate rules of "fair play" for British-American marriages, spoken as if to establish fair trade policy, is one more instance of a transatlantic ironizing of the marriage novel. But the story's open acknowledgment of the rules for marriage as racial—"they were all one race after all"—taps a second, deeper subtext. As a conceptual category, "race" in this moment was pliable to a fault. The term was used variously to signify nation-states, genetic populations, historical cultures, family lines of descent, and designated color groups. James is following a standard usage when he describes his travel writing about European countries as the work of "comparing one race to another."[90] The same sense of a national people as a race is the governing meaning when James describes the white American-British couple as "*inter*marrying." But significantly, meanings shift gear in mid-sentence: Britons and Americans *can* intermarry without fear of breaking any taboo because these national races are, from another semantic perspective, finally "one race." With this slip into a biological or genetic understanding of race, the story momentarily alludes to a world of relations structured by color, a global world that always subtends affluent transatlantic travel but usually remains out of view in the fiction.

What is a subtext in transatlantic fiction was highly visible in transatlantic politics. Stories about British-American marriages echo proposals in the same period for a literal "Race Union" between Great Britain and the United States. The rapid expansion of U.S. industries in the later nineteenth century astonished and frequently alarmed other nations. By 1902 British author W. T. Stead described an imminent "Americanisation of the world" and predicted that U.S. economic expansion would outstrip the reach of the British Empire. As Stead pointed out, the prospect of U.S. dominance was prompting many in Britain to call for the creation of a new polity. Viewing Britain as "the cradle of the race" and America the industrial empire of the future, writers and political theorists began to discuss proposals for forging a new political union on the basis of race.[91] This idea, however radical or unrealistic, was a logical extension of the widely held belief that the United States was already a race union, a nation (as Herbert Spencer put it) consisting of "allied varieties of the Aryan race." Hence, for many, a more formal uniting of the United States with Britain was all but preordained. The proposed union is "as natural as marriage between man and woman," wrote one New York lawyer. "It consummates the purpose of the creation of the race."[92]

As fantastic as a united Anglo state sounds today, the proposal reflected an emerging global order that was altogether real. Any map that charted the world according to the economic centers ringing the Atlantic and the imperial territories that lie beyond would have been a map of "race union"—that is, a federation of white-controlled economic capitals united by their competition for the labor and lands of people of color.[93] The uncharted demarcation DuBois famously called the "color line" was a third global axis, a line that traced a geography of power at the same time that it marked a power of geographic mobility. American travelers favored routes among North Atlantic countries but U.S.-European travel also offered gateways into imperial regions beyond. At the 1876 Philadelphia Centennial fair, the Cook's American World Ticket office advertised the patterns of mobility available to the leisure-class traveler: "Tourist tickets to all parts of the United States, the continent of Europe, Egypt and Palestine, and around the world traveling East or West . . . no matter how extended and complicated the route." Transatlantic travel was embedded in a larger global mobility structured by race, and the politics of the color line meant that the tourists in possession of a "World Ticket" were almost always white travelers.[94]

Was the "consciousness" in transatlantic letters therefore a racial consciousness? Was high literary culture white? Empirically, the answer is no. But the pervasive racial logic that assumed a cultivated subject was white was both a historical fact and a generative problem. The vexed racial logic is most clearly seen in the effort of a number of African American writers to advance the cause of black people through intellectual and cultural achievement. Their productive attempts to wrestle with the color-line dilemmas in the pursuit of "the highest arts" illuminate much of what is ignored or disavowed by white authors. The works they produce, moreover, create a strikingly different American portrait of the "travel-improved" consciousness.

When in 1897 a number of leading African American intellectuals gathered to establish the American Negro Academy, their organized effort to "promote the publication of literary and scholarly works" by black American authors was a dual political challenge. In their charter, the group's stated goal is directed at white racism: the academy will refute "vicious assaults" on the race. Their unstated aim is intraracial. The dedicated purpose of fostering "higher culture, at home and abroad," is a gauntlet thrown down to the accommodationist policies of Booker T. Washington.[95] The academy members, opposing both Washington and the "caste-ridden" white establishment, now set their sights on making high literary expression and culture a vehicle for promoting full political equality for African Americans.

The triangular struggle reflects a racial politics of high culture that is contingent and relational. With shifting responses directed toward two different racial fronts, the academy members marshal notions of Arnoldian cultivation for use in black nationalism and hold up elite learning in the name of enfranchising the black masses. Internal tensions result from this constellation, but so do vital and uncompromising prospects. Both are registered with particular clarity in the writings of academy founder Alexander Crummell, whose books *The Future of Africa* (1862) and *America and Africa* (1891) are among the first works to make West Africa visible in U.S. transatlantic writing. A revered leader and clergyman, the seventy-four-year-old Crummell was in his last year of life when he headed the effort to establish a scholarly society for African American intellectuals. Crummell's stature and long career helped him enlist in the academy such young talents as poet Paul Laurence Dunbar, the essayist and Howard University professor Kelly Miller, and DuBois, then a lecturer in sociology at the University of Pennsylvania. Anna Julia Cooper, a scholar of Latin and Greek who was the principal of the successful M Street School in Washington, D.C., attended the inaugural meeting of the academy and may have been a member. Her collection of essays, *A Voice from the South* (1892), argues for the importance of defending the "untrammeled intellect of the Negro" as a political as well as human right.[96]

When Crummell was a young man, his attachment to Victorian ideals of "civilization" formed a keystone of his vision of racial uplift for black Americans and racial "regeneration" for the peoples of Africa. Civilization ("the scientific processes of literature, art, and philosophy") was for Crummell the heaven-born twin of Christian evangelization, an instrument of the universal redemption God held out to all peoples.[97] And, like Christianity, civilization had been given first to European peoples, who had the obligation to disseminate its gifts to darker races still living in "heathenism." Although Crummell could be famously caustic about European domination ("For three hundred years the European has been traversing the coast of Africa" and "the whole coast . . . has been ravaged wherever his footstep has fallen," leaving behind a "history of rapine and murder" [174]), he shared the Victorian view that the historical fates of races were subject to what he called "God's economy" (196). For Crummell, holding to this view had a particular urgency: how else to explain the devastation experienced by so many native peoples in the "funereal" history (163) of white expansionism except through the hand of God? For this Christian clergyman, to give the power to any other agency than God would be to concede intolerable tenets of white superiority.

Although Crummell's acceptance of this history at times leaves him just short of a blasphemous bitterness, it also supplies a providential vision of a future for "the African people" across the globe. "The aborigines of the South-Sea Islands, of New Zealand, and Australia, are departing like the shadow before the rising sun of the Anglo-Saxon emigrant," Crummell writes, but "amid all theses melancholy facts, there seems to be one exception," the "negro," whose survival and spreading emancipation from slavery bespeaks a divinely chosen role in the future history of the world (163). The same religious underpinnings that compel Crummell to accept white domination as part of a providential design also give him the language to predict black cultural ascendancy. In one essay titled "The Destined Superiority of the Negro," he even claims that the "noblest" future civilization will be produced by African peoples.

More characteristically, however, Crummell in this period tended to use the Victorian discourse of civilization to articulate a vision that recognized West Africa and the Caribbean in the transatlantic circuit of travel and cultural exchange joining the United States and Britain. It was a circuit Crummell himself had hoped to cultivate when, immediately after receiving his degree from Cambridge University, he left England for Liberia and spent the next two decades teaching at Liberia College in Monrovia. The steamship journey from Liverpool to the west coast of Africa, as Crummell portrays it, enlarges the reach of civilized travel rather than departs from it. The voyage "is a grand panorama of sights and incidents," Crummell writes, "bringing to the traveller's sight the Channel with its several isles, the Bay of Biscay, the peak of Teneriffe, Madeira, with its varied and cosmopolitan life, and its beautiful scenery[,] and its aristocratic society" (61). In bringing before the "eye" of the transatlantic traveler the scenery and cities of Liberia and Sierra Leone ("the grand civilization which has sprung up on that benighted coast" [276]), Crummell recasts the Victorian grammar of race and progress to allow black participation in a no-longer-white civilization. Although traditional arts and institutions of African peoples count for little by this way of reckoning, Crummell's rhetoric makes the language of race hierarchy undercut the color line. "Black Yankees" (174) like Crummell, he writes in *The Future of Africa*, for all their "trials" at the hands of whites, have "not been divorced from [American] civilization," and in their fitness for free governance are superior "to the Russian, to the Polander, to the Hungarian, to the Italian" (173).

More important than this recalibration of color, Crummell's version of a Victorian global historiography insists on an independent role for diasporic black people: "America is deeply indebted to Africa" (183). Like William Ferris, a Yale graduate who was another academy member, Crummell's investment in high culture led him to articulate a variant of black nationalism that made the history of civilization impossible to conceive without Africa. Crummell's influence is clear in Ferris's two-volume study *The African Abroad: or, His Evolution in Western Civilization* (1913), an encyclopedic work that recasts world history by making African military and cultural achievement an indispensable part of the ancient world and by claiming the Americas as the second home of the African. Ferris's image of "the African abroad" refashions the black historical subject in a striking way. In Ferris's history, the exported black slave is supplanted by the black traveler, a figure with agency, mobility, and a savvy consciousness.[98]

"How hopeful are the scenes of travel!" Crummell's exclamation in an 1894 letter to a friend signifies the way an Anglo-African transatlanticism remained to the end the frame for Crummell's hopes. "Since my return to London I have been visiting the galleries, the great churches, the Law courts," he writes. Meeting "two black gentlemen" from the Gold Coast in the famous Lincoln's Inn law library and later encountering an impressive "West India gentleman" during his visit in London are travel "scenes" that bolster his faith in transatlantic uplift (89). The pleasure Crummell receives from the sight of black men in London galleries and libraries touches upon the question of class that critics have raised about the institutions like the academy founded by the black American elite.[99] Was the American Negro Academy in essence a gentlemen's club to prove the class bona fides of the black bourgeoisie, status secured by constructing a class difference from the largely unlettered U.S. black population? While resentments and aspirations inflected by class may well have been among the motives of academy members, Crummell's delight at the sight of "black gentlemen" bespeaks a historical variation of the transatlantic "acquisitive mind" that cannot be reduced to a worship of gentility.

In finding pleasure in the sight of black men in London, Crummell's "scenes of travel" appropriate the symbolic capital of spaces of international high culture at a moment when civil space was the most relevant theater of domestic race politics. Once he had returned from Liberia to live in the United States, Crummell's commitment to high cultural advancement changed markedly in its focus. By the time he began his short tenure as the first president of the American Negro Academy, he had become doubtful that learning and letters could join black and white in a shared civilization. Slavery had been abolished, but all around him in the United States Crummell witnessed "the divorce of the black race from all the great activities" in American life: "It is a state of divorcement from the mercantile life of the country; from the scientific life of the land; from its literary life; and from its social life" (206). Yet Jim Crow conditions and global imperialism only heightened the importance of high cultural pursuits for Crummell. In an essay that appeared in the academy's publication series titled "The Attitude of the American Mind Toward Negro Intellect" (1898), Crummell declares that black advancement is a process of active "warfare" and "its main weapon is the cultivated and scientific mind" (294). High culture is not an elevated plane but an arena of "struggle." Crummell's "Negro Intellect" essay shows his advocacy of the "highest arts" (285) for what it was: a counteroffensive against a systemic white campaign directed at the race as a whole. The "Negro curriculum" prescribed by whites, Crummell insists, is no curriculum at all but a "caste education" (297) to make the population an "unthinking labor-machine" (296). Its intent is to make African peoples the only race without intellectuals and thus the world's permanent "serfs." Jim Crow education is not a matter of white "indifference or neglect" (290), then, but the latest instance of a deliberate, sustained effort to "stamp out the brains of the Negro" (291).

Crummell's call for black intellectual cultivation goes hand in hand with his urging of "intelligent impatience" at the exploitation of black labor. A striking phrase, "intelligent impatience" suggests that black scholars and artists share with working-class laborers the need "to demand a larger share of the wealth which [the Negro's] toil creates for others" (296). Crummell expands on the broad "work of intelligence" that is the special responsibility of "scholars and thinkers." The labor of intellectuals finally produces not merely mental constructs or ornaments of beauty, Crummell argues, but forms of action (the work of those "who have got insight into the life of things, and learned the art by which men touch the springs of action" [287]). Crummell's concern with high culture is not a bid for acceptance by the white "cultured classes" ("they have left us terribly alone" [290], as he bluntly puts it); it is rather an enterprise in the service of "the entire social and domestic life of our people" (287).

The overt political context of Crummell's late essays exposes the tacitly "white" consciousness behind most transatlantic high culture at the same time that it aggressively appropriates those territories for the creation of a black public sphere. "Seeing that the American mind in the general, revolts from Negro genius," Crummell writes, "the Negro himself is duty bound to see to the cultivation and the fostering of his own race-capacity" (298). By the end of Crummell's career, his Anglo-African transatlanticism is no longer the domain of an abstract civilization but the transnational geography of a black public sphere—"*our* world of intellect" (288), as he stresses it. The creation of this sphere is not an imitation of whiteness, even though it *is* a pointed appropriation—both imaginary and political—of European geography. This becomes clear as he closes his "Negro Intellect" essay by recounting scenes of black artistic achievements in Europe—Henry Tanner's prize for his painting *The Raising of Lazarus,* awarded in Paris and destined for the "famous Luxembourg Gallery," and the several occasions of "triumph" that Paul Laurence Dunbar received in the "grand metropolis of Letters and Literature, the city of London" (300). The effect of the litany transforms the contours of transatlantic culture. Invoking these scenes, Crummell recasts the European gallery as an exiled outpost of a black "world of intellect" and calls up an African American "republic of letters" (288) that is flourishing most visibly outside the borders of Jim Crow America. High culture will be the home in exile for the "intellectual being" of the race in a hostile age. In his shift from a civilizationist discourse to the language of a literary counterpublic, Crummell shows the power of the public sphere idea to reorder an existing social imaginary.

But literary culture was not the only resource for conceptual reordering. During precisely the same decades as Crummell's career, entrepreneurs had discovered that what Crummell called the "grand panorama of sights and incidents" afforded by travel could be produced at home for remarkable profits by deploying new technologies. By making flat photographs into three-dimensional scenes, stereographs permitted American viewers to feel as though they were physically standing before the Cathedral of Notre Dame or a Cairo bazaar. Even the somatic experience of travel, the sensations of motion itself, acquired a profitable glamour. The rotating painted scenes of mechanical panoramas became increasingly sophisticated in this period, incorporating photographs and later film, and producing more realistic sensations of motion and kinetic visual stimulation. In the "Panorama of the Fleet of the Compagnie Générale Transatlantique," for instance, customers boarded a re-creation of the company's newest steamship to watch ports and coastal landscapes "go by" as the moving pictures created the feeling of shipboard travel and live actors dressed as sailors and officers mingled with would-be passengers.[100] Similarly, the "panoramic vision" that came into existence with rapid rail travel—the ever-changing relation of background and foreground objects, the space-swallowing velocity that made those objects into dynamic moving shapes of color and shadow—was distilled and mass marketed in the new medium of cinema, as films stimulated and then supplied a huge popular appetite for what Crummell called "scenes of travel." French and American companies in particular produced hundreds of scenic films featuring the Alps, the Corsican coast, Africa, and

Italian lakes, with these sites often projected in rapid succession and, in some cases, offered to a viewer seated in a simulated boat (as in a ride called the Maerorama) or in a real funicular car.[101]

However much they might have enjoyed such amusements, of course, few leisure-class travelers would have counted them as contributing to a "travel-improved consciousness." The purchased sensations and pleasures of a shipboard panorama were clearly distinct from the travel experiences of either the wealthy white owner of a "World Ticket" or the black scholar in transit from London to Monrovia. And yet the ingredients that made these commercial amusements so profitable—the onrush of stimulating novelty and sensory delight, opportunities for self-projection—were also the foundation for a new kind of critical consciousness that transatlantic travelers, white and black alike, developed through modes of reflective experience and writing. This sensory foundation was not just integral to the creation of a new black public sphere, as we have seen in the writing of Crummell; it was also the foundation for habits of critical reflexivity that allowed members of that black public to revise the conventional parameters of beauty and the very meaning of travel itself.

W. E. B. DuBois, whose own consciousness had been deeply shaped by his years of study in Europe, extended Crummell's analysis of the connections between race and high culture—now visible, now erased—into a larger project of political appropriation and revision. In his "Criteria of Negro Art" (1926), DuBois looks back to his own late-century transatlantic travel. Like some white American writers, DuBois made the beauty of a European setting—in his case, the "enchantment" of the Scottish landscape—serve as a site from which to critically challenge Gilded Age values. Unlike those white intellectuals, however, DuBois makes the travel topos a site at which to link a critique of materialist values with the question of racial consciousness.

In the high school where I studied we learned most of Scott's "Lady of the Lake" by heart. In after life once it was my privilege to see the lake. It was Sunday. It was quiet.... Around me fell the cadence of that poetry of my youth. [But there came] a sudden rush of excursionists. They were mostly Americans, and they were loud and strident. They poured upon the little pleasure boat,—men with their hats on a little on one side and drooping cigars in the wet corners of their mouths; women who shared their conversation with the world. They pushed other people out of the way. They made all sorts of incoherent noises and gestures so that the quiet home folk and the visitors from other lands silently and half-wonderingly gave way before them. They struck a note not evil but wrong. They carried, perhaps, a sense of strength and accomplishment, but their hearts had no conception of the beauty which pervaded this holy place.[102]

Here the beauty of a foreign landscape has become a test of a type of national character represented by white American travelers. "We want to be Americans," he writes to a black audience, "with all the rights of other American citizens. But is that all? Do we want simply to be Americans?" (993).

Not if it means resting in the "present goals and ideals" illuminated in "the tawdry and flamboyant" manners and blunted perceptions of those rich travelers. For DuBois, the cross-cultural scene of beauty is not a site for the cultivation of an abstract "consciousness" but for a specific work of critical seeing. Examining America's commercial values is part of a project of black world building alert to its own desires and conditions. "Suppose, too, you became . . . rich and powerful," he writes, "what is it that you would want?" (994). Addressing a black audience that surely included many without any direct experience of transatlantic travel, DuBois directs the appropriative desire and self-projection animating this imaginary travel scene ("suppose you, too, became rich and powerful") into a conscious imagining of the agency and citizenship still largely denied to black Americans. In this way, the beauty and privilege associated with transatlantic travel become the occasion for reflection on what "sort of a world we want to create for ourselves and for all America" (995). The sense of mastery and possibility that belongs to the savvy traveler can be cultivated by proxy in the imaginations of men and women who might never leave Atlanta or Boston—or who, alternatively, might follow Chesnutt's path from reading to the twinned activities of traveling and writing.

High-minded and politically inflected, Crummell and DuBois's open effort at world building might seem far removed from the "cheap amusements" of the nickelodeons and panoramas. But it is more than coincidental that the "panorama of sights" Crummell presents to his reader in swift succession—the small isles of the English Channel, the Bay of Biscay joining the coasts of France and Spain, the peaks of Madeira and the "cosmopolitan life" of the West African coastal cities—are remarkably similar to the succession of filmed coastal views that made up the "wonders" of the Maerorama, with its visual itinerary of successive steamboat views of Corsica, Africa, Italy, and finally Marseille. Similarly, the appropriative habits common to both cultivated travel and mass culture amusement are at work in DuBois's effort to turn aesthetic consciousness into reflections on social conditions and possibilities. Aesthetic apprehension is for DuBois always a contextual consciousness that moves between the universal appeal of beauty and the rooted social particulars he calls "the facts of the world," and in a sweeping gesture of revision, DuBois follows his description of Scotland with a lyrical meditation on beauty that breaks open the closed circuit of white transatlantic consciousness.

> After all, who shall describe Beauty? What is it? I remember tonight four beautiful things: The Cathedral at Cologne, a forest in stone, set in light and changing shadow, echoing with sunlight and solemn song; a village in the Veys of West Africa, a little thing of mauve and purple, quiet, lying content and shining in the sun; a black and velvet room where on a throne rests, in old and yellowing marble, the broken curves of the Venus of Milo; a single phrase of music in the Southern South—utter melody, haunting and appealing, suddenly arising out of the night and eternity, beneath the moon. (995)

Here a literary version of a rapid inventory of filmic scenes appropriates the appropriative vision of affluent travel. For DuBois, the consciousness brought to life by beauty and travel was to become a critical tool for an enduring question: "What has this Beauty to do with the world?" (995). It is the primary problem of aesthetics and DuBois never presumes to answer it. Rather, in posing the question, DuBois is able to articulate these very disparate global sites, from the Louvre to the African Veys and back to the Black Belt of the South, as a single constellation. The appropriative imagination, practiced in the lifting out and restructuring of local relations into new angles of vision, could also imagine a deterritorialized world to which no one had yet traveled.

Chapter 2
Realism and the Gordian Knot of Aesthetics and Politics

Matthew Arnold's *Culture and Anarchy* (1869) gave new meaning and prominence to the word "culture." "I shall not go so far as to say of Mr. Arnold that he invented it," Henry James wrote of the word, "but he made it more definite than it had been before—he vivified it and lighted it up."[1] Surely part of what "vivified" culture in the educated vernacular was Arnold's pairing of the word with "anarchy" as its defining antonym. The red-flag urgency of "anarchy" made "culture" its cool and tranquil opposite, an antidote against social and political turmoil. Culture was conceived as a neutral or "disinterested" sphere of human experience, a sphere in which the warring interests of factions could recede in favor of a shared light for intelligent reflection on modern life. W. E. B. DuBois had such a sphere in mind when he wrote in *The Souls of Black Folk* (1903) that African Americans wished to be "co-workers in the kingdom of culture" rather than being relegated to the role of "problem" in the sphere of politics.[2] But DuBois also alerts us to a certain fault line in the Arnoldian notion of culture. So long as the "kingdom of culture" is racially segregated—even so long as it is a solution to segregation, as DuBois wishes—it partakes of the fractious problem of race. As the transcendence or resolution of politics, the sphere of culture is necessarily political.

Hence the doubleness in Wharton's image of a "republic of the spirit," which makes elegantly ironic use of the political figure of a republic to signify a cultural space beyond the "material accidents" of the political. Arnold employs a similar figural turn when he identifies from among the middle classes a "certain number of aliens, if we may so call them," individuals whose developed discernment gives them a special office transcending any narrow interests of British parties or castes.[3] National aliens, spiritual citizens, a kingdom of coworkers—these paradoxical figures begin to capture something of the tension present in any attempt to define aesthetic culture in relation to matters of social power or justice. Yet they are also reminders that the aesthetic and the political each exert a gravitational pull on the other in the Western critical imagination. Whenever one domain is used to leverage the other, they are defined once again as distinct and yet thereby also conjoined. Rarely are they conceptually isolated.

Whether out of protest, class bias, or political hope, the proliferating talk of culture among the educated classes of Britain and America in this period made aesthetic matters into a new kind of nationalist concern. When, only a few years after the Civil War, Thomas Wentworth Higginson published "A Plea for Culture" (1867) in the *Atlantic,* this man of letters was redirecting the energies he had previously used as a Union colonel into a campaign for strengthening art and taste in the nation—an "America of Art." "Our brains as yet lie chiefly in our machineshops," Higginson writes. "What we need is the opportunity of high culture somewhere." His call for the United States to produce "better galleries" and "nobler living" is an early example of the postwar discourse that represented what Arnold called the "inward operations" of culture as a special kind of national resource.[4]

The desire to cultivate a "truly American" literature had carried over from the antebellum era, but in a postwar Arnoldian milieu literary nationalism was now joined with an emphasis on cultural stratification—only "higher" expression could manifest the general national character. Even more incongruously, high art in this moment was charged with bringing harmony to conflicted cities and cultivating fellow feeling in an extraordinarily diverse population. John Sullivan Dwight declared in an *Atlantic* essay that the best music could be a "civilizing agency" for the "mixed people of all races" in American society, restraining radicalism by implanting an "impassioned love of order."[5] The finest art, according to Metropolitan Museum of Art founder Joseph Choate, serves directly "to humanize, to educate, and refine a practical and laborious people." Properly designed parks and civic museums would offer what Frederick Law Olmstead called "a class of opposite conditions" to counter chaotic streets and workaday shops. Confidence in the social powers of art is nowhere so clear—or so curiously literal—than when it was advocated as direct form of mob control. Aesthetic culture, it was proposed, could not only promote national unity, a oneness of heart and purpose, but also ensure "fewer strikes" and industrial labor "more faithfully performed." The secretary of the Academy of Arts and Sciences urged the creation of "Theatres, Operas, Academies of Arts, Museums &c." as the solution to the "gross dissipation" that results "where refinement is not cultivated."[6] Such pronouncements, issued with aplomb, are puzzling to the present-day ear and sound a strange amalgam of faith and fear. Did such calls reflect a species of hope, or a more anxious or calculated posturing? When art is proclaimed to be both intensely "inward" and overtly national, when it is at once disinterested and instrumental, we might begin to wonder at the overdetermined nature of the office ascribed to aesthetic culture.

The stratification of culture in the postwar decades poses similar interpretive puzzles for understanding literary realism. Michael Davitt Bell diagnosed the "problem" of American realism as an unwitting logical contradiction. In calling for fidelity to real life, Bell argued, the realists understood their project as fundamentally "anti-literary"—a disavowal of the values and status of the feminized man of letters—even as their rejection of "style" was inescapably a literary style of its own.[7] But more recently scholars attentive to the era's aggressive stratification of culture have found it implausible to imagine that proponents of realism wished to escape or even disavow the literary. On the contrary, for critics such as Phillip Barrish, Thomas Strychacz, and Mark McGurl, authors writing under the sign of the "real" were strategically elevating what could count as literature, transforming the dross of the real into the gold of early modernism and thereby reserving for themselves the category of the truly literary. From this perspective, realism was an especially effective brand name for distinguishing literary writing from what could now be positioned as lower or more distant kinds of writing.[8]

By analyzing realism through the lens of what Bourdieu calls a "classification struggle," this paradigm based on "distinction" is at odds with an adjacent critical paradigm attentive to "difference"—the social terrain of class, gender, and race that has seemed to another group of critics as the more acute preoccupation of the realists.[9] For critics such as Amy Kaplan, Kenneth Warren, and Nancy Glazener, social hierarchy is also the key to understanding realism, not primarily because it allowed for high literary distinction but because of the realists' intention to address (if only to evade) the dislocations of a hierarchical society, from changing urban conditions and volatile matters of race to the woman question.[10] The interest realists showed in conflicted social relations was not, therefore, merely a pretext for monopolizing the literary; but neither was it a populist project for widening the precincts of high culture to include the sensibilities and interests of more marginalized groups. Instead, the higher position claimed by realists was a position of social supervision. Realism was a powerful preserve for securing the knowledge and values with which to regulate an unsettled social landscape. Like the "distinction" critics, scholars who view realism as a supervision of "difference" do not charge the realists with disavowing the literary; but they *do* see the literary—like other bourgeois institutions of soft power—as able to wield social power "at a distance" through disciplinary norms.[11]

While each of the two critical paradigms offers a trenchant critical angle, when we read them together even these hard-hitting critiques can seem caught in a new version of the vexed, incommensurable demands that turn-of-the-century advocates placed on high culture. Mark McGurl, for instance, asks whether Foucault-influenced critics of realism have really broken with the Arnoldian assumptions they mean to debunk. If we endow elite literature with the power to police modern society, he argues, we may be preserving the notion that "literary culture is the site at which the most socially important beliefs and attitudes are produced."[12] And yet the alternative argument that stresses literary prestige—that, for realists, "low" social materials were really the occasion for generating the private higher consciousness of the elect "art-novel"—is difficult to square with the era's broad pedagogical effort at taking art public. That is, if we credit only the private literary returns afforded by strategies of "distinction," it becomes harder to account for the extensive (and expensive) programs and institutions that the affluent classes invented for the improvement of middle-class taste and the uplift of the masses (or at least the white masses, as we will see). Even from the distance of more than a century, the knotted doubleness of culture—culture is aesthetic because it is beyond politics, and therefore political precisely because it is aesthetic—remains difficult to resolve.

My aim is not to cut through this Gordian knot but to understand the reason for the internal entanglements. The key is to reconsider how and why high culture seemed a likely site from which to address a public sphere that appeared anarchic—and may well have been. That premise becomes more intelligible, I will argue, if we recognize literary realism as a critical practice grappling with a real social formation, a social field that *was*, in truth, irrational if not anarchic. Both the "distinction" and "difference" paradigms for interpreting realism recognize that realists introduced a new emphasis on analytic thought, the first step toward what McGurl calls modernism's "high demand for readerly intellection." But neither critical camp has treated realist analysis—the fictional illumination intended to deepen and extend an understanding of modern life—as critical per se. Instead they have largely positioned realist "intellection" as either a form of political reaction (Arnoldian supervision of a phantom "anarchy") or a chance for aesthetic innovation (a "career opportunity").[13] But what if literary intellectuals were indeed confronting a species of anarchy—namely, a communications revolution that meant the bourgeois public sphere had not collapsed so much as multiplied and mutated into an unfamiliar field of competing publics? And what if the intellectual accents of realism signify not a bid for prestige or an alarmist retreat, or rather not those things alone, but a response to a recognizable demand: the felt need to sort through complex and shifting domains of public representation?

This critical problem seems to me real, not illusory, because it is our own. The vexed relation of art and mass-mediated society has remained a generative problem for literary intellectuals up to the present day, the impetus not just for innumerable books and articles but for distinct programs of critical thought (the Frankfurt and Birmingham schools, for instance) and even whole disciplines like media studies and cultural studies. Still an unstable object, aesthetic culture remains a locus for the office of critical reflection on the political, even—or especially—now that literary culture can no longer claim to adjudicate forms of public representation, nor hope to define the boundaries of collective pleasures and desires. If this enduring brand of critical reflection has a traceable genealogy, its plausible origin was the turn-of-the-century moment when culture no longer appeared to be an orderly jurisdiction and looked instead like an inescapable intellectual problem.

In the campaign to build an "America of Art," a sincere belief in national uplift through art coexisted with a vision of social breakdown. The conjunction matters more than the difference: in either scenario, American progress or American doom, the projection shored up a sense of cultural leadership and helped confer legitimacy on elite tastes and interests by presenting them as national standards. Social obligation and class retrenchment were frequently dual aspects of the same impulse. When Henry Lee Higginson, the founder of the Boston Symphony Orchestra, requested a $100,000 donation to Harvard College from a "public-spirited" relative (you "owe it to yourself, to your country, and to the Republic"), his express motive for the philanthropy was the specter of an "intense and bitter" class struggle: "Educate and save ourselves and our families and our money from mobs!"[14]

Such sentiments reveal the way cultural advocacy and philanthropy could be enlisted for social control. But to see high culture in this period as a program of class domination is to miss the most important aspects of its social power. Advocates of high art recognized that cultural forms invite a transformation of some of the deepest, most vital human responses. "Culture is infectious," one *Atlantic* author wrote.[15] The appeal to culture was ultimately an appeal to pleasure and affect, to senses we appropriately refer to as taste. Though a misnomer, taste is an apt signifier for the range of subtle cognitive judgments and perceptions that make up cultural understanding. Like the sensation of sweetness or bitterness on the tongue, aesthetic taste seems more spontaneous than reflective, belonging more to the body than the mind. Poet William Cullen Bryant, addressing a New York audience on the place of art in countering urban ills, stressed a responsive "sense of beauty" that is the reward of higher art, the "perception of order, symmetry, proportion of parts" that sharpens inward faculties while bringing a heightened interest in the world.[16] The deliberate, nationally oriented campaign to elevate American culture in this period represents an attempt at governance through intimate emulation: the purpose is not to rule but to entice, to refashion feeling and pleasure into a personality possessing an "impassioned love of order."

Of course, the "order" assumed here was not just any order; whatever fell outside the pleasures and restraints of middle-class norms were likely to count as disorder, if not anarchy. But the persistent plea for a higher national culture was not a gambit for imposing the power of one class over others but a program of inner transformation urged upon a broad citizenry. The emphasis on interiority meant that the pleasures of high culture were impossible to coerce but were effective as an offered gift—and effective, I will suggest, whether or not the gift was accepted. Essayists such as Higginson, Thomas Sergeant Perry, and Agnes Repplier saw their charge as a genuine broadening of shared feeling through the medium of art. Howells was the most tireless on this theme. The highest art, Howells insisted, will "widen the bounds of sympathy."[17] At one level, high culture institutions, much like religions, sought to create a oneness of experience in the multitude. A *Scribner's* essay stated "there is such a thing as 'the witness of the spirit,' in art as in religion." The same analogy governs Edith Wharton's retrospective story "False Dawn," from her collection *Old New York* (1924), a story in which a man returning to 1840s New York after a stay in Europe has experienced "something of the apostle's ecstasy" from his awakening to the beauty of Italian Primitive paintings. After his conversion experience he is compelled to "go forth and preach the new gospel" of a rediscovered aesthetic.[18]

The other side of the desire to convert, to encourage oneness, is the desire to identify and mark out difference. The same publications that urged the wide dissemination of the arts also featured attacks on the multifarious expressions of America's "crowd civilization."

First of all, abolish the music halls in which vulgar tunes set to still more vulgar words provide the musical milk upon which the young of the masses are reared. Abolish the diabolical street pianos and hand organs which disseminate these vile tunes in all directions and which reduce the musical taste of the children in the residence streets to the level of that of the Australian bushman, who thinks noise and rhythm are music. Abolish the genuine American brand of burlesque. . . . Abolish the theatre orchestra which plays the music hall stuff. . . . Abolish those newspapers which degrade art by filling their columns with free advertising of so-called musical performers who are of the freak genus.[19]

Even as a merely rhetorical attempt at censorship, the call here to "abolish" mass forms is still revealing. The imperative grammar, the extravagance and sweep, and the repetitive rhythm all attest to an impulse toward total control of cultural expression. Its practical effect is to focus aversion and reify difference through an invented taxonomy ("freak genus"). Both pleasure and denigration, then, are part of the same pedagogical program, an effort to reconstitute a supposedly once-unified public by classifying competing spaces of print, music, and association as part of a wilderness (fit for the "Australian bushman") where there is merely noise instead of music and sensation rather than meaning. But despite the writer's urgency in warning against these features of a "crowd civilization," the warning itself inadvertently recognizes—indeed, names—the presence of something clearly *like* a civilization, another order of perception and expression appearing everywhere in public life.

To widen bounds; to mark the vulgar: these matched imperatives define the controlling energies behind the effort to build an "America of Art." Because it is often compelling only to the few, high art is commonly described as exclusive. But the operative principle behind the emphasis on high culture was not exclusion but choice. That art and literature are embraced only voluntarily made them an effective gauge of the inner life, the site where a subject is "insensibly opened" to what is "humanizing and refining." Hence it is high art's wide diffusion, not its restriction, that was the cornerstone for bringing culture into use in social regulation. Only a real belief in the efficacy of art to transform subjects explains philanthropists' willingness to contribute time and a great deal of money to cultural programs that the target populations could (and often did) choose to ignore. Yet where art was in fact voluntarily embraced, advocates believed the "fine arts" could effect a moral and social transformation: "By abstracting him from the gratification of the senses, teaching him to appreciate physical beauty and to find delight in the contemplation of the admirable accordance of nature, the mind is carried forward to higher aims, and becomes insensibly opened to a conviction of the force of moral worth and the harmony of virtue."[20]

The call for new agencies to diffuse high culture is symptomatic of a profound historical innovation that wed liberal governance to the field of the aesthetic. The notion that art and culture could promote the social good was hardly a new one, of course. There is by now a large body of scholarship confirming Jürgen Habermas's contention that new genres of letters and criticism, emerging in the eighteenth century, encouraged the gradual detachment of art from the authoritative traditions of church and monarchy, and thus helped create an independent public sphere (though still a restricted one) in which the aesthetic judgments of citizens were harnessed to social debate and civic improvement. By the time Matthew Arnold called art a "criticism of life" the idea was a commonplace. What was new in the era of realism, however, was a widespread belief that aesthetic culture, with its power to induce a deep self-transformation of individuals, had a distinctive place in the practical agenda of civil governance. When an 1878 editorial in the *Atlantic* issued a call to establish "agencies for the diffusion of a new culture," only a small number of major metropolitan museums, civic symphonies, and municipal opera companies had been founded, most of them quite recently.[21] Within just a few years, however, an astonishing number of these organizations had been established, creating a web of professionally administered institutions that dominated the production and distribution of fine art and artistic performance in the United States. This remarkable development represents a crucial—if ambiguous—shift in the relation of culture to governance. Tony Bennett argues that while civil and economic developments in eighteenth-century Europe and North America established a separate bourgeois public at a critical distance from the state, in the nineteenth century the same conditions enabled a "reversal" of this relation between culture and the state. Whereas aesthetic institutions had detached themselves from bishops and kings, they were now increasingly organized in a close relation to city and state governance.[22]

Local groups of private patrons originated this system of quasi-public cultural enterprises, but links to state institutions like public schools formed quickly. New York's Metropolitan Museum of Art was founded by financiers and artist consultants in 1870. The Boston Museum of Fine Art, established soon after in 1873, was similarly the venture of private financiers, as was the founding of the Boston Symphony Orchestra in 1881.[23] Philadelphia's Museum of Art, because it was established (in 1877) in the wake of the Centennial Exhibition, represents an early case in which a state legislature was centrally involved in creating the museum. Although the Smithsonian Institution was incorporated in the 1840s, according to director George Brown Goode it was not until 1876 that "the existence of a National Museum, as such" was established in Washington.[24] Crucially, however, municipal and national museums had to be able to perform their public functions at the level of the citizen's private experience. Goode stressed that a museum must be able to transform human subjects from within. "The museum of the past," he wrote, "must be set aside, reconstructed, transformed from a cemetery of bric-a-brac into a nursery of living thoughts." If this potential is fulfilled, "the museum of the future may be made one of the chief agencies of the higher civilization."[25] Circulating collections of specimens were created for schools as the authority of museums flowed "beyond galleries to the lecture hall and beyond the lecture hall to the suburban school."[26]

Institutional links between culture and the state supply persuasive evidence to support Bennett's thesis. The money, bureaucratic studies, and administrative innovations devoted to culture in this period bespeak a new understanding of the aesthetic as offering "resources that might be enlisted in the service of governing."[27] And yet other historical facts are harder to assimilate to a strict Foucauldian model like Bennett's, or to the Gramscian argument developed more recently by David Lloyd and Paul Thomas. If agencies of high culture were designed to produce a more docile, "prudential subject," for instance, why would U.S. institutions deny or discourage African Americans from profiting from culture's pacifying effects? As W. E. B. DuBois made a point of reminding readers in *The Souls of Black Folk* (1903), "to most libraries, lectures, concerts, and museums, Negroes are either not admitted at all, or on terms peculiarly galling to the pride of the very classes who might otherwise be attracted."[28] That cultural institutions excluded African Americans from the population it hoped to cultivate suggests that the subjectivity imagined for the cultivated was more formidable than it was docile. Culture seemed to promise a measure of dignity and agency that the white elite felt it could not afford to extend to black Americans.

An *Atlantic* editorial, "Certain Dangerous Tendencies in American Life," begins to show the Mobius-like turns linking culture and governance.

"We are in the earlier stages of a war upon property, and upon everything that satisfies what are called the higher wants of civilized life," the magazine argued. Workers tend to regard "works of art and instruments of high culture, with all the possessions and surroundings of people of wealth and refinement, as causes and symbols of the laborer's poverty and degradation, and as things to be hated." This perception, the editorial argues, is a confusion of categories that mistakes ennobling works of art for the spoils of luxury. Art and high culture are properly a commonwealth, and as such they represent a civic responsibility rather than an exclusive possession. Those "who believe in culture, in property, and in order, that is in civilization," the essay declares, "must establish the necessary agencies for the diffusion of a new culture, a culture of a higher order" to bring about the "moral education of the people."[29] While the editorial leaves no doubt about the fact that culture was enmeshed in contemporary political battles, it also shows that cultural "agencies" were never able to monopolize public perceptions about the moral meaning of art, and that the views of higher authorities were also in open contest with other ways of understanding the field of culture. If it is true that museums transposed an "order of force" into a refined display of "forces of order" (in Bennett's chiastic formulation), it is still doubtful that these transpositions were ever the closed and totalizing systems portrayed by many theorists.[30] Left out of this theoretical model is any sense of the multitude of other sites and spaces depicting competing understandings of pleasure and modern life—including dissenting views *about* the new network of institutions promoting the "higher order" of culture.

Literary production was enlisted as another of the "chief agencies" for the dissemination of a higher pedagogy. High literary culture was organized around a group of leading magazines, most of them the house organ for one of the major publishing companies. These literary publications—the *Atlantic, Harper's, Century,* and *Scribner's* were the recognized leaders—reinforced each other's authority by reviewing the same books, publishing many of the same authors, taking up a similar range of topics (and mutually ignoring others), and hiring each other's writers and editors.[31] Like other cultural institutions, these journals saw their work cultivating a higher national literature as a public mandate. High culture, in the view of these agencies, was neither a princely possession nor a form of entertainment but a moral resource for the nation, to be administered by professionals who hold a public trust. Howells in particular put forward the novelist as someone uniquely suited for the cultural elevation of the public: "he assumes a higher function, something like that of a physician or priest," and is "bound by laws as sacred as those of such professions" (*CF* 73).

Scholarship on the new prestige of the professions in this period has helped us understand why literary writers were eager to count themselves in the same ranks as doctors and lawyers. But critics have neglected an obvious but crucial fact: even the most elite critics and novelists never did and never could have secured what physicians were able to secure, namely, a legal and cultural monopoly on wisdom and value for a given field of practice. Although realism was a banner that helped build high literary institutions, it remained in perpetual competition not just with commercial culture but also with other brands of writing. This is not to say that advocates of realism did not achieve enduring successes. The "quality" magazines and the authors they promoted won recognition as literary authorities (even from those who declined to read them), and their prestige drew in large numbers of readers. Editors introduced American readers to writers rarely given exposure in U.S. periodicals, including French, German, and Spanish authors as well as a wider range of American authors than is usually recognized. Just as notable, even the failures of realist critics and authors—their failure to acquire a wider readership, for instance—could produce a species of success. Even when ignored, their promotion of high culture served to articulate social distinctions in the public it was aiming to convert. That process is illustrated in Wharton's "False Dawn" when the would-be art "apostle" Lewis Raycie fervently hopes to win adherents and astonishes New York by turning his Manhattan home into an open gallery for exhibiting his collection of Italian paintings. But Raycie is a cultural prophet without a country. As the story describes his desire to share his discovered treasures, it formally traces new lines of cultural difference. For Wharton's readers, Raycie's gallery serves finally to assemble and name the "dumb and respectable throng, who roamed vacantly through the rooms and out again, grumbling that it wasn't worth the money."[32] Raycie's failure frames a self-damning population—the "throng" that is the middle-class version of the "mob"—whose rejection of Raycie's paintings ironically confirms his status as Wharton's culture hero. The story illustrates one of high culture's unique advantages: an ability to win for losing. Prestige can accrue to failure in a mass society.

But the advantages of prestige should not obscure the realities of cultural competition. The new array of "agencies" created to administer the high arts saw themselves in an acute contest with commercial culture. Their efforts to attract were genuine. "The great mass of readers now sunk in foolish joys of mere fable," Howells declares in his conclusion of *Criticism and Fiction*, "shall be lifted to interest in the meaning of things through a faithful portrayal of life in fiction" (*CF* 87). The rivalry with commercial culture for the "great mass" of Americans, though, points up a structural vulnerability. In such competition, the inwardness of high culture, its defining difference, becomes its distinctive problem. How is it possible to make the spiritual property of cultural discernment available as a model? How do the invisible competencies of taste and judgment become visible objects for emulation or, failing that, for intimidation? The solution is ironic, and not without risk: in order to harness the power of culture, put discernment on display. Organized through new agencies and spaces, high culture in this period set out to exhibit itself—to make distinction conspicuous.

Once again the museum offers an apt historical analogy. The metropolitan museum had become a space for instructing the public in selective discernment not simply by exhibiting objects but, even more important, by making visitors and non-visitors alike aware of the invisible knowledge—expertise behind the scenes—that had chosen and assembled the objects exhibited. Museums, in other words, also house what they do *not* overtly display: expert cultural authority. Goode formalized this function when he asserted that museums should have "two great classes" of holdings. The "exhibition series" is visible to the public, "attractively arranged" behind "the clearest of glass." The "study series" ("tens of thousands of specimens"), on the other hand, is "hidden away perpetually from public view" but provides the "foundations of the intellectual superstructure" for the museum. The hidden holdings are the guarantors of museum authority, while the public displays are a visible witness of the curatorial expertise that has assembled the exhibition from out of the storehouse. ("The public," Goode writes, "will take pride in the possession by the museum" of the cache of objects available only to the specialist but "necessary for proper scientific research.") At the same time, public exhibits also make canons of cultural expertise available for study and emulation: "The people's museum should be much more than a house full of specimens in glass cases. It should be a house full of ideas, arranged with the strictest attention to system."[33] Museums offer not only material objects but also the possibility of acquiring a restricted, intangible mastery for the dedicated visitor.

Developments in literature offered similar instances of the direct and indirect display of higher discernment. In an era of competing forms of authorship, books themselves could be a form of artistic exhibition. Private collections and public libraries sought out rare books as well as books of rare learning. Volumes such as Charles Eliot Norton's *Historical Studies of Church Building in the Middle Ages* (1880), Bernard Berenson's *Central Italian Painters of the Renaissance* (1897), Percival Lowell's *Occult Japan or the Way of the Gods* (1894), and Edith Wharton's *In Morocco* (1920) are material embodiments of the unique knowledge and experience described in their pages. Unlike rare editions, such works were not in short supply, but as an object in the hands of a reader or on the shelves of a library they could still advertise a restricted cultural knowledge even as they offered to share it.[34]

The realist fiction promoted by the leading periodicals redesigned the novel around the same paradoxical imperatives of display and discrimination. Though realist novels carry over much of the same thematic materials of the fiction that precedes it—explorations of courtship, family life, and social conduct, representations of moral and social conflicts—the champions of high realism reposition the genre as a form for *challenging* conventional or popular fiction. A less obvious form of exhibition than the museum, the novel is nevertheless made over into a space of instruction through display, a new kind of public space where fictional representation can counter the "distorted and misleading likeness in our books," plays, and commercial spectacles (*CF* 50). The realist novel not only holds out "a faithful portrayal of life" (*CF* 87) but also establishes that there is a specialized knowledge—Howells explicitly calls it "a sort of scientific decorum" (*CF* 73)—necessary to distinguish accurate representations from distortions, fact from fable. That knowledge lies not in the stories themselves but in the habits of perception required to read them. The realist novel makes representation itself not only a medium for fiction but also a distinct cultural practice and a contested terrain. Reading novels with the proper discernment offers the possibility of mastering a special kind of knowledge—according to Howells, nothing less than the "the meaning of things."

Once the novel is deliberately recast as the antidote to "shows and semblances," however, it competes on the same territory of public visibility as the "effectists" of mass culture (*CF* 86, 37). This paradox—that to rescue high culture from conspicuousness, culture must make itself conspicuous—locates the generative rivalry that accounts for much of the controlling energy and creativity of the literature in this period. With varying degrees of perception, realist works recognize that mass culture was remaking the order of the real. Under the pressure of the rivalry, realist fiction begins to resemble the world of spectacle it opposes. But the resemblance is not simply a risk to high culture fiction, it is also that fiction's precondition: the proximity is precisely what makes realist discernment the increasingly specialized, valuable property—in short, the property of distinction—that it is, even as it wed its own fortunes to a commercial culture it could not master.

William Dean Howells, Realism, and the Modern Instance

Like other novels of its time, Howells's *A Modern Instance* (1882) is about a bad marriage; unlike others, the source of the marital trouble is not adultery but publicity. The three-year marriage between newspaperman Bartley Hubbard and his wife, Marcia, reaches a crisis when Marcia accuses him of infidelity. Her suspicions are wrong, and within moments she knows it. Still, the false accusation has the same effect as if it were true: it sets off an enraged confrontation, an impulsive separation, and a dramatic divorce. Howells here could be said to draw on a standard plot device, the threat of adultery, to point beyond it to an even deeper disruption of traditional domesticity. The Hubbards' marriage is not destroyed by intimate betrayal—Bartley is incapable of possessing any fidelity of private feeling to betray. Instead, his only consistent interests and gratifications are the internalized energies of mass publicity, or what the narrator calls Bartley's "newspaper instinct." Similarly, Marcia's disposition consists of female sentiment that has been distorted by commercial culture. Her unrealistic expectations and emotionalism are "distempered imitations" of the melodrama Howells saw as endemic to the era's popular fiction.[35] By presenting an American marriage whose partners are in thrall to the desires and forces of an emergent mass society, Howells reinvented the marriage novel; he would later call it his first truly "realist" novel.

If adultery is a false threat, the energies of mass publicity carry a new kind of sexual tension. Bartley's "newspaper instinct" has the blind but canny force of erotic feeling, with which it is explicitly compared. A reporter for an aggressive Boston newspaper, Bartley dreams of starting an even racier paper that will operate on a method of public seduction. He foregoes any notion of evoking questions of general public interest and identifies the desires of different groups of readers—"local accident and crime," political affairs, religious gossip ("it interests the women like murder"), fashion, financial reports—in order to entice a mass audience to buy the same publication. Bartley defines his journalistic "principle" as simply a matter of meeting demand—"you must give the people what they want" (416)—though it relies on carefully inciting the desires it hopes to gratify.

Bartley's credo is echoed by a theater manager he meets in a bar, a man who stages a new kind of variety show, a "burlesque," performed by all-female troupes. "I give the public what it wants," the burlesque manager announces, which turns out to be "legs, principally" (418). Bartley answers that "it's just so with newspapers, too" (419).

Howells plays the scene for humor, but the comparison of mass-market journalism with burlesque was a pointed critique. By the mid-1870s, the novel's time frame, burlesque troupes had won a large American audience by offering eclectic theatrical novelties that stopped short of any open indecencies.[36] During the 1868–69 theatrical season in Boston, for instance, five of the city's seven theaters featured burlesques imported from England, prompting Howells to write an analysis in the *Atlantic* of the "spectacular muse" of burlesque that had reigned over the season. The troupes consisted of female performers playing male roles in an incongruous collection of skits, songs, dances, minstrel "walk arounds," and topical parodies. Howells's review indicted the burlesque "manager's ideas of public taste," though not without an ironic awareness that the productions actually seemed to have gauged the taste of the public ("honest-looking, handsomely dressed men and women") with distressing accuracy. Howells's objection to burlesque was less its potential for sexual titillation than its deliberate incoherence—the distortions of gender as well as the disconnected jumble of sensational sights. "A melancholy sense of the absurdity, of the incongruity, of the whole," he wrote, "absorbed at last even a sense of the indecency." Burlesque swept in and left nothing untouched: "no novelty remains which is not now forbidden by statute."[37]

With its heedless collection of novelties, burlesque was the antitype to Howells's notion of literary realism. A classical performance of *Medea* Howells attended in 1875 sparked the idea for *A Modern Instance* ("I said to myself, 'This is an Indiana divorce case'"), and the novel he called his "New Medea" was meant to explore the sexual and emotional disruptions that characterized the modern age.[38] Like Howells's novel, a famous burlesque called *Ixion; or the Man at the Wheel* (1863) also took up the theme of modern divorce by way of classical allusion, but did so with the intention to mock and dazzle. In *Ixion*, parodic fragments from classical myth are thrown together in a farcical narrative taking aim at the penchant for divorce among the social elite. Written by F. C. Burnand, the comic production featured popular actress Lydia Thompson in the role of Ixion, king of Thessaly, and her visit to Mount Olympus was the pretext for topical jokes, songs, and dance numbers. The burlesque's deliberate cultivation of incongruities led critic Richard Grant White to label the genre a "monstrous" form of entertainment, and "by monstrous I do not mean wicked, disgusting, or hateful, but monstrously incongruous and unnatural. . . . Its system is a defiance of system."[39]

For Howells, the same "spectacular muse" in burlesque governed mass journalism. The problem with this brand of journalism was not its popularity but rather the source of that popularity in the frisson that comes from gratuitous public exposure. Like a burlesque revue, Bartley's newspaper relies on the excitement generated by the display of what is normally unseen. Howells identifies as the "vice" of mass journalism its compulsion to gather, reproduce, and circulate an indiscriminate constellation of sensational sights: "Why should an accurate correspondent inform me of the elopement of a married man with his maid-servant in East Machias?" asks one of Howells's disapproving characters. "Why should I sup on all the horrors of a railroad accident, and have the bleeding fragments hashed up for me at breakfast?" And, in a revealing inclusion, "Why should I be told by telegraph how three negroes died on the gallows of North Carolina?" (416–17). The newspaper is a burlesque show in disguise, serving up for entertainment the same flavors of racial shock, domestic scandal, and novel sights that spiced the popular stage productions. Driven by exposure for its own sake, mass journalism is for Howells a burlesque of the real.

Howells's novel indicts a long list of the sensational topics exploited by newspapers, naming elopements and railroad accidents as well as suicides, detectives in pursuit of criminals, divorce trials, and murders. But remarkably, this same list of topics is a virtual index to Howells's own plot. The story of the Hubbards' marriage begins in an elopement and, before the novel ends, features Marcia's thoughts of suicide, Bartley's pursuit by detectives, a minor train accident, a major divorce trial, and even a report of Bartley's own murder by gunshot. The novel thus unfolds by way of an uncanny doubling with the very spectacles it names and condemns. Although it may seem curious that Howells's plot is structured by these scandals, the narrative doubling does not compromise Howells's realism; rather, it can be said to *constitute* realism, to show the complexity of its historical formation. For Howells, subjects like divorce do have a genuine claim on the highest public interest, but only in the right kind of narrative frame. *A Modern Instance* is designed to properly expose distorting newspaper exposure in order to permit the discerning reader to tell the difference. The doubling represents a compressed version of the cultural contest that is the very ground for high literary realism, a competition for control over the recently enlarged power of public representation. Howells's aversion to mass forms was not simply a puritanical reflex against low pleasures. Rather, Howells saw that behind the ever more numerous commercial displays and pulp-fiction titles was the power of an expanded market sector to dissolve and rearrange the materials of more traditional institutions of acculturation. Realism was to be a bulwark against the power of the market to remake the real.

Bartley's acuity as a newspaperman gives him a "masterly knowledge" (313) of Boston places and people. But the novel also insists readers realize that Bartley acutely lacks another order of understanding: he had "scarcely any knowledge of the distinctions and differences so important to the various worlds of any city" (336). These additional "worlds," and the "distinctions" necessary to understand them, are not explicitly named. But the comment directs attention to a more expansive point of view than Bartley's, a synoptic vision the novel itself will eventually realize. Through its plot, the novel develops a picture of distinct but interdependent social regions: Bartley's reporter's haunts; the small-scale households of the Hubbards' neighborhood; the indoor world of polite Boston society; a male precinct of professional offices and clubs; and the public space of saloons, restaurants, and theaters, among others. The result is a totality that Howells in his criticism calls "life in its civic relations" (*CF* 39), and the ability to grasp these "various worlds" as a whole is at the heart of Howells's understanding of fiction. Rivals like burlesque and mass journalism also present social life but only by offering incoherent aggregations of events, scenes, and public spaces. What is needed, in Howells's view, is the ability to conceive the increasingly diverse urban worlds as a total social body.

A paradigmatic test of Bartley's "knowledge of distinctions" occurs in the peculiar public space of Boston's new institutions of high culture. The narrator details the way Bartley and Marcia

> went sometimes to the Museum of Fine Arts, where [Marcia] became as hungry and tired as if it were the Vatican. They had a pride in taking books out of the Public Library, where they walked about on tiptoe with bated breath; and they thought it a divine treat to hear the great organ play at noon. As they sat there in the Music Hall, and let the mighty instrument bellow over their strong young nerves, Bartley whispered to Marcia the jokes he had heard about the organ; and then, upon the wave of aristocratic sensation from this experience, they went out and dined at Copeland's, or Weber's, or Fera's, or even at Parker's. (337)

The distinctions in this passage are all implicit. The passage is meaningful only when one sees the meanings *not* grasped by Bartley and Marcia. Readers know that the "aristocratic sensation" the couple experiences at the organ recital actually measures their lack of aesthetic feeling, since those who understand art and culture, who live and breathe in its atmosphere, would never experience the kind of discrete sensation of "aristocratic" elevation felt by the Hubbards. Travel-savvy readers know that Marcia's weariness at the Boston museum means she would experience a fatigue many times greater at the Vatican. By requiring readers to understand by way of the gaps or distinctions in the scene, Howells posits the existence of a larger, unspecified field of knowledge that turns those differences into legible social relations. The effect is to set off the Hubbards' perceptions as examples of a certain kind of (insufficient) understanding, intelligible only to a higher order of sight. Bartley and Marcia are not fictional subjects, alternative selves the reader might emulate or envy or upbraid. Rather, these characters become fictional objects, figures carefully "isolated and analyzed" (*CF* 67), in Howells's critical formula, against a more encompassing horizon of social relations. These are not just objects to be seen but to be *seen through* to a whole that is graspable only by implication. This kind of structure pulls the reader away from the impulse of identification—the immediacy of "reading for the plot"—and instills a habit of what might be called reading for distinction.

Extending and deepening the analysis of "distinctions and differences" is the task of the novel as a whole. The novel will turn the distressing exigencies of the Hubbards' lives into a "modern instance," a representative object that can illuminate a broader social order. It is a mistake to see Howells as a scold or a snob; the Hubbards' deficits in higher taste are important only insofar as they help define "modern" persons who have been formed by their responsiveness to mass culture. The younger American writers who succeeded Howells's generation sometimes painted him as the guardian of a too narrow Victorian gentility, but the primary importance of aesthetic taste for Howells was not propriety or personal refinement. He insisted he was "outside of the rank of the mere *culturists*, followers of an elegant literature," and it was a fair enough claim.[40] For Howells, aesthetic feeling is an index to social differences—a crucial index, it turns out—that points up a defining order of "civic relations" through patterns of difference. The contemporaries of Howells who complained that his realism was given to excessive analysis ("Boston under the scalpel" was the way one critic described Howells's fiction) were closer to the mark than those who have portrayed him as a fussy defender of genteel sensibilities.[41]

That analytic bent is the reason Howells underscores the Hubbards' failed marriage as a meaningful "instance" of modernity. His notion of the fictional "instance"—what he elsewhere calls the "expressive particular"—is a key unit of analysis in realism.⁴² Howells's confidence in a logic of metonymic representation presumes the existence of accessible orders of historical and social relations, orders against which carefully drawn figures could be critically analyzed. In this way Howells realizes in fiction the same modern "museum idea" that George Brown Goode defined for curators and art exhibitors. Goode's definition of a well-organized museum as "a collection of instructive labels, each illustrated by a well-selected specimen," attests to the prime importance of the representative type as the basic unit of meaning.⁴³ The properly selected specimen is a witness of an underlying system or series. Without such series, Goode emphasized, the museum is little more than a "cemetery of bric-a-brac."

The museum object, as Goode described it, is also a specimen of history, an artifact of time. Its ability to represent relies on its place in a temporal sequence, a known cultural history. Howells shares the belief that historical measurement should be one of the structuring principles of fiction. An "instance" is only meaningful as an instance of an epoch, here the order of the "modern." In truly meaningful art, Howells insists, techniques of skillful narration will reveal "the laws of evolution in art and society" (*CF* 9). In all, Howells's realism shares the "museum idea" of the power of disciplined representation. The categories of type and historical sequence operated as a powerful nineteenth-century syntax for converting the amorphous (and wildly overdetermined) concept of "civilization" into vividly realized displays of its constitutive orders—the cultural histories of great nations, the evolution of fine art, the growth of science and technology, the succession of "primitive" cultures that make up the prehistory of civilization. Modeled after the powerful evolutionary principles that had made biology and natural history the supreme sciences, these museum disciplines embodied the desire to give the things of culture the determinate order of an organic law. When Howells asserts that fiction requires "a sort of scientific decorum," he expresses a widespread belief that specialized metonymic display could impart knowledge of the real, invisible order of things. Writers who fail to "body forth human experience" according to realist decorum fall into the error of "falsifying nature," modeling life "after their own fancy" (*CF* 56, 39). Tellingly, Howells relegates these popular forms to the "stone age of fiction" (*CF* 57). The same principles must govern the literary critic as well as the writer. Like the trained "naturalist," the critic is "to identify the species and then explain how and why the specimen is imperfect and irregular"

(*CF* 21). Literary criticism must restrict itself "to the business of observing, recording, comparing; to analyzing the material before it, and then synthesizing its impressions" (*CF* 27).

Yet as powerful as these principles of authoritative display were for agencies of culture like Howells's fiction, realist exhibition never reliably served only one master. Even museum representation could break from the "law of evolution in art and society" into other, more wayward paths. Cultural leaders were acutely aware of this possibility. Boston's first museum, established in 1791, featured wax figures of Franklin and Washington together with oil paintings and live animals. The early museum was likely to offer oddities of natural history, ornaments from exotic places in Africa or China, and sensational technological displays such as a guillotine. Live performances at these museums made unabashed attempts at drawing in large popular audiences; in 1819 the Boston Gallery of Fine Arts featured the "Lilliputian Songsters," two dwarfs whose singing presented "genteel deportment."[44] And, as we have seen, Barnum made the most of the early museum's penchant for eclectic spectacle when he launched himself in show business. The modern museum, however, defined itself through a strenuous differentiation from this kind of array of curiosities. As one museum administrator put it in 1888, "The orderly soul of the Museum student will quake at the sight of a Chinese lady's boot encircled by shark's teeth" or "an Egyptian mummy placed in a medieval chest."[45] Such sheer spectacle is an affront to the discriminating observer. And yet the sting of the affront hints at the museum's lingering affiliation with popular spectacle that prompts the need for disavowal. In 1888, the visual novelties of a Chinese boot or a boxed-in mummy could signify not merely the museum's buried past but its current cultural rival, the welter of mass culture spectacles.

Howells's *A Modern Instance* gives an incisive view of this rivalry between institutions and its place in the formation of high literary culture. On the first night of their arrival in Boston, Bartley and Marcia visit Moses Kimball's Museum theater, a nine-hundred-seat auditorium for popular plays and variety shows. The theater maintained a vestige of its earlier incarnation as a museum in the exhibition gallery lining its first-floor lobby.

They passed through the long colonnaded vestibule, with its paintings and plaster casts and rows of birds and animals in glass cases on either side and she gave scarcely a glance at any of those objects endeared by association if not intrinsic beauty to the Boston play-goer: Gulliver, with the Lilliputians swarming upon him; the painty-necked ostriches and pelicans; the mummied mermaid under a glass-bell; the governors' portraits; the stuffed elephant; Washington crossing the Delaware; Cleopatra applying the asp; Sir William Pepperell, at full length on canvas and the pagan months and seasons in plaster,—if all these are indeed the subjects—were dim phantasmagoria, amid which she and Bartley moved scarcely more real. (302–3)

The lobby's unsorted "phantasmagoria" is antithetical to Howells's realist "instance." The exhibition disregards any distinction between myth and reality, whimsy and solemnity, art and grotesque artifact. Belonging to no one order of nature or history, the objects represent nothing but their own singularity. In *Moby-Dick* Melville often uses something very like this cataloging of curious objects and incongruous exotic allusions to fashion a new lyrical symbolism for his distinctive literary art. For Howells, in contrast, the combined display of disparate artifacts remains an inert if instructive fossil, an example of the "stone age" of popular taste.

The point is not that Howells possessed a more rigid or restrictive imagination than a writer like Melville. Rather, the relevance of Howells's metonymic style lies in its relation to a different social backdrop. Because Howells was writing at a moment when one could witness a Coney Island hotel in the form of an elephant or observe orientalist fashions in the windows of Filene's or Wanamaker's—or even walk past Cleopatra next to Washington on a public poster for a wax museum—the "phantasmagoria" of an exhibition of curiosities could not but resonate with a chaotic-seeming public sphere. For Howells, the fact that a public "appetite for the marvelous" (*CF* 47) seemed to be growing rather than dying out made such taste only more unnatural. In their distortions and factitiousness, these objects are figures for the many kinds of "fantastic and monstrous and artificial things" in contemporary life that Howells identified in his novels and essays, from women's fashions to artificial new American "moods and tastes" (*CF* 10, 9).

A "phantasmagoria" of various urban spectacles is also a thematic preoccupation of the novel—and, indeed, of all of Howells's subsequent novels. *The Minister's Charge,* for instance, includes a closely rendered picture of the pandemonium of a hotel fire, the bathos of a criminal courtroom, and the shocking street theater of a bloody trolley accident—all topics Howells's characters frequently criticize as too sensational when they appear in a tabloid paper. High realism remains intimately bound to what it nominally excludes from the order of the real. The literary realism Howells championed was established in a moment when newly defined orders of culture, high and low, were facing off in open competition. In that sense, realism is a literary language that emerges from the proximity of high and low culture in rivalry, a proximity that calls for vigilant codes of distinction. This is the self-conscious office of Howellsian realism. For all its urgency to purge "distempered imitations," then, realist discourse can never rid itself of what it deems unreal without sacrificing the very basis for realist distinction.

For Howells, realist distinction is also needed for understanding the genre's bedrock institution: marriage. Characters see the Hubbards' marriage variously as vaguely unsatisfactory (Bartley's view) or inscrutably lacking in intimacy (Marcia's view) or fatally short on domestic propriety (Marcia's father's view). But readers are asked to see it as something closer to what another character calls the "hideous deformity" (399) of marriage—eventually, marriage in the form of the modern spectacle of divorce. For Howells the trouble with the Hubbards' marriage is not its singularity but its instructive and *representative* vulnerability to the energies of a rootless commercial society. Howells's novel contends that marriage, like other traditional institutions such as churches and republican politics, is no longer an effective shield against the fantasies of mass culture that, left unchecked, invade intimate relationships and even consciousness itself.

This insight, then, requires one of the finest distinctions in the novel. The Hubbards' marriage is finally not to be seen as a singular "hideous deformity" but as an instructive "modern instance." It is not, that is, a freakish anomaly (however rare divorce was at the time) but a representative case, the result of what Howells said was his "practical and modern" treatment of marriage in the age of mass culture. Only this difference—the analytic value of the "instance"—protects the novel from being what it adamantly opposes, a narrative that exploits for "cheap effects" the "fetid explosions of the divorce trials" (*CF* 71), as Howells put it in his criticism. This is a rather fine line to maintain, to be sure: the same writer who laments tabloid divorce trials is the writer who concludes his novel with a long and dramatically engaging divorce trial. Yet drawing this line, the line that makes visible second-order distinctions about representation, is precisely the point. Howells represents a divorce trial not for cheap effects but for realist effects, which is to say, the effects on the discerning reader, who acquires a mastery over the distortions of mass culture and with that mastery gains a purchase on a social whole—modernity—that is otherwise ungraspable. The right kind of fiction seemed to promise that there was still a unitary public sphere that could recover a single consensual discourse of human meaning.

This realist aesthetic springs from mixed impulses. Howells's pronouncements on realism carry the exhilarated conviction of a truth revealed, even as they convey a profound anxiety in the lower registers. Each was a genuine sentiment, each a tonal counterpoint that increased the resonance of the other. Howells's claims for the social power of high art were astonishingly large, and his convictions about realism amount to a romancing of the power of disciplined representation. "The very highest fiction is that which treats itself as fact": to hear the imaginative promise in this phrase requires recognition of the new excitement and authority ascribed to fact in this era.[46] The prestige of the natural sciences and the recently established social sciences, the remarkable rational leverage derived from statistics, the new professional recognition accorded art and humanities in the university—these and other enterprises held out a disciplinary glamour for the work of fiction. For Howells and many of his contemporaries, realism (a "movement in literature . . . the world is now witnessing" [*CF* 69]) promised a gradual, solid-seeming materialization of an otherwise invisible totality.

Not everyone found an intellectual glamour in the realist "movement." Some observers found Howellsian realism given to cold, bloodless analysis. Critics such as Agnes Repplier and William Roscoe Thayer greeted the renewal of more romantic fiction in the 1890s as a welcome alternative to the fiction of realism's dissecting "anatomists." Debates about realism were waged in competing magazines and other venues, as when a congress on literature organized for the 1893 Chicago Columbian Exposition brought together figures such as Hamlin Garland, Mary Hartwell Catherwood, and Charles Dudley Warner to take sides on what one observer termed the "passion for realism."[47] Despite the detractors, however, those who felt the "passion" saw realism as a singular and truly exciting advance in American letters. With something like the exhilaration of watching a developing photograph, proponents believed realism was bringing into view a social world usually too changeable and fast-paced to be seen steadily.

The other side of this hopeful expectation was a motivating anxiety. Without a language or agency to realize the underlying orders of culture, social life may appear to be only a collection of heterogeneous fantasies and desires. Through the strange eloquence of his personal anxieties, Howells was among the first intellectuals to articulate what are still unresolved questions about the social power of mass culture. His cultural moment, and the institution of realism it spawned, form the prehistory of our own continuing struggle to understand the efficacy of different modes of cultural representation and to grasp the relation—whether corrosive or unifying—between mass culture forms and diverse modern societies. Howells's solution was to define and embrace the literary as a social agent by strenuously distinguishing it from mass rivals deemed unreal. In the disciplinary accents of realism's "order and system," Howells's realism is a dream of reconciliation, an imaginary museum to house desire in the guise of the real.

The utopian impulse in Howells's particular brand of literary nationalism (a "republic of letters where all men are free and equal") tended to cover over its own contradictory premise. Moral force was inherent in the realist vision, as Howells conceived it: the realist writer "feels in every nerve the equality of things and the unity of men; his soul is exalted, not by vain shows and shadows and ideals, but by realities, in which alone truth lives." And literary expression of that vision, Howells believed, would make readers' cultivated perceptions into a route to social transformation. Only realism signified "democracy in literature" because, rather than pandering to a mélange of popular tastes, it promised "the unity of taste in the future" (*CF* 9). The prospect of a "unity of taste," however, also contains an irreducible discrepancy between theory and practice. Howells's genuine democratic ideals were attached to a specialized literary practice, realism, whose effective end was necessarily to produce a delimited, self-selecting readership. Howells increasingly felt the strain of the resulting tension. His ideal "republic of letters" was the simulacrum of a unified culture, an artifact whose principle aim—to join citizens in a single aesthetic public through "taste"—was actually occurring more effectively in the mass marketplace he opposed, even as the more analytic style of realism he promoted was subdividing the field of letters.

The irony was all the more notable for the fact that Howells's success was held up as an example of the national integration that literary culture could foster. Here was a son of the "rough-and-ready West," as James Russell Lowell put it, whose inborn gifts had been recognized and welcomed by the highest literary lights in the East.[48] It is probably more accurate to say that Howells's talent had inspired in the ambitious young writer a keen-eyed study of the eastern literary establishment that he deliberately prepared himself to join. Howells was an outsider whose intense observations from a distance helped him cross the threshold to the inside, and this particular path of career advancement left its mark. For the young Howells, Boston was an object of desire and intense analysis, a combination that energized him and would sharpen his fiction and criticism. His outsider's critical mastery of its "civic relations" was a continuing source of the insider's cultural success. Understanding Howells's work—his social vision and critique, and his later sense of his own critical impasse—requires careful attention to the way the mastery of social distinctions could signify for Howells both a possibility for open mobility (his own professional success) and a threat of implacable difference (the material social divisions he observed). It was a contradiction he would never completely resolve.

The Millionaire in Print: Barnum and Howells

In *The Rise of Silas Lapham* (1885), Howells's rivalry with commercial culture takes the form of an open competition. The novel's central topic coincided with an established genre of the mass press: the portrait of the new American millionaire. Biographies and newspaper profiles of millionaires were tremendously popular in this era, as were capitalist wisdom books such as Andrew Carnegie's *Gospel of Wealth* (1889) and Orison Swett Marden's *Pushing to the Front* (1894). By portraying a millionaire, *The Rise of Silas Lapham* challenges commercial culture on its own turf, and Howells's tour de force realist portrait of Silas Lapham demolishes the competition. It is a fixed fight, certainly, but no less illuminating for that fact. Recognizing the competitive motive underscores the novel's literary control as well as its spirited, almost combative literary energies. Howells lets the press have the first go at his central character Lapham, a paint manufacturer with a "colossal fortune."[49] Bartley Hubbard is resurrected for the task: he reappears as a young reporter, still in his early years of marriage, on assignment to interview Lapham for the "Solid Men of Boston" series (861). Bartley's fatuous sketch describes Lapham as a "fine type of the successful American" (862) in rote formulas. Howells, taking his turn at portraying Lapham, will then expose Bartley's journalistic language as a false kind of representativeness—neither a true understanding of "type" nor a real apprehension of the phenomenon of Gilded Age success. The newspaper sells a polished distortion of a millionaire's life story, one that Howells will first expose and then rewrite, as if to give a whole popular genre its comeuppance.

Howells's novel unfolds as a besting of this shallow newspaper portrait. Where Bartley's Solid Man is blandly genteel, Howells's is brought to life through the quirks of his vernacular speech and manners. Where Bartley's portrait consists of formulaic praise, Howells's presents a closely shaded picture of Lapham's moral hesitations and humiliations as well as his personal recoveries. Nothing in Howells's fiction illustrates quite so well as *The Rise of Silas Lapham* the way his understanding of realism is oppositional, an art defined by the task of uncovering and displaying precisely what rival commercial forms flatten or distort. Yet to see the matter in terms of these oppositions—surface and depth, distortion and real representation—is to define things in Howells's terms. All responsive readers *will* see them in these terms, to be sure; being able to perceive these distinctions is the chief measure of having successfully read the novel. But Howells's defeat of Bartley's vapid journalism is also a backhanded tribute to the power of popular culture. The contest itself tacitly recognizes that other criteria exist for evaluating writing, criteria which, though dead letters to Howells, are alive for vast numbers of readers.

That Howells's distinctions carry with them their own blindness is clear when *Silas Lapham* is compared alongside the single best-selling narrative about the "rise" of an American millionaire. Howells's Lapham is the alter ego of the century's most famous businessman, Phineas T. Barnum, and Howells's novel can be read as the high culture counterpart of Barnum's own narrative. Barnum's autobiography, *Struggles and Triumphs* (1869), is the equal of *Silas Lapham* in the skill with which it manipulates the conventions of the popular success narrative. Both Howells and Barnum rely on the generic figure of the "solid man" for their own very different ends. Howells's novel shows how the attempts by the popular press to grasp the new figure of the rich American are largely bland and undiscerning (Bartley's flat praise of Lapham's "trials and struggles" [863] barely conceals the reporter's derision). The fatuous journalistic language is proof of the need for realist distinctions. On Barnum's side, his self-penned *Struggles and Triumphs* also leverages the popular interest in millionaires' stories and in doing so manages the feat of representing his career in humbug as the very definition of "solid" success. With deft skill, Barnum enlists readers in a game of overlooking the showman's difference from the bankers and industrialists who usually signify American wealth and success. Details of Barnum's advertising tricks and occasional outright lies are to be accepted as proof of the showman's exemplary "integrity, energy, industry, and courage."[50] This apparent erasure of distinctions, however, actually calls for discernment of another kind. Barnum's readers must distinguish between the chicanery of his shows and the shows' innovative success, and between Barnum's bombast and the breakthrough business acumen that recognized in publicity itself a new and expanding international market.

The art of boasting illustrates the difference in these competing narratives. Howells's novel is able to recognize Lapham's tendency to brag as a vernacular trait with its own species of charm. The reader's guide in this respect is Lapham's daughter Penelope, whose affectionate mimicking of Lapham's boasts manages to convey both her better social judgment and her filial loyalty.[51] No reader of Howells, however, can doubt that Lapham's bragging is a liability—not because it is a sign of bad character but because Lapham is unconscious of the fact that he boasts and therefore blind to its effects on others' view of him. Every lapse into boasting proves that he lacks the asset that counts the most in Howells's Boston, the capacity of cultural discernment. But for Barnum, in contrast, bragging is a self-conscious art of considerable complexity. Readers credit Barnum with knowing and exploiting the varying kinds and effects of boasting and recognize the difference between his self-publicized hubris and his profitable mastery of the arts of publicity, the latter as sophisticated as the former is bombastic.

Barnum's account of the building of his new house, for instance, is a study in the manipulation of different forms of self-glorification. As Barnum's readers knew (and Barnum knew they knew), a boastful show of modesty was a prerequisite for any extended self-vaunting. "In deciding upon the kind of house to be erected," Barnum writes, "I determined to consult convenience and comfort. I cared little for style, and my wife cared less." Readers would have recognized Barnum's wink when, in the very next paragraph, he informs readers that the very "style" for this homey domicile was "the Pavilion erected by George IV," the "only specimen of Oriental architecture in England" (163–64). Barnum calls his estate "Iranistan," a choice that, like the mansion itself, stands as a permanent boast. But bragging can neutralize its own offenses if it feeds curiosity. Barnum's account of building the house satisfies his readers' desire to know the details of his extravagance (the real offense would be to withhold them). He describes the furniture, the "expensive water works," and the grounds, with their stables, conservatories, and outer buildings ("all perfect in their kind"), including the "many hundreds" of transplanted trees. If he withholds the most desirable fact, the mansion's actual cost, he offers the next best thing: the preposterous fantasy of possessing an indifference to cost: "The whole was built and established literally 'regardless of expense,' for I had no desire even to ascertain the entire cost. All I cared to know was that it suited me" (164). He ends the passage with a self-deprecating boast, which resolves in a pleasing key any potentially dissonant notes in the self-aggrandizing performance: "When the name 'Iranistan' was announced, a waggish New

York editor syllabled it, I-ran-i-stan, and gave as the interpretation that 'I ran a long time before I could stan!'" (165).

In all, the swagger works because Barnum wholly controls it. Like all lovable rogues, he charms because he doesn't hide his sins but dresses them to best effect as an added seduction. More important, the rhetorical performance is also an index to Barnum's cutting-edge business savvy. The description of the house—like the house itself—turns expenditure into profit, as the structure becomes an advertisement for Barnum's enterprises (a drawing of the house headed his stationery) and a sign of success itself. Responsive readers consumed the boastful writing as entertainment at the same time they studied the book as a manual for career success.

The construction of a millionaire's house is also a central episode in *The Rise of Silas Lapham*. Howells's genius in this plot development is to uncover precisely what a figure like Barnum must suppress if he is to remain in control of his own self-display, namely, the fear of class humiliation. Barnum's narrative conjures for his readers a picture of the showman giving decisive instructions to his master architect. Lapham's architect, in contrast, hearing the rich man's plans for materials and floor designs, is barely able "to conceal the shudder which they must have sent through him" (896). The "shudder" is not concealed from readers, of course; for readers, that glimpse of the architect's aversion is offered them as a sign of recognition of their own superior discernment. To read the novel is to find oneself privy to the discriminations of feeling, crosscurrents of taste, and finely calibrated responses that are wholly invisible to Lapham. Readers are also to recognize the limits to some highly cultivated tastes. When the Brahmin observer Bromfield Corey remarks on the "bestial darkness of the great mass of people" (967), his overrefined views, like Lapham's coarser ones, become an object of critical scrutiny, an example of perception without feeling. Most significantly, the reader's position of higher discernment makes Lapham himself transparent, opening to view the panic and embarrassment that Lapham wants desperately to keep hidden from more cultivated observers (his ignorance about whether to wear gloves to a dinner party at the Coreys' home is a prolonged misery, but "he would rather die than ask this question" [1030] of his young employee, Tom Corey). Lapham's own series of self-critical "shudders"—and these are far more deeply felt—are a record of the distress of a self-made man made helpless by his own upward mobility. Readers are exposed to the agonies of his social uncertainty, the risks of self-exposure that "made Lapham sick" (1033). His own desires are also self-imposed taboos. When Lapham's wife warns him against acting on his deep wish that their daughter marry Tom Corey, he recoils, "shuddering at the utterance of hopes and ambitions which a man hides with shame" (960).

The house is an emblem of Lapham's insufficient taste and not, as with Barnum's, of the prowess of his money. But the house's fate also shows the way Howells recognizes manners as a crucial ingredient of capitalism. Taste is a species of wealth. When the house burns down in a fire accidentally set by Lapham himself, it is not a symbol of the futility of worldly vanity, as a moral interpretation might have it. To the contrary, the sudden ruin is a witness that Lapham lacks sufficient cultural capital. Building the new house has drained him of his money but, more to the point, it has overextended his very limited powers of taste. The property disaster is counterpart to his personal meltdown at the Coreys' dinner party, where (much like his inadvertent sparking of the house fire) his social anxiety leads to accidental drunkenness and his drunkenness to an extravagant display of his inadequate manners. In Boston, Lapham was not a man of means and he never was; he possessed only money—this is the realist insight that Howells uncovers to counter the fantasies of social mobility behind mass-market success narratives. Late in the novel Howells revives a subplot that permits Lapham a moral recovery to counter his economic and social ruin. As in many Howells novels, the moral resolution provides a formal conclusion (Lapham's economic fall is his moral rise); but it also feels distinctly extraneous to the deepest concerns of the novel. It is hard to deny that the novel's real dramatic energies lie in Lapham's crucible of taste as the inside story of Gilded Age capitalism.

Lapham's struggles actually stem from the rewards of wealth. If Barnum's *Struggles and Triumphs* is a hymn to the era's new ways of wealth, *Silas Lapham* is its cautionary tale. Yet it is not clear exactly what the novel is warning against—is it a moral condemnation of the excessive desires and errant speculations of post–Civil War capitalism? Or is it a lesson in taste for the discerning reader, a tacit pedagogy in which the Lapham "type" is the reader's antitype to warn against the pathos of cultural ignorance and its very real costs? This is one distinction the novel will not draw. The novel seems to protest the harsh terms of failure visited upon the Laphams in a capitalist culture and asks the reader to feel sympathy with him, to accord him dignity rather than mockery. But the specter of Lapham's failure also generates competitive energies from within Howells's own narrative, energies that compel the reader to seek success where Lapham fails. Sympathy with Lapham is possible only if the reader disavows any social identification with him; to move past sympathy toward a feeling of identity (as a sentimental fiction would ask) is either to invite self-contempt or to refuse the novel's own terms of realist distinction. Lapham's humiliation serves as a kind of vaccination: his anxieties are the reader's protection, his failure the reader's advance. Howells's novels are among the most brilliant anatomies of class anxieties, feelings that had intensified in the economic boom of the later nineteenth century. But these energies are emotions his novels incite and deploy as well as analyze. As a reading experience, *The Rise of Silas Lapham* can be said to consist of moments of the reader's "shudders" as a system of internally felt distinctions. The cumulative effect is to create Lapham's rounded character as an object of the reader's complex discriminations. The secondary effect, less overt but more fundamentally significant, is the process that fashions its ideal reader as the discriminating subject, a process enacted through internal cues, deflected embarrassment, and sharpened literary apprehension.

The desire that governs Barnum's reader—the open, unembarrassed desire for upward mobility—is what the reader of Howells must most strongly disavow. But from another angle, this difference is also a resemblance. In its way, *Silas Lapham* is, like Barnum's book, a handbook that offers rules for emulation. As one would expect, Howells's rules are nothing like those of Barnum, who codifies his advice as positive axioms ("The Art of Money Getting") and submits his own financial triumphs as proof positive of their correctness. Howells's rules are never stated; they exist only in negative form as the unspoken directives for the reader's acts of distanced empathy and tactical disavowal. But it is no coincidence that the novel's keenest social observers, Penelope Lapham and Tom Corey, are also the characters most clearly positioned for success and wealth. By the end of the novel, Penelope and Tom appear poised to make distinction pay. Tom has recognized the ironic provincialism of his own superior Brahmin tastes; absolving Lapham's shame and marrying Penelope opens up for Tom expansive prospects in the more glamorous form of international trade. And Penelope earns her "rise" into a higher social stratum by making a marriage match equal to her own gifts of sharp perception.

Howells's novel exhibits a culture of money with striking critical acuity. But it is also a document from within that culture and partakes of the same economics of cultural taste it critically portrays. This double resonance is all the more notable for the fact that the cultural dimensions of American capitalism were becoming increasingly troubling to Howells in this moment. He found labor unrest and economic strife acutely distressing, and Howells was almost alone among American intellectuals in his public opposition to the hanging of the anarchists charged in the Haymarket riot of 1887. His novels begin to show a new sense of social dislocation and drift even as he attempts to represent an even larger social landscape. In *A Hazard of New Fortune* (1890) and *The World of Chance* (1893), the costs and violent conflicts of an economics of culture would come in for direct examination. The realities of American life, as much as "unreal" mass forms, were beginning to seem distorted and incongruous. In an oft-quoted 1888 letter to Henry James, Howells wrote that "'America' seems to be the most grotesquely illogical thing under the sun."

After fifty years of optimistic content with "civilization" and its ability to come out all right in the end, I now abhor it, and feel that it is coming out all wrong in the end, unless it bases itself anew on a real equality. Meantime, I wear a fur-lined overcoat, and live in all the luxury my money can buy.[52]

As his dark self-satire suggests, Howells's own aesthetic discernment threatened to symbolize not a future social cohesion but a continuing history of inequality. His belief in the benevolent cultivation of consciousness had begun to seem ever more distant from the dream of a "republic of letters," threatening to leave taste and distinction as capacities that amount to little more than an eye for a fine overcoat.

Twain, James, and Publics

The rift Howells faced between his principles of realism and an unrealized dream of civil unity is instructive. In formal terms, the rift was structural. Realism's reliance on the mass forms it opposes ensures that it never achieves the closed mastery it seeks. And the "inequalities of knowledge" that are the ground for high literary discernment risk becoming a symbol of economic inequalities.[53] But that dilemma also motivates the realist vigilance for maintaining perceptions of cultural difference, and the process of erecting and displaying the difference between literary values and mass forms is what the realist novel itself performs. Lack of mastery was thus the energizing tension through which realist writers created increasingly complex literary codes of distinction. Writers achieved their distinctive styles by risking—at times even courting—a confusion in readers' minds between those writers' use of literary irony and the cultural objects they ironize. Charles Chesnutt and Edith Wharton offer critical portraits of social worlds (the South and the coteries of the urban rich) that were already objects of mass fascination and, by doing so, flirted with the voyeuristic market desires they mean to critique. The exotic reversals and elaborations of ironic distinctions in James's moral dramas often spin away to form a melodrama of their own, an aesthetic effect that made many contemporary readers suspect James himself of moral perversity. Henry Adams, whose novels and early essays endorse Howells's faith in analytic distinctions, later finds apocalyptic collapse in that very analytic cast of mind.

While the "analytic instinct" that (in James's words) "rises supreme" in the later nineteenth century failed to govern cultural tastes, it allowed Howells and others to reinvent fiction writing as a special vocation and a vital cultural authority, an authority structured from within by the conditions of modernity it profoundly, warily examined.[54] This position in the social landscape, more than any set of features or unified worldview, gives high literary realism its shape and force. Yet the question that haunts Howells's vision of a "grotesquely illogical" America remains: high literary culture acquired authority and prestige, but to what end? Did the powers of discernment credited to the realists amount to more than what Howells sometimes feared—a badge of cultural capital alone?

Mark McGurl is surely correct that the contest for literary prestige cannot be reduced to a matter of petty "careerism" inasmuch as it partakes of the profound human struggle to win recognition, a struggle that is not only existential—Hegel's dialectical "desire for the desire of others"—but also inescapably social.[55] That no individual author could succeed or fail outside of a collective field of competing positions makes for the resonance I have noted between realism's authorial strategies and the social conflicts it portrayed. But, taken on their terms, the realists aspired to more than career success or even the elevation of public taste. The intellectual cast of realism was not designed merely to explore or profit from "inequalities of knowledge"; it also represents a wish for knowledge *about* something. Whatever their other motives, realists cultivated critical thought in the name of greater social understanding, and even a dedicated aesthete like Henry James declared a hopeful belief in what he called the "civic use of the imagination."[56] But this genuine critical impulse was also the source of a threatened impasse. For the realist, to recognize a "unity of taste" as a wholly quixotic goal would likely lead to Howells's eventual sense of futility. Yet to concede that talk of a civic dimension to high art is disingenuous would be to accept and embrace high art as an instrument of social control. Then again, to give up any claim of art's social relevance would reduce high literary values to nothing more than the self-satisfied preferences of the elite.

A threat of an impasse of this sort lurks within high literary realism almost from its inception. The majority of those who inhabited the actual America, as it turned out, preferred the commercial arts to the hoped-for "America of Art"; beyond the possibility for securing an author's own prestige, then, could the "analytic impulse" cultivated in realism achieve anything other than a sense of social disappointment or cultural disdain? Mark Twain would sidestep this dilemma, but he managed to do so by finessing if not altogether flouting the tenets of realism. Ironically enough, it was Henry James, the artist possessing the most analytic narrative style, who eventually may have developed the most far-sighted ideas about the "possible fine employments" for literature in an age of mass culture.[57]

After Twain became a canonized figure in American studies—or "hypercanonized," as Jonathan Arac argues—critics tended to lose sight of the idiosyncratic nature of his career.[58] Although he shared the realists' belief that the best literature possessed a special order of social knowledge, he was far less alarmed by the expansion of commercial culture and new media publics—though Twain was ultimately more skeptical that *any* spaces of public representation, literary or otherwise, could recover enduring meaning. Twain's canny literary understanding can be glimpsed most clearly in the ways he would choose to defy literary codes, usually with an eye to how he could profit from the transgression. When Howells began serializing *A Modern Instance*, Twain claimed that the portrait of Bartley Hubbard—a figure George Washington Cable described as the insufferable type of "our national 'smart Aleck' "—was based on Twain himself (Howells denied it).[59] In identifying with the novel's undiscerning anti-hero (or pretending to), Twain's act of misreading is proof he understood perfectly the proper way to read a realist novel—but Twain's own trump move would be to decline to take up the cultured position of the realist reader.

Howells had become a literary insider by mastering the tastes of the Boston illuminati (and then subtly helping make them seem old-fashioned), but Twain earned success by mastering a performance culture of popular public lectures and storytelling in which he honed strategies for comically deflating authority. He went on to fashion those comic techniques and moods into a species of fiction that won acceptance from northeastern literary magazines. But even as he acquired recognition from the literary establishment for his talent as a novelist, Twain cultivated a persona at odds with the cultured man of letters and turned a range of comic techniques, from sarcasm and vernacular voices to bravura feats of linguistic surprise, into a distinctive kind of literary narrative. Like Whitman, Twain was by turns defensive and derisive about the more analytic styles of high literary writing. His tribute to Howells's work is telling: "you make all the motives & feelings perfectly clear without analyzing the guts of them."[60]

Henry James was Twain's target here, indicted (along with George Eliot and Hawthorne) as a writer who *did* gut his subjects with excessive analysis. Twain had little patience for the cerebral intricacies of James's fiction ("I would rather be damned to John Bunyan's hell" than read *The Bostonians*, he wrote to Howells).[61] And the few essays he wrote on literary topics tended to import the satirical tones from his humor pieces for use in puncturing high literary authorities. In an 1898 essay on the French writer Paul Bourget (an intimate of James and Edith Wharton), Twain offers some of his only comments on the art of what he calls "novel-building." He states his conviction that the novelist is the "one expert who is qualified to examine the souls and the life of a people and make a valuable report," but his positive assertions about the value of novels amount to no more than a few sentences. His critical position emerges instead by way of a humorous skewering of Bourget's much anticipated travel book on the United States. Although American critics were eager to read Bourget's forthcoming observations, Twain feigns alarm: "I feared for my country," Twain writes, because Bourget "had gotten his equipment in France." With this wry image, the analytic criticism favored by advanced tastes ("I saw by his own intimations that he was an Observer, and had a System—that used by naturalists and other scientists") becomes a risible picture of "equipment" trained on a national "bug": "The bug may not know himself perfectly, but he knows himself better than the naturalist can know him, at any rate."[62]

Initially, Twain's adherence to comic modes of writing cost him full acceptance by academic critics. Van Wyck Brooks was sure that "the making of the humorist was the undoing of the artist. It was the suppression of his aesthetic desires, the degradation of everything in which the creative instinct feeds."[63] But literary historians would eventually credit his innovative techniques of irony and comic penetration with as much analytic acuity as James. Howells himself had classified Twain as a "romancer," but Twain's willingness to address slavery and the enduring problem of race eventually made him as central to the literary history of realism as James and Howells. With his sustained preoccupation with masks, language games, and complexities of identity, Twain has been recognized as a sophisticated "theorist of representation" and a savvy "analyst of cultural performance."[64] Twain, too, makes inequalities of knowledge into both a generative literary technique and a literary subject, as he explores the cultural divisions and acts of social exploitation that become newly visible in games of knowing. Who is in on a joke and who is duped, who is self-deceived and who is exposed, who knows more in order to appropriate or invade, and who knows enough to fool or evade: these dynamics animate the reader's tangle with the Twain text even as the text maps out social games as simple as a small-town hoax (a con game with a jumping frog) or as large as an imperial slaughter (the Connecticut Yankee's Gatling-gun massacre).

Given that Twain shared the realists' concern with authenticity, then, it is all the more notable that he was untroubled by the machinery of mass culture. Part of the reason is no doubt the origins of his art in popular theater. Lawrence Levine argues that Twain's career was a holdover from an earlier world in which Shakespeare plays, symphonic bands, and charismatic speakers drew large audiences of both educated and working-class patrons.[65] But despite his start in local forms of populist entertainment, the phenomenon that was Mark Twain in fact belongs the new mass culture of the postbellum world. Like Barnum, Twain was among the first figures to understand the synergy possible between electrifying live performances and newspaper publicity, a circuit that could simultaneously report an event and advertise the performer for a national and even an international audience. Twain's own early career as a newspaper correspondent, dispatching pieces from Hawaii, San Francisco, or Nevada to media networks reaching across the continent, anticipated the "army of subscription salesmen" who would later sell his works door-to-door in all corners of the country. Twain saw mass markets not just as a means for distribution but also as a source of new material, as he deftly adapted best-selling genres (detective fiction, time-travel stories, historical romance, plantation tales, travel writing) and media sensations (Siamese twins, séances, fingerprinting) for use in his fiction.[66]

In contrast with Howells's sense of a critical impasse between literary and commercial publics, Twain saw the gap as an opportunity for a profitable convergence between the two domains. His ability to fashion literary analysis at the level of humorous shock and surprise counters Howells's worried assumption that the "effectists" of mass performance produce nothing more than meaningless sensation. As Jane Thrailkill has argued, the laughter that conducts meaning in a novel like *Huckleberry Finn* is both a "bodily event" and an act of critical reflection, an expression of both feeling and meaning.[67] Twain's intimate knowledge of disparate publics, together with his canny understanding of the new commodity that was publicity itself, were crucial to creating what became his unmatched linguistic freedom. And yet, despite his extraordinary success, Twain suffered from his own sense of confronting something anarchic, as if the very linguistic freedom he had discovered by traversing such different publics carried the germ of meaninglessness.

The formation of high literary culture created a gap that Howells feared was an impassible distance between literary sensibility and social agency. Twain might be said to have closed that gap only to open what appeared to be an abyss. The performative ironies of Twain's writing operate through what Sacvan Bercovitch has analyzed as unstable reversals of meaning, moments that retrospectively revise the reader's understanding of earlier moments in the text. In the "deadpan" humor of *Huckleberry Finn*, for instance, the reader can never rest easy in the knowledge that she is in on the joke; what looks like Huck Finn's merely playful early pranks on Jim, for instance, cannot remain harmless foolery after we've discovered the later hoax that is Jim's unnecessary "rescue" from slavery. In these moments of reversal, something innocent belatedly may become recognizable as satire, or something satirical resolves into the sinister, and our own acts of interpretation are able to gull us into a trap. Through this perspective, Twain's humor is at its most serious when it seems the most comical, for by the rules of his high-stakes game of literary deadpan, the moment when readers laugh is also the moment Twain may be laughing at his readers, having darkly "persuaded us that he's a Comic Writer."[68]

Inasmuch as such reversals of meaning occur in time, they occur not just in the mind but in the body, bringing a "severe set of shocks" through which one feels Twain's "nub" or "snapper" as a tangible jolt. With its emphasis on a dynamic but uncertain phenomenology of inversions and jolts, Twain's art of the mediated shock resembles a literary version of the sensory emphasis in mass fiction and commercial amusement. By dropping a "snapper" effect into literary culture, Twain shows that the aesthetic meaning of a novel is no less dependent on the nerve-filled body in high culture than it is in low. At the same time, the experience of reading *Huck Finn* also begins to unsettle the institutional pleasures associated with literary discernment and interpretation.[69] Unlike the realists who sought to distinguish civil relations from commercial distortions, Twain saw meaning everywhere; no one place was the space of retreat where one could use the operations of culture to extract social meaning or rule out the meaning of other public worlds as mere sensation or noise. But though meaning is everywhere, it is everywhere subject to the same fate as the human bodies and collective cultures that produce it: complicity with cruelty, and susceptibility to delusion and decay. In *Huck Finn*, and especially in the late writings of the "dark Twain," the comforts of culture—meanings shared through myths, language, and icons—increasingly turn into what Bercovitch calls the "trap of culture," and interpretation itself begins to look like culture's last, best trap. Despite the comic warning at the beginning of *Huck Finn* that those seeking a moral will be "shot," the reception history of Twain's famous novel proves that we are unable to forego the need to find a self-redeeming interpretation for Huck's story, even when it confirms a willingness, if not an institutionalized compulsion, to misread Twain's damning novel.[70]

The entertainment of reading *Huck Finn* has never broken free from the discomfort (which might be pleasure) of trying to decide just what theft or rescue or flight is supposed to mean for the reader—or, indeed, the author—of *Huck Finn*. If this ambiguity hints at a historical relation between Twain's fiction and the commercial culture of hoaxes, thrills, and publicity stunts he knew and sometimes imitated, the same interpretive ambiguity also became the foundation for a pedagogical industry that has been among the most efficacious projects in U.S. literary culture. Twain looked rather skeptically on coordinated efforts to instruct or raise public taste, so there is no small irony in the fact that Twain himself became the central figure in the vast pedagogical project to institutionalize "conscience-driven forms of American liberal interpretation." But the large success of the institutional Twain might be said to confirm the instincts of the historical Twain, inasmuch as academic efforts at teaching a unified meaning for Huck's story and Twain's art keep proving that American society is *not* in fact a unified culture.[71]

Unlike Twain, Henry James perceived a threat to the value of the literary from the era's new forms of publicity and print production, and his fiction and essays from the 1890s show his preoccupation with the new "flood" of print. But it is also in this moment that he begins to write essays that meditate on a rather different, less hostile role for the "high aesthetic temper" in the changed landscape of mass expression, as if his sense of immersion in the "flood" also initiates a critical sea change for James himself.[72] In "The Question of the Opportunities" (1898), James still retains what he calls his "slightly affrighted" view of the "flood of books" claiming their place in American literature, for he recognizes that their vast numbers and the expanded reading public they address have altered forever what "literature" actually is.[73] The "comparatively small library of books" that defined literary value in the past can no longer serve as an adequate measure. The quantity of print and the "huge American public" that consumes it have made fluid and unfixed the very qualities that constitute the literary: "Whether, in the conditions we consider, the supply [of texts in print] shall achieve sufficient vitality and distinction really to be sure of itself as literature" is all but impossible to say, especially when "all this depends on what we take it into our head to *call* literature" (653). But at the same time he records his apprehension, James emphasizes his sense of excitement—"the drama and the bliss, when not the misery" (652)—at viewing the dizzying changes. The very contingency of literary value, James stresses, means the possibility of unexpected creativity, of "new light struck out by the material itself" (653).

The prospect that altogether new literary values might spring from mass conditions brings a sense of critical exhilaration, an escape from "foregone conclusions and narrow rules." To be sure, a reading audience counted in the millions ("or rather the fast-arriving billion") brings no guarantee of literary achievement—and for James, it also brings positive dangers, such as the "mechanical reverberation" of the war lust he heard in the American press.[74] Yet whatever the risks, for James such massive numbers are also certain to bring artistic "opportunities."

But if the billion give the pitch of production and circulation, they do something else besides; they hang before us a wide picture of opportunities. . . . It is impossible not to entertain with patience and curiosity the presumption that life so colossal must break into expression at points of proportionate frequency. These places, these moments will be the chances. (653)

The forms of expression likely to emerge from such conditions, moreover, represent not just possibilities for fresh literary illumination but also a new kind of literary field. Although the gargantuan scale of print production is likely to foster "extravagantly general" writing, James argues that the same threat of homogenization may well encourage counteracting strains of innovation, strains that "may get individual publics positively more sifted and evolved than anywhere else" (654). The introduction of plural "publics" here is crucial. James imagines multiple kinds of literary value able to coexist, related yet distinct, on a plane "subdivided as a chess-board, with each little square confessing only to its own *kind* of accessibility" (653). The metaphor of a chessboard conveys James's attempt to think his way past a purely hierarchical scheme of literary value without severing the link between literature and cultural criticism. James's chessboard figure insists that literary value must remain social; an image of congruent literary "varieties" permits him to conceive of a reading public with at least potential communication among its parts, even as it recognizes that the force of "individual genius" may work in different ways to draw in disparate kinds of readers. Accepting multiple "varieties" of the literary means the notion of a uniform system of privileged literary representation—a realist museum—must be sacrificed. But the sacrifice brings returns: the more dynamic model of a multiform field of literature developed through a creative "reaction" to mass leveling promises to preserve a critical function for literature now recognized as contingent.

Literary possibility is also the keynote in "The Lesson of Balzac" (1905). James claims in this essay that a "critical spirit" can survive in the novel despite the genre's transformation into a mass "article of commerce." The commercial machinery of innumerable publishers, editors, interviewers, and producers, he asserts, has made the novel a thing of "easy manufacture" and a "bankrupt and discredited art."[75] In these conditions, James turns to the example of Balzac to recover the figure of an "emulous fellow-worker" (121), of the novelist as a "craftsman" and the novel as a "handmade" object of deliberate care (134). In the course of the essay, however, James's most insistent lament—that at present an enormous "array of producers and readers" together generate "production uncontrolled" and uncritical (134)—gradually becomes his most striking and hopeful suggestion. His own talk of a background world of producers and production seems to prompt James to realize that a novel can be conceptualized not as an object at all but as a practice or activity, one that is necessarily shared by readers as much as by the novel's author. The "faculty of attention" (128) that makes for the vitality of the worthy novel, James argues, is replicated in readers prepared to go as far as the author in the critical pursuit of a given literary subject.

Balzac is thus the "fellow-worker" of any individual who rises to the bait of his "intellectual adventure" (127). For James, no other novelist equals Balzac in offering an "intensity of educative practice." The practice is never without the reward of pleasure; James insists that Balzac offers "entertainment" as much as instruction. But so comprehensive and penetrating is the picture of life produced by Balzac that an extraordinary density of "significance, relation and value" is opened for the reader's analysis: "It is a prodigious multiplication of values, and thereby a prodigious entertainment of the vision—on the condition the vision can bear it. Bearing it—

that is *our* bearing it—is a serious matter, for the appeal is truly to that faculty of attention out of which we are educating ourselves as hard as we possibly can" (128).

By conceiving the novel as a literary practice rather than an object, James presents literature as the creative labor that produces a public as it multiplies relations of shared "significance." Hence the essay's concluding image that recasts the space of the novel from a museum or exhibit to a collective workshop: "It will strike you perhaps," James notes to his audience, "that I speak as if we all, as if *you* all, without exception were novelists, haunting the back of the shop, the laboratory, or, more nobly expressed, the inner shrine of the temple; but such assumptions, in this age of print—are perhaps never too wide of the mark" (138). Although James retains his allegiance to the distinctions of literary discernment, the "uncontrolled" production in the age of mass print supplies the very conditions for a collective creativity able to foster multiple publics. Moreover, the excesses of the age of print also appear to create the possibility for a strange conjunction or communication between the "shop," the "laboratory," and the "temple," all of which are sites for a population James addresses as a confederation of novelists—a conceit that redefines the identity of the novelist as much as it does the public.

Chapter 3
Women and the Realism of Desire

In his *Atlantic* essay on the 1869 Boston theater season, "The New Taste in Theatricals," Howells describes the actresses impersonating men in the popular comic plays called burlesques. Although "they were not like men, [they] were in most things as unlike women, and seemed creatures of a kind of alien sex, parodying both. It was certainly a shocking thing to look at them with their horrible prettiness, their archness in which was no charm, their grace which put to shame."[1] For Howells, these cross-dressing performers were vivid proof of popular entertainment's ability to deform even the most fundamental of human categories, the identity of sex. By creating the illusion of an "alien sex," neither woman nor man, the burlesque impersonations stood out as one of the "monstrous and artificial" inventions that Howells found everywhere conspicuous in commercial culture. Yet, as Howells surely knew, the burlesque shows told a truth, even if it was the skewed truth of a visual pun. The "unreal" creatures onstage, that is, bespoke a new social reality: the striking presence of women in public life. As the male-costumed actresses moved and spoke onstage, they evoked the recent entry of women into what had been male roles and traditionally male social spaces outside the home.

The increasing participation of middle-class women in public life was one of the most striking features of post–Civil War culture. Observers stressed the changed look of U.S. civil society, its transformed countenance. In the workplace, one journalist writes, there is "scarcely an occupation once confined almost exclusively to men in which women are not now conspicuous."[2] Commercial consumption, too, had a female face. The advent of the highly theatrical world of department stores, for instance, was perceived as a feminine transformation: "The lady-element of Broadway is one of its most dazzling features." Thorstein Veblen even contended that the essential purpose of the middle-class wife was no longer to nurture and instruct in private but to advertise affluence in public, to display her husband's wealth through her clothes, accessories, and manners—hence, even *as* wives, women had become public creatures. In 1904 when Henry James returned to the United States after a long absence, he described an American world in which the presence of the "new" woman had become "the sentence written largest in the American sky."[3]

As James's image of skywriting suggests, women's new visibility dazzled as well as provoked. Even the way debates about women's status circulated in public discussion acquired a startling, capital-letter conspicuousness—a stark legibility as the Woman Question, a revolutionary profile as the New Woman, an international publicity as the American Girl, a threatening incarnation as a modern Amazon. The sight of women in public seemed to demand a new definition of womanhood. But the contemporary emphasis on visibility—the sense that a large, unanswered question loomed on the social scene, that it crowded every street and workplace—suggests that the issue was as much about the nature of the public sphere as it was about the nature of women. To the Reverend James Weir, the *sight* of women seemed inescapable, a fact that seemed to change the very idea of public life: "we see forms and phases of [women's] degeneration thickly scattered throughout all circles of society, in the plays which we see performed in our theatres, and in the books and papers published daily throughout the land."[4] Weir was very certain about the changed nature of the modern woman (she had suffered "degeneration"); but exactly what was the sphere of the modern public now that it was "thickly" crowded with such a variety of female "forms," from actresses, authors, and reporters to book and newspaper depictions? Was the domain of literature, books, and the press still a sphere of public reason, a site at which the mind can think with and through other minds?

Scholars have recognized for some time the pivotal role of gender in the formation of literary realism. There is little doubt that anxieties surrounding women triggered phobic reactions and aided compensatory efforts at constructing a "masculine realism." But critics have given less attention to the way women's entry into public life was also an opportunity, a chance to use fictional lives to redefine and explore what it might mean to be a subject in public. As women began appearing outside the domestic sphere, they made it difficult to retain an idea of a public culture that was, at its purest, a meeting of the minds. The public woman could seem all body—an excess of mobility, desire, and outsized will. This was especially true in mass culture, where women's rather small, incremental gains in social agency grew to larger-than-life dimensions and occult forms: dazzling celebrities, outsized images on posters, "priestesses" of consumption, star reporters, voracious women readers—all exciting or distressing reminders that social relations were too mixed up with desire, corporeality, and commerce to be easily sifted out into a set of common concerns amenable to rational-critical debate. However unreal these different effigies of public womanhood might have seemed, they represented a reality in need of direct critical analysis. Like scientists and other critical professionals, realists hoped to bring the enigma of the public woman into analytic understanding, a project that was often as compelling for women writers as for men.

In many respects, the divide between mass culture and literary culture created a divide in the portraits of women. Onstage or on the screen she is a powerful visual icon, all color, vivid style, and movement, whereas on the pages of the realist novel—as on the anatomist's table or the data of a scientific study—she is often a more passive object, frequently in the grip of social or biological forces. Representations of women often remained caught in this static duality: over here she is an ungovernable agent, over there a still, even tragically arrested object. But precisely the analytic habits of realism, I will argue, allow these polarized portraits of women to enter into a more dialectical relation, making it possible to critically explore a woman as both a conscious agent and a social creature, both a mind and a body. The puzzle of public womanhood is a vexation and a motive for close literary analysis, a spur to develop methods of narrative dissection able to reach new depths of human interiority and yet a site where interior consciousness is seen as inseparable from desire and corporeal feeling.

"Personating" in Public

Public talk about "woman," of course, usually referred to the lives of a relatively limited group: middle-class white women who were lucky enough to receive (or, less happily, merely to desire) the kind of education their brothers received, women who might contemplate paid work as a route to autonomy or status rather than a means of survival. Working-class women were present all along in the world of labor and in city streets without seeming to have invaded public life, a telling indication that the public sphere was not an aggregation of actual spaces but a mediated path to authority and self-representation. The fact that publicness is a result of mediation, moreover, helps explain the unlikely origins of the public womanhood of the 1870s and 1880s: ironically, the public woman was a creature of the antebellum private home, where wives, daughters, and maiden aunts acquired a new kind of symbolic capital as private beings.

In the antebellum era, women had developed a distinct sense of womanhood that was private and domestic. The spiritualized femininity they invoked had its essence in a piety defined against sexuality and in domestic instincts that were opposed to marketplace calculations. These women authors repeatedly effaced their professional status, taking pseudonyms, disclaiming any aspirations to high art, and expressing anxiety about their public exposure ("I have a perfect horror of appearing in print," as Sedgwick wrote)—all disavowals that actually aided their rise as public figures.[5] While their ambivalence about publicity was no doubt real, their disclaimers about fame also made fame possible: only by circulating a private, spiritualized model of women's identity did women authors achieve public attention both for themselves and for their vision of private womanhood.

Popular domestic fiction also gave women a worldly visibility in even more material ways. Domestic authors compared their literary production to needlework and other intimate fireside occupations, yet their commercial success ensured that their names and faces became icons in a mass marketplace. For authors like Harriet Beecher Stowe and Fanny Fern, the machinery of advertising, sales figures, biographical sketches, lithographs, tours and personal appearances, press sightings, and celebrity photographs made the women's home lives, and even their bodies and styles of dress, into objects for public display and consumption. Unauthorized reprinting of their essays and stories produced self-perpetuating circuits of publicity; like their visual image, their words spread through an almost automatic, decentralized production that further heightened their public recognition.[6] The champions of women's spiritual, home-centered identity acquired a status that was decidedly public, commercial, and quite frequently political.

But public visibility for women was not limited to hearthside writers. The dancer Fanny Elssler and singer Jenny Lind were among the first female performers in America to acquire national celebrity through new networks of mass publicity. The personal lives of stage performers such as Lydia Thompson and Adah Isaacs Menken began to supply material for secondary dramas that ran in syndicated gossip columns. In the footsteps of reformers like Stowe, women lecturers became celebrities whose activities on behalf of various causes also brought attention to their lives. The antilynching activist Ida B. Wells and the feminist Charlotte Perkins Gilman were as often condemned as they were lauded, but both responses heightened their public profiles.

In a multitude of forms, femininity thrived in modern publicity. To observers like the Reverend Weir, however, the public nature of print or the stage necessarily compromised a woman's true identity. Francis Lieber, an influential writer on political topics, declared that "woman loses in the same degree her natural character ... as she enters into publicity."[7] Henry James gives the same sentiment to his character Basil Ransom, a Southern traditionalist, in *The Bostonians* (1885). When Basil observes Verena Tarrant give a public speech, the sight of a "virginal" young woman addressing a crowded assembly produces for Basil a paradox of "sweet grotesqueness."[8] For Basil the incongruity of female subjectivity showcased in a public exhibition was not just an irony but a provocation. Howells's reaction to the "horrible prettiness" of the female burlesque troupe was rooted in the same feeling of witnessing a public transgression of a fundamentally private or domestic female identity.

There is a note of gender panic if not misogyny in the chorus of voices raised against women's increased public visibility. But critics' contempt was not for women's essential nature (now frequently idealized) but for their degradation in the new media of modern publicity, the largely ungoverned machinery of image and print that was producing what Weir calls the "thickly scattered" representations of and by women. Still, it is difficult, and at times impossible, to tease apart contemporary anti-woman sentiments from concurrent anxieties about the raft of new cultural technologies that churned profit out of the words and images "published daily throughout the land." For the things that most worried critics about the popular culture industry matched closely with what was most worrisome about women: both, it was feared, had a susceptibility to unchecked fantasy, a tendency to wander from the real. Precisely in their spiritual nature, women were apt to discount or simply fail to apprehend the necessities that determined worldly systems and orders. Similarly, the productions of mass culture, beholden only to profit, were blithely indifferent to either traditional social orders or the rationalized orders advanced by science and professional experts. Hence the widespread tendency to see the mass culture industry itself as feminine in nature and feminizing in cultural effect, where "feminine" signifies the unconstrained power of feelings and wishes to overwhelm the order of the real. In the words of one male writer, the consumer demand of the vast female audience is the "Iron Madonna who strangles in her fond embrace the American novelist."[9]

The desire to assert a contrasting professional virility for fiction writing can be detected at many levels.[10] Quite clearly, anxiety about the cultural exposure of women—her exposure *in* popular culture as well as *to* it—is an animating energy in high realist literature. But for male and female writers alike, the disorientation that results from shifts in gender norms is a conscious resource as well as trigger for phobic reaction. In high realism a historical sense of sexual vertigo is subject to a profound, self-conscious analysis. Male panic is as much on display in this writing as the female exposure that produces it. Moreover, the disorienting new publicity for women was a provocative subject for women writers just as it was for men, and though the values of realism closed down avenues for some women writers they helped create professional opportunities for others. Above all, the association of women with commercial culture made women *representative* in an Emersonian sense. If women were exemplary cultural objects, they were also a crucial topic for exploring the vicissitudes of the thinking, feeling human subject who faced the far more theatrical, mediated world of the later nineteenth century. Within realism, it is largely women and women's stories that pose the most profound meditations on human agency, embodied consciousness, and the authenticity of the self that were the realists' chief concerns in an age of mass culture.[11]

Howells's first-person account of his confrontation with the "shocking" womanhood staged in burlesque plays offers an instructive point of entry: what can read like a phobic confession is in fact a canny delineation of the sexual dynamics and obsessions with embodied subjectivity that would structure high cultural art. Howells makes no attempt to disguise his distress at the production. The "prettiness" of conventional feminine faces and figures performing aggressive male postures and gestures is for him a "horror to look upon" (639). One actress dressed as a prince "had a raucous voice, an insolent twist of the mouth, and a terrible trick of defying her enemies by standing erect, chin up, hand on hip, and right foot advanced, patting the floor. It was impossible, even in the orchestra seats, to look at her in this attitude and not shrink before her" (640). As Howells's emphasis on his own act of looking suggests, the performance requires a literal seeing—a forced revision or recognition—of women as active agents. After decades of rhetoric underscoring an ethereal, transcendent femininity, the sight of women possessing erect, defiant bodies and insubordinate voices makes them seem an altogether different sex. One woman who had appeared to shrink in the opening sketch "seemed quite another being when she came on later as a radiant young gentleman in pink silk hose and nothing of feminine modesty in her dress except the very low corsage" (642). The transformation did not come from any illusion that the actresses were men—if anything, the body-revealing costumes emphasized their identity as women. Rather, it was the comic but pointed sight of women inhabiting the role of the worldly, self-possessing, and self-asserting agent that converted the performers into an "alien sex."

Howells is confounded by the change, as much for what it reveals as what it distorts. The theatrical staging seems to unveil a species of interior truth, not in spite of the artifice of the performance but through it, and the theatrical setting, Howells recognizes, allows for glimpses of intimate insight. At one point the actresses add to their male imposture a racial mimicry of minstrel dances, a double impersonation that reveals an "infuriate grace and a fierce delight very curious to look upon" (641). The stage role seemed to bring one woman such pleasure that she must be "at something of a loss to identify herself when personating a woman off the stage" (642). The power of playacting cannot be limited to the stage and leads Howells to ponder the actress's offstage identity, only to lead him to see the theatrical role as a more fitting—because happier—context for the woman she is. The activity of "personating" uncovers otherwise undetectable truths about subjectivity, truths revealed by evidence of "delight" and physical "grace."

Similarly, Howells's own identity as a man, as he openly portrays it, begins to seem a corresponding act of impersonation. Acknowledging the evident pleasure of the female performers, Howells describes his own reaction as a parody of traditional male agency. The sight of an actress who, "coldly yielding herself to the manager's ideas of the public taste, stretched herself on a green baize bank with her feet toward us or did a similar grossness," evokes a chivalrous alarm: "It was hard to keep from crying aloud in protest, that she need not do it; that nobody really expected or wanted it of her. Nobody? Alas! there were people there . . . who plainly did expect it, and who were loud in their applauses of the chief actress" (639). As if joining the performance in a hapless role of his own, Howells casts himself as a male rescuer only to underscore the absurdity of his response in a mock-heroic self-portrait.

Through Howells's self-scripted melodrama of gender anxiety, the paradoxical artifice of a stage performance makes selfhood and human agency at once more transparent and legible, and yet more subject to mutability. The shock of seeing an "alien" femininity, even in a comic stage play, actually provides for a new and striking inside view of male and female selves. Howells is clearly unnerved by the funhouse distortions of the burlesque, but he also experiences the strong draw of a femininity electrified by the medium of publicity and its ability to reveal as well as refract. Despite his tones of disapproval, recognizing the performers' "fierce delight" leads Howells to open speculation about what he knows he *doesn't* understand: the consciousness and desire of women who eagerly appear in the trappings of men. Howells's musings on theater and the effects of burlesque begin to point up ways that gender organizes the key terms of analysis in high realism—its terrain of psychological insight as well as public exhibition, its reflection on agency as well as social determinacy, its obsession with forms of intimacy and wayward desire as well as with social estrangement and public disguise.

These are the terms of analysis governing James's *The Bostonians* (1885), a novel in which the public woman is the muse for the postbellum culture of commercial spectacle. James explores the iconicity of the public woman as a figure that casts doubt on the premise (or at least the wish) that the modern social world can be understood through a disembodied discourse of reason. When the wish for reason becomes indistinguishable from desire, the public woman becomes the scapegoat for a lost ideal of the literary public sphere.

As embodied in the novel's protagonist, Verena Tarrant, the female spirituality once defined as domestic and religious in nature has become a public sensation. Under a quasi-occult inspiration, Verena gives rapturous speeches on social topics. For Verena's liberal-minded audiences, the young woman's public spirituality holds no contradiction: her talent for oratory is a feminine "genius" for feeling and speaking that quite naturally should be shared with a world in need of enlightenment about women's rights, the power of love, and other higher truths. For Basil Ransom (the "stiffest of conservatives" [856]), on the other hand, public femininity is an inherent contradiction. Verena's success before the era's "great popular system" of urban audiences is little more than a commercial scam, an "exhibition of enterprise and puffery" (1200), and her "genius" is merely the vibrancy of a feminine sexual attractiveness that has been improperly placed on public display. "It was simply an intensely personal exhibition," Basil insists, "and the person making it happened to be fascinating" (856). Olive Chancellor also recognizes the "danger of vulgar exploitation" (876) in Verena's public career. But for Olive, who joins league with a group of women reformers, the danger that Verena will fall victim to *private* exploitation—heterosexual marriage—is even greater. Clearly in love with Verena, Olive gives financial backing to Verena's career and initiates a domestic intimacy by bringing her to live in her home, an arrangement akin to the "Boston marriage" that was recognized at the time as a substitute couplehood for two women living under the same roof. For both Basil and Olive, Verena's "intensely personal" exhibitions have an erotic draw that is inseparable from a troubling publicity.

Basil insists there is "no place in public" for Verena, yet Verena's story reveals the postbellum public world precisely as a place where the female image thrives and proliferates. Like the domestic novelists who became celebrities of the hearth, Verena gets her start by sharing her "gift" before intimate gatherings in private homes and then circulates before wider and wider publics of strangers. Finally, in the climactic scene in the novel, Verena's scheduled performance before a sold-out audience in the Boston Music Hall registers the world of full-fledged celebrity that had been erected around women performers. Verena's public "gift" has been converted to publicity in its most expansive, commercial sense, and her appeal even spreads through copies of her reproduced image. Before she appears onstage, she is already presented to the "gaze of hundreds" (1115) who see her likeness in countless iterations of mass-produced theatrical posters and distributed handbills. Though mass-produced, these images are anything but impersonal. With an artful economy of effect, James captures the erotic attraction generated through these multiplied reproductions by showing us Basil's fiercely jealous reaction to the posters and handbills themselves: their sight made him "wish he had money to buy up the stock" (1200).

Verena's posters, a public site of sexual cathexis, recall the lithographic posters that took the place of block printing in theatrical advertisements beginning in the 1870s. The surviving posters from this period give a bravado stylization to the charismatic sexual power of female stage performers, featuring such sights as color drawings of gigantic Amazon maidens or dancers towering over puny male admirers. In *The Reign of the Poster* (1895), published in Boston, Charles Knowles Bolton compiled a catalog of some of the pictorial posters that had become a ubiquitous form of advertising. Bolton describes the personalized erotic attraction that had become part of the public experience of everyday life through the poster displays: "Ladies (on paper), like prospectuses, are ever attractive, and how many glad moments these poster beauties have given us as we passed from window to window!"[12]

Verena's posters, of course, would have displayed a notably different iconography than the "poster beauties" advertising burlesque troupes or popular plays. Her look and public appeal more closely resemble the style of celebrity singer Jenny Lind ("the most popular woman in the world"), who won fame through a carefully staged female artlessness, wearing her white dress as a signature costume and singing "Home, Sweet Home" before packed houses.[13] But in picturing the multitude of posters with Verena's image, James clearly aligns her power with the magnified mass appeal of the female performer, and the narrator similarly describes her as a "rope-dancer," an "actress," a "prima donna," and a "vocalist." For Basil, the charismatic appeal on display in Verena's handbills and posters compels him both to romantically pursue the soon-to-be star and to seek to terminate her public stardom. Success would restore the boundary between public and private: by seeking to acquire Verena's consent to marry, Basil means to return her public "charm" to a private home, a goal that goes hand in hand with his effort to publish an essay in the "Rational Review," a name that evokes (and perhaps parodies) an idealized print culture of male reason.

James presents the "great popular system" (856) of mass publicity not only as feminized public sphere but also as a distinctive trait of modern America. At this stage of his career, James aimed to write novels that were "very national, very typical . . . very characteristic of our social conditions."[14] But, notably, this effort at writing a national story was actually a sign of James's *international* tutelage in higher literary practice: his inspiration for writing a "very national" novel about the power of female publicity was his close study of, and, in some cases, personal acquaintance with, the French and Russian realists whom James met in Paris in the 1870s and 1880s.[15] The portrait of "social conditions" in *The Bostonians* is less a product of James's direct observation and notation than of the most advanced techniques in Anglo-European fiction writing, where the tenets of realism signified the most advanced or "modern" brand of literary production. James's source for *The Bostonians*, we might say, was the cafés and salons of Paris. What is more, the perception that feminized publicity was intruding on the literary public sphere was far from being an American phenomenon; in Paris in particular, the tyranny of the "poster beauties" was widely discussed and debated. Within American realism, then, transnational institutions of mass culture were crucial to the construction of the national framing of womanhood.

Conservative intellectuals in France in this period were even more alarmed than Americans were about the convergence of female beauty and commercial publicity on display in theatrical posters and advertisements. No other mass form demonstrated as clearly the ease with which the erotic appeal of women could erode the boundaries preserving art and civil society from the distortions of commercial culture. The stylized figure of a female performer created by poster designer Jules Chéret became such a familiar character that she was soon referred to as "the chérette." The problem with the color poster, which advertised the new world of Parisian music halls, circuses, and café concerts, was that it *too closely* resembled a work of art, and thus contaminated the domain of the aesthetic with the frantic energies of modern commerce: "Triumphant, exultant, brushed down, pasted, torn in a few hours and continually sapping the heart and soul with its vibrant futility, the poster is indeed the art, and almost the only art, of this age of fever and laughter, of violence, ruin, electricity and oblivion."[16] If the domain of art was inseparable from the inconstant world of commerce, critics of the poster feared that art was unlikely to foster contemplation or critical reflection—even though their own voluminous critical writing *about* the relation of art and commerce suggested otherwise.

Parisian traditionalists were as distressed as Boston authorities by mass genres like the poster. But, despite the immense popularity of posters among Parisians and the stylistic innovations of French designers, both French and American critics took the poster as a sign of an *American* force of cultural degradation. Parisian conservatives lamented that "art is undergoing a daily process of Americanization." Barnum was the face of this troubling *américanisme,* and French critics linked the degraded art of the poster to the celebrity showman. For Alfred Jarry, however, that meant the corrosive power of Barnum's arts of publicity could be harnessed for injecting iconoclastic energies into the staid world of French theater: "BARNUM is within our walls, by which we mean that he would fill them to breaking-point if he were so inclined, with his cornucopia of wonders, just as easily as he has submerged them with his posters."[17] An image of mass culture as innately American had currency not only within the United States, then, but in international literary space Pascale Casanova calls the "world republic of letters."

It is intriguing, therefore, to imagine Henry James, who is living in Paris for extended periods at precisely this time, confronting the "Barnum associations" of his childhood on the walls of the French city. Analyzing the "great popular system" of American publicity was not only an opportunity to reflect on contemporary conditions of his native land; it was also a chance to seize the national material—"Barnumized" mass culture—that might generate international literary value through analysis of an extraliterary domain that Europeans associated with America. For the purpose of grasping this dialectic, the art of the poster offers a revealing point of comparison with literary realism. In most respects, theatrical posters followed an aesthetic distinctly at odds with James's realism. Whereas theatrical posters celebrate the charismatic, the categories of James's *Bostonians* are analytic. When James looks to the categories of gender, region, and nation to understand Verena's remarkable appeal, the occult energies of the new culture of public performance become the critical *object* of realist categories with their more rationalized basis for the accurate representation of social life. Such categories provide a taxonomy for "our social conditions" through which a crisis of modernity—what Basil calls the "damnable feminisation" (1111) of American culture and what James, in more neutral terms, calls "the situation of women"—can be clearly seen and measured. Significance lies in the typical rather than the extraordinary, the analytic and not the scenic or the theatrical. Or, as James summarized the realist project, the novel provides "a more analytic consideration of appearances."[18]

This analytic turn is the key to realism's interest in uncovering psychological depth. Against the dazzling but opaque surfaces of the stage performance or the lithograph poster, the realist novel counters with a penetrating view of the human interior, a dissection made possible by what James calls the "discoveries" of realist analysis that fathom the unseen from the seen.[19] Thus, even as *The Bostonians* is at times wickedly satirical (so much so that a good many Boston denizens felt personally insulted), its grounding in a context of specific material conditions still yields rich portraits of motive and feeling. Basil Ransom's character, for instance, his defining lines and tones, are always focused through the lens of his social situation as a Southern white man. The "intimate connection" (846) Basil feels to the South opens to us a range of affect and lived relations—passions, resentments, reflexes springing from a code of honor and shame, an unconscious drive for vindication—that Basil himself keeps closed from others' view (and, at times, closed even from himself). Olive Chancellor is likewise what James calls a "representative woman" (1064) whose complexity of character unfolds along lines of a concretized human background. Her shades of feeling and her mixed motives are the animated substance of a distinct type of modern womanhood, a social type—the reformer-spinster—that the narrator describes as "visibly morbid" (810). The narrator takes delight in slyly ridiculing many of Olive's beliefs and contradictory motives. But, at the same time, the novel's analytic penetration also offers psychological insight into Olive that is rendered with considerable sympathy and, at times, with a breathtaking lyricism, as in the moving, anguished self-revelations that come to Olive during her isolated vigil on Cape Cod. With its "solidity of specification," the realist novel connects identifiable social forces with resulting textures of character to create a density that is missing from—because irrelevant to—the high wattage of conspicuous fame within mass culture.[20]

Yet even as *The Bostonians* demonstrates the potency of realist methods, it points up a contradiction in those methods. Analysis through "social conditions" supplies a scaffold for psychological depth, but such analysis also introduces a troubling uncertainty about the question of individual agency. Self-determination begins to seem a fragile and constrained human capacity at best, and at worst a human delusion. At one level Basil and Olive represent two strong wills locked in a struggle to control Verena. But as the portrait of each character is deepened through a web of social reference, the question of just what a human will *is* becomes more equivocal. As exemplars of contrasting "social conditions," Basil and Olive eventually seem merely to be repeating in a different arena the war that had issued from the intractable differences between North and South, or from an ancient battle between men and women. Their antagonism seems scripted by larger forces, and as individuals they begin to resemble unwitting actors, mere puppets of those forces. In that sense, a theatrical culture thus begins to seem a site not for distorting but for actually apprehending a deeper historical and social truth about the tenuousness of human agency. This truth is something James's otherwise anti-theatrical novel seems forced into acknowledging in the resolution of its plot, as the representation of characters' will blurs with an overtly theatrical "personating." Basil, for instance, at the height of his determination to possess Verena, is shown repeating a role already written and performed in a fated moment of history. His sense of possessing a unique, self-directed mission is marked by the narrator through an obvious allusion to the mission of another aggrieved Southerner (and professional actor), John Wilkes Booth: "There were two or three moments during which he felt as he could imagine a young man to feel who, waiting in a public place, has made up his mind, for reasons of his own, to discharge a pistol at the king or the president" (1198). Basil's "unique" will now looks to us like a reprised role.

Thus theatrical surface may, in its illusion, yield as much insight as does analytic depth. Olive, too, is in the end pulled into an ambiguous stage role that seems at once a defiant act and a scripted submission to external "conditions." Rushing onto the music hall stage when Verena fails to go on, Olive is described as repeating a historical role of martyr: "offering herself to be trampled to death and torn to pieces," she might have resembled "some feminine firebrand of Paris revolutions, erect on a barricade, or even the sacrificial figure Hypatia, whirled through the furious mob of Alexandria" (1217). Here is the Jamesian answer to the female burlesque troupe. Deliberately overdrawn, colored by a melodrama verging on ridicule, this picture of Olive absorbs the charisma of the female performer into realist analysis of the "visibly morbid" womanhood. Yet this culminating scene is also a moment the novel does not directly portray, as if the novel is unwilling—or perhaps unable—to dissect the actual spectacle in its moment of performative power. These realist characters are in the end equivocal social actors. In *The Bostonians,* the analysis of women and publicity describes a broader dilemma: the more rationalized the analysis of human lives, the more uncertain the question of human agency—but also the more compelling the figure of woman as a representative of modern subjectivity. Among its other critical insights, the distinctly cerebral brand of literary analysis undertaken in realism discovers the power of a corporeal figure—the public woman—that is no longer explicable as merely an unreal spectacle.

Incommensurate Art: Constance Fenimore Woolson

In *The Bostonians* women are caught between the distortions of publicity and the restrictions of domesticity, between crass public exposure and private effacement. The dilemma as James paints it is exaggerated. But its polarized terms trace a structure of feeling that organizes a large number of novels and stories in this era, fiction in which middle-class women confront a divide between private and public worlds that makes each seem insufficient and yet unable to be bridged. In *The Tragic Muse* (1890), James replays the same dilemma in a higher theatrical culture of serious drama. But James's novels also implicitly contain a third position from which women might circumvent the dilemma—namely, *his* position, the role of realist author with a critical standpoint from which to analyze the predicament and thus transcend it intellectually.

For the most part, the possibility of realist authorship as a role *for* women goes unrecognized in James's stories themselves. The omission is significant. The European novelists acknowledged most often in the official genealogy of American realism were men, and Balzac, Flaubert, Zola, and Turgenev were among the most oft-cited models, even while Austen, Eliot, and Sand were some of the strongest influences on realist practice. Worldly rather than religious in orientation, professional rather than commercial in status, the role of realist writer was in large part defined in contradistinction to the women novelists who so successfully established the mass market for domestic fiction in antebellum America.

High realism was not the sealed province of men, of course. But genres, as social creations, carry the sediments of gendered experience, silent articulations of norms for the sexes that inform their linguistic patterns. Such traces are important to a history of high realism in American writing, in the first instance for the way gendered norms operate to encourage or to constrain would-be authors. Who gets to be a real (realist) artist? The issue really begins from a different corner: who *wishes* to be a realist artist? Many successful women writers—even some who sought to publish their fiction in the most prestigious magazines and publishing houses—never enlisted under the realist banner. By the mid-1870s, fiction writers such as Elizabeth Stuart Phelps, Louisa May Alcott, and Elizabeth Stoddard were painting a wider field of experience for women than was portrayed in the domestic novels of an earlier generation. Still, in both formal and thematic ways, their stories and novels mark their own exclusion from a domain of high culture—indeed, they often count that exclusion from high art as one of the defining features of women's experience.

Harriet Prescott Spofford recalled the reordering of literary criteria as a termination of her brand of expansive psychological fiction. "You wonder why I did not continue in the vein of 'The Amber Gods,'" she wrote to a friend. "I suppose the public taste changed. With the coming of Mr. Howells as editor of the *Atlantic,* and his influence, the realistic arrived. I doubt if anything I wrote in those days would be accepted by any magazine now."[21] At the same time, however, the constraints of the high realist ethos could also supply conditions for an oppositional creativity. In Elizabeth Stuart Phelps's novel *The Story of Avis* (1877), for instance, Phelps measures her heroine's distance from institutions of high culture to create a space for a narrative mode rich in visual symbol and characterization. The protagonist, Avis Dobell, aspires to become a painter—to acquire "that most elusive of human gifts,—a disciplined imagination"—and travels to Florence and Paris where she studies under master teachers. But unlike the expatriate artists of James or Wharton, Avis is never directly represented in a European museum or gallery. The narrative quickly forecloses any description of her artistic training and returns her to rural Massachusetts where, in the isolation of her "little bare studio," she is visited by a series of ecstatic, unformed aesthetic visions. The tension between the fullness of Avis's artistic vision and her distance from established aesthetic institutions expresses perfectly Phelps's own creative position, as she wrote vivid, innovative fiction while remaining largely outside the high literary establishment.

The title character in Constance Fenimore Woolson's story "Miss Grief" (1880) is a woman who has written passionate creative works—"unrestrained, large, vast, like the skies or the wind"—not unlike the visionary paintings of Phelps's Avis Dobell.[22] In contrast with Phelps's emotionally expansive treatment of Avis, however, Woolson brings to Miss Grief's story the sharp, analytic dissection more typical of realists. Woolson's critically penetrating style—James lauded the "high value" of her "careful, strenuous studies" and her "remarkable minuteness of observation"—brought her recognition from the high literary establishment, recognition never accorded Phelps.[23] Even so, it is difficult to read "Miss Grief" without the distinct sense that, in disposition if not technique, Woolson was closer to the Phelps-like artist Miss Grief than she was to the successful male realist who narrates Woolson's story, a man proud of his stylistic "good taste" and transatlantic urbanity. Woolson can be seen as a realist who turns her critical eye on the high cultural establishment promoting realism. With skillful indirection, Woolson probes precisely the kind of "high value" critics accorded fiction like hers and discovers urbane aesthetic values entangled in currents of erotic abjection and subtle cruelties.

"Miss Grief" is actually Aaronna Moncrief, an American woman living in Rome who makes repeated calls at the home of the narrator, an American writer, until she finally manages to meet and implore him to read her manuscripts. When his servant, having misheard the name, first reports a visit from a "Miss Grief," the narrator is bemused: "Grief has not so far visited me here" (6). He continues to refer to her with that name even after he discovers and then conveys with an unstable sympathy that hers is indeed a life of grief: aging, living in poverty and ill health, Moncrief holds to a dim hope that her unpublished plays and poems might yet find responsive readers. This misnaming of Miss Grief distills Woolson's central ironic device, the formal distancing of a woman's misery so that its pathos cannot be viewed except through the eyes of a sophisticated man of letters. Moncrief's suffering is thus realized (or made realist) but only through the storytelling of a mediating literary authority; one cannot tell her grief apart from his "Miss Grief."

How, then, to read female grief? The question is implicit in a narrative that returns to the shopworn theme of a dying woman while disabling the sentimental narrative codes for portraying female suffering. The question is also posed at the level of plot: how will an accomplished, complacent transatlantic novelist ("I model myself a little on Balzac" [8]) read the writing of an isolated, untrained woman? Woolson answers that, in essence, he actually cannot read her—at least not with the kind of interpretive mastery that has made him a literary authority. Initially irritated at being cornered into the task by a "shabby, unattractive" (9) woman, as he reads the narrator is quickly "inspired and thrilled" (18) by the strength of her passionate expression. He recognizes her superior artistic gift and tells her so: of the two, she is the "greater power" (39). But he also finds her "unrestrained" creations literally unaccountable. He has no workable critical terms for either her "passion and power" (18) or what he deems her flaws. Neither sublime nor grotesque, the aesthetic logic of her art—"like the work of dreams" (27)—is simply outside his ken. Certainly it exceeds the realist aesthetic of his own fictional "studies," a point confirmed when he agrees to send one of her manuscripts to an editor in his literary circle. Though "impressed by the power displayed in certain passages," the editor declares that the "impossibilities of the plot" make the piece unpublishable (31).

Woolson in this way presents her reader with an aesthetic fissure. The story identifies extraordinary literary works but supplies no critical access to their force and beauty, no explanation of their aesthetic power. The disjunction remains to the end: Moncrief dies and her manuscripts remain unpublished and unknown. The effect is to make the reader imagine a species of powerful literary meaning that Woolson's own story, for all its ironic perceptiveness, cannot directly tap. The narrator's realist vision begins to seem limited, neither definitive as art nor authoritative about the real, and the values of Howellsian realism are thrown into relief. Whereas proponents of high realism criticized the work of many women writers as simplistic and naïve, Woolson's story in effect turns the tables: the sophisticated narrator is finally too limited in imagination to fully understand the works of this untrained woman, while her works become figures of a "greater," inaccessible literary power that is anything but simple.

Another strand of Woolson's plot, however, hints at an ironic—and damning—connection between these incommensurable literary values. The narrator's failure to redeem Moncrief's powerful writing is matched by his romantic success in winning over a socially prominent younger woman, Isabel. A marginal character, Isabel is characterized only as someone unable even to intuit the force of Moncrief's artistry. The poems shown her by the narrator she deems "mixed and vague" and prompt only her condescending pity: "Her mind must have been disordered, poor thing!" (32). At hearing this proof of Isabel's lack of comprehension, the narrator's thoughts reveal a subtle but crucial pattern of affective response, a pattern in which aesthetic taste and sexual feeling generate a complicated species of gratification:

> Now, [the poems] were not vague so much as vast. But I knew that I could not make Isabel comprehend it, and (so complex a creature is man) I do not know that I wanted her to comprehend it. They were the only ones in the whole collection that I would have shown her, and I was rather glad that she did not like even these. (33)

Isabel's failure to be moved by the poems that move him actually heightens the narrator's romantic attraction to her. For the narrator, it is precisely Isabel's difference from the "unrestrained, large" beauty of the poetry that makes her desirable: "Isabel was bounded on all sides, like a violet in a garden bed. And I liked her so" (33). Behind the apparently simple matter of what one "likes," Woolson quietly insists, are rules of decorum for gender roles, rules that are tied to both artistic and erotic feeling.

Hence the skepticism the reader feels when the narrator, in the name of fulfilling what the now dead Moncrief would "like," decides to withhold her work from ever appearing in print: "I keep it here in this locked case. I could have published it at my own expense; but I think that now she knows its faults herself, perhaps, and would not like it" (38). What Moncrief would "like" as the fate of her poems, as with Isabel's dislike of their contents, turns out to be entangled in what the narrator likes in a wife (a "bounded" nature) and prefers in dead women writers of genius (enduring obscurity): "When I die," the narrator confides, the Moncrief manuscript "is to be destroyed unread."

> Not even Isabel is to see it. For women will misunderstand each other; and, dear and precious to me as my sweet wife is, I could not bear that she or anyone should cast so much as a thought of scorn upon the memory of the writer, upon my poor dead, "unavailable," unaccepted "Miss Grief." (39)

The narrator's elegy for Miss Grief is simultaneously a willful entombment of her writing. Though his perfect "good taste" remains in force to the end, the lines hint at his eerie satisfaction at the eternal silence of her unread works. His twin tributes to the "poor dead" writer and the living "sweet wife" sound a Poe-like note that echoes an earlier melodramatic outburst from Moncrief's grieving aunt that "all literary men" are "vampires" (34).

Woolson herself, quite unlike her "Miss Grief," enjoyed considerable literary success. Her five published novels sold well—*Anne* (1880) was the most popular—and her short stories won consistent critical praise. Woolson also published her own criticism as a frequent contributor to *Harper's* and the *Atlantic*. Yet, in spite of her popular and critical acceptance, Woolson found it difficult to escape unhappiness and suffered from poor health and financial strain. Even though her own career was proof that women could write with a forceful literary style ("I have such a horror of 'pretty,' 'sweet' writing that I should almost prefer a style that was ugly and bitter, provided it was also strong") and garner high recognition, Woolson seemed to believe women authors were all but fated for lives of grief. "Why do literary women break down so?" she wrote to Edmund Clarence Stedman. "It almost seems as though only the unhappy women took to writing."[24] In 1894 at age fifty-three, Woolson either fell or jumped to her death from the second-story balcony of her room in a Venice villa.

Woolson's mastery of realist technique often operates as a second-order analysis of realism and high art. Her fiction follows the contours of analytic reason in order to trace the relay points at which reason is revealed as an instrument of cunning or desire. Conscious or unconscious motives and interests retrospectively expose rational criticism—often wielded by men against women they desire—as limited, cruel, or self-deceived. In "At the Chateau of Corinne," for instance, a man admits his attraction to a Katherine, a woman writer, immediately after he has denounced "literary women" in general, Madame de Stael in particular, and Katherine's own poetry most directly. The sequence makes clear that his erotic attraction intensifies through Katherine's visible humiliation. Similarly in "The Street of the Hyacinth," when a young American painter belatedly realizes that her work is "extremely and essentially bad," her abjection as an artist brings on three marriage proposals. Realist knowledge for Woolson is a tragic knowledge, a recognition that analytic reason or the pursuit of high beauty may well uncover truths, but that what is uncovered may be neither lovely nor particularly rational.

Motion and Motionless Seeing

Like Woolson, other women writers such as Sarah Orne Jewett, Mary Murfree, Celia Thaxter, and Mary E. Wilkins Freeman published their work in the premier journals such as the *Atlantic Monthly* where it was deemed to be "truly artistic" by male editors. As writers who offered sharply etched portraits of rural regions and small-town life, they aided the collective project of portraying the United States with "unexampled fullness" in fiction, a central realist goal that would produce the literary equivalent of an authoritative map or an empirical study.[25] Yet the same virtues that earned them the status of artists—their skilled observation of distinct local cultures, their deftness of narrative touch in crafting shorter forms—also permitted the male literary establishment to conceive of their work as belonging to a feminine aesthetic distinguished from a broader literary mastery. Although women regionalists rely on the realist categories of secular time and specified place, the islands of rural life and the shorter narrative forms that characterize their work set them apart from the realists who wrote with ambitions for large sociological reach.

Just as important, perhaps, the women characters in regionalist fiction were by definition women who *belonged,* who were indigenous to the Maine islands, the Tennessee mountains, and the New England villages that defined the horizons of social life in regionalist fiction. In contrast, the representative value of women within high realism was precisely their ability to dramatize a loss of belonging that artists and intellectuals identified with a fraught modernity. When the status of women becomes a literary topos for modernity, "the most salient and peculiar point in our social life," as Henry James puts it, woman supplants nature as the phenomenon most in need of interpretation. Signifying a new mobility of selfhood, she embodies the most visible aspects of social change, from energies of organized reform (James's *The Bostonians* and *The Princess Cassimassima,* Howells's *Annie Kilburn,* John Hay's *The Bread-Winners*), to possibilities for a cosmopolitan American culture (James's *Daisy Miller,* Woolson's European stories, Henry Adams's *Esther,* Wharton's *Custom of the Country*), to the clamorous icons of the emerging commercial culture, the "Iron Madonna" of feminized spectacle. Precisely in her mutability, the enigma of woman could contain the key to understanding the future. Finding the male domains of politics and history too narrow to grasp the emerging world, Henry Adams saw the fate of modernity in the fate of women: "I should drop the man, except as accessory, and study the woman of the future."[26] When the commercial civilization was judged to be a flat or empty production and commercial men its flat producers, women were often made to signify depth. Within high literary culture women yield an inside view of consciousness that is at once objectified and closely realized, a literary object brought to life in deft and often astonishingly vivid detail. Woman became a gendered representative of human subjectivity and its travails, a modernized counterpart to Emerson's "representative man" in a restless, unheroic age.

For women writers, of course, the "situation of women" was at once a literary topic and a condition of their lives. In the late 1880s and 1890s, women began to fashion this double status into an object of their own brand of literary mastery and to make an open claim on high culture. Their works therefore illuminate in particularly vivid ways the place of women in American society as both a modern consciousness and an enigmatic cultural object. The demand for critical detachment was, in a sense, both a woman writer's burden and her advantage: for her, the need for distance from the woman question could require nearly acrobatic techniques of self-scrutiny. The difficulty of this position might explain why the most accomplished of these women writers all claimed to find literary wisdom in the study of science. Kate Chopin declared that "it's impossible to ever come to a true knowledge of life as it is—which should be everybody's aim—without studying certain fundamental truths" of natural science. Immersion in science, Chopin contended, is the only saving antidote for women writers who continue to produce "hysterical" and "false pictures of life."[27] Edith Wharton was a passionate student of Darwinism, hereditary biology, and anthropology, among other disciplines, and scientific practice was her model for successful fiction: the worthiest fiction "probes deep enough to get at the relation with the eternal laws." The literary critic, too, requires a "disciplined acquaintance with his subject" that is the equal of the professional scholar of "history or paleontology."[28]

The appeal of science for writers like Chopin, Wharton, Pauline Hopkins, and Charlotte Perkins Gilman lies in a mix of intellectual excitement and cultural authority. Scientific knowledge for these authors bespeaks creativity, thought freed from convention. Tropes and allusions borrowed from science frequently mark the places where their fiction diverges most sharply from inherited patterns. Just at the moments when her *House of Mirth* (1905) is most vulnerable to melodrama, Wharton turns to images derived from science. She supplies a botanical description of her heroine's rootless "tentacles of self," for instance, or riffs on the "men and women . . . like atoms whirling away from each other in some wild centrifugal dance," tropes that concentrate emotion through a controlling analysis.[29] But the more significant appeal of science for these women may have been the disposition of the scientific observer, a posture distinguished by analytic power and a keen intellectual command over external objects of study. In science's mode of critical detachment, women writers found the means to dissect a social situation they also lived day-to-day from within.

Wharton called it the posture of the "drawingroom naturalist." To view lives and social relations from this position was to possess at once deep human insight and "high impartiality," with each capacity strengthened by the other. In her volume of collected criticism, *The Writing of Fiction* (1925), Wharton offers what may be the most concise distillation of realist practice. The "creative imagination," Wharton writes, merges "the power of penetrating into other minds with that of standing far enough aloof from them to see beyond, and relate them to the whole stuff of life out of which they but partially emerge. Such an all-round view can be obtained only by mounting to a height."[30] Giving primacy to analysis over sympathy, to discipline over identification, Wharton and others reinvented the domestic novel as an acknowledged high art open to the woman writer. To the same degree that these women acquired realist credentials, however, their fiction frequently prompted a proportional unease—even outright distaste—in many of their contemporaries. "Mrs. Wharton sits at her desk like a disembodied intelligence," one reviewer remarked in 1905, "acute and critical and entirely unsympathetic."[31] *Like* a disembodied intelligence but also very much an embodied presence: the complaint itself pictures Wharton at her desk, a woman in the flesh. The contradiction here is instructive: the very success of a woman like Wharton at mastering the impartial gaze of the high realist artist creates an almost reflexive return of attention to her status as a woman, placing her under the scrutiny of others' eyes as a body as much as a mind. Although this was a predicament not usually imposed on male writers, it could also offer an awareness of the artist's inescapable existence as a corporeal being, an observer and a creature observed. This knowledge in turn brings a new consciousness of the internal fissures of high realist art. For these women writers, the allegiance to science and its critical powers coexists with a keen sense of what it can mean to be a scientific object.

Both aspects of this creativity—the inspiration of science and women's status as scientific object—were dominant notes of the time. Science in the later nineteenth century was a success story, enjoying the same spectacular expansion as the national economy without its volatile cycles of boom and bust. That heightened prestige found enduring form in university programs, museums and exhibitions, professional associations, and well-funded institutes, all of which gave scientific enterprise a new and decisive social authority. And across the disciplines there was a consensus about the scientific importance of studying sexual difference in general and women in particular. Rapid social change "necessarily induces a perturbation in the evolution of the races," scientist Paul Broca wrote in 1868, "and hence it follows that the condition of women must be most carefully studied by the anthropologist."[32] Scholars like Broca were cautious, if not overtly fearful. Other scientists such as Elsie Clews Parsons saw in the same "perturbation" of sex roles a promise of sure progress for society and for the status of women. Parsons, the first female professor of anthropology at Columbia University, mused that the United States would someday have to build a "Museum of Women" to show "a doubting posterity that once women were a distinct social class."[33] In works such as *The Family: An Ethnographical and Historical Outline* (1906) and *Old-Fashioned Woman: Primitive Fancies About Sex* (1913), Parsons popularized an anthropological approach to debunking contemporary social and sexual conventions. But Parsons's confidence in an untroubled advancement for women was almost as singular as her career. Among scientists of this period, the more prevalent view held that fixed sex traits and slow evolutionary forces defined a female nature that was subjected to social change only at great peril.

That more alarmist perspective imparted a sense of urgency to the collective project of defining, measuring, categorizing, comparing, and representing womankind. The result was a heterogeneous display marked by a style of representation that could be called scientific realism. Parsons fancifully imagined a museum of women for the future, but clearly the museum already existed, dispersed in the textbooks, exhibits, case studies, and lectures devoted to empirically realizing "the condition of women." Taxonomy lends an air of fixed identity to a status in flux. The "sensitive white woman" ("subsisting on fiction, journals, receptions"); the "bachelor woman" (an "interesting illustration of Spencer's law of individuation and genesis"); the "educated woman" (whose "nubility" and "fecundity" were in question); the "female hysteric"—these and other labels delineate sharp lines for the otherwise amorphous phenomenon of the modern woman.[34] Visual representations supply a realism of physiognomy and link white women of the middle class to "primitive" women of other races. Exhibits of female skulls, life-size wax "Venuses" or medical effigies with dozens of removable parts, and "absolutely lifelike" mannequins in ethnographic displays, such as the twelve life-size figures of Native American, African, and Polynesian women at the 1876 Philadelphia Centennial, were all contributions to a vast realism of gender artifact.[35] One scientist, Edward A. Spitzka, a practitioner of the dubious anthropometric discipline of brain-weight measurement, defined a cranial hierarchy that began with the lowest brain-weight specimen, that of an anonymous Bushwoman (794 grams), and ascended to his highest specimen, which happened to be the brain of a male realist novelist, Ivan Turgenev (2,012 grams).[36]

The disciplined modes of observation trained on women are one measure of the seriousness with which questions about the status of women figure in scientific discourse. Suggesting by turns alarm and an exhilarated curiosity, the proliferating scientific images signify a felt need to bring women within new techniques of empirical representation. Science is thus another domain that featured a new visibility for women in this period. In contrast to the tendency of earlier scientists to subsume women under the study of mankind, in the later nineteenth century women hold a central place in efforts to empirically realize the true order of civilization, its laws, its powers, and its natural evolution. But, as is true for all scientific objects, this imperative for empirical knowledge brings with it a tendency to depict woman as static and without agency. Her passivity is axiomatic, the result of method. Efforts to explain her nature by way of social law and natural forces make woman into a product of those laws—frequently, into their manifest victim. Visually, woman as seen through the empirical lens is inert, arrested, and, at the furthest extreme, perfectly lifeless—a type, a symptom, a corpse. Perhaps the most openly aestheticized portrait in the scientific canon was offered in Johann Bachofen's influential study of ancient cults, *Das Mütterecht,* where the origin of Western law and civilization, in triumph over "the seductions of Egypt," is "imaged in the death of Candace of the Orient (Cleopatra), and in Augustus' contemplation of her lifeless body."[37]

The icon of the beautiful corpse is one pole of female representation. Its opposite is the galvanized actress from popular culture, all motion and outsized vibrancy, a figure that inflated women's incremental gain in social mobility into the hyperbole of a dazzling mass fame. Against Bachofen's lifeless Cleopatra, we can juxtapose the sensational Broadway performer Adah Isaacs Menken, who became a national celebrity in the 1860s playing the leading male role in *Mazeppa; or, The Wild Horse of Tartary.* At the famous climax of this melodrama, Menken, as Prince Ivan Mazeppa, bursts across the stage nearly nude (in flesh-colored tights) and bound to a live horse galloping full stride. In contrast with this electric spectacle, Bachofen's tableau is a frozen allegory of scientific sight. Law and the reign of reason commence in Augustus's observation of a lifeless woman, a figure for dynamic, sensuous Nature that has been arrested in death and thus mastered. In Menken's wild ride, in contrast, the syntax of the allegory is precisely reversed. On the stage, it is the dynamism of a female spectacle that arrests the observer, who is reduced to looking on in passive wonder. To be gazed upon is a source of power, while looking is a form of subjection, an enthrallment. ("The intensely emotional situation that Miss Menken displays," wrote one editor, is expressed in grand actions whose "significance scorns interpretation.")[38] Stillness and motion, observation and display, analysis and sensuous feeling, science and spectacle: these contraries order the field of representation that is the matrix for the portrait of women in realist fiction. Efforts to define woman's essential and unchanging traits are indirect witness to the change and uncertainty of her status. The field defines power and passivity as exclusive properties, opposite poles that are given to sudden reversals of position.

At the heart of much realist writing, then, by men and women alike, is an urgency to observe women that responds to the charged poles of this field of representation. In Henry James's *Portrait of a Lady* (1881), the observation of a woman supplies both method and story. An activity the narrator calls the "conscious observation of a lovely woman" is the primary occupation of the novel's main characters, all of whom follow closely Isabel Archer's courtship "career" in Europe.[39] It is the word "conscious" in this formulation that bears the strongest accent. More than his earlier fictions about young women, *Daisy Miller* (1878) or *Washington Square* (1880), for example, this novel brings the act of watching itself under close scrutiny. The supreme importance of discernment in the literature of high culture fosters a self-reflexiveness about observation, and in James's work this secondary subject moves increasingly into the foreground. As a result, readers found in James's fiction a sometimes startling intensity of vision. "No word or look or action in [the characters'] lives had escaped the author's attention," wrote one reviewer. "His observation and knowledge seem to grow keener with each new novel. But where will it end?" For some, James's vision was too coolly scientific, a rigor "without pity."[40] But in *The Portrait of a Lady* the novel makes clear at all levels that the practice of watching— "the sweet-tasting property of observation" (231), as the narrator calls it—is never dispassionate. Observing Isabel (there are "plenty of spectators" [344]) will involve efforts to know or possess or exploit or love her. Vision is transitive. It is also very often erotic, charged with pleasure, in ways both generous and sinister.

But importantly, the conscious observation of Isabel never includes the sight of her dead. The fact is significant even if it is not, in the end, definitive; as a genre the nineteenth-century realist novel features a remarkable number of dead women. A genre that develops an increasingly dense background of social conditioning for human action, high realism often resolves vexing questions about women's subjectivity (what does she want? is she free?) by locating a social explanation—or at least social closure—in her death. Even a woman's suicide is oftentimes less an act of agency than a nearly unwilled surrender to social or natural forces. In realism there is an aesthetic logic, hence a beauty, in the death of a woman. Anna Karenina, Emma Bovary, Tess D'Urbervilles, Lily Bart, James's own Millie Theal—these compelling protagonists all illuminate most clearly the cunning conditions of their worlds at the moment they cease to live.

James considers the possibility of Isabel's death and gives it a striking aesthetic resonance. By the time she recognizes her mistake in marrying Gilbert Osmond and the duplicity that engineered it, the idea of death has become something deeply affecting: "To cease utterly, to give it all up and not know anything more—this idea was as sweet as the vision of a cool bath in a marble tank, in a darkened chamber, in a hot land" (769). Isabel's sudden wealth had given her a field for independent action rare for a woman, but in the end even her sense of having chosen and acted freely—"If ever a girl was a free agent, she had been" (609)—has the feel of an illusion imposed from without. But importantly, against the novel's own gravitational pull toward death Isabel retains a measure of agency, a power to reflect on the conditions that have entrapped her. "Conscious" observation, then, belongs to Isabel, too. In this she differs from Daisy Miller, the heroine of James's most popular study of the "young feminine nature." Daisy Miller's rash indifference to European decorum is less a trait of moral innocence than a lack of a discriminating consciousness, which at first appears to be a freedom to act but ends as a vulnerability that issues in her death. Isabel, in contrast, becomes not only the object observed but a rich source of interior perception that mirrors what James in his preface calls "the posted presence of the watcher," the penetrating "consciousness of the artist."[41]

Consciousness for James is authorial, a form of agency if a limited one. In that respect Isabel is like Madeleine Lee, the protagonist of Henry Adams's novel *Democracy* (1880), a woman watched by others who develops an ability to see that equals that of the keenest of her observers. Examining closely the workings of national politics and politicians, Madeleine "got to the heart of politics, so that she could, like a physician with his stethoscope, measure the organic disease." Yet where Madeleine expects to gaze on the living, breathing body of American governance, she sees instead a Washington revealed as a series of "elaborate show-structures" peopled by mechanical mannequins and "wax images."[42] Once again, the (realist) truth about the social world turns out to lie in the distressing power of illusion and spectacle. The highest rule of the Republic is no better than the machinations of low entertainment.

In possessing a penetrating consciousness, these women characters share the savvy of the most discerning observers who study the "situation of women." As rich as their developing vision comes to be, however, because they are women the power of Isabel and Madeleine to observe remains a force incommensurate with what James calls the realist heroine's "fate." The gap between her sight and her social fate is revealed in women's self-examination. Observing themselves, women are at once the discerning subject *and* the paralyzed object, unable to escape the body despite the critical illumination supplied by the mind: "Madeleine dissected her own feelings and was always wondering whether they were real or not; she had a habit of taking off her mental clothing, as she might take off a dress, and looking at it as though it belonged to some one else, and as though sensations were manufactured like clothes."[43] Like the tragic knowledge uncovered in Woolson's fiction, self-scrutiny by women often tends toward a realization of their own social entrapment.

The paradox has its most famous expression in the "vigil" chapter of *The Portrait of a Lady*, a tour de force of psychological revelation. The reader in this chapter follows the furthest reach of Isabel's unfolding self-comprehension while, in the external narrative frame, Isabel neither speaks nor moves. Her consciousness painfully alive, Isabel in her person is perfectly still, locked in a disposition of "motionlessly seeing."[44] Her power to see and understand her own fate is matched with a paralysis that bespeaks her final restriction in marriage. This concentrated image of Isabel's self-understanding expresses a "far-reaching sadness" (755). Yet it is an "exquisite" sadness, too: the beauty lies in a previously unknown truth now brilliantly realized in a completely transparent, motionless image. Isabel's vigil thus distills a whole aesthetic mode. In this realist mode, the more a woman is consciously known, and the greater her own consciousness of the social world that made her, the more likely she is to become a tragic still life, a portrait of woman as beautiful, silent, and unmoving.

But the trope of a woman's "motionless seeing" was not always a marker of tragedy. Isabel Archer's reverie was perhaps the most famous instance, notable for James's stylistic feat of writing a passage of sustained free indirect discourse that defies literary laws of gravity. But the figure of a silently thinking or daydreaming woman was appearing in many other cultural and scientific sites as well, where she seemed to promise new knowledge and perhaps even a new species of human agency. Manet's portraits of gazing or distracted-looking women, for instance, were causing a sensation in the transatlantic art world. Jonathan Crary has shown the way the blank stare of the woman at the center of *In the Conservatory* interrupted trained tendencies to see a female subject as either a beautiful object or a subject given purely to feeling or fantasy. Manet's woman *might* be fantasizing (but about what?), and she is clearly beautiful; but the opacity of her facial expression blocks any easy interpretation and makes the fact of attention itself into a critical problem. In scientific circles, human attention had become an acute research problem as well. As scientists gave increased attention to the sensory apparatus of human perception—the biological basis of vision, stimulation, and psychology—the activity of observation itself demanded new investigation. What Crary calls "the relocation of perception into the thickness of the body" meant that different states of reverie, hypnotic thought, and attention held out the possibility of yielding new scientific knowledge.[45]

William James's *Principles of Psychology* was among the first scientific studies of the physiological foundations of distraction and attention. In his chapter "Attention," James dissects the complex mental activities that can occur during a state of "dispersed attention" or daydreaming, and the description reads like a record of Isabel Archer's physical state during her extended reverie: "The eyes are fixed on vacancy, the sounds of the world melt into confused unity, the attention becomes dispersed so that the whole body is felt, as it were, at once, and the foreground of consciousness is filled, if by anything, by a sort of solemn sense of surrender to the empty passing of time."[46] Although William James notes that "most of us" fall into such states regularly, scientists often associated more extreme or pathological states of dispersed attention with women.[47] At the same time, however, women were also associated with a range of somnambulant and trance-like states that were increasingly thought to be potentially creative. Like Isabel's ability during her reverie to connect fragmentary glimpses and subconscious observations into a breakthrough in cognitive understanding, the distracted or dreaming subject was able to conduct a somatic version of thinking. In such states, Crary writes, "sensations, perceptions, and subconscious elements could loosen themselves from a binding synthesis and become floating, detached elements, free to make new connections." A lapse from focused, externally directed attention could signify a creative consciousness able to think with and through energies of desire, sociality, or revolt.⁴⁸

The scientific study of perception offers a new context for interpreting Charlotte Perkins Gilman's now classic story "The Yellow Wallpaper," a story in which a woman's bodily experience becomes an alternative mode of thought. "The Yellow Wallpaper," which Gilman wrote in southern California and sent to Howells in his editor's study a continent away, combines the polarized figures of the spectacular female body and the quiet, unmoving consciousness in a striking new way, transforming the realist property of consciousness into a hallucinatory performance. In this portrait of a lady as a morbid "case," the unnamed female narrator suffers a "slight hysterical tendency," or at least that is the diagnosis of her physician husband. Observation has become aggressively clinical. The narrator is carefully observed by her husband, and by his sister who is deputized to answer his "professional questions" in his absence. The story thus makes clinical observation into an unacknowledged domination, just as it makes her seeming illness and bed rest into an unnatural entrapment (he "hardly lets me stir without special direction").⁴⁹

Gilman's protagonist has been warned away from self-reflection—"John says the very worst thing I can do is think about my condition"—but she develops a critical consciousness nonetheless. To call it a consciousness is somewhat misleading, however. Gilman's narrator possesses none of the lucidity of Isabel Archer, none of the dark comprehension of Madeleine Lee. It is by *not* directly comprehending her "condition" that the woman creates from her mind a grotesque expression of that condition: rather than analyze her social condition she imagines a monstrous, living "woman" trapped in the wallpaper of her bedroom. In Gilman's story, the topos of "motionless seeing" is intensified and grotesquely literalized until the protagonist's own alienated vision becomes a collection of ugly, frenzied phantoms, which she begins to mimic bodily. Gilman refuses the figure of the beautiful corpse: in contrast with the tragically beautiful stillness at the center of so many realist portraits, the narrator's arrested state begins in an enforced submission and ends in convulsive movement. Like the neurologists studying somatic states of drifting attention and pathological excess, Gilman describes a somatic version of thinking, allowing detached or dispersed elements of attention to recombine in a new mental state. While this distressed mental condition is, by itself, unable to articulate what it knows, a combination of mental vision and bodily movement expresses a shocking, corporeal version of female self-reflection.

Jane Thrailkill has emphasized how the intense "psychophysical experience" depicted in Gilman's story resonates with the "psychophysical way nineteenth-century readers seemed to experience the story." Reviewers tended to emphasize the eeriness and "chill alarm" they experienced while reading it, and Howells called the story "blood-curdling." While this astute interpretation helps reveal the way Gilman's interest in women's corporeality resembled the interests of contemporary scientists, it overlooks the social dimension of Gilman's sudden staging of a "home-shocked" wife in the space of a literary public.[50] For part of the *sensation* (in both senses) of Gilman's story is the shocking way she reclaims the publicity value of the public woman, refusing either to tranquilize her condition through a realist aesthetic of tragic beauty or to perpetuate the illusory social agency that women performers were allowed to mime in titillating ways on the popular stage—all while still drawing analytic power from both domains, literary and commercial. Instead of enacting an enthralling but misleading performance of (male) agency like the burlesque actress, Gilman's woman performs a shocking physical performance of her own deformed and restricted condition.

Although Gilman meant to denounce the notion of innate female hysteria, she shared scientists' interest in exploring how and what the body knows. In "Wallpaper," the narrator's perverse perceptions and panicked, defiant movements are able to "speak" what her conscious mind cannot. There is no social power in her concluding hysterical performance—"I've got out at last!"—except as a dark parody of a self-determination she does not possess. Unlike the thrilling ride of Adah Menken's famous *Mazeppa* performance, a feat of daring that lives up to the male heroic agency she is representing theatrically, Gilman's woman crawls along the floor in the grip of a delusion. Her protagonist lacks even the minimal agency of a character like Isabel Archer, a woman who can consciously know even if she cannot freely act.

But as a literary object, the abject condition of Gilman's woman also implies its own opposite. A woman *can* have the ability to see and act under her own powers, but this species of agency is represented in the person of the author, and Gilman as author usurps entirely the expertise of the physician husband. The story is thus Gilman's superior diagnosis of his wife, a trumping of specious medical knowledge with a form of literary analysis rooted in principles she shared with leading researchers (a reviewer called it "a striking and impressive study of morbid psychology, in the shape of a story").[51] Gilman, who had immersed herself in evolutionary biology and sociology from a young age, extracted from science a tone of fearless and authoritative speech, a resource earlier women writers had borrowed from religion, and used it to critically undo what she perceived to be harmful fictions, including fictions of science itself. Gilman's particular writerly gifts thrive in these creative crossings, which achieve the startling force of the female stage performer, one whose moves are the flash of intellect and the shock of convention dissected and dismissed with breathtaking agility. This was a performance in the strongest sense of the word, an ideal projection of a masterful agency that possesses the power to renew belief, for the author as well as the audience, in the reality of the human capacity it represents. Gilman achieves this feat, moreover, by recognizing a coincidence of opposites in polarized figures of womanhood: the illusion of power in the stage performer's audacious movements and the unique self-understanding of the reflective woman's consciousness.

Chopin and the Realism of Desire

In much realist fiction, self-reflection tends to lift a woman's consciousness from her immediate surroundings. As with the "motionless seeing" that transforms Isabel Archer, a woman's reflective consciousness can for a time eclipse her awareness of the quotidian world, including her own body. A distinctive reversal of this pattern, however, is one of the important innovations of Kate Chopin's fiction. Rather than bringing mental detachment, in Chopin self-reflection brings a new awareness of the body, of its immediate sensations and varying states of corporeal consciousness. A typical moment of this kind occurs in *The Awakening* (1899), when Edna Pontellier lies alone on a bed during a pause in an afternoon outing. She will later decide she is in love with her afternoon companion, Robert Lebrun, one of several consequential realizations for the married mother of two children. But in this moment, lying at rest yet still awake and observant, Edna's own body becomes the object of her consciousness.

How luxurious it felt to rest thus in a strange, quaint bed, with its sweet country odor of laurel lingering about the sheets and mattress! She stretched her strong limbs that ached a little. She ran her fingers through her loosened hair for a while. She looked at her round arms as she held them straight up and rubbed them one after the other, observing closely, as if it were something she saw for the first time, the fine, firm quality and texture of her flesh.[52]

In this scene of self-reflection, "observing closely" is as tactile as it is visual, and Edna's thoughts are reflections on the pleasurable strangeness of her sensations—the feeling of an unfamiliar bed beneath her body, a sense of novelty at the sight of her own arms. Here the iconic figure of the prone woman is no longer a beautiful, lifeless object; but neither is her body merely the point of origin for her reflective thought. Once again, observation is a woman's path toward agency, but the new consciousness Edna acquires is not purely cognitive; here and elsewhere the "awakening" of her understanding is more physical than analytical. Consciousness in Chopin is always sensory consciousness, awareness of and through the body's senses.

Hence the odd accuracy of the formulation, penned by a (hostile) contemporary critic, that *The Awakening* was a novel of "soul dissection." Influenced by Flaubert and Maupassant, Chopin brought the sharp delineations of French realism to her portraits of American women. Her scalpel-like style, dispassionate and exact, was recognized as the kind of "consummate art" that elevates fiction to the status of high art. But the object of Chopin's art, the self or "soul" she depicts, is less the social identity favored by realists than the sensuous interiority of the romantic poets.[53] A marriage of Flaubert and Whitman, *The Awakening* is a close analysis of the diffuse, even chaotic sensations of the embodied consciousness. By bringing sensory impressions and erotic feeling into the purview of high fiction, Chopin's realism insists that consciousness is subject to the mutabilities of the body and its desires, a view that follows realist truth-seeking to a point that undercuts realist aspirations for intellectual mastery even as it thereby gains access to a new order of realism.

Because of her lifelong immersion in Francophone culture and literature, literary realism likely had different compass points for Chopin from those it had for most northeastern writers. By the time Chopin began to publish fiction, she had moved from New Orleans back to St. Louis, the home of her French-descended maternal family, following the death of her husband, Oscar Chopin. But her two collections of stories, *Bayou Folk* (1894) and *Night in Acadie* (1897), were deft portraits of the rural Louisiana towns and affluent Creole culture she had known during her married years. The stories were critically praised and Chopin was received as a particularly skillful contributor to the genre of local color fiction flourishing in the leading journals. Like most "quality" local color writing, these stories betray little overt concern for the emergent mass culture that so often troubled (and creatively spurred) intellectuals in the Northeast. And yet, viewed as a genre, local color writing reveals its own rivalry with mass culture precisely in its studied elimination of any trace of mass forms. By depicting rural regions and small-town life as islands of authentic culture, local color fiction tacitly identifies mass technologies and genres with a corrosive modernity, an order deemed impersonal, disruptive, and likely to carry destructive human desires.

Chopin's early Louisiana stories largely share these implicit generic values. In "At the 'Cadian Ball," a threat of sexual exploitation (a wealthy landowner hopes to seduce an Acadian girl) brings into view class tensions between Acadian farmers and Creole planters. The culminating scene at a traditional Acadian ball, however, allows these tensions to be contained as finally harmonious parts of a distinctive regional world.

The big, low-ceiled room—they called it a hall—was packed with men and women dancing to the music of three fiddles. There were broad galleries all around it. There was a room at one side where sober-faced men were playing cards. Another, in which babies were sleeping, was called *le parc aux petits*. Any one who is white may go to a 'Cadian ball, but he must pay for his lemonade, his coffee and chicken gumbo. And he must behave himself like a 'Cadian. Grosboeuf ... could recall but one disturbance, and that was caused by American railroaders, who were not in touch with their surroundings and had no business there. "Ces maudits gens du Raiderode," Grosboeuf called them.[54]

Chopin's story works as an extension of the genre of ethnography: her fictional plot poses and then works through a potential social disaster, but does so in a literary form that guarantees the ethnographic integrity of the local. The interests of Cajuns, Creoles, and black folk may collide, but the Cane River area—like the ball itself—has the resources to contain the conflicts within the bounds of a self-sustaining world.

What cannot be admitted into this world is modernity. "American railroaders," envoys of technological speed and translocal relations, prove far too disruptive for admission to the ball. Neither are they admitted into the story: because the railroad workers are fundamentally anti-local ("not in touch with their surroundings"), the episode is never directly narrated in this local color narrative. The modern rail system unified and transformed the postwar nation, but its speed, impersonal power, and force of dislocation have "no business" in Cane River culture and no place in local color fiction except as a token of what is dangerous and inassimilable to local "surroundings."

Although "At the 'Cadian Ball" is inhospitable to the stories of railroaders, it is not quite accurate to see it as hostile to the railroad. After all, it is the national rail system that transports Chopin's manuscript to the editorial offices in Boston, and the same rail lines deliver copies of *Bayou Folk* to readers scattered at sites from Florida to Chicago and San Francisco. Thus the public circulation of the story relies on a system of production that the story—and the local color genre—tries to cordon off from any meaningful relation to the local. For some critics this structural discrepancy reflects the fact that local color writing is a largely uncritical a mode of literary consumption, a genre that packages quaint or vanished ways of life for more affluent metropolitan readers.[55]

The critique seems especially applicable to popularity in the 1890s for nostalgic plantation fiction, a phenomenon that rested on operative irony: that the "memory" of a pre-industrial world of gracious rural living and racial harmony was the product of a prodigious mass industry. New systems of transport, distribution, and merchandising were behind not just popular plantation fiction but the endless production of such commodities as sheet music and trading cards, Mammy dolls and clocks, decorative wares and ad campaigns, all of them disseminating pleasing fantasies of an authentic and harmonious Southern past.[56] Some of Chopin's sketches of Southern life are hard to differentiate from this nostalgia industry. The short fiction that launched her writing career includes tales of devoted slaves ("Beyond the Bayou") and old-timers who perform the symbolic labor of carrying fond memories of slavery days ("Aunt Polly," "The Benitou's Slave").

But Chopin's stories also feature significant departures from the profitable conventions of local color fiction, suggesting that this popular genre could be used to export ideas and sights that were neither traditional nor modern in any simple sense. In Chopin's "Nég Créol," for instance, readers are lured with conventional scenes of picturesque poverty in the New Orleans French market, only to be taken to a room that reveals the far more startling poverty of a dying woman and the poor black man who brings her food. Though the woman's physical pain and death are not softened or made quaint, Chopin's portrait insists on the scene's accuracy (it exists offstage where "the audience does not follow in imagination beyond the wings") and thus its dignity. In "Lilacs," Chopin leaves out the urban glamour available to a young Parisian singer to depict instead the pleasure and "excitement" the woman finds in her annual stay inside a convent, dwelling on the intense love she shares with one of the women there ("What ardent kisses! What pink flushes of happiness mounting the cheeks of the two women!").[57] Such scenes are not nostalgic glimpses of traditional mores but pictures that confer value on still unrecognized lives and unacknowledged affective bonds. Social recognition will have to come—if it comes—in a world yet to be; these scenes belong to the future, not to the past.

As Chopin began to move away from regionalist studies, her fiction increasingly featured scenes and objects from city life and critically explored urban experience through the lens of women's lives. In one respect this moved her closer to the concerns of other realists like Howells and Wharton. But, read closely, these narratives exhibit a remarkable departure from the more familiar realist suspicion of urban consumer culture. Mass objects and experiences are not fetishes that infect or distort human life but rather potential portals into different states of consciousness. Consumer culture reveals rather than obscures. Indeed, for understanding the lives of women in particular, consumer culture offers privileged glimpses of the truths of the body, the suppressed wishes, possibilities, and dissatisfactions that cannot be articulated at the level of thought or language.

In "A Pair of Silk Stockings," an unexpected windfall of fifteen dollars affords a struggling homemaker hours of "calculation" that preempt any other thoughts: "It was during the still hours of the night when she lay awake revolving plans in her mind that she seemed to see her way clearly toward a proper and judicious use of the money."[58] But in a large department store, Mrs. Sommers's calculations give way to a revelation as affecting as that of any realist heroine. Her revelation, however, occurs at a lingerie counter, and comes solely through her sense of touch.

An all-gone limp feeling had come over her and she rested her hand aimlessly upon the counter. She wore no gloves. By degrees she grew aware that her hand had encountered something very soothing, very pleasant to touch. She looked down to see that her hand lay upon a pile of silk stockings. A placard near by announced that they had been reduced in price from two dollars and fifty cents to one dollar and ninety-eight cents; and a young girl who stood behind the counter asked her if she wished to examine their line of silk hosiery. . . . She went on feeling the soft, sheeny luxurious things—with both hands now, holding them up to see them glisten, and to feel them glide serpent-like through her fingers. (817)

Stroking and gazing at the colored silk transports her to a new mental state, one that displaces altogether her economic calculations ("she was not thinking at all") and propels her toward seeking other pleasurable sensations—the softness of kid leather, the shine of polished boots, wine and black coffee consumed in a quiet restaurant dining room.

Although Chopin parses this state of mind as closely as James does Isabel Archer's, Mrs. Sommers's consciousness is not a rumination on her social predicament but a new state of sensory awareness that reorders her relation to her body: "Her foot and ankle looked very pretty. She could not realize they belonged to her and were a part of herself" (818). The ability of the department store to transform her consciousness and her sense of her own body reflects the successful strategies of retail entrepreneurs and marketing experts who had redefined shopping from labor to a highly pleasurable species of leisure. The transition, which occurred over several decades in the United States, was especially noticeable in London when Harry Gordon Selfridge—a Wisconsin native who pioneered many of the innovations at Marshall Field's in Chicago—opened a new department store in the West End in 1909. Primed by Selfridge's own promotion blitz, British journalists declared that the work of shopping had now become "an Amusement" and a "delightful pastime."

Women's presumed susceptibility to aesthetic and sensory pleasure—their love of music and textures, their responsiveness to color and attractive surroundings—was the cornerstone of the modern department store. Selfridge's London store coordinated an array of techniques that maximized "eye appeal," including theatrical lighting, glass cases, painted backgrounds, and elaborately designed window displays. For marketers, forms of mass entertainment were a conscious resource: they "perceived the theater, and later the cinema, as the model of how to turn images into consumer desire." But visual stimulation was not the only source of pleasure. Selfridge, who had introduced the first restaurant in Marshall Field's, found ways for the store to integrate vocal and symphonic concerts, tea and foods, restful comforts like reading, and even rooftop ice skating. His bargain basement was similarly designed to appeal to every sense at once: "What a shining feast for the eyes are the ribbon tables; what filmy piles of blouses are here . . . what a forest of silken and velvet flowers; what delicious scents are wafted to us from that mound of tinted soaps." The chance to enjoy "the feel of a fine fabric" made this non-domestic space into a site of rare stimulation and corporeal experience.[59]

Induced by her surrender to the feel of silk, the trance-like state of Chopin's protagonist might well have confirmed the worry (or for some, perhaps, the hope) that the only public role for women was the desiring consumer rather than the rational citizen. When women left the home for the metropolis, to many they seemed an incarnation of mass feeling or standardized fantasy, "an army of furs and feathers."[60] But Chopin brings the analytic habits of realism to examine this species of affective experience not as an undifferentiated realm of fantasy but as a site of sensory perception that is precognitive and yet still socially meaningful. Like the woman in Manet's *Conservatory* painting, Chopin's protagonist in "Silk Stockings" cannot be classified by an outside observer, and her very opacity signifies a new kind of interpretive problem. On the trolley she rides after leaving the department store, a man gazes at Mrs. Sommers's "small, pale face" but cannot read her: "It puzzled him to decipher what he saw there" (820). The real cannot be grasped by even the keenest outside observer who expects to find knowledge in legible social facts or relations. But by giving an inside view of a woman's sensory transformation, Chopin finds meaning in the realm of fantasy: "In truth he saw nothing—unless he were wizard enough to detect a poignant wish, a powerful longing that the cable car would never stop anywhere, but go on and on with her forever" (820). Her longing exceeds the Howellsian categories of high realism, with its suspicion of the effects of consumer culture on female desire. Here it is the embodied life of a subject—her sensations, appetites, and revealed wishes—that must be read in order to reach the real.

Attuned as it is to desire and bodily pleasure, commercial culture in Chopin is not dismissed as a theater of illusion. Objects in a department store can awaken unknown or forgotten internal dispositions. In their clarity and immediacy, the physical pleasures experienced by Mrs. Sommers become facts that overwhelm the reasoned motives and plans that had governed her life. In turn, her life as wife and mother temporarily becomes something far more ghostly or unreal, defined by a "wish" for its endless deferral. Chopin's realism does not dispense with the distinction between fact and fantasy, but it does insist that desire and sensory perception can be among the most telling data for understanding social experience. Her short story "An Egyptian Cigarette" (1897) makes the point even more emphatically. When a woman smokes a narcotic cigarette, it opens up a hallucinatory dreamscape that, although imaginary and wildly fantastic, conveys a woman's keenest feelings and social understanding ("He will never come back").[61] There is still a secure referential status for this imagery; these wild scenes and exotic objects are chemically induced phantoms of a woman's brain. But the physiological basis for the fantasy also gives analytic weight to the unreal images, and the woman emerges from her "dream" with knowledge she had not previously possessed.

That elliptical story was written just before Chopin began work on *The Awakening*. Though little more than a sketch, the brief story's unwillingness to heed the Howellsian opposition between unreal spectacle and narrative truth anticipates one of the defining features of Chopin's novel. Although *The Awakening* returns to Louisiana settings and customs, its local color texture is in key moments overwhelmed by charged symbols expressive of Edna Pontellier's sensations and interior life. Creole social codes govern life at Grand Isle, the gulf resort where Edna and her family spend a holiday. But interior changes ("new conditions in herself") enable Edna to live increasingly out of sync with the web of social life that surrounds her. *The Awakening* can be read as the text in which desire fractures the ethnographic authority of local color fiction. Edna is neither an illustration of enduring Creole culture nor a "modern instance" of an anomie that can be blamed on mass culture.

The music, smells, light, and sea at the resort all serve to foster her awakening. Hearing a skillful piano performance, for instance, is a key catalyst: it was "perhaps the first time her being was tempered to take an impress of the abiding truth" (549). Her first swim, in a moonlit ocean, is an even more dramatic event, bringing "exultation" at her new ability to propel her body through the waves, and then an "appalled" sense of fatal isolation as she becomes aware of her distance from the shore. Edna receives "abiding truth" in these moments, but just what truth is in this novel is left undefined. Knowledge is no longer a product of the thinker's intellectual mastery over external objects but a temporal process Chopin calls "awakening," a change in a state of consciousness akin to the passage from sleep to wakefulness that cannot be abstracted from the body of the sleeper.

As if to mark her departure from the realist coordinates of truth, Chopin twice interrupts her own narration of Edna's history to sound a lyrical refrain.

> The voice of the sea is seductive; never ceasing, whispering, clamoring, murmuring, inviting the soul to wander for a spell in abysses of solitude; to lose itself in mazes of inward contemplation.
> The voice of the sea speaks to the soul. The touch of the sea is sensuous, enfolding the body in its soft, close embrace. (535)

Like Whitman's leaves of grass, the sea here is both nature's pastoral bower and a medium of metaphor. The poem-like passage distills the novel's aim to identify the self with the body, and meaning with affect and desire. Thought ("inward contemplation") has become erotic solitude. Voice is a medium of touch. This is Whitman's nature, not Emerson's: the natural world bespeaks the spirituality of the flesh rather than a transcendence of matter to reach ideal meaning. When nature speaks, it reaches the human soul through pleasure and desire, a benevolent language of sensory "embrace."

But the source of Edna's awakened self is not nature alone. The same stimulus for her spiritualized desire comes by way of "gorgeous" objects of the bourgeois household, including luxury chairs, a satin gown worn with diamonds, "good, rich wines" (624), and garnet-colored cocktails. In giving lyrical affirmation to any sensuous object or medium that moves her protagonist, Chopin realizes Howells's fear that the modern marketplace would allow desire—not intellectual discernment—to ratify the real. By failing to observe a sharp distinction between nature and market commodities, or between contemplation and corporeal touch, Edna does live in the kind of zone in which empirical facts and material objects exist alongside intangible desires, inarticulate experiences, and half-formed thoughts—just the kind of unsorted "phantasmagoria" that critics feared women would import into public life. But while it is true that Edna's desire-driven reality is not congruent with the ideal of a rational-critical public, scientists and other thinkers were discovering the same mixed, corporeal conditions for rationality and for human experience in general. To be sure, scientists—and a good many realists—saw their task as finding techniques to purify human reason by extracting it from bodily experience.[62] But other thinkers, artists, and cultural producers attempted to draw upon these corporeal conditions for other ends. In a variety of new genres, a heightened mix of real objects and subjective projections made readers aware that modern life often entailed dwelling in what Margaret Cohen calls a "twilight epistemology." In the city-scenes sketches Cohen calls panoramic literature, in urban *flânerie*, in the phantasmagoric environment of the department store, and later in the cinema, the subject enters "a state where objective knowledge, externally verifiable experience, socially sanctioned fictions, and individual phantasmatic projection interact in unstable and unruly fashion," creating relations that are uncertain and yet open to new ways of drawing meaningful connections.[63]

The "phantom referentiality" in this zone presents a troubling challenge to the norms of rational-critical debate. But, by the same token, the very problem of referentiality in this twilight calls for new *analytic* exploration, redirecting observation to a corporeal reality whose very mix of desire and empirical fact present an open field of inquiry. To undertake this exploration, however, intellectuals would have to accept a wider domain of signs and experiences as legitimately meaningful and potentially public; a literary public sphere that has merely expelled all that it deems unreal will be unable to bring whole tracts of experience and consciousness into its field of critical reflection. Chopin was prepared to take the step of recognizing desire as publicly expressive and potentially communicative; few male realists were similarly prepared to entertain this possibility. The difference, I contend, was Chopin's willingness to count fantasy, affect, and desire—including desire mobilized by consumer objects and spaces—as part of a horizon of communicative experience.

Taken by itself, of course, the new apparatus of consumerism did not constitute a deliberative public sphere; any social interactions and identifications it happened to cultivate were by-products of the market imperatives of private acquisition and profit. But in Chopin's expanded version of realism, a woman's experience at a lingerie counter or amid "gorgeous" household objects might be as socially revealing as coffeehouse debates or the arguments in Basil Ransom's favorite publication, the *Rational Review*. If the powerful tactics of a consumer culture became adept in this moment at mobilizing female desire, those market strategies could not easily suppress the contradictions of the new consumerism—the tension, for instance, between sensuality, abundance, and female desublimation on one hand, and the discipline of labor and gendered divisions necessary for industrial production on the other.[64] Like early cinema and department stores, Chopin was willing to annex needs and desires that were traditionally excluded from the public sphere and to include those half-articulated feelings within an inventory of public concerns, with the result that ideological contradictions—maternal sacrifice *and* feminine erotic agency, self-fulfillment *and* codes of familial duty—were reproduced and variously transformed, heightened, or blurred in the pages of her fiction, as they were on the screen and the stage.[65]

Whitman saw in nature and bodily desire the spiritual license to disregard law and custom, and Chopin's song of the self partakes of the same radical potential. Beginning in the 1970s, feminist critics championed *The Awakening* as a literary declaration of independence from the patriarchal constraints of nineteenth-century marriage and motherhood. Edna's struggle is often seen as a dismantling of what Chopin calls the "mother-woman," a bourgeois deity whose sacralization goes hand in hand with women's social subordination. But the novel's primary energies have less to do with a vision of gender equality or autonomy than an ethos of erotic liberation. Edna's pursuit of love and vitalist sensation leaves her indifferent to the dictates of duty. The faces of her children bring her real joy, but in their absence the bonds of kinship become negligible. Because social and familial structures matter less the more Edna's awakening intensifies, the novel's political valence is largely implicit. What are the consequences if female desire and feeling are authorized as literary truth, as a portrait of the real? In *The Awakening*, social roles and constraints are not so much critiqued as sloughed off and left to the side. The radicalism of Edna's story lies in the ease—and the sensuous pleasure—with which she escapes a life that had come to seem numbing and pointless.

Did white women like Edna simply have agency all along? That possibility is one of the startling implications of Edna's unhindered choices and actions. Because Chopin's novel shifts the authority of realism from social types and civic relations to the truths of the body, Edna's will-to-desire is matched with a freedom to act. The only "inward agony" (648) she experiences comes when she observes the bodily violence of a birth; the sight seems either to affront her with the fact of physical pain as a power superior to pleasure or perhaps to reassert the claims of her own children as the flesh of her flesh. In either case, even as it brings an ideological contradiction to the surface (maternal love and individual desire), this "scene of torture" still leaves Edna with a power of agency. Almost immediately afterward, she enters the sea unclothed for the swim that is the novel's concluding scene and final ode to the sensuous embrace of nature.

That this last act of freedom is a likely act of suicide, however, clearly tempers the notion of Edna's agency. If the ability to take action is only the freedom to end her life, Edna's character is little different from the heroines in the museum of realism, the beautiful corpses of the Anglo-European novel. Yet if Edna's choice is the last and surest expression of an ethos of corporeal truth, then the scene is not her death but a final glimpse of a consciousness that lives in the body and its senses: "There was the hum of bees, and the musky odor of pinks filled the air" (655). By ending the novel with these words, Chopin leaves readers in a "twilight epistemology" that invites—indeed, requires—one to reflect on the value and weight to give these traces of Edna's desire and sensory perception before one can make any critical judgment about her social position.

Virtually no contemporary critic saw Edna's story as heroic. Only a few saw it as tragic. The fact that readers all conceded Chopin had created "flawless art" seemed only to heighten their sense of unpleasantness; the novel was deemed "sordid," "morbid," even "repellent."[66] For these readers Edna seems to have possessed an uncanny likeness to the "horrible prettiness" Howells saw in the comic burlesque performers who exploited the incongruity of feminine bodies in male costumes and roles. For all of Edna's femininity, her sexual agency struck readers as a kind of realist cross-dressing that produced an incongruous, hybrid figure of modern womanhood. Chopin was surprised by the novel's stinging reception (though recent scholarship suggests that it was her illness and other difficulties—not social ostracism—that probably caused her to publish next to nothing after *The Awakening*).[67] Although later critics re-created Edna as a feminist martyr, Chopin's contemporaries may have grasped something closer to the truth Chopin intended for Edna's story: a portrait of the unheroic, limited agency of a protagonist who lives by the vicissitudes of desire. But after Chopin's death, her experiment in analyzing female desire would have its own public career, becoming a forerunner to later aesthetic production and an occasion for new agencies of critical analysis.

Chapter 4
Celebrity Warriors, Impossible Diplomats, and the Native Public Sphere

The birth of an American mass culture industry coincides with the "Long Death" of Native peoples' sovereignty in the trans-Mississippi West. In 1871 the U.S. government halted the practice of making treaties with Native nations, closing down what had been an already circumscribed form of diplomatic recognition for tribal sovereignty. Diplomatic standing vanishes, while mediated representation explodes: in its new spaces of virtual existence, from newspaper photographs, dime novels, and Wild West shows to its apotheosis in the cinema, mass culture creates an expanding iconic life for Indians as they are steadily dispossessed of their lands and free lives.

Native peoples pose an especially trenchant test of ideas about American mass culture and the literary public sphere. This is not only because the image of the red body became such a striking phenomenon of mass publicity but also because intellectuals from several different nations began to construct a pan-Indian public sphere at precisely this moment, adapting and directing literary expression and cultural criticism for use in recovering a Native "thought world." The treatment of Native peoples supplies damning evidence for the argument that mass culture was fundamentally imperialist—that it was fueled largely by white nationalist passions and served the interests of those who controlled capital and power.[1] But analyzed together, the co-emergence of mass culture and a Native literary public complicates the narrative of a "refeudalization" of the environment for public reason by mass culture and uncovers the historical roots of critical public reason—its contradictions as well as its possibilities—in fraught moments of transcultural contact. "The first Indian show," according to Chauncey Yellow Robe, occurred when Columbus "imported" American Natives "for exhibition before the Spanish throne."[2] Yellow Robe's comment bespeaks a sphere of public discourse able to criticize governments and analyze exploitative commercial spectacles. But it also begins to suggest a deeper genealogy for public reason that will be hard to disentangle from a history of racial display. To understand the peculiarities a post-Custer American culture, I contend, we need to go back to earlier moments in what Joseph Roach has theorized as a history of "circum-Atlantic performance," a history in which ongoing contests for what will *count* as reason are frequently violent, distinctly aesthetic (a matter of sensuous forms), and always implicitly or explicitly transcultural.

Barnum, Pokagon, and the Impossible Indian Diplomat

P. T. Barnum provides a telling example of the way mass culture entertainment could be constructed on the ruins of diplomatic representation. In his best-selling autobiography *Struggles and Triumphs,* Barnum recounts the coup he achieved in 1864 when he managed to convince a delegation of Plains and southwestern chiefs who had met with President Lincoln to come to New York from Washington. The chiefs, he learns from a translator, would never permit themselves to be displayed as curiosities before a paying audience, so Barnum uses tactics that sustain the illusion that he and his patrons wished merely to pay tribute to the tribal leaders as honored guests. The ruse amounted to a grandly enacted wink, a display of Yankee wit overcoming Indian ferocity.

In exhibiting these Indian warriors on the stage, I explained to the large audiences the names and characteristics of each....
"This little Indian, ladies and gentlemen, is Yellow Bear, chief of the Kiowas. He has killed, no doubt, scores of white persons, and he is probably the meanest, black-hearted rascal that lives in the far West." Here I patted him on the head, and he, supposing I was sounding his praises, would smile, fawn upon me, and stroke my arm, while I continued: "If the blood-thirsty little villain understood what I was saying, he would kill me in a moment; but as he thinks I am complimenting him, I can safely state the truth to you, that he is a lying, thieving, treacherous, murderous monster. He has tortured to death poor, unprotected women, murdered their husbands, brained their helpless little ones; and he would gladly do the same to you or to me, if he thought he could escape punishment. This is but a faint description of the character of Yellow Bear." Here I gave him another patronizing pat on the head, and he, with a pleasant smile, bowed to the audience, as much as to say that my words were quite true, and that he thanked me very much for the high encomiums I had so generously heaped upon him.

Barnum's trick is a feat of doubling: each chief is simultaneously a fearsome killer and a fool. The double bind holds even after the men discover the ruse. Their anger at the sustained deceit resonates with a long history of Native protest, but in Barnum's narrative, the chiefs' anger can only prove the risible pride of a savage: "Their dignity had been offended and their wild, flashing eyes were anything but agreeable."[3]

More critically revealing than Barnum's descriptions of soulless "monsters" is his spectacle of false homage. The Cheyenne (War Bonnet, Lean Bear, Hand-in-the-water), Kiowa (Yellow Buffalo, Yellow Bear), Apache (Jacob of Caddos, White Bull), and other chiefs in the delegation had been led to believe that their visit to New York was an extension of their diplomatic mission to Washington.[4] Barnum pretends to receive them as dignitaries who had come to the East to represent the interests of rights-bearing peoples, and he organizes carriage promenades through Central Park and ceremonial visits to public schools, public outings that trick the chiefs into serving as unwitting advertisements for Barnum's show. But these acts of deception are not simply Barnum's false pretenses; they are his comic premise. Barnum seizes on and sells the pleasure afforded white people at the picture of Indians believing and behaving as if they possessed a standing that is in fact illusory.

But there is also something true about Barnum's false pretenses. Barnum's ruse succeeds by finding an ingenious way to present the Indian diplomat as an impossibility, a living oxymoron: whatever his words, intentions, or gestures, on Barnum's stage they can signify only threat and unreason. Inasmuch as the chiefs were in fact a Native delegation, therefore, Barnum's success cannot but have a broader significance. Did Barnum's sham praises and trumped-up excursions tell a slant version of the truth about the state visit just completed in Washington? Whether the Lincoln administration during that summit had merely pretended to recognize the delegation as leaders owed respect for their status as representatives cannot be ascertained empirically. But the historical record shows that the administration's reception of tribal heads had become by this time a species of official playacting. One administration critic stated it outright: by pretending to negotiate with Indians as independent nations while really undermining tribal governments, the Bureau of Indian Affairs operated on a foundation of "falsehood."[5] Barnum's ruse, then, was less a showman's singular trick than a theatricalization of U.S. Indian policy, a policy that enacted a show of negotiation structurally at variance with a white intraracial understanding that the leaders of Native American peoples did not possess the status that officials pretended to recognize and pledged to respect.

Within the year, the notorious Sand Creek massacre would make this operative policy starkly apparent. After armed clashes throughout the summer between U.S. troops and Cheyenne and Arapaho fighters, the Colorado territorial governor declared amnesty for all Indians willing to locate on reservations. A Cheyenne leader, Black Kettle, took his people to the banks of the Sand Creek near Fort Lyons as directed. Despite Black Kettle's surrender, a regiment under Colonel John Chivington attacked the camp in late November and cut down hundreds of people, most of them women and children. Every corpse was mutilated in some way, with body parts later displayed in a Denver theater.[6] That scalps, breasts, and sex organs became the literal representations of the Cheyenne is a grotesque inversion of the hollow recognition given only months before in Washington to a Cheyenne chief as a living representative of his people.

Easterners were largely appalled by the massacre. Barnum could not have drawn his crowds—certainly not the same crowds, anyway—had he presented the limbs and organs from the massacre rather than the living Indians of his show. Yet the trophies on the Denver stage and the showman's entertainment in New York draw on the same controlling idea of Indianness. Barnum's spectacle relied on the absence of any understanding by the chiefs of what everyone else in the museum audience saw and heard, a (manufactured) ignorance made all the more striking by the physical presence of the men onstage. To his audience Barnum's Indians are bodies but they are not selves, not human subjects with full capacities to understand and communicate. In virtually the same moment, the question of Indian comprehension is the critical factor in the events that culminate at Sand Creek. In the weeks before the massacre, Colonel Chivington had gone on record with his view that negotiation with Indians was a strict impossibility. The proof was their racial inability to grasp white words in any meaningful way: "It is simply not possible for Indians to obey or even understand any treaty. I am fully satisfied, gentlemen, that to kill them is the only way we will ever have peace and quiet in Colorado."[7] Chivington's Indian is a creature whose inability to comprehend white meanings is matched by his innate propensity to kill white people. In crucial respects this representation of the Indian is also Barnum's, a double figure as fearsome as he is uncomprehending. With brutal frontier exaggeration, the notion of the Indian as a body without a reasoning mind finds its ultimate expression in the collection of body parts of dead Cheyenne and Arapaho on a stage in Denver.

After his museum burned down in 1865, Barnum's next large enterprise was the Great Traveling Museum, Menagerie, and World's Fair (featuring "Fiji Cannibals, Modoc and Digger Indians, and representative types of Chinese, Japanese, Aztecs, and Eskimos"), which staged large-scale pageants under movable tents. A later exhibition launched in 1884, the Ethnological Congress of the Barnum and London Circus, convened an even larger cast, listed under the Barnumized taxonomy of "Cannibals, Nubians, Zulus, Mohammedans, Pagans, Indians, Wild Men." The "Congress" brought foreign men and women to U.S. cities, but Barnum's show was not meant to cultivate a sense that people from distant points had been brought near. Instead, this exhibition, staged in more cavernous arenas, signified faraway global territories "where a white man never trod before." The show, in other words, was not intended to evoke an assembly of diverse peoples but to call up an unfolding history of white-native contact in a context of imperial discovery. In the 1890s Barnum dramatized the allegory directly in gigantic productions of *Columbus and the Discovery of America* with a cast numbering in the thousands.[8]

When civil and state authorities organized their own allegory of Columbian origins, commercial techniques of racial spectacle were annexed to a monumental public venture. The 1893 Chicago World's Columbian Exhibition devoted its exhibit halls in the fair's neoclassical "White City" to technological displays and artistic achievement; engines, maps, and artworks were objects attesting to the intellectual capacities of the dominant peoples of Europe and the New World. In the fair's ethnological villages, in contrast, populations were represented not with wrought objects but with representative bodies, as re-created Indian camps and villages from countries such as Algeria, Dahomey, Ireland, and Egypt were located in the Midway entertainment zone alongside amusement rides and souvenir shops. Cody's Wild West troupe performed to large crowds in an outdoor arena near the fairgrounds, earning profits of up to a million dollars during the Chicago season.[9] The fair made clear that in the intervening decades since Barnum's exhibition of the delegation of western chiefs, agents of the state and private entrepreneurs had cross-cultivated new and intricate ways of drawing on the publicity value of red Indians.

In a ceremony to mark the fair's "Chicago Day," Simon Pokagon, a Potawatomi from southwestern Illinois, came forward to ring a replica of the Liberty Bell. The resulting visual tableau promised an elegant solution to the problem of how to express the aspirations of a democratic republic in an age of empire. The sight of a Native American sounding the symbol of U.S. sovereignty created a continuity of national meaning by way of balanced contrast, the red body linked with the state symbol of liberty. As the prelude to a succession of official speeches, the image also reflected the fair's artful synthesis of mass culture techniques of racial display and the discursive reason of public culture. The visual set piece could achieve in a single moment what the speeches could only attempt in a discursive sequence: the formal equipoise necessary to contain the internal tensions of an empire of liberty.

The content of Pokagon's address, "The Red Man's Greeting," however, dissolved the visual composition—the literal composure—of an approved racial tableau.[10] Pokagon was counted a "civilized Indian" because of his training in white institutions and his conversion to Christianity. Whereas most of Pokagon's nation had been forced out of the Midwest, a group of largely Catholic Potawatomi had managed to avoid expulsion from their lands through cooperation with federal authorities. Already considered a hybrid, a civilized Indian was deemed a fitting figure for representing the amalgam of Indian origins and U.S. global destiny brought together in the public ceremony. And Pokagon's address fulfills to the letter what was expected of this "civilized" genre, as an oratory in English composed to mark a solemn civil occasion. But swerving radically, Pokagon also redefines the occasion to be commemorated: it is not an anniversary but a "funeral," the passing of a free red continent. "On behalf of my people, the American Indians, I hereby declare to you, the pale-faced race that has usurped our lands and homes, that we have no spirit to celebrate with you the great Columbian Fair being held in this Chicago city, the wonder of the world. No, sooner would we hold the high joy day over the graves of our departed than to celebrate our own funeral, the discovery of America." The civilized Pokagon, with his command of English letters, marks for his audience the absence of any elegy for this loss: "Shall not one line lament our forest race, / For you struck out from wild creation's face?"[11]

Pokagon's "Greeting" becomes that missing English elegy. Printed and distributed at large fairs and other sites by Pokagon and his Chicago lawyer, C. H. Engle, Pokagon's address (sometimes appearing under the title "The Red Man's Rebuke" or "The Red Man's Lament") and his activities as a speaker and writer made him an "Indian celebrity."[12] Insofar as his speech sounded notes of elegiac mourning, it risked assimilation to the nationalist trope of the vanishing Indian, the figure of tragic necessity that confirms and solemnizes the epic destiny of a white republic on the continent. But Pokagon insists on using the fair's apparatus of public history to detach continental geography from a Columbian epic. Pokagon's address replicates the story of the "young republic" as the history of a confederated Indian people, a sovereign "forest race." So narrated, there is no providential design to this history, only contingency: "But alas! The pale faces came by chance to our shores" (233). When "base ingratitude" is the payment for early Native assistance, Pokagon passes racial judgment on white settlers as "barbarians" and rules accordingly: "As the United States has decreed, 'No Chinaman shall land upon our shores,' so we then felt that no barbarians as they, should land on ours" (234).

As that imitative "decree" suggests, Pokagon does not reject the discourse of civilization but instead effects a transvaluation of its feats of material power. The city of Chicago, Pokagon acknowledges, is the "wonder of the world" (233); the "great Columbian show-buildings stretch skyward" (233); the railroad is a creation "greater in strength, and larger far than any beast of earth" (234). Pokagon does not dispute what should count as civilization nor challenge its proof in material transformation; he merely redraws the picture of its unparalleled power.

The cyclone of civilization rolled westward and the forests of untold centuries were swept away; streams dried up; lakes fell back from their ancient bounds; and all our fathers once loved to gaze upon was destroyed, defaced, or marred, except the sun, moon, and starry skies above, which the Great Spirit in his wisdom hung beyond their reach. (234)

Improvement and defacement are both synonyms for civilization, two accurate names for the same phenomenon. Pokagon speaks of both together, and in doing so traces a hitherto submerged fissure in the language of civilization. When spoken by Pokagon, English words, conventions, and meanings contain a divided and warring world where white "success" is grammatically identical to red "sacrifice." As a civilized Indian, Pokagon was to have reconciled this divide in his person and speech. Instead, his address draws in stark terms a destructiveness internal to civilization itself.

If the division cannot be erased, it can be rationalized. Pokagon knows well this species of reason, which dictates that Indian loss is a hard truth but truth just the same, "the unalterable decree of nature" (237). But Pokagon rejects this appeal to nature, just as he insists on the double valence of civilization. His recounting of a past period of intercultural peace thus becomes the most damning chapter of Pokagon's history of post-Columbian civilization.

> The few of our children who were permitted to attend your schools, in great pride tell us that they read in your own histories, how William Penn, a Quaker, and a good man, made treaties with nineteen tribes of Indians, and that neither he nor they ever broke them; and further, that during the seventy years while Pennsylvania was controlled by the Quakers, not a drop of blood was shed nor a war-whoop sounded by our people. (235)

Pokagon emphasizes a convergence of language: the seventy years of peace in Pennsylvania is the only episode for which red people and white histories recite the same version of events. As a common narrative, the Pennsylvania peace reveals that European settlers and Indians belong to the same history—to the same temporal order and geography—and not to different phases of a natural order. This brief history of peace is the exception that proves the rule of war, but it is also the anomaly that disproves the rule of war as nature's law.

Recounting this diplomatic history is among the most important aspects of Pokagon's address. He stands before the assemblage of state officials and private citizens, we should remember, because he is *not* a diplomat; that is, he is accorded public speech only because he is neither a national enemy nor a representative of a nation recognized as sovereign. Speaking from this position, Pokagon's language has a status that is uncertain at best. In his pointed remarks about the perfidy of settlers, Pokagon makes a bid at influencing public opinion, and might even have changed the way some in the audience viewed the treatment and standing of Native peoples. But he faces the problem that, in a post-diplomatic world, the speech of a self-described "red man" is apt to be received as merely decorative, as a species of exotic style rather than rational meaning. At the time Pokagon composed his address, large and powerful networks of mediation filtered Native expression in just that way: in an era of Indian shows, dime novel westerns, and racial pageants, even Pokagon's English words and literary conventions would be unlikely to signify as a language of public reason, circulating instead as a red idiolect that in effect could be seen but not heard. (Pokagon also unwittingly heightened the likelihood that his speech would be received as merely ornamental by selling copies that were printed on birch-bark parchment.)[13]

But even with these unfavorable conditions in place, by recalling a history of successful treaty making Pokagon is able to invoke a different scene of reception in which his "red" words and gestures would signify the possibility of real diplomacy. His return to Pennsylvania treaty history, that is, locates the ideal (if not the reality) of a scene of diplomatic reason, a site at which distinct peoples—Quakers and nineteen Indian nations—together arrive at a commensurable sense of justice, a sense that is ratified by a history of peace. He thus remembers in public what mass culture *and* white critical publics are proficient at forgetting: the possibility of an order of rational meaning that could be discovered or, more precisely, historically *made up* between white and red peoples. Dominant public opinion was largely impervious to recognizing any such diplomatic order of transcultural meaning. After all, in 1893 the Indian diplomat was not just an oxymoron but a factual impossibility, and even schools that accepted Native students tended to see the successful education of an Indian as effectively erasing her red nature at the moment of inculcating reason. But by invoking an absent scene of diplomatic reason, Pokagon's speech becomes a kind of palimpsest, carrying within itself the memory of a diplomatic public in which red words and red bodies—precisely *as* embodied signifiers—could be the vehicles of a transcultural order of meaning. Remembering (or inventing) this time and place allows Pokagon's speech to locate a public that does not exist but that some day might come to be.[14]

The Transcultural Public Sphere and Practices of Unknowing

When Pokagon delivered his speech, the conditions for what I have called a diplomatic public had vanished, but his act of rhetorical recollection could perform a certain kind of cultural work. The significance of his recollection is clearer if we return to the earlier moment in Barnum's museum auditorium, a moment when white-Native diplomacy was still a technical possibility but very close to being overtly closed down. Barnum's show is illuminating, I have suggested, because it literally dramatizes the refusal of a white public to acknowledge a Native leader as an eligible agent of diplomatic reason. Instead, the trick of false homage ratified a particular discourse of red unreason, as the audience's collaboration in Barnum's ruse allowed white observers to see and experience the "true" nature of the red man: uncomprehending, naturally violent, and not to be trusted. While the hoax may have been the brainchild of Barnum's theatrical imagination, it was also an index to the racialized knowledge that rationalized the U.S. Indian policy of the postwar era.

Just as crucial to this scenario, however, was the fact that this knowledge rested on the audience's active *unknowing* of what was plainly before their eyes. The hoax on the chiefs was also an act of white self-deception insofar as it licensed Barnum's patrons to misrecognize the obvious: before them were leaders of peoples seeking fair conditions of peace who were aware of the treatment due dignitaries and whose capacity to comprehend white ways was proven by the very need to conduct the ruse. Although the notion is counterintuitive from our present-day vantage, Barnum's auditorium *could* have been a site at which numbers of white U.S. citizens not only responded to curiosity about exotic-seeming peoples but also witnessed all that the chiefs meant to demonstrate and perform, namely, their cautious pledge of goodwill and their desire to find and enact terms of mutual understanding to ensure the rights of their respective peoples.

This possibility is no less important for having been foreclosed. It was not ignorance that led the Plains chiefs to participate in Barnum's enterprise; they knew very well the sort of exploitation a public appearance could entail and expressly refused it. Nor were their efforts at diplomacy—in Washington and, as they believed, in the public diplomacy of New York—attempted without awareness of the imperialist conditions governing past and present relations between Indian nations and the United States.[15] It was precisely their awareness of those conditions that prompted the chiefs to undertake forms of direct diplomatic address. No international courts or codes, and not even earlier federal treaties, could constrain the United States from the outside; Indian nations could only seek (yet again) to elicit recognition and agreements from a polity that claimed controlling rights of dominion, or else contest that claim through warfare. Lincoln's commissioner for Indian Affairs, William Dole, asserted that Native tribes were reliant on the state's prevailing "sense of justice."[16] The Plains and southwestern chiefs saw their trip to New York as a venture that would bring that "sense" into a space of collaborative display and open action. That the encounter was rigged does not negate the fact that a different sense of justice—the one Barnum and his audiences elaborately mimed, for instance—might have been realized rather than mocked in that performative space.

In arguing that a "sense of justice" was at stake in Barnum's show, I mean to invoke a quite literal understanding of "sense." Appearing in person before white eyes, undertaking excursions and promenades, standing for ceremonial introductions, accepting greetings and delivering translated (or mistranslated) messages from their peoples—these and other activities made for a material site of showing and sensory reception, an experiential domain in which meaning is fashioned through what is seen, enacted, and exchanged. In this regard, Barnum's show and Lincoln's summit meeting alike can be linked to a tradition of Native-European contact of which the key historical form was the treaty.

Treaties, of course, were never neutral instruments of peace; over time they functioned as a proven mechanism of dominance that aided the process of Indian removal and U.S. expansion through land sale. But before the practice was rescinded, treaties were also the primary means for fashioning mutual terms of understanding regarding tribal land rights and legal standing as well as federal powers and obligations. Treaties were collaborative, even as they were coercive in greater or lesser degrees. They were also expressly performative, issuing from discrete dialogic actions that unfolded in time and space. David J. Carlson points out that during the British colonial and early U.S. national periods, "speaking of an Indian 'treaty' referred not only to the written agreement itself, but also to the act of negotiation and the actual meeting where it was reached."[17]

A treaty was thus a site of sense-making, a place and process where differing protocols, personages, and expressive styles came together, in advance of any governing discourse, and fashioned commensurate forms out of otherwise incommensurate systems of meaning. Cognition was insufficient; words alone could not achieve agreement, or even Indian acquiescence. To produce and ratify a treaty required kinesthetic transmission and exchange. The choreography of European diplomatic protocols merged with the ceremonial oratory, gift giving, and storytelling that characterized indigenous styles of negotiation—the "forest diplomacy" that had governed intercultural relations among Native peoples long before any European conquest.[18] Because of their overtly performative nature, treaties, according to Constance Rourke, were "our first American plays."[19] Recently Eric Cheyfitz has stressed the importance of treaties as intercultural forms that are inextricably both expressive and legal. Calling the treaty an "expressive matrix" in which law is enacted as drama, Cheyfitz points to this historical genre as the "prelude and complex basis" for the body of federal Indian law that has shaped, and continues to shape, Native letters and oral expression.[20] Although treaty making changes markedly over time, the history of treaties shows legal powers bound up with intercultural aesthetic expression and transmission.[21]

It may seem perverse to situate Barnum's deceptive show in this context of aesthetic diplomacy. But it is in fact his perversion of this tradition—his strategic use of the kinesthetic medium of diplomatic exchange—that defines his place within it. Barnum's commercial success ironically confirms the aesthetics of Indian diplomacy; he is able to sell off, as it were, the sensory or aesthetic dimensions of diplomatic contact in the form of sheer spectacle. The show works only because it mimics the processes of shared sense-making that motivated the chiefs to journey to Washington and New York. But Barnum and his patrons simultaneously disavow the very diplomatic basis on which the show depends: by making the interactive understanding of diplomacy the pretext for an exploitative hoax, they displace mutuality by superimposing a monocultural "sense of justice" that willfully creates and then pretends to expose the Indian incomprehension the audience pays to see. The result is a bad-faith empiricism: Barnum's sleight of hand offers paying customers vivid "proof" of the inborn ignorance of the red man, giving white observers license to pretend to witness what they have in fact imposed.

Because Barnum's bad faith was highly profitable here, of course, it is hardly surprising that he exploited a space of public intercultural contact in this way. Barnum's exhibition converted a space of public diplomacy into a node in the fast emerging networks of mass entertainment, moving Indian shows a step closer to the massive outdoor Wild West shows of the 1880s and the endless reels of celluloid westerns that would follow soon after. From this angle, Barnum's Indian show looks like a striking corroboration of Jürgen Habermas's contention that the mass culture of the nineteenth century eroded the public-sphere conditions of the eighteenth by enabling profit-driven circuits of representation to crowd out the chances for more marginal views to enter public discourse.[22] But, by the same token, Indian shows like Barnum's can also raise questions about the way we have understood the concept and history of the Habermasian public sphere. Joseph Roach's study of transatlantic performance culture, for instance, gives a different perspective on Barnum's commercial venture and makes it harder to see his Indian show as a corrupting alteration of a purer space of public culture. Roach's *Cities of the Dead: Circum-Atlantic Performance* gives compelling evidence that what Habermas calls the bourgeois public sphere was from its inception both highly theatrical and emphatically commercial, especially when it came to the charged public encounters among European, Native American, and African populations that were at the foundation of the new Atlantic world.

Roach demonstrates that even as print became a medium for creating a shared sense among strangers of belonging to a community of "freeborn" individuals, performance spaces such as markets, theaters, and street processions were also crucial interanimating sites of public culture, sites that operated in concert with print circulation to fashion self-conscious notions of a reflective public life independent of the king or the state. It was no coincidence, Roach argues, that the publications that generated operative standards of critical reason for public discourse, such as *The Spectator* and *The Tatler,* were also intensely interested in what Addison called the "infinite Variety of solid and substantial Entertainments." Plays, the novelties of street life, and "the grand Scene of Business" were favorite topics.[23] In an age of global contact and colonies, a new diversity of bodies and goods were concentrated in urban shows and markets, and the attention, glamour, and anxiety those bodies generated made commercial spectacle foundational to the public sphere. Roach enlarges the field of sites and mediations we need to recognize as the conditions for a modern public—not just lending libraries but slave auctions and Indian melodramas, not just coffeehouses and newspapers but Mardi Gras parades and Caribbean funeral rites. At the "point of convergence of entertainment and commerce," Roach argues, live social dramas stimulated the exercise of reflective reasoning in print, just as published travel reports and social views became the stuff of live performances.[24] These interactive nodes of print and orality—"orature" is Roach's term, borrowed from Ngugi wa Thiong'o—became crucibles for forging identities, alliances, and symbolic expulsions and for calibrating standards of legitimate behavior and rational thought.[25] What kind of person can be sold and what kind of person does the selling? Who belongs to a sovereign nation and who doesn't? Questions like these, unasked but also unfixed, were answered tacitly and revised perpetually in the performative public sphere where stage actors and other social surrogates articulated the cultural self-definitions and intercultural relations of the new and highly volatile transatlantic world.

If we follow Roach's model of public culture as structured by a collaboration of performative and literate techniques, Barnum's Indian show begins to look like an exemplary instance of the public sphere rather than a distortion. Not only did his popular shows animate the era's spectacular fiction and reports about red Indians, the performances themselves were easily transposed to print when Barnum recounted them in an autobiography that became a massive best-seller. And because Barnum's show was so directly tied to a context of Indian diplomacy, it belongs to one of the performance "genealogies" that Roach explores at length, the pivotal "Mohawk embassy" that visited London in 1710. This delegation of American sachems—three Mohawks and an Algonquian Mahican, along with their translators and sponsors—visited Queen Anne's court to negotiate a joint Anglo-Iroquois alliance for the purpose of confronting the French and their Huron allies in Canada. Their diplomatic visit was the occasion for a spate of public appearances—not just at court but at an opera, a special performance of *Macbeth*, a cockfight, a military review, a missionary society, and the Board of Trade—as well as the inspiration for two issues of *The Spectator* among other accounts in print. The "Mohawk Kings," as Londoners called them, thus mobilized multiple sites of public mediation in their successful diplomatic mission. Far from an intrusion by the primitive or premodern, the Indians were a participant in the development of this most modern of institutions we call the public. This scene of modern public diplomacy in England, Roach demonstrates, was patterned after the ceremonial orature of American "forest diplomacy," the repertoire of gift exchange, wampum handling, recitation and song, and "pen and ink work" that had adapted intertribal practices of the Iroquois Confederacy to the trade and peace negotiations Indians conducted with British and French settlers.[26]

The Mohawk embassy reminds us that long before the chiefs' summit with Lincoln in Washington, Indian diplomacy played out in a field of mediation that was already scenic, commercial, and sensory, a context in which shows and promenades were as vital as documents and signing ceremonies. But major diplomatic events like the London meeting—deciding alliances and strategies that shaped the future of the Atlantic world—were easily erased from the Anglo-European understanding of diplomatic history. The long history of intercultural exchange between white and red peoples is, as Roach puts it, a history "particularly subject to forgetting," and transatlantic encounters like the Mohawk visit to London were always poised between possibilities for mutuality and occasions for negation, the acts of amnesia necessary to the knowledge that red peoples could not reason or coexist with white ones.[27] Barnum's show is also exemplary in its performance of this modern amnesia. As we have seen, it is a performance that still offered the sensory experience generated by diplomacy, but one that ritually excluded Native American diplomats from any intersubjective life or meaning, producing them as mute, uncomprehending objects whose only expressive meaning became the violent threat signified by the mere presence of a racial body. The hoax Barnum played on the delegation erased the *too-evident* fact of a previous collaborative understanding with the chiefs, a fact that had to be in place but then forgotten if the audience was to have the pleasure of confronting menacing red bodies and besting their uncomprehending, "blood-thirsty" nature.

After the Plains chiefs discovered the deceit, Barnum's bemused reaction to the Indians' injured "dignity" trivializes their anger. But when we restore the diplomatic context that Barnum and his audience willfully forgot, the chiefs' anger suggests a very different critical reaction to this public encounter. It is clear that the Indians' sense of "dignity" was of a piece with their diplomatic self-presentation and intercultural address, the kinesthetic practices designed to be a medium for addressing a white public and for interacting with the powers of the state. And those state powers really were at issue in Barnum's auditorium, for by *negating* a public diplomatic event—by enacting pragmatically what Colonel Chivington said overtly, that it is "not possible for Indians to understand any treaty"—Barnum's hoax eroded the conditions for peaceful negotiations with the Plains and southwestern nations and demonstrated the weapon of forgetting that the state could and often would enforce as policy. The chiefs' anger, then, was not simply offense at being treated with a lack of respect. Surely the anger also signified the chiefs' larger critical understanding of what the hoax performed: a willful, aggressive erasure of the space of public intercultural exchange.

Native Americans who hazarded the uncertain, changeable grounds of intercultural diplomacy acquired an education in U.S. public culture—and in some respects, saw it more clearly than white intellectuals. Pragmatically and critically, the chiefs in Barnum's show learned that entering the space of appearance, speech, and print we call public means submitting to a test, not defined or secured in advance, that determines whether one's expression will be intelligible—whether it will count as public meaning or merely as non-public noise and local color. The public sphere is not an open market of ideas and entertainment but an arena in which the styles and modes of speech and performance determine what will count as reason. Rational reflection and attempts at persuasion are largely secondary phenomena, signs that a given instance of speech or expression has passed the test and managed to acquire recognition *as* public speech. The test is therefore less conceptual than formal, a test of whether one's material *modes* of expression are sufficiently rational to signify meaning. For the chiefs, the test was as weighty as it was simple. When are claims intelligible and thus negotiable and when are they merely signs of unreason? What sorts of actors can address civil society as rational subjects, and not risible objects?

By contesting the ability of the chiefs to appear as diplomats, Barnum's show illustrates in a particularly vivid way Michael Warner's analysis of public discourse as speech that tries to characterize and thereby project its own field of reception, and thus to define in advance what is publicly intelligible. Any public effort at persuading, entertaining, or publicizing is preceded by conscious or unconscious choices of style, lexicon, and protocols of address, a tacit aesthetics that attempts to imagine and conjure into existence the concrete social world it wishes to address—the kind of world that will say, yes, that claim is reasonable, that joke is funny, that sight is arresting and worth paying to see. For this reason, public speech is as much a matter of poetics as of abstract reason or ideology, but a poetics in which the stakes can be very high: success or failure determines what sort of speech will be able to enact an "imaginary coupling with the state" and thus to call on the state's monopoly of legitimate force—its police and military powers—to enforce a particular social imaginary.[28] In its aggressive act of forgetting, Barnum's show distilled the struggle over conditions of intelligibility that were always a civil battle for Native peoples, whatever the climate for war or peace. Can an Indian be a diplomat, a speaker who offers intelligible claims and proposals? When the delegation of chiefs appeared in New York, they proffered a sensory field of signs and gestures—their clothing and bodily postures, their speech and outdoor processions—as a field for intercultural mediation, but the public reception was such that every word and movement was framed to signify savagery rather than diplomacy. Implicit in this public reception, then, was an ominous "sense of justice," unspoken and imposed rather than reasoned, that would have its starkest expression in the dramaturgy of butchered bodies on the stage in Denver.

Indian Thought Worlds: Parker, Eastman, Bonnin

At a moment when commercial culture, dominant opinion, and state law all tended to cast the Indian subject as something other than a civil agent, the effort by Native American writers and intellectuals to construct a pan-Indian critical public was an inherently complex undertaking. In 1899, within a few years of delivering his address at the Chicago fair, Pokagon died just before turning seventy years old. Although he had received some formal education and religious training in white institutions, Pokagon had relied largely on improvised channels for addressing a white public, seizing the opportunity that came with his assigned role as an iconic red man at the Chicago fair, for instance, and devising his own system of print distribution with the help of his lawyer. But a younger generation of Native American writers and thinkers were emerging who had institutional ties to school administrations, universities, and museums, and who began to appear in literary journals and to sign contracts with established publishing houses. Some, like Senecan scholar Arthur C. Parker, had family ties to Christian missions and U.S. civil institutions that went back a number of generations; others, like Gertrude Bonnin (a Yankton Lakota also known as Zitkala-Sa), were the first in their families to have any sustained contact with English speakers or institutions, often through the system of boarding schools for Indian children. For this younger generation, intertribal contact networks running through these institutional sites made it seem possible to bring together an association of Native minds to analyze the predicaments and resources of diverse nations as a set of common concerns. The prospect, moreover, seemed not just possible but urgent: in the absence of a treaty system, after the massacre at Wounded Knee, and with the dire effects of the Dawes Act policy of land allotment intensifying the long U.S. assault on traditional institutions of tribal governance, for many Native intellectuals there seemed few other means to try to navigate a troubling political landscape.[29]

One formal expression of this public came in 1911 when a six-person executive committee set out to organize the Society of American Indians (SAI). Unlike the many white organizations that took up what they called the "Indian problem," the society permitted only Native Americans as members, although white people were welcome to become SAI associates. The policy reflects a central premise of the organization: Native Americans possessed unique knowledge with which to reflect on Indian affairs and on American society more broadly. The fact that SAI members sought to mobilize that knowledge through public channels of print and cooperation with white civil and governmental agencies, however, often put them at odds with traditionalist leaders and with nationalist movements organized around religion.[30] The society drew on existing forms of public communication, issuing a statement of purpose, publishing journals (the *Quarterly Journal* and the *American Indian Magazine*), circulating reports, and holding conferences. That these were cultural forms the SAI shared with white publics, however, can obscure the fact that this Native public circulated some distinct notions about reason itself—some of which would be *more* intelligible in the performative arenas of mass culture than in the existing domains of a print-based public.

When Arthur C. Parker, as editor of the *Quarterly Journal*, published a list of seven charges against "American civilization," he made the curious decision to name before all else the dispossession of Indian thought. Parker's first charge is that the United States "had robbed a race of men—the American Indian—of their intellectual life." The choice was not the idiosyncratic concern of a bookish scholar, though Parker did prize scholarship, and his collaborations with Frank Putnam of Harvard and Columbia's Franz Boas reflected his position as a leader in his field. Rather, his chief reason for stressing intellectual before material or social deprivation was Parker's conviction that Native thinking, so discounted by Anglo-Americans, was in fact the foundation of all else in Indian life.

> In his native state the Indians had things to think about. These things in their several subjects were a part of his organized mental and external activities. . . . *Human beings have a primary right to an intellectual life, but civilization swept down upon groups of Indians and blighted or banished their intellectual life and left scattered groups of people mentally confused.*

For Parker there exists a clear need for a restitution of intellectual rights: "The Indian must have his thought world given back."[31]

By positing the domain of thought as a lived, existential "world," however, Parker's definition was not congruent with the way rationality was tacitly understood in the public he was speaking from and addressing, a print public with an indefinite audience of Native and non-Native readers. Most obviously, what Parker called Indian thought was not the rationality of literacy: before European contact and to a large extent after, the thought worlds of Native peoples were not structured primarily by letters or by print but were ordered through "mental and external activities," as Parker puts it, the forms of reasoning that were expressed not just in speech or reflection but in practices of everyday life. In contrast, the mechanics of print circulation tend to favor a particular understanding of thought as an invisible, placeless activity that unites the minds of private reading subjects. With the rise of bourgeois print culture, public reason was increasingly seen as "a neutral, relatively disembodied procedure for addressing common concerns" as opposed to embodied practices that were demoted to the status of "private, local, or merely affective and expressive."[32]

Of course, even the kind of thinking that constitutes rational-critical debate is an activity as well; public reason is not the invisible operations of minds but the product of a concrete set of expressive and worldly practices that bespeak a particular way of life. Habermas's historical study and the rich body of scholarship on European and American print culture that followed it have made us aware of the webs of concrete topics, idioms, reading practices, market conditions, and circulation sites that make up that way of life. The bourgeois public sphere, therefore, is also a "thought world," as Parker would put it, and is ordered by its own context of "mental and external activities." But crucially, it is a thought world that can more easily ignore or discount its own enabling context. The reading practices of its members, the figural or poetic dimensions of their language, the distinct social imaginary through which they characterize public and private, civil and uncivil—these features can be taken for granted and therefore forgotten, the mere vehicles of the supposedly unitary human reason they transmit.

The inherent tension between the pragmatic or material dimension of the bourgeois thought world and its self-understanding, between its particular social conditions and its definition of human reason, however, could sometimes emerge to become a palpable problem—even a perceived crisis. I have been arguing throughout this study that the emergence of mass culture represents just such a crisis, an event that prompted intellectuals to distinguish, under the sign of the literary, the higher human faculties from the lower and thereby recover a field of public representation that could continue to transmit purer expressions of human thought. Mass media forms, in contrast, favored strongly visual vocabularies and direct appeals to desire and sensation; by suppressing and stigmatizing such vocabularies, high culture hoped to restore a public sphere of reason, aesthetic truth (realism), and critical thought. But for Native writers, the bourgeois public sphere itself already posed a palpable tension, precisely *because* it favored an ideology of disembodied reason. Print culture offered Indians conditions for a species of critical speech; and yet to represent an Indian thought world from *within* those conditions was to picture an embodied world and thus to speak from athwart conflicting ideologies of thought.

Charles Alexander Eastman (Ohiyesa), a Dakota Sioux author, physician, and activist, presented the tension between the two as something he experienced at an affective level. Eastman wrote of the dissonance he felt when his medical fieldwork for the YMCA in the 1890s brought him back into contact with the Native "philosophy" familiar from his youth, a style of thought that had been "overlaid and superceded by a college education" and his conversion to Christianity. As described in his autobiography *From the Deep Woods to Civilization* (1916), Eastman's discussions of Christianity with tribal elders produced unexpected results: he was at a loss to refute their "logic," while he found that his "close contact with the racial mind" was strangely consoling.³³ But what Eastman represents as a felt confusion at the level of subjectivity is also textual effect, a kind of formal mark or fissure that registers orthogonal definitions of reason: brought together in his text, the "logic" of a "racial mind" and the implicit logic of public reason allow two thought worlds to coexist, if uneasily, while remaining distinct.

What registers as dissonance in this text takes a different, more generative form in a number of other published works by Eastman. In *The Soul of the Indian*, he posits a sphere of spiritual belief that has its essence outside language ("the Indian does not speak of these deep matters so long as he believes in them"), and then tries to find a way to represent that world faithfully for non-Indian readers.³⁴ Similarly, in several collections of sketches and stories, including *Red Hunters and the Animal People* (1904), *Wigwam Evenings* (1909), and *Old Indian Days* (1907), Eastman and his wife, Elaine Goodale Eastman, helped innovate a species of local color fiction, stories in English that combine a realism of ethnological detail with literary equivalents of Dakota storytelling conventions. The fiction may have been Eastman's way of attempting to resolve the tension between the intellectual practices he acquired through higher education (he was a graduate of Dartmouth and Boston University medical school) with what he called the "philosophy in which I had been trained."³⁵ The integration succeeds in creating a new literary form, but it also represents a *return* to a modality of communication we have characterized as orature, a form in which oral or embodied speech and gesture is produced "alongside or within mediated literacies."³⁶ And we have seen that, especially where and when sites of orature have been a connective passage between American Native and European peoples, they have been distinctly unstable—creative and productive, but also subject to erasure and sometimes violent forgetting.

Glimpses of that charged instability crop up in and around the Native print public. When Eastman eventually turned away from his life as an activist-author and lived much of his last years alone in a cabin near Ontario, for instance, it is instructive to ask (even if we cannot answer) why he withdrew. Was his decision to stop publishing books a sign that a Native thought world could not in fact be recovered? Or was his public silence proof that it could be and that Eastman had finally recovered it, precisely by withdrawing altogether from thinking in and through a mediated public? Carlos Montezuma (Yavapai), an SAI member who was an even stronger advocate of integrationist policies, also returned at the end of his life to live on a reservation in a simple shelter that recalled the dwellings of Yavapai pre-reservation camps. Robert Allen Warrior (Osage) contends that Eastman, Montezuma, and other intellectuals from the "post–Wounded Knee" generation discovered too late that cooperation with white public institutions only strengthened the destructive impact of federal Indian policy. By directing their energy and thought at a reading public, Warrior argues, these Indian intellectuals largely released themselves from accountability toward Indian constituencies and instead placed their faith in white reform principles and organizations. Rather than redefining the terms of public debates, their writing served instead to supply "a market for books and articles about Native traditions and lifeways" for white consumers who favored romantic primitivism over serious consideration of the realities of Native American life.[37]

By Warrior's reckoning, then, the site of literary orature created by this generation of Indian authors proved to be "impractical," or worse, when it came to resisting federal depravations. But Warrior himself acknowledges that the practical success or failure of the SAI intellectuals is not the only measurement of what was created by the early pan-Indian public. Clearly, white consumption of Native letters could be another form of forgetting. Yet Warrior also counts the SAI writers of this era as the foundation of a multigenerational lineage of Native intellectuals that precedes his own, a generation now often writing and teaching within U.S. universities. The emergence of this generational history has not resolved the tensions faced by early Native intellectuals; Indian scholars writing today, Warrior argues, inherit new versions of the complex critical problems of inhabiting an "interlocutorial role" in dialogue with European-descended disciplinary traditions.[38] But the generational history itself points to another dimension of the original pan-Indian public. If print culture made transcultural sites of orature more vulnerable to white co-optation (as Warrior argues), print also allowed the audience and the terms of reception for Native writing to mutate over time. Today, largely through the efforts of Indian scholars, the work of writers like Eastman, Parker, Montezuma, and Gertrude Bonnin circulate among new Indian and non-Indian readers who might (or might not) take up those texts in ways very different from the ways the original reading audience did.[39]

Academic publics in particular often have a long temporal horizon. Warrior's own published work is proof of the way print mediation can reevaluate and transform the reception of writing—white *and* red—across time; Native critical reflection, Warrior insists, has been "a process centuries long." This means that the very instability of forms of Native orature—

the volatility inherent in speaking across different thought worlds, the styles and resources that crossing can generate—is also a source of analytic power for contemporary Indian critics.[40] And the ruins of diplomatic speech, I have been arguing, were the grounds of similarly productive tensions and instabilities in work of the first generation of Indian intellectuals as well: analytic insight often resides in the transit across orthogonal thought worlds, a process that becomes legible in print as formal and experiential moments of incommensurability.

Another example of this generative tension is visible in the writing of Gertrude Bonnin, who draws on canons of public reason not just to represent an Indian thought world but to analyze a process of "deculturation," the deliberate dismantling of inherited systems of meaning that make that world cohere. Bonnin, who studied at Earlham College in Indiana and Boston's New England Conservatory of Music, returned for a time after college to the Yankton reservation where she had grown up. Coming back after her immersion in English and literary genres, her return meant both a reentry into everyday Dakota life and a recognition that there was "material for stories" in that life. In 1900 and 1901 she published fiction and autobiographical stories in *Harper's* and the *Atlantic* (pieces later collected in 1921 as *American Indian Stories*) and brought out a book of traditional Sioux tales, *Old Indian Legends* (1901), publishing under the name Zitkala-Sa. Like Eastman and Parker (who published English versions of Iroquois legends), Bonnin created print artifacts that presented traditional stories and contemporary everyday activities as part of an integrated world. But alongside her print portrait of Dakota life, her writing stages scenes from a print-based world of white education, a world in which techniques for inculcating literacy are of a piece with efforts to extinguish Dakota practices.

Her autobiographical stories in particular offer compressed, artful accounts of the techniques used at Indian boarding schools for breaking apart the forms of compound understanding—a fusion of the mental and the physical—that animated traditional Sioux society, forms that were now legible in print at a moment of their dissolution. Bonnin's "Impressions of an Indian Childhood" and "The School Days of an Indian Girl" are an intimate record of the bewilderment and fear she experiences upon entering at age eight a Quaker-run boarding school for Indian children. The force of the account lies in its creation of a textual disjunction, a marked incongruity between the girl's overwhelming feelings and the school's "iron routines" that treat Indian children as passive bodies. During Bonnin's first days at the school, for instance, the rooms and routines designed to cultivate order are for her a chaotic sensory assault.

> We were led toward an open door, where the brightness of the lights within flooded out over the heads of the excited palefaces who blocked our way. . . . The strong glaring light in the large whitewashed room dazzled my eyes. . . . A large bell rang for breakfast, its loud metallic voice crashing through the belfry overhead and into our sensitive ears. The annoying clatter of shoes on bare floors gave us no peace.[41]

Because Bonnin only rarely depicts school instructors or administrators, the narrative creates the sense of a strange, almost automated landscape of "large buildings" that exist to separate Indian bodies from their beliefs and memories. An invisible, impersonal power dwells just outside the range of the narrative point of view, even though this "civilizing machine" drives everything that occurs in the story.

> I remember being dragged out [from a hiding place under a bed], though I resisted by kicking and scratching wildly. In spite of myself, I was carried downstairs and tied fast in a chair. I cried aloud, shaking my head all the while until I felt the cold blades of the scissors against my neck, and heard them gnaw off one of my thick braids. Then I lost my spirit. (55–56)

By eliding any picture of who carries her, ties her down, or cuts her hair, the narrative finds an ingenious way to represent the dictates of an educational ethos that seems to have no worldly origin or location—no elders, artifacts, places, or expressive practices. This ethos or force is only an inexplicable rationale that makes itself felt through the "iron routines" demanded of the Indian pupils. In its eerie ability to concretize an absence, Bonnin's language depicts an ideology of placeless, universalizing reason that is able to blindly dismantle the worlds it deems to lack reason.

The Indian child's body is disciplined in the name of cultivating her mind, but the process really works in reverse: the ministrations of white schooling close down an interior "spirit" as they civilize the red body. Bonnin thereby exposes the deculturation that occurs under the sign of education. Yet in her very reversal of the meaning of education, there is also an expressive example of one of the important ends to which Bonnin directs her mastery of English literary codes. Here and elsewhere, Bonnin uses the leverage of literary irony to detach the practices of a white social order from its controlling symbols. The code of propriety governing bourgeois dress, for instance, reappears as immodest display: "As I walked noiselessly in my soft moccasins, I felt like sinking to the floor, for my blanket had been stripped from my shoulders. I looked hard at the Indian girls, who seemed not to care that they were even more immodestly dressed than I, in their tight-fitting clothes" (52–53). The estranging effect becomes a critical mirror for reflecting to a largely white audience the vantage of the Indian who is otherwise made to occupy the position of visual object.

That aim is realized most pointedly in a scene Bonnin describes from her college days, a state competition in which she represented her school in an oratory contest. Before she delivers her speech, Bonnin looks out at an auditorium of white faces and prepares herself to confront an audience of observers who reflexively see an Indian as a mere object or picture—in this case, a literal picture at its most derogatory, the sign of the squaw.

> There, before that vast ocean of eyes, some college rowdies threw out a large white flag, with a drawing of a most forlorn Indian girl on it. Under this they had printed in bold black letters words that ridiculed the college which was represented by a "squaw." (79)

So crudely reduced to a sign of Indian stigma, the picture of the red body becomes the figure through which Bonnin gives an oppositional expression of the interiority she is not believed to possess. She does so most obviously in her speech, a superior performance of English oratory that wins the intercollegiate competition. More subtly, and with more complex implications, Bonnin also proves the point by writing and publishing her account of the event, expressing in print the interior life of feeling she will not display in the public hall. Anger, elation, and increased loneliness are the successive emotions given artful expression in her written recollection. All are signs the readers of *Atlantic Monthly* would interpret as the marks of the literary self, the writer who disciplines thought and feeling through the uniquely public privacy of the crafted literary text.

Yet defeating the picture of the "squaw" with English eloquence does not count as success in Bonnin's work and she retreats from her own lettered persona almost as soon as she has represented it. Here and throughout the narrative she reveals that every advance in her mastery of English letters widens the estranged relationship between Bonnin and her mother, who had wanted the girl to remain with her on the Yankton reservation: "The little taste of victory did not satisfy a hunger in my heart," she writes of her prize in the competition. "In my mind I saw my mother far away on the Western plains, and she was holding a charge against me" (80). Bonnin's story depicts a rift in what had been a more cohesive, lived world, a rift that gives rise to an ineradicable, self-perpetuating desire to overcome absence through literary expression. The divide between worlds, in other words, is presented not as a simple opposition but as a generative experience of difference that was the basis for her literary and political expression. As Jane Hafen (Taos Pueblo) points out, Bonnin's public role became increasingly "more entrenched in an aboriginal persona" the further removed she was from her Dakota origins.[42]

The generative tension of this brand of literary orature makes a virtue out of a structural rift: print mediation allows Native American writing to function as both an expressive medium and a vehicle of critique. Bonnin focused on Indian education, but as we will see, within the space of public print Indian intellectuals also conducted their own version of the critical scrutiny of mass culture—Wild West shows, film, and historical spectacle. But their distinct vantage on the space of mass culture also meant that Native Americans saw possibilities for using the energies of mass culture in the service of their own post-diplomatic analysis and expression. Because Native authors are attuned to the material dimensions of public speech and appearance—because they recognize these material dimensions in print culture as well as mass spectacle—their participation in both spheres is alert to what might be fashioned from the ruins of an absent diplomatic public.

Indian Celebrity and Counterfactual Diplomacy: Standing Bear, Yellow Robe, Geronimo

In the decades after the United States terminated treaty making, the business of Indian shows expanded spectacularly. Buffalo Bill Cody's first show was staged in 1883 and started a vogue for large-scale productions, often staged in outdoor arenas and featuring hundreds of participants. Rival Wild West shows as well as smaller companies sprang up to capitalize on the "Indian show craze." Although these productions were collaborative, little in the pageantry itself acknowledged the continent's long history of red-white treaties and trade. Instead, these shows usually offered a live-action allegory of a logic of war, dramatizing actual historical battles between Native fighters and the U.S. cavalry, and fitting tribal dress, customs, and lifeways to a narrative schema that framed the militarized settlement of western territories as the "Drama of Civilization."[43]

Cody's shows featured many of the very Sioux fighters and leaders who participated in the Plains battles of the 1870s, and a reenactment of Little

Big Horn was often a highlight of the show.⁴⁴ In replaying these historic fights, Indians were asked to perform in the public sphere as a disciplined and formidable military power, not at the direct behest of the government (though the participation of Indian performers required government permission) but in response to the popular demand of a market. Their public role was thus less that of a savage or even an enemy than the role of the celebrity: unlike Barnum's chiefs, the show Indians in Cody's productions were neither monstrous nor risible but estimable agents accorded a certain elegiac nobility as warriors.⁴⁵ Through the extravagant performances, the recognition and glamour awarded Indian warriors was mutually conferred on U.S. military forces, as what had been chaotic operations on the real battlefield were choreographed for thrilling public displays.⁴⁶ Roosevelt recognized the legitimating publicity attached to the Indian warrior when he enlisted Geronimo to appear in his inauguration parade. When a skeptical bureaucrat asked why the new president would invite "the greatest single-handed murderer in American history" to appear in a state procession, Roosevelt answered, "I wanted to give the people a good show."⁴⁷ A good show in this context meant not just a spectacle that could entertain the crowds but the presence of a celebrity Indian able to radiate a species of public agency—a new warrior publicity—that could be shared by the head of state.

By the time Roosevelt was in office, the market in military glamour had largely replaced the public diplomacy that had been available (if very often abused) in the era of Lincoln. But the ghost of an absent Indian diplomacy still haunted the scenic encounters of the later shows. Luther Standing Bear, an Oglala Sioux who had attended the Carlisle Indian School and was working in Philadelphia, told of attending a traveling show that featured Sitting Bull, where he was startled to hear a white impresario give a wholly false rendition of the chief's address (in Lakota) to the audience. Sitting Bull believed his group was en route to the White House ("My friends, we Indians are on our way to Washington to see the Grandfather, or President of the United States"), and he spoke to the Philadelphia audience of having ended his days as a warrior and his plans to shake hands with the president. The white "translator," however, pretended that Sitting Bull was speaking about the Battle of Little Big Horn and about having killed Custer by his own hand—a sensational "fact" trumpeted in advertisements that Standing Bear knew to be false. The ruse was one more deliberate elision of diplomatic speech, but one for which we have a record of the reaction of a Native American observer. In recollecting the Philadelphia performance in his book *My People the Sioux*, Standing Bear poses a question that is really a form of complex critical analysis: "What sort of Indian agent could it have been who would let these Indians leave the reservation without even an interpreter, giving them the idea they were going to Washington, and then cart them around to different Eastern cities to make money off them by advertising that Sitting Bull was the Indian who slew General Custer!"[48] It is telling that Standing Bear underscores not just the profit motive behind the deceit, and not just the pretext of a diplomatic meeting in Washington, but also the pivotal role of the Indian agent, the government official who exercised the carceral power of the reservation system and without whom a commercial tour for Sitting Bull would not have been possible. By stressing the agent's role, Standing Bear points to the amalgam of state authority and commercial publicity behind the appearance of the bankable celebrity warrior, an appearance here directly predicated on the erasure of diplomatic speech.

For many contemporary critics of the Indian shows, such manipulations were a sufficient reason to oppose the industry—though Standing Bear (as I discuss below) was not among those who took this position. Richard Henry Pratt, the founder of the Carlisle Indian School and a leading Anglo advocate for Indian assimilation, attacked the industry not only for exploiting performers but also for perpetuating backward tribal habits, as he saw them, and for encouraging white people to hold to a view of the Indian as incorrigibly "wild."[49] In 1914, a former Carlisle student, Chauncey Yellow Robe, published a critique, "The Menace of the Wild West Show," in an SAI journal. Yellow Robe was probably influenced by Pratt, a former mentor; but like Standing Bear—and *unlike* Pratt—he criticized the shows for more than just "commercializing the Indian." The deeper problem, he suggests, is what happens to public appearances and expression that could and should have been diplomatic.

Beginning with the men and women Columbus exhibited "before the Spanish throne," Indians have been displayed by state power, presented by and before the kings, presidents, and governments that use Indians and their expressive styles as a means to publicize their own authority rather than to conduct intercultural communication. And the intervening centuries have only introduced new ways to make Indian performers reenact their own diplomatic silencing. For Yellow Robe, film re-creations of the massacre at Wounded Knee were the most galling confirmation of this erasure. The massacre, he stresses, was a "criminal act without diplomacy," an exercise of power by the state that obviated any channel of negotiation.

"The tragedy was reproduced for 'historical preservation' in moving picture films and called 'The Last Great Battle of the Sioux,'" Yellow Robe writes, but these films were not a historical record of a battle; they were the cinematic repetition of an act of forgetting: "The whole production of the field was misrepresented and yet approved by the Government." Shows and films distort a record of state crime ("criminal act without diplomacy") by placing it under the sign of historical necessity and thereby erasing from view yet again the option of negotiation that could have prevented the massacre.[50]

Standing Bear, as we have seen, was also attuned to the reciprocity between Indian shows and state power, but he did not oppose the whole industry—indeed, Standing Bear was himself a performer in both Wild West shows and Hollywood films. His father and brother Henry had ties to shows as well. Although he didn't hesitate to criticize individual productions—he was especially outspoken about films that used white actors in Indian roles—Standing Bear did not share Yellow Robe's view that Indian shows necessarily presented the Native American as an archaic, "savage being."[51] As even opponents acknowledged, sometimes unwittingly, Indian shows offered performers a kind of agency or public identity that was "enthusiastically applauded."[52] As a report in 1890 lamented, "the show business is a constant incentive holding forward a glittering prize to every Indian boy."[53] One Indian Affairs commissioner, trying to end the cozy relationship between Indian agents and show managers, complained that performers who travel in Indian shows "become self-important" and learn that white people, "whom they have been taught to regard as examples of civilization," will pay handsomely to watch battles and other simulated "deeds of blood."[54]

For the commissioner, the shows were a regressive retreat, a lapse into "old ways" that allowed Indians to escape from the real "battle of life."[55] (Reformers who frowned on the theatrical warfare in the shows often used martial language to describe the civil sphere they urged on Indian peoples—the "battle of life" that is "modern" society. But it's safe to say that Native Americans had learned that lesson about American modernity long ago; Ely Parker, the Seneca writer and scholar, wrote to a friend in 1881 of his late sense that the "gladiatorial contests of modern life" may not have been worth fighting.)[56] For performers such as Standing Bear, however, participation in Indian shows was not a retreat from the modern "battles of life" but an effective way of joining them. As Cody's translator and managerial assistant as well as a leading performer, Standing Bear recognized as well as anyone that Indian shows were part of a modern industry, one in which what he called the "exterior life" of Indians had a commercial currency.[57] But this "glittering prize," Standing Bear knew, was a form of *political* currency as well—a form of value that was not just traded by Indian performers for wages, and not just exploited by unscrupulous managers for unearned profits, but also a form of public currency that could be bartered in the interest of a given Indian nation and traded for Native control over the publicity value of Indians' "exterior life."

Such a currency mattered all the more at a moment when overt political channels and reforms had proved to be largely destructive; Standing Bear would come to call citizenship "just another hoax."[58] With a clear-eyed understanding of the way "glittering" publicity was of value to the state and the marketplace, Standing Bear viewed Indian shows as an opportunity to refashion the kinesthetic dimensions of Indian expression for modern political conditions. After his time with Cody's company, performing in Europe as well as the United States, Standing Bear was recruited to California where he served as a consultant for the Hollywood producer Thomas Ince and performed as an actor in westerns alongside Douglas Fairbanks and William S. Hart. He also performed songs and dances and taught classes in sign language at the Southwest Museum in Los Angeles in this period, continuing the lectures he had been giving during his career with show companies. Standing Bear deliberately increased his profile as a performer—circulating photographs of himself in full regalia for his letterhead, advertising himself as "An Official Sioux Authority"—at the same time that he criticized stage managers and film directors who produce inaccurate pictures of Indian life and castigated white authors who do "irreparable damage" by writing books about the Indian that aid in "distorting his true nature."[59] Stage shows, films, and exhibitions were part of the way Standing Bear understood his battle *against* an array of commercial and civil authorities, those figures who, from the Pine Ridge agent he despised to the white ethnologist who criticized one of his book manuscripts for lacking "knowledge," were perpetually trying seize, co-opt, or sell the "exterior" life of the Native.[60]

Performative modes of expression were not an expedient strategy of "playing Indian," a compromise necessary to get white citizens to listen to the rational arguments of red people.[61] Rather, these forms of Native publicity represent an effort at post-diplomatic expressivity, an attempt at world building that looked to the mass communicability of Native styles and signifiers as the materials for securing greater recognition and protection for Native societies. Charles Eastman also viewed public shows in this light. The choice to appear before audiences in "our ancestral garb of honor" or to perform acts of "surpassing agility" as dancers or horsemen was not an atavistic expression of primitivism but a modern form of public agency—Eastman calls it a "new line of defense of the native American."[62] The phrase is telling; although he often couched his support for commercial exhibitions in terms of education and outreach, this formulation suggests he saw publicity as a species of power, a "line of defense" specific to an era when the state strictly controlled the tribes' mobility and access to resources, but one in which public entertainment venues—"the circus tent and sawdust arena"—prized at least certain dimensions of Indian expression.[63]

A similar critical perspective is implicit in the book dictated by Geronimo. For this brilliant warrior and strategist, the work he called "book-making" meant something far different from the writing of Native intellectuals who published with established presses and journals. Geronimo only published a book because he was a prisoner of the state; had he never been incarcerated at Fort Sill, Oklahoma, it is doubtful he would have agreed to narrate the story of his life and people, as he was finally persuaded to do by a white educator, S. M. Barrett. For Geronimo, "book-making" meant structured sessions of oral dictation to his kinsman, Asa Daklugie, who translated his words into English for the text that Barrett recorded and edited.[64] But while he had no connection to the pan-Indian public sphere that was being created by Native intellectuals, analysis of *Geronimo: His Own Story* shows that this famous Indian warrior pragmatically understood public culture—both print culture and commercial shows—as a space in which to barter his celebrity for returns that might benefit Apaches. As an unlettered man of color who acquired international fame, he illuminates the conditions of mass culture by way of his strange career as an inmate-celebrity, and Geronimo's book is among the most revealing windows on the fate of Indian diplomatic speech in the modern public sphere.

The stardom conferred on Geronimo is complex and in some respects puzzling. After nearly thirty years of the "Apache wars," he surrendered in 1886 and was eventually incarcerated at Fort Sill. But Geronimo was already a mass celebrity on the order of Mark Twain and Theodore Roosevelt, with a face recognized by millions from photographs and cartoons and a life of popular legend. For one performance in Oklahoma, sixty-five thousand spectators traveled by train and crowded into bleachers to see him kill a buffalo.[65] So ecstatic were citizens at seeing him ride by in Roosevelt's inauguration parade ("Hooray for Geronimo!") that a disgusted member of the inaugural committee complained the Apache seemed to be "Public Hero No. 2," as if the celebration were Geronimo's installation in public office as well the new president's.[66] Yet oddly, his mass fame had already begun to build when he was still an insurgent battling U.S. troops as an avowed enemy. "When he surrendered," observed one of the scouts he had fought, "he had been doing his [recent] brand of renegade stuff for about nine years, and during all of those years an innumerable throng of enthusiastic press agents vied with each other in spreading the name and fame of Geronimo, not only throughout the United States, but throughout the civilized world wherever newspapers were read."[67]

One can only speculate as to why the man dubbed "the Apache terror" became so significant, even beloved, an international figure. Roach's discussion of "the celebrity as effigy," however, offers a relevant frame of analysis. Performers, especially when they signify pressing "relationships of difference," are often simultaneously despised and revered. The potential for triggering contradictory emotions is something of a prerequisite for outsized fame; celebrity status is more likely to descend on figures able to project "strength and vulnerability" in the same public appearance. It is this instability of meaning, according to Roach, that allows a celebrity to do the work of conferring an "illusory fullness of being" on the mass audience that he or she attracts, mobilizing a "simultaneous push and pull at the margins of collective identity" that gives a stability to the center.[68]

Certainly few could match Geronimo as a figure of strength. And when "the tiger of the human race" became a prisoner of the state, the result seems to have been a new quality of vulnerability shadowing and thus highlighting his displays of strength.[69] Noting that "a lot of people was really scared of [Geronimo]," an Iowa Indian named Blaine Kent recalled watching the line of people who would walk past Geronimo selling photographs of himself as he sat at a table with "a ball and chain on him down around the ankle" and "guards behind him with guns, too."

> Old Man Geronimo, well he has good sense just like anybody else in putting on a show. . . . He was sitting there and people come by. . . . He don't say a word. Just look right at them. Don't smile. Don't laugh or nothing. Somebody will come along, look at his picture, and throw down a dollar bill, maybe a five dollar bill, and he grabbed that and stick it in a pocket. Won't even give them any change back.

The commander at Fort Sill where Geronimo was imprisoned complained that "the old Apache deserved to be hanged rather than spoiled by so much attention from civilians.'"[70] But the public attention was not a reward for supposed crimes; rather, the contradiction he appeared to embody—a still fearsome warrior held in chains—is likely to have made Geronimo a unique mediator of collective feeling.

The comments from Blaine Kent suggest Geronimo was in on the act—that he was not an unwitting bystander inured to his own celebrity but rather that he understood intimately the marketplace for the exhibition of Indians. Geronimo became adept at extracting money for his fame, selling the buttons off his coat, from an ever-replenishing supply, and learning to print his name in order to sell autographs. He eventually added handmade bows and arrows to his inventory. To his biographers, Geronimo's willingness to sell artifacts of himself reflects a wily entrepreneurial streak they find ironic or bemusing—the warrior-turned-Apache Willie Loman.[71] But it seems evident that Geronimo understood a good deal more than his biographers did about the conditions of Indian publicity. The dictation process of his "book-making" and the content of his book itself silently explicate those conditions and show that Geronimo, like Roosevelt, keenly understood that celebrity is not an identity but a currency that can be traded for returns not limited to money.

Geronimo never sought his fame as a goal in itself. He had no wish to publish his life story and turned down the proposal until Barrett offered money. Nor did Geronimo go willingly to the expositions at Omaha and Buffalo. Barrett reveals this fact only in a brief footnote that acknowledges Geronimo was "sullen and took no interest in things" during much of his time at Fort Sill (162). But this revelation of Geronimo's hostile indifference is hard to reconcile with the chapter describing his visit to the St. Louis World's Fair, an engaged, detailed account of many of the sights and sounds on the Midway. Even more striking, the St. Louis chapter—which comes after several chapters of often bitter denunciation of U.S. deceptions and poor treatment of the Apaches by the government—concludes with a tribute to the white American public: "I am glad I went to the Fair," he declares. "I saw many interesting things and learned much from the white people. They are a very kind people and peaceful people. During all the time I was at the fair no one tried to harm me in any way" (161–62). By including this gloss, Geronimo rewrites the distinction between the state and civil society as the difference between sources of potential "harm" (soldiers and agents) and sources of relative safety and amity (the "peaceful people" he met at the fair). This distinction, then, appears to identify a public sphere in the traditional sense—an open space or context for the voluntary association of an audience of strangers. At the same time, however, Geronimo reminds the reader that he was accompanied at all times by armed guards ("The Government sent guards with me when I went [to the Midway shows], and I was not allowed to go anywhere without them" [156]); for *him* the domains of state and civil society are merely two dimensions of a larger social system of carceral confinement. In Geronimo's America, the penitentiary and commercial fairgrounds are superimposed spaces: they are not identical geographies but also not discrete spheres. He may address "peaceful people," but there is no distinct public sphere in which his words or other expressive forms are able to break free from a context of state power.

In explaining the gap between Geronimo's "sullen" resistance and his apparent change of heart, Barrett points to Geronimo's religious conversion: "The St. Louis Exposition was held after he adopted the Christian religion and had begun to try to understand our civilization" (162). But Barrett's explanation does not answer why Geronimo stresses his *inability* to understand white ways, especially his supposed ignorance of the mechanical rides and Midway stage shows that Geronimo almost surely had seen at earlier fairs. In his book he writes with bewilderment of the "little house" that moves (a Ferris wheel) and the odd "canoe" (Shoot-the-Chute) he finds too unstable to set foot in. By the time of the St. Louis fair, Geronimo's third such exposition, the mechanical rides and stage shows could no longer have been the mysteries he depicts. But Geronimo emerges in this chapter as a version of the uncomprehending Indian warrior, one who is overawed even by the mechanical entertainments beloved by white children—a legendary fighter who confesses that a Shoot-the-Chute "looked too fierce to me" (160). It is impossible to say whether this textual version of the unknowing Indian was subtly shaped by Barrett or whether Geronimo was knowingly reprising in print a role he knew played well in public arenas. In either case, Geronimo's print appearances—as an inside guide to Apache life, a savvy warrior, and a show Indian—were popular roles that pleased the white public Geronimo had come to know well.

Still unanswered, though, is why the once angry and indifferent Geronimo would agree to exhibit himself at all, whether at fairs or in print. The chance to earn badly needed money was likely a partial motive. And as a prisoner, of course, he was not able to refuse the directives of authorities when they chose to insist on show contracts.[72] But a stronger clue to his motivation lies with the book's final chapter, a direct appeal to Roosevelt, to whom the book is also dedicated: "I am thankful that the President of the United States has given me permission to tell my story. I hope that he . . . will read my story and judge whether my people have been rightly treated" (167). Although Geronimo seems closely attuned to a mass audience, and even characterizes that potential public in flattering terms, that public is finally not the audience he addresses most directly. Implicit in the formal features of the book is a pragmatic understanding of what sort of print artifact—the book equivalent of his coat buttons and autographed photos—will successfully circulate in a mass market. But for Geronimo himself, the book is an object of quasi-diplomatic value that he can offer to the head of state in hopes of gaining what he wants the most: permission from Roosevelt for the Apaches to travel back to their homeland. "Our people are decreasing in numbers here and will continue to decrease unless they are allowed to return to their native land. Such a result is inevitable" (169).

The final words of Geronimo's book show us the terms of this, his largest gambit.

Could I but see this [return] accomplished, I think I could forget all the wrongs that I have ever received, and die a happy contented old man. . . . If this cannot be done during my lifetime—if I must die in bondage—I hope that the remnant of the Apache tribe may, when I am gone, be granted the one privilege which they request—to return to Arizona. (169–70)

Here Geronimo expressly offers to trade a fiction of public contentment and balanced scales for the right of return for Apaches. There is additional evidence that this attempt at bartering his celebrity for the release of the surviving Apaches at Fort Sill was Geronimo's governing intention. Days after his appearance in the president's inaugural parade, Geronimo was allowed to meet with Roosevelt in person. The plea he makes at the end of his book echoes the request he made of Roosevelt at that recent face-to-face meeting: "Great Father, other Indians have homes where they can live and be happy. I and my people have no homes. The place where we are kept is bad for us. . . . We are sick there and we die. White men are in the country that was my home. I pray you tell them to go away and let my people go there and be happy."[73]

Officials at the War Department opposed Barrett's efforts to produce Geronimo's book; Barrett had to acquire direct permission from Roosevelt to override their authority.[74] It was Geronimo's mass appeal, and perhaps Roosevelt's sense of celebrity kinship with the warrior, that gave him access to public speech—speech that is sometimes sharply critical of the United

States—and even allowed Geronimo to make direct appeals to the head of state. But if Geronimo's fame gave him the means to lobby the president, his mode of address also shows how far this form of speech is from the kind of diplomatic speech that is expressive of national sovereignty. "Great Father, my hands are tied as with a rope," he said to Roosevelt at their meeting in Washington. "I will tell my people to obey no chief but the Great White Chief. I pray you to cut the ropes and make me free."[75] His capture and exhibited charisma has made him a "public hero" with a public voice, but Geronimo can only concede Roosevelt's controlling authority over the Apaches and plead his case as a prisoner of war.

Yet even as Geronimo acknowledges the absence of a recognized Apache sovereignty, at this site of ruined diplomatic orature Geronimo is still able to speak of and for the Apaches as a nation, invoking the conditions that are the foundation of national life ("our native land"), stating his rationale for defying the government (the president's "people desired the country of my people"), and bearing witness to the illness and early death of many of the Chiricahuas held at Fort Sill.[76] Unlike the chiefs in Barnum's show, Geronimo has no illusion that he will be received as the emissary of a rights-bearing people; in fact, he is at pains to make sure that his audience sees that he is a captive who is held against his will. But implicit in his self-representation is both an analysis of his celebrity status and an attempt to refashion it by bringing diplomatic expression to a space of Indian exhibition and imprisonment from which diplomacy had been exiled.

Geronimo's analytic interest in performance is evident in the close attention he gives to other Midway acts in St. Louis. It seems more than coincidental that all the performers Geronimo mentions are brown or black people. He describes Turks ("strange men with red hats") who demonstrate flashing swordplay (156); unfamiliar Native peoples he joins for a roping contest; the "little brown people"—indigenous Iggorrotes from the Philippines—"that the United States troops captured on some islands far away," and others (160). What interests him most about the "strange people" is not their color or caste per se but something that might be described as a comparative racial agency. Which performers possess the greatest skill and strength? Who has a keener eye? The Turks with their scimitars earn Geronimo's respect: "They would be hard to kill in a hand-to-hand fight" (156). He dismisses the Iggorrotes as substandard performers who should not have been invited to appear at the fair. Geronimo gives particularly close attention to a black escape artist who manages to free himself from the ropes that bind him. His curiosity about these acts seems partly vocational, an insider's appraisal of the abilities of fellow performers. But alert as he is to his own conditions of captivity, his observations also suggest an attempt to study and calibrate the skills on display in relation to a background of controlling white power. Geronimo could not have viewed as insignificant the fact that the Iggorrotes, whom he scorns for their feeble drumming and dancing, were from a tribe that had been captured by U.S. troops in a faraway homeland. By the same token, Geronimo's description of the black escape artist resonates as the tale of a racial captive.

> In another show, there was a strange-looking negro. The manager tied his hands fast, then tied him to a chair. He was securely tied, for I looked myself, and I did not think it was possible for him to get loose. He twisted in his chair for a moment, and then stood up; the ropes were still tied but he was free. I do not understand how this was done. It was certainly a miraculous power, because no man could have released himself by his own efforts. (156)

Attended by his guards, Geronimo watches a black man release himself with neither the help nor the hindrance of the manager who bound him. The performance revises the alchemic combination of strength and vulnerability that is behind Geronimo's celebrity: Geronimo must ask Roosevelt to "cut the ropes and make me free" (and is refused), but the escape artist slips his bonds himself. Though it is based on illusion, the performance still allows onlookers to see a special ability by which the artist transcends the carceral constraint he simultaneously insists that they acknowledge. This species of "miraculous" agency cannot exist apart from the stage, but the performance concretely realizes the deep wish for release and sovereignty that motivates Geronimo's "book-making" and that gives material shape to his appearance in print.

Public speech and performance can make intelligible what is counterfactual. Like all aesthetic expression, these are forms of agency that have no direct control over levers of power but have the ability to make visible and literally *sensible* new forms of expressive meaning that then can become part of a shared social imaginary. Geronimo's book, like all speech in the public sphere, has no political agency in itself; but like the escape artist's ability to free himself from bondage, his book is able to hold up before an audience a counterfactual possibility: recognition and restoration of the sovereignty of Apache nationhood. For all of Geronimo's fame, his contemporaries did little to acknowledge or protect that sovereignty; the idea of mobilizing U.S. armed forces to protect land rights promised to Indian peoples was all but unthinkable.[77] But Geronimo's literary public would come to include future readers like Leslie Marmon Silko (who would make the trickster performer Geronimo a character in fiction) as well as critics and scholars of a future discipline, Native American literary studies.[78] In and of themselves, these publics cannot bring about the recognition of Apache sovereignty either. But they do give a life in letters to an alternative sense of justice, extending and renewing the damaged diplomatic overture Geronimo made when he addressed Roosevelt in the hope that "he will cause my people to receive justice in the future."[79]

Chapter 5
Black Bohemia and the African American Novel

In 1900, the debut issue of the *Colored American Magazine* featured an essay on Leo Gowongo, "A Magician of Note." "He is a native of Antigua, B.W.I., with a mixture of Hindoo and Negro blood," an editor explains, "a young man of pleasing appearance, with piercing eyes, and whose every action shows energy and intelligence."[1] Readers are invited to assess this pleasing appearance for themselves: the article includes four photographs of Gowongo performing in his tailored black tuxedo. The evident pleasure the *Colored American Magazine* editors take in Gowongo's polished professionalism may well reflect the importance the black elite invested in public achievement. And yet, as a professional entertainer, Gowongo also places the figure of the successful "New Negro" in a somewhat different context than critics have used to assess the politics of cultural uplift.[2] This man of "energy and intelligence" qualifies as a suitable representative of the race, but he is not a public figure in the manner of a writer, businessman, or political activist. Rather, his status as a public man is based solely on his ability to *appear* in public—his ability to command attention, admiration, and profit by presenting his person before an audience of strangers. (The published photographs not only confirm his public status, they restage and extend it into print culture.) Because of his distinct relation to commercial culture, Gowongo can begin to illuminate in new ways the opportunities and dangers of entering public space in Jim Crow America.

As a magician, Gowongo joins two cultural types, the folkloric trickster and the modern black entertainer, both of whom risk racial stigma or punishment in order to perform a display of exceptional skills. By performing as a black showman, Gowongo will necessarily share a close proximity to the blackface minstrel. Whereas the minstrel banks on public blackness as a source of entertaining ridicule, the black performer stakes a claim to public space as a site of professional skill and financial reward, and Gowongo, with his tuxedo and glossy photographs, stands at the nexus of a high-stakes contest that masks itself as leisure entertainment. African American entertainers in this moment venture into commercial theater, music, and dance for gain and recognition, but they do so when public visibility for black people is more charged than at any time in U.S. history. Black and white people both use mass culture as another space in which to play out a struggle over the meaning and limits of black civil agency after slavery. Career, money, and cultural power are the prizes, injury and abjection the risks.

Like other intellectuals in this moment, African American writers produced a penetrating critical analysis of mass culture. But for black intellectuals, this new network of cultural industries posed critical problems that went largely unrecognized by white thinkers. Commercial culture was threatening for African Americans in a quite literal way: the great capacity and reach of mass production flooded private homes and civil spaces with defamatory images of black people, reinventing minstrelsy for an age of mechanical reproduction. At the same time, for black intellectuals the existing domains of science and literary culture were far from secure institutional spaces in which to differentiate a discourse of public reason that would recognize black civility. Even mainstream magazines discovered profitable ways to trade on derisive manipulations of the black image. The illustrated magazine *Leslie's Weekly*, for instance, ran a series it called "The Blackville Gallery," which placed mocking captions beneath photographs of poor African Americans, and the feature quickly became popular with white readers.[3] Looking back at this turn-of-the-century moment, Langston Hughes saw a catch-22 logic waiting for the black writer: precisely by making a bid for literary authorship, one would likely be marked with a status akin to the lowest of mass amusement performers. When Paul Laurence Dunbar published his dialect verse, the white world responded with the "encouragement one would give a sideshow freak (a colored man writing poetry! How odd!) or a clown (How amusing!)."[4]

For black intellectuals, mass culture was less an invasion or corruption of a sphere of public reason than an arena that magnified and, in some respects, clarified what was already at stake when black people ventured into public life. African American writers found that in *both* traditional publics and spaces of mass spectacle, signs of one's civil identity were liable to convert in an instant into marks of criminal depravity, risible pretensions, or other forms of incivility. Their critical analysis brings a particular urgency and informed insight to the literary intellectual's self-designated office of scrutinizing mass culture conditions. But black writers simultaneously discovered that they can only conduct that analysis from outside high literary culture, at the site of a black counterpublic where the distinction between high and low culture gives way to new possibilities for reimagining the facts of race.

Chesnutt and the Limits of Realism

When Charles Chesnutt confided to his journal his hope to someday secure a place in "literature," he understood literature to offer both a professional vocation and an elevated future self. In this sense, Chesnutt was the first African American author to imagine himself in the terms Howells and James established institutionally for the fiction writer, terms in which the activity of novel writing could bespeak one's high artistic distinction and a matching professional standing. In a revealing turn of phrase, however, Chesnutt characterized that literary public as an incarnation of "the Northern mind." Chesnutt recognized high literary culture less as a freestanding order of excellence than a set of concrete tastes and intellectual habits that had a specific worldly location. The literary world to which he aspired was analytic, urban, and—from Chesnutt's point of view—regional. What was more, the "Northern mind," Chesnutt recognized, had become newly interested in "the southern Negro."[5] As a young black man in the South, Chesnutt had acquired his astute literary understanding against high odds; now the largely unlettered life of Southern African Americans had become an object of literary interest. Whether this state of things represented a professional advantage for Chesnutt (as he hoped) or an added liability (as he sometimes feared) was difficult to predict when he began to pursue publication in earnest in the 1880s.

His prospects were uncertain because the white Northern interest in African Americans was mercurial and mixed. Black folk life, like other rural cultures, had acquired an intellectual interest for some Northerners as a unique part of American vernacular history, and scholars and amateurs began collecting folk artifacts, stories, and beliefs for their ethnological value. Thomas Wentworth Higginson, for instance, became fascinated with Southern black folk songs, which he compared to "those strange plants seen in museums alone."[6] Chesnutt sometimes remarked dryly on the ethnological glamour that African American folk life held for Northerners. Both their fascination with black culture and their concern for the black plight, he observed, has something to do with their distant vantage: "Men are always more ready to extend their sympathy to those at a distance, than to the suffering ones in their midst." But Chesnutt was hopeful that the unique social position of African Americans in the South, recently liberated from slavery but struggling against a new Pharaoh, would interest Northern readers in his fiction: "they lend a willing ear to all that is spoken or written concerning their character, habits, etc."[7] The growing interest of the leading northeastern magazines in regionalism also enlarged the audience for fiction about the South.

Yet, along with these strains of social and ethnological interest, Northern readers possessed a literal economic interest in the South and its black population. The propertied classes in the North had been steadily investing in Southern land and industries since the end of the war, and as the Northern economy grew, so too did their Southern portfolios. Investors did indeed wish to know the "character, habits, etc." of Southern black people, but for very different reasons than Higginson's in his hunt for rare folk melodies. Finally, as economic ties grew stronger, white Northerners also began to evince a new species of *disinterest* in the South—that is, a growing tendency to look away from "the Negro Problem" in favor of more pleasing evocations of Southern pastoralism and a courtliness lost to the urban North.

Chesnutt's first significant publications reflect his close and canny study of these aspects of Northern interest in Southern life. The local color tales Chesnutt began publishing in 1887 bespeak a literary tact so finely tuned as to cross over into the tactical. Chesnutt's stories, collected in *The Conjure Woman* (1899), follow many of the narrative conventions established by authors of plantation fiction such as Thomas Nelson Page and Joel Chandler Harris, whose *Uncle Remus: His Songs and His Sayings* (1881) successfully collected African American folktales in a form of regionalist fiction. Like Uncle Remus, Chesnutt's Uncle Julius is a freedman with a rich collection of stories from his younger days on a plantation. The figure of the older black storyteller was indispensable: told from the point of view of a rustic black man, the pastoral scenes and black folkways from the Old South could be recalled fondly without necessarily suggesting a compromising sympathy with the vanquished slave system.

That potential difficulty was resolved—or at least evaded—through the vehicle of black speech, the instrument of dialect. The typography of black dialect usually strikes present-day readers as tortured and denigrating, but it was precisely the opacity of the printed "black" speech that served for Chesnutt's contemporaries as a linguistic sieve to separate ethnological meanings from the abjection of slavery. Chesnutt mastered these forms and likewise their regionalist appeal. As Caroline Gebhard has argued, for an author who could *also* demonstrate a mastery of high literary writing, an ability to write dialect offered a significant form of cultural capital.[8] By excelling at dialect and a literary representation of the South, Chesnutt also proved his intellectual mastery of the region that was the "Northern mind." Chesnutt's first conjure tales appeared in the *Atlantic*, and the collected volume was published by the premier Boston firm of Houghton Mifflin.

What distinguishes Chesnutt's tales from others in the genre, however, is the way a canny assessment of the "Northern mind" is actually the subject or content of the stories themselves. In each successive tale, Uncle Julius recounts a different incident of plantation conjuring—a magical spell or charm that turns human beings into objects like trees and animals—to two white listeners, John and Annie. This married couple from the North had purchased a grape vineyard and moved to North Carolina. Like Chesnutt's readers, the two white Northerners are drawn to Julius's lore as strange or picturesque tales from a vanished way of life. Uncle Julius himself is no conjurer and never claims to be. But so skillful is Julius in understanding the psychology of his listeners—John's self-satisfied sense of property and rationality, Anne's readiness to suspend disbelief in return for the pleasures of sentiment—that his tales always manage to win from them some prized object or opportunity.

Julius's verbal dexterity, then, is its own form of charm or occult ability, and Chesnutt redoubles its ironic power by making the conventions of plantation fiction obliquely expose the violence and humiliation at the heart of Southern slavery. In "Po' Sandy," for instance, Julius tells of a slave he once knew who could not bear to be separated from his wife. On the eve of his being sold away from the plantation, Sandy asks his wife to use her conjuring power to turn him into a pine tree so that he will not have to leave her. She does so, turning him back into a man each night under the cover of darkness. One fateful day, however, Sandy is cut down for lumber. "When she seed de stump standin' dere, wid de sap runnin' out'n it," Julius recounts, "en de limbs layin' scattered roun', she nigh 'bout went out'n her min."[9] The trope of conjure allows Chesnutt to realize in fantastic terms the dehumanization of chattel slavery without erasing the man's human subjectivity. In an act of subtle analysis, the bleeding sap and the horrific accuracy of the severed tree "limbs" use dialect imagery to pinpoint the irrational realism of slavery's living property and the violence of its dehumanizing conceit.

Despite the darker undertones of many of the stories, reviewers praised their ability to "charm." It is a fitting term, if inadvertently so: Chesnutt's own writerly dexterity was a kind of literary charm or transformation that allowed him to use his knowledge of the psychology of a Northern audience to win interest and sales. Like other African American authors, Chesnutt was drawn to figures of occult or exceptional power: the conjurer, the trickster, the wily storyteller—all figures who hide canny, unsuspected abilities in the guise of a more benign-seeming capacity to entertain white people. But crucially, Chesnutt's own power was to be the exceptional agency of the literary, the secular magic that distinguished high art from mere writing. Without disavowing a kinship with the vernacular storyteller, he still relies on a hierarchical distinction between the ex-slave Uncle Julius and Chesnutt's own standing as a man of letters. He relies, in other words, on the difference of the literary, on the concentrated capacity for analytic discovery and critical vision cultivated in a history of narrative convention and style, in order to express what an impoverished freedman had neither the intellectual training nor the social protection to say. The sphere of the literary, Chesnutt believed, would allow him to directly address the civil relations of the contemporary South as no black or white author before him had done.

To that end, Chesnutt quickly set his sights on other genres. "I think I have about used up the old Negro who serves as mouthpiece," he wrote in a letter of 1889, "and I shall drop him in future stories, as well as much of the dialect."[10] His aim was not merely to make a name for himself as an author of the highest kind of narrative art. Like the advocates of realism, Chesnutt also believed that high aesthetic achievement could subtly change and develop what Henry James called the "civic imagination." For Chesnutt, the imperative task was the "elevation of the Whites." Whatever their station or even their goodwill, white people in America were held back from "moral progress" by a "subtle almost indefinable feeling of repulsion toward the negro." Believing with other proponents of high art that literary forms work at the deepest levels of inwardness, Chesnutt had faith that literature could help effect a crucial social shift in the "public mind": "The negro's part is to prepare himself for social recognition and equality; and it is the province of literature to open the way for him to get it—to accustom the public mind to the idea; and while amusing them to lead people out, imperceptibly, unconsciously, step by step to the desired state of feeling."[11]

At this juncture, artistic achievement and civil advancement (in large part through *white* uplift) were compatible goals in Chesnutt's mind, and he was certain that the literary public sphere—the "province of literature"—was a public region in which African Americans would acquire recognition for their civil equality.

Once *The Conjure Woman* volume appeared, Chesnutt began publishing works about contemporary life in more of a realist vein. In 1899 Houghton brought out a collection of his short stories, *The Wife of His Youth and Other Tales of the Color Line* (1899), and soon after issued his first novel, *The House Behind the Cedars* (1900). But in November 1898, as these works were being readied for print, an incident of mass violence against African Americans occurred in Wilmington, North Carolina, an event that left Chesnutt "deeply concerned and very much depressed." He wrote to Walter Hines Page, the white editor of the *Atlantic,* that the attack was "an outbreak of pure, malignant, and altogether indefensible race prejudice, which makes me feel personally humiliated, and ashamed for the country and the state."[12] The massacre galvanized Chesnutt to write a new novel, *The Marrow of Tradition*, a fictional examination of the November election fraud and subsequent riot that weaves the stories of fictional families around a quite accurate retelling of the real political firestorm.

In *Marrow of Tradition,* Chesnutt returns to the question of the mixed and wavering interest of a Northern audience in the material—both economic and literary—of the South. But in *Marrow,* Chesnutt produces a fundamental shift in the way he represents "the Northern mind." In this novel Northern observers are no longer a body of passive readers, consumers looking for picturesque glimpses into another way of life. Now they are also the producers of knowledge about the real, the sociologically minded analysts who examine the South to try to determine the truth about race relations and economic conditions. Yet as Chesnutt's plot unfolds, this realist Northern mind is shown to be the credulous audience of a white-authored show of staged humbug, and spectacle proves all too compatible with the instruments of Northern realism.

Before the outbreak of open violence in the novel, the narrator describes a visit to Wellington (Chesnutt's fictional name for Wilmington) by a group of Northern observers.

A party of Northern visitors had been staying for several days at the St. James hotel. The gentlemen of the party were concerned in a projected cotton mill, while the ladies were much interested in the study of social conditions, and especially in the negro problem. As soon as their desire for information became known, they were taken courteously under the wing of prominent citizens and their wives.[13]

What follows is a series of "elaborate luncheons" and field trips that allow the Northern delegation to see and discuss these local social conditions in the company of their white hosts. "Whether accidentally or not," the narrator notes dryly, "the Northern visitors had no opportunity to meet or talk alone with any colored person in the city except the servants at the hotel"— these, however, "seemed happy enough" (556). A Northern delegation, prepared to study and analyze social conditions, has become the unwitting audience for a rigged show. What they see in their guided visits to a selected black church, a mission school, and other sites is the "spectacle of a dying race, unable to withstand the competition of a superior type" (555).

Although critical categories like "types" are supposed to allow an analyst to ascertain the real, here they actually help reproduce and rationalize an elaborately staged "spectacle" of a deficient race. Chesnutt's narrator becomes the ironic ventriloquist for a manufactured realist narrative about the "degeneracy" of the current descendants of the loyal Negroes who had flourished under slavery. It is a sad tale of the largely futile attempts at black education and of the unnamed crimes by certain black men that have brought on the "rough but still substantial justice" of lynching (555). The sorrowful story, however, has a happier aspect: whatever the burdens on white people, the black people are more than content. "Surely a people who made no complaints could not be very much oppressed" (556).

This live action drama of "local conditions," then, is really white fiction dressed up in blackface. Chesnutt underscores the point brilliantly when he makes the last stop on the visitors' itinerary an actual show.

> In order to give the visitors, ere they left Wellington, a pleasing impression of Southern customs, and particularly of the joyous, happy-go-lucky disposition of the Southern darky and his entire contentment with existing conditions, it was decided by the hotel management to treat them, on the last night of their visit, to a little diversion, in the shape of a genuine negro cakewalk. (556)

In this "little diversion" of a genuine cakewalk, African Americans are unwittingly made to perform their own political contentment, in the form of a literal performance of black folk practice. As Chesnutt presents it, all dimensions of Northern interest in the South, from economic investigation (masculine fact-finding) to questions of race relations (feminine social concern) have been diverted by white fictions of race relations and the manipulation of pleasing black customs. The costs of this diversion, Chesnutt insists, are potentially catastrophic, and as the plot unfolds he makes his indictment even sharper: the cakewalk performance supplies the means for a white man in blackface to pin his capital crimes on a black man, an act that starts a contagion of violence.

In this, the most realist of Chesnutt's novels, he demonstrates the skepticism about theatrical spectacle that we would expect of a protégé of Howells. But Chesnutt's analysis emphasizes what critics like Howells tend to downplay, namely, the extraordinary appetite mass audiences had not just for fantasy but for commercial displays of the real. Wax museums, true-crime magazines, photographic entertainment ranging from stereographs to cinema, Cody's re-creation of actual Plains battles—these and innumerable other modes of mass entertainment proved the immense profitability of what Miles Orvell calls the "appetite for replication" and Vanessa Schwartz calls "the public taste for reality" at the turn of the century. Schwartz emphasizes the new conditions of urban modernity that made everyday experience seem more factitious; "real life was experienced as a show at the same time that shows became increasingly lifelike."[14] However much urban life may have helped generate a taste for the real, rural lifeways and "authentic" exotic customs were among the most avidly reproduced and consumed products.

Authenticity helped make the Old South a lucrative brand. Alongside its timber, cheap labor, and other resources, the South had become a leading exporter of "pleasing customs" to international audiences. The cakewalk, a tradition of competitive dancing rooted in black plantation culture, was a favorite entertainment in the Northern states as well as in Europe. Madison Square Garden would draw thousands of people to watch black dancers compete for top prizes. Elaborate re-creations of plantation life, including massive "panoramas" of Old South scenes, toured widely in the North and West and were featured at world fairs. One gigantic show billed as "Darkest America," which toured throughout the country in the same year as the Wilmington massacre, was produced by an all-black cast and management, and featured a sugar plantation, a cotton gin, a prizefight, and a black ballroom scene, to mention only a few of the extensive sets. Sheet music, minstrel shows, and stage dramas were likewise cultural products that circulated in a national market for antebellum figures and scenes.[15]

Although Northern interest in Southern vernacular life had provided Chesnutt with a point of entry into the literary marketplace, his sense of personal and political humiliation at the Wilmington massacre seems to have altered sharply his perspective on "the Northern mind." In the wake of the massacre, Chesnutt analyzes the "pleasing" re-creations of Southern life with a sense of urgency and alarm. As presented in *The Marrow of Tradition*, these white pleasures cannot be separated from a complex web of other passions—sexual panic, supremacist rage, fury at black ownership, a sense of righteous indignation that fuels a political coup and a racial massacre. The mass production of racial realness has unveiled the racist desires behind what now appears to be either the pretense or the impotence of Northern discourses of social fact and type.

The novel left Chesnutt's own Northern audience taken aback. The reviews in the leading literary magazines had little praise for it and sales were tepid. Despite his earlier enthusiasm for Chesnutt's fiction, Howells wrote a review that was decidedly mixed, calling the novel a "bitter, bitter" book even as he conceded that Chesnutt's portrait of Southern race relations was wholly just and "presented with great power." Most strikingly, Howells assessed Chesnutt's ability as a novelist in terms that cast the author as a black stage entertainer.

> Mr. Chesnutt, it seems to me, has lost literary quality in acquiring literary quantity, and though his book, "The Marrow of Tradition," is of the same strong material of his earlier books, it is less simple throughout, and therefore less excellent in manner. At his worst, he is no worse than the higher average of the ordinary novelist, but he ought always to be very much better for he began better, and he is of that race that must first get rid of the cakewalk, if it will not suffer from a smile that is more blighting than any frown. He is fighting a battle, and it is not for him to pick up the cheap graces and poses of the jouster.[16]

According to Howells's trope, Chesnutt should be waging the battle for recognition within the domain of realism but has succumbed instead to playing the cakewalk performer who traffics in mannered "poses."

The review enacts a puzzling slippage: qualified praise for Chesnutt's "power" gives way to a put-down for presenting the "cheap graces" of a racial clown, while disapproval at Chesnutt's bitterness turns into an accusation that he offered up a damning "smile." How is it that Chesnutt's most skeptical evaluation of racial theater earns for him this comparison with the black minstrel? *The Marrow of Tradition* clearly subscribes to the Howellsian tenets that define worthy fiction as the literary corrective for the distortions of mass spectacle. Perhaps no other work of fiction in the era offers a more pointed examination of the emergent institutions, from the national press syndicate to mass entertainment, that were drawing together all regions of the country in a single national market. Howells had previously criticized blackface minstrelsy for its willful projection of a theatrical "lie" that appealed to sensation; Chesnutt can be said to have expanded Howells's criticism into a full-length novel, with a plot intended to reveal the harm to lives, families, and American civil relations from the racial spectacles reuniting North and South at the expense of African Americans. Yet in response, Howells places *Marrow* at a remove from the highest "literary quality" and closer to the theatrical gestures of a black stage performer.

The answer to the puzzle lies in Chesnutt's reinterpretation of the nature of mass spectacle. Chesnutt goes much further than Howells in his critique of the lie of minstrelsy and argues American civil relations are themselves shot through with minstrelsy's exploitative use of the black body as spectacle. The fault, then, cannot be pinned on a distortion of the real in the sphere of commercial culture. Rather, Chesnutt points to minstrelsy and other white manipulations of black life for the truth they expose about civil society more broadly, the reality that under the rule of Jim Crow all black people who enter any kind of public space must present themselves as a racial spectacle or sign—as a human stigma. Even in a literary public, a black subject risks a slippage from critic to hapless racial performer.

Two related moments in *Marrow* make this point most powerfully. The first comes when the innocent black man, Sandy, has been framed for a murder and presumptive rape, crimes that had really been committed by a white man who had disguised himself in blackface. Chesnutt's plot thus links minstrelsy with the literal theft of a black man's identity and to a criminal distortion of that identity into the phantasm of the black rapist. As the white people call for Sandy to be lynched, Chesnutt depicts the town reconstituting itself as an audience for a second racial show, another spectacle created from the appropriation of a black body. "Already the preparations were under way for the impending execution," the narrator explains.

A T-rail from the railroad yard had been procured, and men were burying it in the square before the jail. Others were bringing chains, and a load of pine wood was piled in convenient proximity. Some enterprising individual had begun the erection of seats from which, for a pecuniary consideration, the spectacle might be more easily and comfortably viewed. . . . Railroads would run excursions from the neighboring towns in order to bring spectators to the scene; . . . Several young men discuss[ed] the question of which portions of the negro's body they would prefer for souvenirs. (634)

Chesnutt never gives this audience their wished-for spectacle; his plot averts the lynching at the last minute. What he makes visible instead is the avidity of a white community to become spectators at the death of a black man as a sensational visual event.

Northerners are part of this audience as well. Chesnutt emphasizes that the mass press creates its own version of the anticipated lynching as a spectacle in print: "All over the United States the Associated Press had flashed the report of another dastardly outrage by a burly black brute,—all black brutes it seems are burly,—and of the impending lynching with its prospective horrors. This news, being highly sensational in its character, had been displayed in large black type on the front pages of the daily papers" (645). Newsprint itself is here a visual spectacle: like the story it tells, the large type reproduces "the negro's body" in inked letters as a display of sensational blackness. These visual artifacts, whether a blacked-up white man, a large newsprint headline, or a Jim Crow sign hanging in a railroad car, belong to the same family of signs: all circulate in public as material instances of black stigma. The doctrine finds its fullest logical expression in the theater of lynching, where the black body becomes the literally self-evident sign of his own racial abjection, with the body and stigmatic meaning made finally, wholly identical. The ability to turn body parts of a black person into private souvenirs bespeaks the African American's violent exclusion from civil society.

The other black townspeople in Wellington know how to interpret such signs perfectly.[17] As the preparations are made for the lynching, Chesnutt writes, there is a sudden "disappearance from public view" of the black population (603). For African Americans under Jim Crow, any appearance in public requires a de facto acceptance of the stigma of blackness, or what the dissenting opinion in the 1896 *Plessy v. Ferguson* case called "a badge of servitude." Minstrelsy and other forms of racial entertainment merely capitalize in various ways on the conditions that already obtain in civil society.

Chesnutt's other dilation on this theme comes in his representation of the riot. For all its fury and confusion, the hours-long rampage (planned in advance by white supremacists) is still a form of deliberate racial spectacle. Chesnutt's protagonist, the black physician Miller, is hurrying through the streets during the violence when he is shocked by the sight of a black man's corpse. What he "shuddered at was not so much the thought of death, to which his profession had accustomed him," the narrator notes, "as the suggestion of what it signified." Miller realizes that the "dead body of a negro" defines the real role for the black person in public: to perform his own nonexistence as a black citizen. Hence, "the negroes seemed to have been killed, as the band plays in circus parades," the narrator remarks, "at the street intersections, where the example would be most effective" (687).

The corpse's "example" instructs Miller in the realism of racial spectacle. In that moment Miller realizes that his public life as a middle-class professional is a hollow fact with no social purchase. He had believed that his education and accomplishments would elevate his status and help advance the cause of African Americans, but the "circus"-like display of abjection is the only black role that can receive any public recognition, at least as long as white supremacists control public space and print media. From one perspective, *The Marrow of Tradition* is the most far-reaching instance of the realist ambition to use literary distinction to critically penetrate mass spectacles. Chesnutt uses that critical insight about mass spectacle to profoundly reinterpret civil relations. The enormous postwar industry of commercial entertainment and communication, Chesnutt insists, is not an unreal world of capricious fantasy. It is not a sphere apart at all but rather a field of expressive conditions existing wholly within the civil relations of postbellum society and increasingly a chief engine of civil power and change. The problem with mass culture is that it is *too* real—it produces, distributes, and sells artifacts of the real that often anticipate if not also create social reality.

Chesnutt takes the critical powers of realist fiction, therefore, to a new level of insight. But from another perspective, Chesnutt's literary critique succeeds too well. Chesnutt had turned to Northern literary culture both to make his critique and to escape the professional straits he described for Miller. Unlike the segregated Southern public that obviated the professional authority of Dr. Miller, the "province of literature," Chesnutt believed, could supply a space of reflective difference for cultural criticism on questions for which Chesnutt possessed exceptional knowledge. And, as long as Chesnutt could secure contracts with publishers, he did practice that critical function. Howells recognized this fact in another subtly ambivalent formulation: "In that republic of letters, where all men are free and equal he stands up for his own people with a courage which has more justice than mercy in it."[18] Chesnutt speaks freely in the world of letters, it is true; but he does not entirely escape the conditions that bind his protagonist Miller. In writing a "bitter" novel, according to Howells, Chesnutt falls short of realism's requirement for the "passionless handling" of social material. And yet in the same breath Howells acknowledges that any novelist, black or white, could not write about an "atrocity" against his race without some degree of passion.

I am not saying that [Chesnutt] is so inartistic as to play the advocate; whatever his minor foibles may be, he is an artist whom his stepbrother Americans may well be proud of; but while he recognizes pretty well all the facts in the case, he is too clearly of a judgment that is made up. One cannot blame him for that; what would one be one's self? If the tables could once be turned, and it could be that it was the black race which violently and lastingly triumphed in the bloody revolution at Wilmington, North Carolina, a few years ago, what would not we excuse to the white man who made the atrocity the argument of his fiction?[19]

Unable to be sufficiently detached, Chesnutt is judged too histrionic ("bitter, bitter") to qualify as a realist. He is, in other words, too much of "the race that must rid itself of the cakewalk"—he is too black—to signify as an author of the highest "literary quality" on a subject as politically charged as Jim Crow oppression. And yet this passion is also to his credit: for who would not write a bitter book, Howells asks, if he were black? But even this recognition of equal feeling posits an inequality of professional standing when literary quality rests on "passionless handling." To reveal oneself as bitter is to reveal oneself as black, and to be a black author is to be racially excluded from the detached objectivity that is Howells's prerequisite for realist analysis. Even within high literary culture, then, Chesnutt remains racially marked, a "stepbrother" with the artistic liability of his race's civil subjugation.

With considerable precision, Chesnutt's career traces both the critical powers and the racial limits of realist analysis.[20] Howells had defined realism as the analytic representation of civil relations; but at the point at which civil relations turn into civil abjection—the point when the stigma of Jim Crow abjection is imposed through a national consensus effected in the law, in public streets, and in mass media—writing high literary realism becomes impossible for a black author. Chesnutt was admitted to the "republic of letters" yet judged a professional stepchild unless he could somehow write of American civil relations with neither partisan anger nor the cakewalker's smile. Neither seems to have been a possible path for Chesnutt (or for any other African American aspirant to the high literary novel in this moment), and he largely retreated from writing for the northeastern literary public. After the publication of *Marrow of Tradition,* Chesnutt dropped his literary career to devote himself to the stenography business he owned. And in that commercial sphere, where writing entailed the formal reproduction of others' words, Chesnutt found wealth and professional success.

Commercial Improvisations: Black Bohemia and the Unwritten Epic

The minister Charles H. Parkhurst of New York was certain that African Americans would be a pariah race kept forever outside American civil society: "they never, never, never will contribute, in any part, toward forming the national type of the Americans of the future."[21] Chesnutt was equally adamant (at least in 1900) that African Americans would someday join with white Americans in "a complete racial fusion." His essay "The Future American" (1900), published in three parts in the *Boston Evening Transcript,* predicts that "slowly and obscurely" the Caucasian, Negro, and Indian populations in the United States will together create a single "American race." Despite their diametric predictions, Parkhurst and Chesnutt understood race in the same general terms: both saw blackness as a biological identity currently at odds with a "national" race. Chesnutt, of course, believed this state of things unjust, and in his essay he makes a point of noting that "color" in the United States reflected "a social structure" only. Skin color has "proved no test of race," and the notion of "a pure Aryan, Indo-European race has been abandoned in scientific circles." But he is convinced that biological race in its "popular sense" would remain a tacit foundation of the national identity. The makeup of the American race, however, will be transformed. In a far-distant time, he argues, the "Negro element" will have been so thoroughly absorbed into the general population that color will signify no social opprobrium, for all Americans will be a people of color, regardless of whether they are called white or something else.[22]

Chesnutt's understanding of race here, like Parkhurst's, is genetic and generational. By their reckoning, the facts of descent will determine over time the natural history of a single "American race." But in contrast with this racial realism, other representations of blackness, less tethered to categories of color and genetic descent, were emerging in the same moment from the spaces of mass culture, even as mass venues trafficked in some of the most racist depictions of African Americans. In theaters, dance halls, and commercial music it is possible to see the marks or signs of a denigrated blackness loosed from the logic of natural history and revalued as the material for creative expression. In stage performers like Leo Gowongo and the Broadway performer Aida Overton Walker, the grace and skillful gestures of a black body were able to speak a public corporeal language of "energy and intelligence." The expressivity that black entertainers discovered in commercial culture, of course, had only a limited ability to counter the racism that dominated most mass circulation. But the overdetermined interest in blackness evinced by mass culture also opened up possibilities for new public improvisations of the meaning of black lives and expression.[23]

Urban culture was central to the new improvisations of race. A new density of sites for commercial entertainment in major cities permitted black musicians, nightclub performers, and songwriters to make a living in show business, or at least to attempt it. In an 1887 *New York Sun* article, the Sixth Avenue district of midtown Manhattan was described as "black Bohemia," an area with clubs, dance halls, and cabarets that formed the African American cultural center for some decades before the rise of black Harlem. The writer and composer James Weldon Johnson recalled that alluring world of "Negro Bohemia" as a distinct area of clubs and other establishments "where one got a close-up of the noted Negro prize fighters and jockeys" as well as "theatrical performers." When Johnson re-created the district for his novel, he stressed that it was a location that generated a new kind of black celebrity, hosting the performers whose "names and faces were familiar on every bill-board in the country."[24] The billboard conspicuousness of black fighters and vaudevillians made the area a destination for pleasure seekers, while the concentration of black audiences drew aspiring performers and artists. Johnson, for instance, arrived in 1899 with hopes of producing a comic opera he had written with his brother. Beholden only to profit, mass culture rewarded novelty, visual flair, and self-display, and thereby produced a paradox: African American performers in New York, Chicago, and other urban centers discovered that racist styles and caricatures circulating in commercial culture yielded more easily to creative transformation than did the more staid racial typing of literary culture. Both Johnson and poet Paul Laurence Dunbar wrote novels about black Manhattan, works that highlight a creative tension between literary values and commercial culture that carried special relevance for African Americans.

Dunbar's novel, *The Sport of the Gods* (1901), portrays the ragtime clubs and theaters of New York as a vital but seductive world of potentially ruinous risks. In most respects, the novel was an unlikely work to come from Dunbar. Several books of poems, including *Oak and Ivy* (1892) and *Lyrics of Lowly Life* (1897), had established Dunbar's reputation as a deft poet of Southern scenes and vernacular language. When *The Sport of the Gods* appeared, the novel was a marked departure from the gentler tones of his other published works. If *The Marrow of Tradition* was "bitter," Dunbar's novel verged on nihilistic.

The Sport of the Gods follows a black family from its "own beloved section" in the South to a bewildering world in the urban North, the same journey masses of African American migrants were beginning to undertake.[25] Like Dreiser, Crane, and other novelists of modern city life, Dunbar finds an impersonal destructiveness concentrated in northern American cities. But the ruin of the Hamilton family begins in the South; urban life only extends and intensifies it. When Berry Hamilton is falsely accused of theft, his employer (and former master) has the man sent to the penitentiary and his family forced from their home. The Hamiltons' thrift, having steadily built up the family savings account, has only made them more vulnerable to the false accusation. Even crueler ironies follow. Berry's wife, Fannie, and teenaged son and daughter attempt a new life in New York ("a city that, like Heaven, to them had existed by faith alone" [43]), but they come to grief when a real crime—son Joe's murder of his lover—and family estrangement are the ultimate issue of the father's false imprisonment.

"Whom the gods wish to destroy," the narrator proclaims, "they first make mad" (50). Like the novel's title, the narrator's commentary sounds a note of tragic drama. The relentless misery visited upon the Hamiltons, however, is rooted in the work of white perfidy and betrayal, not the design of capricious gods. Dunbar uses allusions to Greek and Shakespearean tragedy to pointedly misname the white racism that causes the family's destruction. But the narrator's dark turn on ancient drama has a second significance as well. *The Sport of the Gods* is not only a caustic debunking of Southern local color myths but also, more subtly, a memorial to the unwritten high epic of black American life. Enslaved and then stigmatized, the mass of African Americans had been relegated to the "lowly life" of vernacular culture and shut out from what one white character calls "higher civilisation" in America (30). Thus the Hamiltons' arrival in New York is for Dunbar the grim start to what can be only an ironic form of tragic irony: the fall of the already low.

Awaiting them are the destructive worlds of "coon-show" theater and whiskey joints. "If he be wise," the narrator warns the "provincial" from the South, he will shun New York.

But if he be a fool, he will stay and stay on until the town becomes all in all to him. . . . Then he is hopeless, and to be elsewhere would be death. The Bowery will be his romance, Broadway his lyric, and the Park his pastoral, the river and the glory of it all his epic, and he will look down pityingly on all the rest of humanity. (47)

The pride of Joe Hamilton, a shallow dandy, and the dreams of Kitty Hamilton, an aspiring stage singer, are the poignant, self-damning ambitions of people who can know nothing else. Johnson, a friend of Dunbar, reported that the poet spoke with "self-reproach" of the limits of dialect writing, and surmised that his ambition had been "to write one or two long, perhaps epical, poems in straight English that would relate to the Negro."[26] Some scholars have questioned Johnson's account and suspect he misconstrued or overstated Dunbar's supposed self-condemnation of his dialect poetry.[27] But it remains the case that much of the power of Dunbar's blues tragedy (it has its own Tiresias in a drunk named Sadness) comes from the novel's deliberate disjunction between the "low" world of black Bohemia and the absent "glory" of a high black epic that is invoked but unwritten.

Despite the novel's marked indictment of black club life (a "social cesspool"), Dunbar himself was a leading figure in the rise of popular black theater. He created the "Senegambian Carnival" for the famous dance troupe of Bert Williams and George Walker who, with Walker's celebrated wife, Aida Overton Walker, became a phenomenal success in the United States and Britain. Dunbar's all-black musical *Clorindy, or The Origins of the Cakewalk,* written with Will Marion Cook, toured the country in 1898 and propelled the cakewalk into a national dance craze. Dunbar was thus a key figure in the transition that brought local black styles of music and dance into mass circulation.[28] When one knows this fact of Dunbar's biography, his novel's harsh judgment on black Bohemia (Kitty had formerly sung "simple old songs," but in New York she turns to "detestable coon ditties which the stage demanded" [74]) poses an apparent contradiction. Is it Dunbar, a successful theatrical songwriter, who finds these songs "detestable," or is it only his neo-Greek narrator? Does a displaced anger at restrictions imposed by white literary culture account for the Hamiltons' harsh degradation in black New York? Like the cruelty of white "gods" who destroy black lives for sport, Dunbar permits his characters no real escape from "dishonor" and isolation, as if to act out the ability of white literary authorities above him to insist that a black author keep to vernacular forms.

More suggestive, however, are the hints in *The Sport of the Gods* that Dunbar knew well the creative excitement in black urban culture, the "sense of triumph" (72) and exhilaration released in stylized expressions of black street life. When the Hamiltons are taken to a show on one of their first evenings in Manhattan, Dunbar's description of the music and dancing betrays an almost ineffable appeal the narrator is hesitant to admit. The performers are oddly costumed and poorly made-up, but "they could sing, and they did sing, with their voices, their bodies, their souls. They threw themselves into it because they enjoyed and felt what they were doing, and they gave almost a semblance of dignity to the tawdry music and inane words." Kitty is "enchanted." Joe is "lost, transfixed." Even their fretful mother is "divided between shame at the clothes of some of the women and delight with the music" (59). The moment seals their unhappy fates but the same instant supplies a "grand" feeling that gives them new hope and self-regard.

Dunbar clearly knew how to conjure strong feeling through popular song. Moreover, he was skilled enough to help turn minstrel traditions and stagecraft toward more artful productions. Like *Abyssinia, Sons of Ham, Octoroons,* and other black-authored shows, Dunbar's *Clorindy* was recognized as moving away from the coarser racism of white minstrelsy. This is "a coon show in name only," one white critic wrote of *Abyssinia,* for "in reality, it was a most serious near-grand opera for which we were totally unprepared."[29] Dunbar's reflections on black New York capture conflicted but generative divisions in black America—the divide between blocked ambitions for higher cultural expression and the profits from popular art; between a middle-class "dignity" always out of reach and a vital urban aesthetic that risked shame and stigma from its proximity to the low; and between the inhospitable conventions of high forms and the euphoric beauty of a street life that could also bring grief.

For Dunbar, these aesthetic divisions also seem to have represented personal conflicts. In a sketch Dunbar published in the *New York Sun,* "The Negroes of the Tenderloin," he depicts "careless, guffawing crowds" that threaten moral and social ruin, even as letters from Dunbar's fiancé (later his wife), the author Alice Dunbar-Nelson, urge him to give up his affinity for the "sporting" people and pastimes of that section of New York.[30] But whatever the source, the artifact of irony that was Dunbar's blues epic conducts an implicit analysis by way of its formal disjunctions. *The Sport of the Gods* bespeaks a sense of poetic exile from a high cultural authority, an aesthetic shadow that silently indicts the systemic exclusion of African Americans from full civil agency in the life of the polis. In contrast with the analysis conducted by authors like Howells who rely on a single set of civil relations to uncover the real, Dunbar represents the expressive power of a "low" aesthetic by framing it through what would have been an epic "glory" in a world ruled by other civil gods. At the same time, Dunbar's sharp sense of cultural and racial divisions is also the matrix for both narrative innovation and theatrical renovation.

While Dunbar's literary irony conducts a critical analysis of a divided civil society, his novel also hints at the fact that such extraliterary forms as blues laments and popular theater contain their own pragmatic analysis of commercial culture, generating a species of knowledge about race and racial signifiers that comes from commercial praxis itself. When Dunbar's Kitty Hamilton becomes a "celebrity" of the black stage, it portends ill; the novel's only other female performer, Kitty's mentor, Hattie, has just been murdered. But the real-life star of Dunbar's cakewalk musical *Clorindy*, Aida Overton Walker, enjoyed a markedly different fate. Although her early career was restricted to cabaret musicals like *The Cannibal King* and *A Lucky Coon*, Aida Walker was eventually heralded as an innovative choreographer and a performer in mainstream Broadway productions. *Variety* called her "the foremost Afro-American stage artist."[31] A career on the stage, though, violated the rules of propriety that many middle-class African Americans believed would help advance the race. "I am aware of the fact that many well-meaning people dislike stage life, especially our women," Walker wrote in a 1905 article in the *Colored American Magazine*. Urging bourgeois deportment and behavior, educated "race leaders" tended to shun the signatures of black identity—styles of speech, dress, and gesture—that white people had long distorted and ridiculed. But Walker in effect reversed this tactic, using theatrical self-display to reclaim signs of blackness as markers of modern grace and professional skill. Arguing that the contemporary stage was a true profession, Walker's essays in the *Colored American Magazine* present her career as precisely the sort of "uplift" work that dominated the black middle-class agenda. There are many "honest and well deserving men and women of color in professional life," she wrote of black entertainers, "who will compare favorably with men and women of other races in this profession or other professions." "Those before the lights must do their part," and we must "work together for the uplift of all."[32]

Asking black stage performance to signify bourgeois mobility was a tall order, however, when pleasure, profit, and sexuality were the undisguised energies of the urban stage. The break in Walker's early career came when, as a young unknown, she agreed to be photographed dancing the cakewalk for the American Tobacco Company's trading card. The other models for the photo shoot were a team from California who had recently arrived in New York, Walker and Williams. The trio that became the first black star entertainers thus had its origins in a commercial venture of the most straightforward kind, an advertisement; the mass reproduction of their stylized dance moves—the angled limbs, the costumes, and brown faces—were circulated purely for the sake of trade. But paradoxically, the commercial nature of urban black performance may have made it easier to detach and transform images of the black body in mass culture than was possible in other spheres. Aida Walker's beauty, for instance, and her savvy in presenting it, allowed her to refashion the sensual appeal of her stage roles in such a way that African American dance moves signified a transracial feminine charm. Her cakewalk steps, her Salome dance, and other movements were widely imitated, especially among affluent white women. In private lessons, public demonstrations, and magazine interviews, Walker transmitted her gestures and techniques ("don't forget your eyes, [for] a little flirtation— just a little—is a prime requisite") along these commercial routes to a large audience that not only consumed but also themselves performed her "black" styles.[33]

The success enjoyed by Aida and George Walker and Bert Williams was an anomaly. More often it was white performers and producers— Johnson called them "pirates"—who profited from popular interest in the innovative styles of African American performers. In addition to their easier access to mainstream venues and financial backers, white people could more freely negotiate elements of sexuality in the music and dances than could the black performers they imitated. In a 1906 interview Aida Walker noted that, while white companies featured love scenes in virtually every production, during her ten years in professional musicals "there has never been even the remotest suspicion of a love story in any of them" because of "popular prejudice against love scenes enacted by negroes."[34]

The color line fostered vigilance, on the stage as well as off. "You haven't the faintest conception of the difficulties which must be overcome," Walker said to her interviewer, "of the prejudices which must be left slumbering, of the things we must avoid whenever we write or sing a piece of music, put on a play or a sketch, walk out in the street or land in a new town. No white can understand these things, much less appreciate them."[35] Although black and white entertainers could perform the same "black" numbers, African American performers had to exercise a sharpened self-consciousness about the social meaning of possessing a brown body, whether on the stage or on a public street. The need for constant self-reflection was a burden. But it is also the case that "the ten thousand things we must think of every time we make a step," as Walker phrased it, gave black performers a unique analytic understanding of the nature of racial signs. Walker describes a pragmatic black social knowledge that inheres in an everyday repertoire of movement, posture, and gesture— knowledge that informs and animates black performance but is also shared by every African American. Black styles were marketable as well as punishable, exciting and upsetting, richly creative as well as vulnerable to racist ridicule. As a result, black performance was appropriated quite as often as it was disdained, and this highly dynamic field of meaning demonstrated that blackness was not the rooted biological identity proclaimed by scientists but a lived experience that was the basis of a separate form of knowledge.

Johnson's novel about black New York emphasizes the changeable nature of racial signs. *The Autobiography of an Ex-Colored Man* (1912) represents the division between high and low spheres not as the cruel snare that Dunbar depicted but rather as a permeable boundary, a cultural divide permitting forms of transmission even while it further segregates the civil valuation of black and white lives. Johnson's novel offers a second-order analysis: his literary form devises a way to articulate the pragmatic or implicit analysis enacted in black commercial performance.

Johnson's protagonist, a sheltered young man light-skinned enough to pass for white, arrives in Manhattan after an aborted college career in the South. Johnson is even more direct than Dunbar about the "fatally fascinating" power of the city: "To some natures this stimulant of life in a great city becomes a thing as binding and necessary as opium is to one addicted to the habit."[36] But "the Club" at the center of Johnson's novel (based on the real Ike Hine's place) is more than the haunt of drinkers and hustlers. Among its patrons are people like "the Doctor," an African American medical school student from Harvard unable to give up gambling, and the black "minstrel" who will "never essay anything below a reading from Shakespeare" when he accedes to requests to perform at the Club (65). White producers and performers who "made fortunes" from publishing ragtime and who "came to get their imitations first-hand from the Negro entertainers they saw there" (65) are regulars as well. Like the photographs on the Club wall, which group portraits of boxers with giants like Frederick Douglass, the Club houses a promiscuous mix of high and low figures. Vital differences thrive.

The unnamed protagonist, a classically trained pianist, is dazzled by the music and creativity of a black world he has never before known. At the same time, the millionaire he meets at the Club becomes his entry to the world of the white elite (in whose penthouses he performs the ragtime he has only recently learned) and his ticket to Paris, London, and Berlin, where he lives as a white man himself. Crossing color and class lines in this way teaches him the possibilities for fertile cultural transmissions; the wealthy

Germans he meets in Berlin are expert ragtime players, and the black people of Martinique and Haiti are often "more Frenchy" than Parisians. But Johnson's narrator does not lose sight of the way cultural hierarchies still operate to limit and define the meaning of a "Negro" life. Because the African American has been typecast as the "laughing, shuffling" clown, black people's efforts to elevate themselves socially are viewed as risible playacting: "In this respect the Negro is much in the position of a great comedian who gives up the lighter roles to play tragedy. No matter how well he may portray the deeper passions, the public is loath to give him up in his old character; they even conspire to make him a failure in serious work, in order to force him back into comedy" (102). Like Dunbar, Johnson objects to the racist reflex that would oppose black expression to the higher forms of a putatively white civilization. Exclusion from epic and tragedy is not a sign of black deficiency but an index of the civil oppression of black lives.

But the "future Negro novelist and poet" who pushes past artificial restrictions can capitalize on a chance for literary innovation. Where others presume a vacuum, the future author can "give the country something new and unknown, in depicting the life, the ambitions, the struggles and the passions of those of their race who are striving to break the narrow limits of traditions" (102). The passage can be said to gloss the fictional *Autobiography* itself. Johnson's novel, with its plot conjoining Cuban cigar factories, railroad porters' boardinghouses, and black nightclubs with Berlin opera houses and Paris cafés, was among the first works of fiction to portray the diverse cultural terrains of African American life. But Johnson also exceeds conventional limits by looking to commercial culture—not just literary culture—as a site that could cultivate a critical understanding of civil relations and race.

This conviction, unusual for an intellectual, reflects Johnson's distinctive life. As a young man, Johnson had left a public life in the professions—he had studied law and passed the Florida bar, and served as a school principal—for the chance to join the entertainment world. He and his brother Rosamond had migrated to New York with hopes for staging their musical *Toloso*, a satiric take on American military expansionism. "The United States had, the year before, annexed Hawaii, and was at the time engaged in the Spanish-American War," he wrote in his memoir *Along This Way* (1933), and "we decided to write a comic opera satirizing the new American imperialism." The musical was never produced. But Johnson, who met Dunbar and other luminaries such as Oscar Hammerstein in this period, became a successful figure in entertainment circles. It was in this "alluring world" of black commercial culture—a world of "greatly lessened restraints" but "tremendous artistic potentialities"—that Johnson theorized an early notion of a black aesthetic rooted in vernacular expression. "I began to grope toward a realization of the importance of the American Negro's cultural background and his creative folk-art, and to speculate on the superstructure of conscious art that might be reared upon them."[37]

The same desire to bring formal artistic resonance to vernacular forms such as ragtime, the rural black sermon, and Jubilee songs becomes the central obsession of Johnson's narrator in *Ex-Colored Man*. Richly beautiful in themselves, these "lower forms of art," the narrator predicts, also "give evidence of a power that will some day be applied to higher forms" (54). The point was not to erase the distinction between higher "conscious art" and vernacular forms; instead, the commercial milieu of New York convinced him that black forms reflect aesthetic power and critical insight conducive to the highest aesthetic expression, and he formulated a plan to translate the signature styles of African American identity into the recognized artistry of "higher forms." His goal was to have black cultural forms retain racial meaning—to bespeak collective African American experience and feeling—but to cease to signify all that falls short of civility. Although he sees rural and religious forms as an untapped resource, it is the mixed and unpolished cultural marketplace of urban black Bohemia that inspires the narrator's critical theory.

Just as commercial culture alters the way the narrator thinks about imaginative art, it is also the matrix for a new critical understanding of blackness. In *Autobiography of an Ex-Colored Man*, race is as much a matter of imaginative force as one of fact. Despite his own ability to live as a white man, the narrator never loses sight of the sometimes fatal realities of life for black people; his witnessing of a lynching makes the point with horrific vividness. (Johnson's own seizure by a lynch mob in Jacksonville had a similar life-altering effect.) But the novel also allows the reader to see the nimbus of invisible, almost magical belief and assumption that always surrounds the real-world facts of race. There is a "dwarfing, warping, distorting influence which operates upon each and every coloured man in the United States," the narrator writes. Its power stems from the fact that virtually all "thought and activity must run through the narrow neck of this one funnel" of race status (15). This influence is irrational and destructive, yet it also inculcates an almost ineffable species of social knowledge. Echoing Aida Walker's comments about the "ten thousand things" in the mind of the black performer, Johnson's narrator states that the black person's thoughts "are often influenced by considerations so delicate and subtle that it would be impossible for him to confess or explain them" (15). African American subjectivity is thus a kind of "freemasonry" (16), a pragmatic interior knowledge that is not a racial trait or a fact of birth but a manner of seeing and understanding akin to a sixth sense and shared by black people alone.

This element of mystery or opacity at play in racial difference, Johnson suggests, has a creative dimension. The "warping" effect of racial stigma has as its other side the power to imaginatively bend or refashion the collective fantasies that define racial identities. What Johnson calls a racial "freemasonry" reflects this creative or productive side of racial stigma: everyday racial experience produces a pragmatic epistemology in which warped or fantastic signifiers sometimes bespeak the most fundamental social realities. Like Johnson's conceit of an "ex-colored man," black authors often found that impossible or illogical figures were often the most accurate representations of black experience and American civil relations. In trying to find a literary form for this indwelling knowledge or "freemasonry" about the reality of social warping, the materials of commercial performance offered more than did the tenets of high realism or the nation's new institutions of literary culture.

Fantasy and Discredited Knowledge

Because of this lived epistemology, fantasy and romance are often the ironic materials of an African American version of social realism. Carla Peterson identifies "a second flourishing" of the African American novel that occurred during the period 1892–1903, "breathing new life into a form born years earlier with William Wells Brown's *Clotel*." This surge of creativity, Peterson shows, relied on a unique set of plot patterns and critical assumptions that could only have taken shape outside the dominant literary culture. Whereas most leading white literary authorities believed the tenets of realism would produce the more socially discerning fiction, black novelists tended to rely instead on the materials of romance in order to articulate social knowledge. "In constructing their texts as sites of memory that invent traditions," Peterson writes, "African American novelists appropriated the form of the historical romance but subverted many of its values."[38] Novels by Chesnutt, Francis E. W. Harper, Pauline Hopkins, and others fashion the genre's preoccupation with family lineage into a counterfactual language for remembering a ruptured past. The white novelist Albion Tourgée wrote that in the wake of slavery, African Americans had "no family tree." But black novelists bend the conventions of domestic fiction and romance in order to reimagine continuities where white authorities see only "an inheritance of reproach."[39] Romantic revelations of hidden kinship, family reunions, and mythic templates of memory allow novelists to reclaim a historical consciousness. Moreover, the same romance materials serve a critical function, revealing the way custom, law, and civil power are not a record of the real but instruments that often erase or block knowledge of black lineages.

Still other works of fiction depart altogether from any effort to represent black experience in terms of lineage and family life. Rather than refashioning conventions of the domestic novel, these authors looked to discourses of science and history. But scientific disciplines, too, presented obstacles to conveying what Toni Morrison calls "the discredited knowledge of black people."[40] Black intellectuals faced a double bind: science and scholarly histories were as apt to stigmatize black people as was the sphere of commercial culture, and the realisms of science and historical fact offered no real haven from the distortions of black identity. But within the counterpublic of the black literary sphere, writers surmounted this dilemma by romancing the language of scientific discovery and historical fact in fantastic narratives, yoking scientific discourse with fiction for the task of reimagining the facts of race.

An unpublished story by DuBois is a notable example of this species of fiction. "A Vacation Unique" was likely written around 1889 while DuBois was studying in the philosophy department at Harvard. The story, which exists only in incomplete fragments, tells of two Harvard undergraduates, one white and one black, who decide to earn money during their summer vacation by touring as "two readers giving 40 or 50 entertainments" around the country. The black student has convinced his classmate that the most profitable course would be to undergo a "painless operation" that temporarily renders him a Negro. The novelty of two black Harvard students will provide a unique spectacle ("Niggers at Harvard!"), and they will profit from the world's "gaping" surprise.[41]

The cynical plan diverts the theme of black entertainment to a framework of scientific speculation. In a reverse minstrelsy, the Harvardians will turn the "astounding incongruous role" (221) of black intellectuals into a form of public entertainment. At the point at which DuBois appears to be fashioning a Twainian fable of ironic racial doubles, however, the storyline veers into an altogether stranger terrain. After the white student has been transformed into a black man, he discovers that he has entered the coordinates of an entirely different domain of space, a "fourth dimension": "By reason of the fourth dimension of color," the black student tells him, "you step into a new, and to most people, entirely unknown region of the universe—you break the bounds of humanity" (221).

DuBois was borrowing from C. H. Hinton's "What Is the Fourth Dimension?" a story from his *Scientific Romances* (1884), and from Edwin A. Abbott's *Flatland*, a widely read science fiction novel that had appeared in a second edition in 1884. And like Hinton and Abbott, DuBois uses fiction to frame a counterfactual world of theoretical ideas. "Outside of the mind you may study mind, and outside of matter by reason of the fourth dimension of color," the black student tells the other, "you may have a striking view of the intestines of the fourth great civilization" (223). But in the story itself, DuBois offers little theoretical speculation of the kind written by Hinton and Abbott. Instead, the fantastic operation that has turned a white man black opens to the real-world experience of black life in America. Scorn and abjection are basic conditions of that life, something immediately made clear from the caustic way the black student addresses his newly transformed "fool." To exist in this dimension is to live in a limbo in which the world, for all its gaping, does not recognize you as a subject: "your feelings no longer count, they are not a part of history" (223). To live in this dimension is also to glimpse the amorality that is the hidden secret and future "death warrant" of "Teutonic civilization" (225).

Because the black student, as narrator, addresses his "fool" in the second person ("you"), the reader experiences by proxy what it is to be addressed as a creature belonging to the "fourth dimension" of blackness. When you are not receiving taunts or stares, you are subject to demands to recognize white magnanimity: "Hostess is cordial: letting you know how nice she can be to colored people; she mentions casually the vast debt owed to Anglo-Saxon race because of the interest her people had in your people and pile of clothes sent to Tuskegee last winter" (224). The story, with its second-person narrative structure, thus requires any white reader to undertake his or her own experiment in racial transformation—or would have, if the story had ever reached print. That it was not completed and published is a reminder that the "fourth dimension" was in fact a social reality: what DuBois called the "inner life" of African Americans was obscured or ignored in most public life and was thus an invisible dimension of human existence for most white Americans. Through his scientific parable, DuBois turns inside out the stage performances of blackness, exposing the warping force that constantly conditions what appear to white eyes to be the objective facts of black identity. The mocking invective the narrator directs at his newly black "fool" is a mimicry of the white hostility and contempt that train the black subject in the tricky arts of public self-staging.

Other examples of racial scientific romance, almost as provocative, did succeed in coming into print. Sutton Griggs's novel *Imperium in Imperio* (1899), originally self-published, imagines a secret organization of black people devoted to building a powerful "empire" within the United States. This black nation, a kind of inverted image of the invisible order of white supremacists who make up the Ku Klux Klan, imagines the scattered strength of the black U.S. population as an organized political power to be reckoned with. Through the creative license of fiction, *Imperium* turns the imposed "freemasonry" of internal racial vigilance into a stealthy armed force and a potential black republic.

A similar transformation occurs in James Corrothers's story "A Man They Didn't Know" (1913). Corrothers, a Chicago author and pastor, had earlier teamed with Bert Williams and others in the world of vaudeville. His insider's knowledge of black popular culture shows through in his comic tale of black urban life, *The Black Cat Club* (1902), a parody in dialect about a literary society whose members are razor-toting toughs from the Chicago streets. Corrothers later regretted publishing a story with such low subject matter and language. But it is striking that when he committed himself to "literary English," his more serious-minded stories included historical fantasy.[42] In "A Man They Didn't Know," Japan and Mexico have formed an alliance with Hawaii, now in secession, to declare war on the United States. African Americans, deserting the U.S. army in large numbers, become a kind of independent armed force that is initially inclined to side with the invaders. Eventually, though, the title character leads ten thousand black men against Japanese troops in a decisive battle in southern California. Ninety thousand more black troops help secure the victory. For Corrothers and Griggs, fiction is an aggressive weapon against history. Faced with the defeat and humiliation of black people in the post-Reconstruction era, Corrothers and Griggs imagine African Americans as a dominant national power. Blackness no longer signifies the low and the dependent; instead, those values are precisely reversed as black men step forward and become the new embodiment of American will and military potency.

For DuBois, Griggs, and Corrothers, scientific romance was a creative alternative to an overly restrictive brand of literary realism. Within the precincts of fantastic science and counterfactual history, writers could draw on an aura of higher scientific authority to address the topic of race while allowing for the free transformation of racial signs and hierarchies. One of the most fascinating texts in this vein of racial fantasy is Pauline Hopkins's novel *Of One Blood* (1903). Appearing in serial form in the *Colored American Magazine,* of which Hopkins was the literary editor, the novel is a deliberate amalgam of scientific speculation and exotic romance. Like DuBois's story, the novel begins at Harvard where a young "genius," Reuel Briggs, suffers a keen awareness of his abjection as a black man. He passes for white among his fellow students but still carries the shame of his subordinate status. Asked what he thinks of "the Negro problem," he refuses comment: "I have a horror of discussing the woes of unfortunates, tramps, stray dogs, cats and Negroes—probably because I am an unfortunate myself." In the logic of realist and naturalist narrative, early death is the likely fate for most urban "unfortunates" and, ominously, Reuel possesses "morbid thoughts."[43]

Hopkins thus initiates her story with the codes of Howells's literary Boston, invoking the "self-possessed, highly cultured New England" (15) elite and the achievements of Harvard scholarship. In the first scene Reuel is even studying an actual psychology text written by William James ("The Hidden Self," later reprinted in *The Will to Believe*), from which Hopkins quotes several passages. But, as if reversing the inside of a glove to make the lining become a new exterior, Hopkins takes from the James essay a notion of spiritual identity ("the hidden self lying quiescent within") that brings about a wholesale inversion of the anticipated narrative structure. "The wonders of the material world," Reuel tells a friend, "cannot approach those of the undiscovered country within ourselves" (7) that normal science has yet to explore. From this metaphor of a terra incognita, Hopkins spins out an Africanist fantasy of mesmeric visions, secret birthmarks, the recovery of an occult science, and the restoration of a rightful king—Reuel's "hidden self" and true identity—to an ancient black civilization surviving within a secret city in Africa. Hopkins trades museum realism for archeological fantasy of the most romantic kind.

The setting in an ancient African city, however, reflects a serious scholarly interest. Like many black intellectuals, Hopkins was drawn to theories of "Ethiopianism" that argued ancient Egypt was a civilization derived from black Africa. Her study *A Primer of Facts Pertaining to the Early Greatness of the African Race* (1905) surveys the scholars and classical authors who supported the claims for a black Egypt. But Hopkins is also distinctly aware of the fact that imagery of Africa and ancient Egypt had become a mainstay of mass culture. A joking (and racist) white character who has joined Reuel on the North African journey looks around him and pronounces it a fit set for "Barnum's circus." The "Arabs, camels, stray lions, panthers, scorpions, serpents, explorers, etc.," he cracks, are his chance to break into show business: "There's money in it" (81). Regardless of her own interest in Egyptian classicism, Hopkins was prepared to enlist the proven entertainment value of imperial spectacle, and her story features familiar plot turns such as pouncing leopards and the discovery of heaps of jewels. But the Barnum joke turns out to be on the white jokester when the discovery of Telassar, the secret city, reveals African art that rivals "the galleries of Europe" and an occult science only "in its infancy" in the West (105). Deliberately transposed from realism to science fiction, her retelling of the "story of the Negro" is a praise song to the dignity and cultural wealth of a civilization "hidden" in the fourth dimension of world history.

Hopkins's novel puts excess in the service of critique. Where Dunbar's blues epic is structured by the divide between high literature and commercial spectacle, Hopkins fuses both high and low materials in an ungainly doubling, confident that both spheres will bear witness to the same truth: behind the stigma of blackness is an unrecognized dignity and agency, an identity or "blood" that her novel reclaims and redeems. The novel multiplies its signifiers of race almost past the point of intelligibility. By the end of the novel, the "blood" that explains and defines Reuel Briggs has acquired almost every conceivable association: biological descent, an inherited mesmeric power, Ethiopian civilization, Christian universalism, a pan-African nationalism, and an aristocracy of royal lineage. Despite any number of internal contradictions, all remain suspended together as affirmed meanings of black racial identity—all *except* for an idea of African American blood as the caste stigma of a subordinated people, the one identity codified in U.S. law and custom. That stigmatic meaning, of course, could not be dissolved by fiction, however inventive. But fiction *could* expose by way of contrast the poverty of the racial imagination that had been fixed in the law, and could also circulate creative improvisations that "warp" and thus transform the signifiers of blackness for a black literary public that would grow larger over time.

Chapter 6
Wharton, Mass Travel, and the "Possible Crash"

Edith Wharton loved the sensation of speed. In *The Custom of the Country,* when Wharton writes of the "rush of physical joy" that comes from flying in an open car at twilight through the wintry boulevards of Central Park, the passage bespeaks her infatuation with motorcars and their mechanical power.[1] For Wharton, local motor flights and transatlantic travel were fundamental conditions of living. Henry James always pictured her "wound up and going"; in alarm and bemusement his letters define her through "her dazzling, her incessant braveries of far excursionism."[2] Wharton loved speed, almost as much as she loved stillness—the contemplative space of gardens, the quiet stimulation of indoor conversation, the nearly motionless concentration necessary for the work of writing. These contraries—mobility and reflective stillness—inform Wharton's complex stance as an observer of modern manners and give shape to her profound ambivalence about what Dale Bauer calls "the increasing speed of cultural production" in the early twentieth century. Wharton was fascinated as well as alarmed by the rapid changes in customs, family life, and material culture that were erasing the nineteenth-century world of her youth. Her own day-to-day living could be as divided as her views. Writing in the morning quiet of her bedroom, Wharton would satirically dissect the modern "goddess[es] of velocity" who traveled on yachts and high-speed automobiles and the men of wealth they pursued, married, and divorced. She would then emerge in the afternoons to instruct her driver to prepare the Panhard motor for the swooping journeys that prompted friends to dub her the "Angel of Devastation."[3]

Wharton's attraction to the "rush" of velocity bespeaks a biographical contradiction, but within her fiction speed and mobility operate as crucial if surprising elements of a distinct form of literary analysis. Wharton shared the realists' wariness toward mass culture and viewed "the new facilities of communication" as largely destructive—although, like Veblen, she saw the rich as the equal of vaudeville showmen or tabloid papers when it came to staging extravagant spectacles.[4] But Wharton also saw that the power of commercial culture operated not just through discrete mass genres but also through the global spread of mass-produced goods and expanding travel routes for tourists. Gillette razors and Ford motorcars were also angels of devastation of a kind: their infiltration of the "uttermost parts of the earth," Wharton wrote, has succeeded to the "deep detriment" of more rooted cultural forms. Certainly for Wharton the forces of the new commercial "order of things" seemed to threaten literary culture and the kind of aesthetic sensibility she prized most.[5] At the same time, however, the very energies of modernity that fueled the new emergent order—technologies of speed and mobility, the pleasures and hazards of trading the familiar for the novel and the transitory—are also absorbed into Wharton's literary practice, transforming both the texture and the critical vision of the novel of manners she inherits from Austen and Eliot.

Wharton's literary use of velocity is clearest in her enduring preoccupation with high-speed travel. It is present in the journeys that structure her plots, the travel-related tropes that are the keynotes for her characters, and the specific forces of travel (mechanical speed, imperial reach, intercontinental communication) that are the material conditions for Wharton's own ability to write and publish. Velocities of modernity animate her novels with a sense of risk just below the surface of social routine. Featuring rapid shifts in location and increasingly curious, deracinated (anti)marriage plots, Wharton's fiction transforms the novel of manners, creating a form that is less a chronicle of local social patterns than a record of the disruption and global dispersion of those patterns. By linking money and mobility, by connecting continental and marital crossings, her stories of rich travelers who "inter-married, inter-loved, and inter-divorced each other over the whole face of Europe" and beyond become a kind of index to the global powers that are otherwise missing from the surface of the fiction.

These mechanical, commercial, and imperial forces are the absent cause of particular narrative textures, creating a record of "modernity as embodied sensation" and lived experience, to borrow from Arjun Appadurai.[6] Rapid change and dislocation are sensations her characters find variously thrilling, reckless, and disastrous while only vaguely apprehending any connection between these feelings and their underlying conditions. Out of this reformulation of manners, Wharton's fiction registers forms of social and somatic vertigo that have less in common with any sentiment in Austen or Thackeray than with the aesthetics of disaster and bodily thrill informing a host of contemporary commercial amusements, from the re-creation of shipwrecks and massive fires to automotive stunts and films of speeding trains. Precisely because Wharton's fiction recognizes the extraliterary sensations and apprehensions accompanying high-speed travel, her literary analysis is able to uncover and explore the distributions of risk that lie behind a key mass sentiment, the diffuse apprehension that "something may happen to somebody."[7]

Manners, Machines, and Modernity

As defined by social theorists, modernity is less an epoch than a tempo. The modern life confronting Wharton and her contemporaries was the result of specific accelerations, velocities of change fueled by wealth and new technologies. Faster trains and steamships, telegraph cables, the expansion of European empires and of U.S. territorial reach, the rapidly growing volume of print and consumer goods that spanned these global territories—these and other innovations created a global geography of rapid transit, a new alignment of space that resulted from technologies of speed. Between 1875 and 1925 (a period roughly matching the span of Wharton's lifetime), the global travel and contact that had been under way for several centuries entered what historian Roland Robertson terms a "take-off phase." The exponential change meant that the category of place was increasingly transformed by new modalities of time. Living in Rome or Bombay, traveling to North Africa or New York, all became very different enterprises when cables, phones, and motorcars made these places of local dwelling into sites of instant relay. Anthony Giddens describes this transformation as "a 'lifting out' of social relations from local contexts of interaction and their restructuring across time and space."[8]

For any observer attuned to the new transitivity of social relations, such restructurings could not but change the terrain of customs and manners. In Wharton's fiction, vehicles of transit have become a major social institution: ships, cars, and trains are machines that govern manners. In *The House of Mirth*, for instance, Lily Bart's emotional life and social fate rely on the itinerary of a yacht. An invitation from her friend Bertha Dorset to travel the Mediterranean on the Dorsets' steam yacht allows Lily to escape the threat of ruinous gossip in her Manhattan circle. Though she knows Bertha's social world is ignoble, it is the only world in which Lily can imagine finding security and pleasure. Carrying her away from the danger of social ruin, the transatlantic cruise seems to embody both safety and luxury—indeed, safety is for Lily the ultimate luxury. Yet at the moment she believes herself most secure, Lily is headed for a fall. An episode in Monte Carlo is marked, in no less than four passages, by the metaphor of a disastrous crash. When Lawrence Selden gets his first glimpse of Lily in this setting, for instance, he sees a young woman "on the verge of disaster" and thinks of her as someone about to be "fatally involved" in a "possible crash" (222). The yachting trip, promising safety, instead delivers Lily into a danger that Wharton expresses through the trope of a violent accident.

The foreground of the novel still presents the more compressed and coded field of manners—the drama of subtle gestures, allusive speech, the covert glance. Lily's is a world governed by the reign of social appearances, overseen through the mutual surveillance of a community of recognized insiders. But a poetics of disaster figures at the margins and locates the dynamic energies of an industrialized mass society that exists behind or beneath the nuanced calibrations of manners. It is telling that Lily's figural "crash" in Monte Carlo, a public humiliation in a fashionable restaurant, precipitates her descent to the less illustrious society of the "Gormer set" whose social life is organized around "motors and steam-launches" (244). The members of the Gormer circle imitate the cosmopolitan mobility of the established elite, but in doing so they reproduce leisure-class travel as merely frantic, heedless movement, a social life in a constant state of near violent transit. In this world a crash seems just a matter of time: Lily experiences the "sense of having been caught up into the crowd as carelessly as a passenger is gathered in by an express train" (244).

Wharton stylizes the heedlessness of the Gormer set not merely through the figure of a speeding train but more specifically through Lily's internal "sense" of train travel, the remembered sensation of being hustled impersonally into a powerful mechanical vehicle. Evoking kinetic excitement as well as foreboding, the figure identifies with surprising precision a species of consciousness that is born of modern travel. Wharton places a good deal of weight on this figure. Lily's "sense" of being caught up in an express train echoes an earlier description of her anxious foreboding in Monte Carlo. When Bertha Dorset and a male guest one night fail to return to the Dorsets' yacht, Lily feels an immediate sense of alarm—as well she should, since she will become the scapegoat for the lovers' exposed affair and will be expelled from both the yacht and the Dorsets' social circle. Lily first expresses her alarm as the fear of a train wreck: "What happened—an accident to the train?" (210). What the narrator calls "the peril of the moment" (211) is a marital and social peril, but the sense of danger reverberates through the chapter and indeed the whole novel as the physical danger of an accident. The trope returns, for instance, in Lily's subsequent "sense of being involved in the crash, instead of merely witnessing it from the road" (212). And the same figure governs Lawrence Selden's internal thoughts. His musing likewise derives a distinct "sense" from the anticipation of a violent accident: Selden wonders "to what degree was [Lily's] dread of a catastrophe intensified by the sense of being fatally involved in it" and concludes that "whatever her . . . personal connection" with the "disaster" to come, she "would be better out of the way of a possible crash" (222).

The theme of the disastrous wreck or car crash would become a major focus for modernist and postmodernist fiction, from *The Great Gatsby* with its fatal auto accident to the work of present-day writers like J. G. Ballard, whose novel *Crash* features characters who violently desire the ironic star status of car accident victims. As a literary trope, the high-speed accident signifies the tremendous powers and desires, seductive as well as menacing, generated by the velocities of twentieth-century life. In its turn to a phenomenology of the modern crash, however, fiction was a distinctly belated cultural language. The literary crash arrives decades after medical discourse attempted the first systematic articulation of what it meant for human lives to enter the altered time and space of high-speed travel. As early as the 1860s, medical authorities tried to pin down the "power of locomotion" on the human nervous system. The most telling evidence, all agreed, was likely to surface in the aftermath of a train accident, an event of alarming frequency and yet one that by definition could not be predicted or rationalized.

For medical theorists, the train accident presented a whole new kind of human injury, arising from "the helplessness of a human being in the midst of great masses in motion." The distinctive harm came not merely from the higher likelihood of death or maiming; it was also produced by the passenger's near-constant awareness of the "close possibility of an accident." In the words of one traveler, "it is impossible to divest yourself of the notion of instant death to all upon the least accident happening." When rail travel became more routine, such fears were more easily suppressed. But, as medical writers saw it, sublimation carried its own costs. When an accident did occur, regardless of whether a passenger suffered any bodily harm, the sudden, overwhelming return of terror created a deep traumatic injury, a mental wound or collapse resulting from "fright only." The risk of "railway brain" or "fright neurosis," as researchers called this injury, was shared by any and all passengers: everyone who traveled by train had to adapt in some fashion to the always pending possibility of "instant death to all."[9]

For Wolfgang Schivelbusch, the process of adjusting to the shocks and stimuli from technological transformations like railway travel gave rise to an "industrialized consciousness." Whatever the scientific validity of constructs like "railway brain," the medical discourse of shock was an attempt to come to terms with the "interiorization" of industrial conditions demanded of the modern subject. An industrialized consciousness sounds like a non-literary consciousness; certainly the mental strains associated with the train crash, from fearful suspense to traumatic shock, seem incompatible with the creative powers necessary for literary writing. When Charles Dickens in 1865 walked away unharmed from a minor train accident he felt "not in the least fluttered" (and had the presence of mind, in fact, to climb back into the compartment to collect a manuscript before leaving the scene). But four days later, even briefly describing the event in a letter was disturbing enough to cause him to halt the attempt at writing about it: "But in writing these scanty words of recollection I feel the shake and I am obliged to stop." His only reflections were negative: he would not attempt to turn the experience into fiction, he noted, nor did he plan even to speak of it to investigating authorities.[10] For this most prolific of novelists, the consciousness that issued from an accident marked a kind of limit to literary consciousness.

While the interiorized shock of the railway accident was at odds with writing fiction, novelists eventually began writing *about* mechanical crashes and disasters, making scenes of destruction and the feelings of victims, survivors, and observers into literary objects. Originating the themes later developed in fiction like Ballard's *Crash*, Zola's 1890 novel *La Bête Humaine* told of crime and destructive lust enacted on speeding trains and in railway yards. Zola's narrative refashioned the medical trope of internal shock into various forms of expressive desire and spectatorial pleasure: "Flore was standing there, looking too. She loved accidents: any mention of an animal run over, a man cut in pieces by a train, was bound to make her rush to the spot."[11] The object of Flore's avid interest in this scene is the head of a decapitated man. If "railway brain" named the injured consciousness of the accident victim, the dead victim's head and Flore's excitement at holding and gazing at it are objects that convert the interiorized shock of a disaster into two external, polarized forms: the perverse delight of the living, and the abject unknowing of the dead. Literary objects like severed heads and girls who "love accidents" were shocking in their own way, of course; but these externalized objects might be said to recover or restore the interiority of the literary subject (Zola as a productive writer, Zola's outraged or savvy reader) from the kind of inexpressive state that had momentarily silenced Dickens.

Although Zola's novel generated scandal, the idea that an accident or disaster might generate pleasurable excitement was hardly an unfamiliar notion in 1890. The new amusement industry had already made destructive fires, crashes, and natural disasters a particular specialty. At the height of their popularity, the resorts at Coney Island staged six or seven disaster spectacles a day, from re-creations of historical floods and fires to scenes of fictitious battle in which an American warship defeated a foreign naval threat. Shipwrecks and sea battles may have reinforced a sense of removal from the site of danger inasmuch as spectators watched from grandstands on shore (in crowds sometimes reaching twelve thousand). But other attractions allowed visitors to step inside the scene of the disaster and to realize their own role as witness within the re-creation itself. A Dreamland extravaganza called "Fighting the Flames," for instance, featured six-story tenement buildings and two thousand performers, and the crowd watching the firemen as part of the production was hardly distinguishable from the paying audience.[12] The mode of amusement that Bill Brown calls "Coney Island realism" was designed to let patrons participate in dire scenes that were neither purely fictional nor fully actual. Freed from the "moral(izing) teleology" of the melodramatic stage play or sentimental novel, the mass amusement disaster was able to extract sensational effect as a kind of purified surplus value.[13] Thrill-seekers were not depraved accident lovers like Zola's Flore; it mattered that these disasters, while lifelike, were not the real thing. But for producers and consumers alike, the (tenuous) fictionality of the disaster spectacle was an acknowledged license for enjoying smash-ups and destruction.

From a certain standpoint, there is something contemptible about extracting amusement from the scene of a lethal disaster, however harmless the thrill itself. That standpoint, I have been suggesting, is a stance or subject position we can plausibly call literary. Critics in literary magazines like *Harper's* viewed thrill-seeking crowds with varying degrees of derision. To Maxim Gorky, the appetite of the Coney Island crowd for visual shock and sensation was really a form of latter-day "slavery."[14] Even a gleefully impious novelist like Zola presented the avidity for violent spectacle as one of the more beast-like traits of the human animal. But if the literary perspective returns moral evaluation to the mass enjoyment of the aesthetics of disaster, the literary observer who surveys the thrill-seeking crowd also possesses a tacit pleasure—a literary pleasure that the mass observer has foresworn. The literary subject enjoys the security of speaking (which is to say, writing and reading) from a position outside the foundational modern knowledge of the "close possibility of an accident." Literary speech presumes conditions of public communicability that writers and readers alike are able to think of as continuous if not timeless, located in human minds and imaginations rather than bodies. The thrill-seeker, in contrast, anticipates temporal and material rupture. Awareness of the proximity and unpredictability of a disastrous physical accident is the ground of the mass culture disaster. The pleasure and relief provided by the disaster spectacle is predicated on the "helplessness" of the modern subject living amid mechanical forces and physical "masses in motion." Rides and re-creations might playfully invert the condition of helpless subjection, but they also heighten awareness of the condition itself.

Mass amusements found ways to articulate this foundational knowledge, whose central truth is indeterminate: "something may happen to somebody." This axiom, voiced by an ordinary observer of urban life at the turn of the century, contains a prophecy that will eventually come true—but for whom? The disaster spectacle momentarily supplies images of particular agents and specific victims, allowing the spectator to count herself a bystander who observes the scene unharmed. But proximity to a scene of destruction, real or fictional, only reinforces the disaster epistemology with its mix of certainty and indeterminacy: sometime soon some kind of accident will happen to somebody. This indeterminacy offers a species of protection, even if it can never deliver security. The crowd for the mass amusement crash is an early incarnation of the "mass subject" that Michael Warner has theorized as the postliterary subject born of electronic mass media. As news, film, and television learned to cultivate techniques and topics that could draw the interest of millions, the "discourse of disasters" has proved to be irresistible, a mass "fetish." Among the complex reasons why plane crashes and disaster films have mass appeal is the tautological reward they offer precisely by being massively popular. Viewing a mediated disaster, the mass subject enjoys the pleasure of social belonging and a sense of public standing—even though the freedom such pleasures seem to promise is based on the unfreedom of the consumer, who cannot trade mass publicity for the public agency she thought she was buying.[15] Bill

Brown identifies a somewhat different version of the rewards that come from the genre of the spectacularized disaster. As early film learned to integrate documentary images of real destruction and codes of narrative cinema, "disaster became the privileged mode for effecting the recreational sublime," a heightened experience "wherein the audience, witnessing personal panic made public, publicly shares its own panic."[16]

For the literary subject, in contrast, aesthetic experience and critical insight depend on the difference between those literary faculties and anything resembling mass pleasure or panic. Howells condemned the "bloodless sports of the modern amphitheater" as the antithesis of the literary.[17] Wharton's sense of the difference was distinctly personal. In an autobiographical sketch published in *Harper's,* she described a core self in terms of an interior "something" that always remains apart from the arena of mass publicity: "something in me has always resisted the influence of crowds and shows, and I have hardly ever been able to yield myself unreservedly to a spectacle shared with a throng of people."[18] The language of resistance and yielding here acknowledges that "crowds and shows" can exert a powerful gravitational pull, but Wharton identifies her capacity to speak as a self-reflexive subject ("something in me") with her ability to remain apart from the body of the crowd. The literary language of her novels is likewise reflexive, viewing social formations from a certain remove.[19] Accidents frequently appear in her fiction, but the smash-up is almost always figural. The work it does is analytic, connecting different linguistic planes through the larger grammar of the narrative. There is nothing in Wharton's fiction like the imagistic jolt of torn bodies one finds in Zola or even Fitzgerald, a self-described student of her fiction. But while Wharton's accident tropes always operate at the analytic level of the figural, they usually turn out to be advance signposts pointing to literal forms of destruction and injury. In Wharton's fiction, literary language repeatedly seems to lose its exemption from the collective panic and indeterminate risk that enter with the knowledge of a "possible crash." The pleasure of the reader, like the freedom of the traveler, keeps slipping into the unfreedom of the accident victim.

Through tropes of disaster and speed, Wharton revises the ancient meaning of dread. Instead of the fear of an absent or invisible power like a god, dread in *House of Mirth,* as we've seen, is expressed through the anticipation of a distinctive kind of modern event, the high-speed accident. The accident had become an occasion for mass amusement because rapid travel itself had become a mass experience. Though train travel had introduced a new order of speed early in the nineteenth century, it was only in the 1880s and 1890s that inland and intercontinental travel had become a phenomenon involving massive numbers of passengers and far higher rates of speed than ever before. The increasing coordination of railway and ocean steamer lines in the later half of the nineteenth century produced significant new levels of international trade, but it was ultimately passenger travel, the transport of humans, that had the most profound effects. British railway travel increased twentyfold during 1840–70, with a comparable rate of increase taking place in America during a somewhat later period. Oceanic travel surged with the mass emigration from Europe to America and the British Dominions, with spectacular increases in 1880–83 and 1900–1913. Ocean liners became increasingly larger in size and more diversified in accommodations; the most successful companies learned to combine a large capacity for steerage bookings with luxuriously appointed cabins for wealthy tourists and businessmen. Eventually the famous Cunard Company innovated the tourist class accommodations to reach middle-income shipboard travelers. As other steamship companies followed suit, transatlantic travel became so widespread as to verge on the commonplace.[20]

Although the emergence of a system of mass travel helps confirm Schivelbusch's account of an "industrialized consciousness," the process did not produce a uniform mentality among travelers. Everyone had to pass the "new thresholds of demand and danger" in modernity, but not every modern subject shared the same sense of increased vulnerability.[21] The domain of travel also registers a new kind of triumphal subjectivity, a sense of almost unlimited agency and an ability to extend the sovereignty of the self throughout the globe. The son of a leading industrialist expressed this sense of expansive agency in rhapsodic cadences: "I could step on any steamship and be transported to any point in the Seven Seas; I could board any train and ride from Portland, Maine, to Portland, Oregon." Mobility in space was of a piece with the global reach of modern communications: "Because I was my father's son, I could walk into any telegraph office, compose as long a message as I wished, sign his name, and walk out."[22] No small part of the luxury of this power of mobility was the sense of personal security, the luxury of feeling inured to harm and thus free of dread. But this sense of personal security was not in fact personal—or not merely so. It rested on a historical process of militarized security that was creating a new geography of travel routes out of projects of imperial expansion. Although emigration and tourism made North Atlantic routes the most heavily traveled, in the wake of imperial expansion steamship lines were increasingly adding passenger routes in the Pacific, to South and Central America, and to the Caribbean.[23]

Just how closely passenger travel was related to commerce and military ventures was illustrated in 1899 in the wildly successful effort by the American Line to book its luxury liner *Paris* for a West Indies cruise to the sites of the Spanish-American War. After stopping in Haiti, Puerto Rico, Trinidad, and Jamaica, the *Paris,* which only a year before had served the U.S. Navy as the auxiliary cruiser USS *Yale,* took its four hundred passengers to excursions of famous war sites along the Cuban coast. The highlight of the March cruise was the formal ball aboard the *Paris,* anchored in Santiago Harbor, with music supplied by a Cuban band and the Fifth United States Infantry band.[24] *Mirth*'s Lawrence Selden, in response to his ambivalent feelings for Lily Bart, flees to this newly reopened Caribbean travel route, something Lily learns when she reads a newspaper announcement that Selden was one of the passengers to set sail "for Havana and the West Indies on the Windward Liner Antilles" (188).

Lily's own escape—a flight across the Atlantic to the Mediterranean—is never described in the narrative, but its very omission can be read as an indicator of the revolutionary speed that distinguished modern travel. No sooner does Lily receive the yachting invitation than we turn the page to find her in Monte Carlo. The wax seal Lily uses for personal letters, "a grey seal with *Beyond!* beneath a flying ship" (163), could have served as equally well as a travel industry logo as it does a signature for Lily's personal yearnings. Steamship lines vied for the "Blue Ribbon" for fastest transatlantic trip, an industry competition that eventually reduced Atlantic crossing to four and a half days. At times steamers found themselves in head-to-head races, with passengers on deck doubling as spectators for their own competitive journey, though on more than one occasion such races ended with a ship run aground during the final race to port.[25]

By evoking Lily's social risk through the dangers of high-speed transport, Wharton makes us aware of what otherwise remains largely invisible in this novel. As in most Wharton novels, the actual sources of wealth for the rich—the economic markets and the era's rapid imperial expansion—are nowhere depicted. But in the "motors and steam-launches" that propel the plot, the novel locates the mechanical power, speed, and economic expansion that were transforming the globe. As a result, Wharton's fiction is structured around a tension between closely observed communities, with their local rituals and inherited gender roles, and the sweeping forces of a new economic world seen only obliquely but felt on every side. The latent power in these forces, their significance for her characters as for Wharton herself, was a persistent anxiety and an enduring interest, and the figure of the anticipated crash pinpoints a convergence of impersonal powers and anxiety about those powers."[26]

Lily's "sense" of an impending wreck, then, can be seen as an internalized register of powers that remain out of sight. The crash that eventually ruins her is precipitated by gossip and social intrigue, old-fashioned harms to be sure. But the narrator paints Lily as a modern accident victim caught in forces far more impersonal, contingent, ruthless, and eventually fatal. Lily's vulnerability to Bertha's social power is finally an economic vulnerability; if she is to travel at all, Lily must travel on someone else's yacht, according to someone else's itinerary. As a result, she is in the wrong place at the wrong time and, as the scandal of Bertha's affair begins to surface, Lily grasps that she will not be able to be a bystander. It is precisely because she is *standing by*, a body on the margins of the plans and power of the rich, that she will take the force of the crash. When the scandal hits, Bertha virtually throws her overboard: she announces to the dining party in Monte Carlo that "Lily will not be going back to the yacht" (227). As deliberate as Bertha is, Lily's fate is not a structured, ritual punishment but an incidental harm, the indifferent destruction that comes to the accident victim. Lily and Selden's diffuse fears about train wrecks and metaphorical crashes are realized in the wake of the Dorsets' yachting trip and the callously wielded power it makes visible on the social scene.

At the level of critical analysis, Wharton's evocations of rapid transport become signs of the social recklessness and potential for destruction in a mass society. The narrator calls the Gormers' journey to Alaska a "tumultuous progress across their native continent" (247), a phrase that allows the forward motion of mechanized travel to signify the agitated, ungoverned energies of modernity that make the overtones of "progress" ironic if not wholly false. Figuring nouveau riche society as "the rush of travellers," Wharton condemns a world that "scarcely slackened speed—life whizzed on with a deafening rattle and roar" (244). Yet, while the novel indicts this "life" as crass and thoughtless, it is hard to deny that the energies signified in the "possible crash"—motion, power, suspense, the anticipation of novel sensations and arresting sights—are the very energies that give the novel its dramatic tension and excitement. It is hard to deny, in other words, that Wharton herself recognizes and indeed uses the modern currents of feeling that Selden and Lily both register as the sense of impending accident. This tone of anxious anticipation is the novel's keynote. Generated as it is through evocation of mechanical speed, the "possible crash" is a structure of feeling that can be said to transform—to modernize—the genre in which Wharton wrote. The nineteenth-century novel of manners was built on the close examination of local social life, the contained worlds of parishes and country towns. In *House of Mirth,* intercontinental travel and the evocation of travel disaster make us see social worlds not as self-contained locales but as communities cut through by larger, far more impersonal governing forces. In Wharton's fiction the questions of most concern are no longer social regulation and marital resolution but reckless pleasure and potentially fatal risk.

In shifting the novel of manners to this new social terrain, Wharton's novel is arguably the forerunner to the fictional studies of disaster undertaken by Ballard, Don DeLillo, and other novelists of the "risk society."[27] The shift represents a significant literary development, but the shift itself comes from the loss of a secure difference between the detached literary subject and the indeterminate mass subject, the subject who dwells in the possibility of a crash. The transformation of Wharton's fictional field is the result of a breach that opens the space of the literary to the energies of panic, pleasure, and dread "shared with a throng of people." But while such a transformation erodes the existential security that Wharton, for one, seemed to find in an ideal of literary culture, it also might be said to renew or redirect the analytic office of the literary. When Wharton rewrites the literature of manners for an era "in which crashing is a permanent condition," it also makes possible a new analysis of risk that uncovers determinate patterns in the indeterminate condition of modern subjection to risk.[28] Her focus on the gods and goddesses of velocity shows the way management of risk, psychic as well as material, is never accidental.

Compared to the vast majority of people who inhabit the lands that travelers merely visited, the wealthy had the means to protect themselves from the most serious kinds of harm. Like Selden's escape from New York through the reopened Caribbean route, the journeys of wealthy travelers taking flight from personal disaffections or romantic failures followed a set of military and economic routes that were the grid, as it were, for the dominant global powers. Wharton's characters often flee their sense of personal risk or loss, the merely metaphorical "crash," by making literal journeys along these intercontinental routes, tracing paths in which losses and upheaval were far more likely to fall on the poor or on native populations than on the leisure-class travelers. Why then is the dread associated with modern risk felt keenly by so many of Wharton's characters, figures who belong to the class she called "world-compellers" and the social group least in danger of physical harm?

Wharton's fiction can be said to enact a distribution of risk, a careful managing of the modern sense of danger through a narrative process that is both revealing and evasive. In contrast to earlier novels of manners, the stakes in Wharton's novels are dizzyingly high. When Lily Bart flirts with Lawrence Selden, she also flirts with real poverty, and eventually with the question of her own survival. When the much-married Undine Spragg uses up a husband, the result is usually cataclysmic, a suicide or the abandonment of a child. The gentler ironies attending courtship and marriage in Austen's novels have given way to harsh incongruities and startlingly destructive forms of kinship: compulsive serial divorces (*The Custom of the Country, Glimpses of the Moon*), bizarre intergenerational love triangles (*The Mother's Recompense*), and forms of incest (*Summer, The Children, Twilight Sleep*). Though these novels tend to focus on the affluent, Wharton can be said to reintroduce internal class lines by depicting extreme consequences that fall overwhelmingly on the most economically vulnerable: children and single women. Even the most socially polished woman can, like Lily Bart, find herself facing privation and physical threat. A very young and poor woman like Charity Royall in *Summer* is doubly at risk. The downward mobility and sexual vulnerability that shadow the lives of so many of Wharton's women make the inequities of modern conditions visible within the white middle and leisure classes.

Yet these internal fault lines can be said to obscure as much as they reveal. Absent from Wharton's novels is any appreciable recognition of the people most at risk in modernity: the poor and the colonized populations for whom travel routes represent labor rather than leisure and imperial intrusion rather than escape. I return later to these absent populations when I discuss Wharton's nonfiction writings on early twentieth-century globalization. Their absence suggests another possibility about the trope of the possible crash: that the dread and exhilaration called up in aesthetic re-creations of disaster may cover up as much as they reveal about conditions of modern risk. First, however, it is instructive to consider the way Wharton's novels acknowledge—if not always fully consciously—an internal impulse to redistribute modern threats and vulnerability. The process of redirecting risk, of displacing, exaggerating, or transforming a sense of threat, is one of the activities that characterize the modern "crash culture."[29]

Once again, the "possible crash" is a pivotal trope in this regard. Like the narrator, Selden in *House of Mirth* views Lily as someone headed for a smash-up. But it is significant that the novel's most complex rendering of *Selden's* position is also rooted in the trope of the travel accident. Selden practices a technique of "personal detachment," as the narrator calls it, designed to protect him from desire he wishes to keep at a distance (195). When he sees Lily in Monte Carlo as a woman "on the brink of a chasm" (200), his concern for her is also a feeling of self-protective removal from her plight; he is on the other side of the figural chasm. But even his sense of detachment carries a trace of the emotional risk he wishes to acknowledge in Lily's life only: "The feeling he had nourished and given prominence to was one of thankfulness for his escape: he was like a traveller so grateful for rescue from a dangerous accident that at first he is hardly conscious of his bruises. Now he suddenly felt the latent ache, and realized that after all he had not come off unhurt" (195). The internal practice of viewing others as potential victims of some future harm ("on the brink") may betray one's own sense of threat. A habit of detachment may be entangled in a wish to disavow feelings of vulnerability.

Of course seeking a feeling of detachment by imagining something as catastrophic as a "dangerous accident" is more than a little knotted in logic. Here and elsewhere, Selden (or the narrator who supplies figures for his thought) betrays an imagination of disaster that seems at odds with his cultivation of intellectual distance. But Selden's turn to the site of an accident to explain his psychic injury was far from unique; in fact the train crash had actually been the means by which medical forensics had rationalized the concept of invisible injury and its concomitant problem of psychic integrity. Medical theorists who studied train accident victims were anxious to show that seemingly imaginary injuries of the survivors—especially male survivors—were in fact real, even if the injury was psychic. One authority wrote that a man who might initially "congratulate himself upon his escape from immediate peril" often suffered belated symptoms, including tears, sleeplessness, and waking to a sudden "sense of alarm."[30] Could a man of "great mental activity and vigour" really become enfeebled for no substantive physical reason? Could he really be only "'hysterical' like a love-sick girl"? The prospect was so unlikely that it demanded a neurological explanation grounded in some species of bodily injury.[31] Selden's effort at personal detachment from his feelings for Lily replays this rationale almost perfectly but displaces it to the figural level. The vehicle of his metaphor, a "dangerous accident," supplies a physical cause to account for the realization that emotionally "he had not come off unhurt." It is a fairly tortured way to acknowledge feelings of love, but this is complexity with a purpose.

The linguistic turns serve to uphold his difference from a feminized subject ("love-sick girl"), and Selden's literary use of the accident trope performs a cognitive mastery of feelings of panic and dread.

Yet this literary turn is also a compulsive return, especially when we read it in the context of Wharton's recurring use of the accident trope. At times the figure of the traveler at risk begins to look like an authorial tic, a narrative thought Wharton cannot stop thinking. In *The Mother's Recompense,* for instance, when evoking the crisis of the protagonist Kate Clephane, the narrator returns again and again to the trope of the travel accident as if it were a hidden secret rather than a figural likeness. Kate is compared to a "traveller" who has "skirted an abyss" and glimpsed "the depths into which she had not fallen"; to a "traveller" on a "ledge above a precipice"; and finally to a "traveller" who has "fallen asleep in the snow" and wakes to great pain.[32] The novel's reliance on managing a diffuse sense of risk through the figure of a possible accident makes visible what social theorists have identified as a central phenomenon within modern social systems, the felt need to master unpredictable harm. In her complex uses of the accident trope, Wharton brings the literary power of detachment to the distinctive species of modern dread, the ineradicable possibility of a crash. But Wharton's *attachment* to the crash as the vehicle of a recurring metaphor presents us with a picture of literary detachment that is inseparable from a compulsive return to what literary language can never master.

National, International, Global

In at least one respect, Wharton obscured the profound changes signified in the modern culture of travel. Though she saw destructive effects in modern commercialization, Wharton was largely blind to the damage that global travel inflicted on colonized peoples. This blindness is thus an unstable ground on which Wharton's sense of internationalism was founded. Her sophisticated sense of the international is, we might say, a cover or alibi for her inattention to the global. If a position of detachment can mask feelings of vulnerability (as with Selden), by the same token Wharton's sense of leisure-class vulnerability could blind her to the far more pervasive risks facing the poor populations, risks that go largely unnoticed in her picture of modernity.

In an essay of 1927, Wharton cited the motorcar as one of the machines to "internationalize the earth." Mechanical power and modern commodities had created a "new order of things," an order Wharton found both absorbing and repelling. "The whole world has become a vast escalator, and Ford motors, and Gillette razors have bound together the uttermost parts of the earth." But as the American brand names suggest, for Wharton this international "order" was also national, the result of a distinctly American process of commercial globalization. "The universal infiltration of our American plumbing, dentistry, and vocabulary has reduced the globe to a playing-field for our people; and Americans have been the first to profit by the new facilities of communication which are so largely of their invention and promotion." Wharton's picture of this commercial global order as an Americanized order is crucial, since it is the source of both blindness and insight in Wharton's understanding of modernity. By casting the "new class of world-compellers" as Americans, driven by distinctively American excesses, Wharton analyzed as largely destructive the "infiltration" of the globe by U.S. interests: "We have, in fact, internationalized the earth, to the deep detriment of its picturesqueness, and of many far more important things."[33]

At a moment when most Americans greeted U.S. expansionism as an unequivocal force of progress, Wharton's view was far more wary and critically discriminating. But while this way of reading globalization prompted a disapproving view of American commercial powers, Wharton's critique rested on a distinction that allowed her to embrace European empires as America's opposite, as global orders that cultivated rather than destroyed the things Wharton found most important. Yet this crucial distinction—between America and Europe, between empires that raze and those that preserve—was not only a political distinction but an aesthetic one. The criterion for telling the difference was the criterion of beauty: while Americanization destroys beauty, European imperialism reveres and protects it. Art and beauty are the keys to her understanding of global politics, a fact that put art and artists more deeply within the sphere of the political than Wharton was otherwise prepared to admit.

To understand these interrelated criteria, we need to begin with Wharton's sense of the beginning: her own transatlantic childhood. Wharton describes herself in her memoir, *A Backward Glance,* as "the offspring of born travelers." Her deepest sensibilities, as she saw it, were formed by the "happy misfortune" that forced her parents to leave for Europe when she was a very young child in order to live more economically abroad than was possible in New York in the years after the Civil War. Living and traveling in Europe, Wharton believed, imprinted on her for life a "background of beauty and old-established order."[34] And from the first Wharton conceived this order of beauty through an opposition to New World "ugliness." In an autobiographical piece titled *Life and I*, Wharton writes of her return from her early years abroad that "I shall never forget the bitter disappointment produced by the first impressions of my native country. I was only ten years old, but I had been fed on beauty since my babyhood, & my first thought was: '*How ugly it is!*' I have never since thought otherwise, or felt otherwise than as an exile in America."[35]

Significantly, though, Wharton eventually came to see a "pathetic picturesqueness" in the New York world of her youth. As she described it in her memoir, this was a beauty she perceived only after world war and modernization brought about its "total extinction." But the moment when Wharton sees the "compact [American] world of my youth" as one of beauty is also the moment she identifies that vanished America with Europe. This lost American world is not only defined in opposition to modern technology ("telephones, motors, electric light, central heating . . . , X-rays, cinemas, radium, aeroplanes and wireless telegraphy were not only unknown but still mostly unforeseen") but is remembered as a transatlantic outpost of "an old tradition of European culture."[36]

America and Europe, then, are less geographic places for Wharton than they are movable sites of contrasting aesthetic value. Seeing a belated beauty in nineteenth-century New York makes that spot a lost island of European culture. By the same token, Wharton saw the "standardizing" practices of modern American trade opening the world to vast commercial "infiltration." What Wharton called "the growth of modern travelling facilities" meant the dissemination throughout the world of a set of commercial habits that she associated with the national culture of the United States. Indeed, Wharton saw "the modern American as a sort of missionary-drummer selling his wares and inculcating his beliefs from China to Peru."[37] The results were for Wharton largely lamentable, even though the drama of American commercial imperialism was the subject she urged as worthy of serious fiction. But the most striking thing about the way Wharton cast global trade as American is the way it permitted her to locate a national explanation for what were far more complicated global processes. Conceiving global trade as American allowed Wharton to separate cultivated travel—the source of her own aesthetic perceptions—from a destructive commercial travel, when in reality both art and commerce (like the Europeans and Americans who largely controlled them) were quite literally traveling in the same global circles.

In her memoir, for instance, it is Americans who pursue "feverish money-making" and get rich in "railway, shipping or industrial enterprises."[38] For these Americans, travel means cash and movement means profit. Even leisure travel for the rich American is merely a displaced form of acquisitiveness, an insatiable appetite for novelty. Wharton's *Custom of the Country* offered a fully drawn portrait of moneyed Americans as a "new class of world-compellers" who were also world travelers (803). In this novel, which follows the transatlantic adventures of the divorcée Undine Spragg, Wharton explored the "taste for modernity" that theorist Walter Benjamin identified both with fashion and with travel. An analysis of fashion, Benjamin argued, "throws light on the significance of the trips that were fashionable among the bourgeoisie during the second half of the [nineteenth] century." The most "trifling symptoms" of fashion, even the "switch from a cigar to a cigarette," reflect an enthrallment with the "tempo of modern life," the "yearning for quick changes in the qualitative content of life." Like travel, fashion is finally an attraction to speed, a "switching—at high frequency—of the tastes of a given public." Benjamin thus concurred with Georg Simmel that the essential drive behind fashion "is fully manifest in the passion for traveling, which, with its strong accentuations of departure and arrival, sets the life of the year vibrating as fully as possible in several short periods."[39]

Travel, in short, gives speed—gives a vibrating "life"—to time itself. Though Benjamin and Simmel saw the twin passions for fashion and travel as characteristic of bourgeois culture generally, Wharton's *Custom of the Country* presents the merger of feminine fashion and intercontinental travel as a distinctively American phenomenon. What attracts Undine to Europe is not only the literal fashions of Paris couture but the fashionable hotels where Americans gather and enclose themselves in a luxe life of their own making. Undine's restlessness represents an appetite for sheer novelty, for change in everything from dresses to husbands, which the novel identifies as characteristically American.

As more than one critic has observed, while Undine's cultural ignorance makes her nothing like Edith Wharton, there is still something about the character's voraciousness and love for the "rush of physical joy" that echoes portraits of Wharton offered by some of her contemporaries (754). And in her memoir, Wharton herself owns up to the "state of euphoria" she enjoyed for over two months when she indulged in a chartered yachting trip in the Aegean. Although she stresses that the trip was an uncharacteristic extravagance ("my prudence vanished like a puff of smoke"), she also describes her travel as a wondrous excess of joy akin to the excessive wealth of the rich industrialist. On "that magical cruise nothing ever seemed to occur during the day to diminish my beatitude, so that it went on rolling up like the interest on a millionaire's capital."[40] Mobility and money, Wharton saw, were interchangeable. Tellingly, Wharton used some of the proceeds of her first novel to buy her beloved Panhard motorcar. To illustrate the novelist's "motor-mania," one critic points to Wharton's "graphic account of a near-fatal accident suffered by a friend, in which her profoundest horror is reserved for the destruction of 'the beautiful car.'"[41]

But in contrast with these portraits drawn by friends—and perhaps in part because they contain truth—Wharton tended to present herself not as a restless traveler but as someone far more rooted and home-centered. In her letters, her memoirs, and even her photographs, Wharton emphasizes her devotion to personal dwelling places—to gardens and rooms and local surroundings. Put another way, Wharton recasts herself from an American traveler to a settled expatriate, a transformation that converts transatlantic travel into a form of dwelling, a rooted way of life. In her descriptions of "the compact and amiable little world" of her social circle in prewar Paris, Wharton's life seems to stand as an antidote to the rootlessness of modernity. Whereas London society reminded Wharton of the rush of travel— "the stream of new faces rushing past me often made me feel as if I were in a railway station rather than a drawing-room"—Paris represented an increasingly rare "continuity of social relations," a place for the cultivation of intimate and enduring human ties.[42] France was a place where Wharton cultivated not only lasting friendships but also the domestic arts of gardening and home decoration, first in her Paris town house and later in the country home of Pavillon Colombe she built in 1922.

These ties distinguished Wharton from most American tourists and even from the younger, flashier Paris expatriates such as Fitzgerald and Hemingway. Yet to accept at face value Wharton's description of her Paris circle as a small society of homey Old World seclusion would be to overlook the astonishing degree to which members of this "amiable little world" directed power in the world at large. Studying the political writings of many who belonged to Wharton's coterie in the Faubourg Saint Germain has led one scholar to conclude that "most of those who frequented the salons to which she belonged were affiliated in some fashion with French colonial enterprise."[43] The French journalists, diplomats, and writers in her circle were some of the chief architects of the empire erected by the Third Republic. Similarly, Wharton's American intimates in Paris were strong proponents of U.S. expansionism and wrote some of the most influential works in favor of solidifying an American empire. The American scholar Archibald Coolidge, for instance, whom Wharton credits with having introduced her to Parisian literary circles, gave a lecture series at the Sorbonne that later became his pro-imperial volume *The United States as a World Power.* Wharton's onetime lover, the political journalist Morton Fullerton, wrote a series of articles urging the United States to become a "predominant" power in the Caribbean. Naval superiority in the Atlantic and Pacific, Fullerton announced, was necessary in order to fulfill the nation's "destiny." In *Problems of Power,* the book Fullerton published from his articles, he declared that Americans "are marching to the step of an imperial movement."[44]

The closed circle of Wharton's friends and acquaintances, then, turns out to have possessed a remarkable global reach. It was through this "little world" that Wharton met General Hubert Lyautey, a leading figure in the French expansion into Indochina, Madagascar, and Algeria. When Lyautey was serving as the resident-general of the French Protectorate in North Africa he invited Wharton to travel through Morocco under the auspices of his colonial office. Wharton's account of that trip, her travel book *In Morocco* (1920), might be described as an aesthetic revisioning of the facts of empire. Although Wharton prized the "continuity of social relations" she found in her Parisian society, the imperial relations these men and women promoted globally, of course, brought discontinuities of the most profound kind. Wharton recognized the contradiction, if obliquely. Her own attempt at a resolution in her Morocco book, however, elided as much as it admitted. Wharton acknowledged the destructive effects of colonialism only to set that destruction in opposition to an imperial "appreciation" for beauty, a force of aesthetic preservation and discernment that Wharton located in French colonial rule.

Unlike imperial enthusiasts such as Fullerton or her friend Paul Bourget, Wharton never justified European expansion in the name of progress. In fact, Wharton puts the notion of the colonizer's modern improvements under the scorn of quotation marks: "Before General Lyautey came to Morocco," Wharton writes, "Rabat had been subjected to the indignity of European 'improvements,' and one must traverse boulevards scored with tram-lines, and pass between hotel-terraces and cafes and cinema-palaces, to reach the surviving nucleus of the once beautiful native town." The greatest sin of the "modern European colonist," Wharton insists, is the "harm" he does to "the beauty and privacy of the old Arab towns."[45]

But just as the destruction of beauty is for Wharton the most damning fact about colonialism, so too does aesthetic value become Wharton's chief criterion for defending the most recent "French intervention" in North Africa. For Wharton, General Lyautey is exceptional because of his exceptional sensibility: he possesses "a sense of beauty not often vouchsafed to Colonial governors" (23). In Wharton's Morocco book, French military intervention figures almost wholly as aesthetic preservation. Elaborating Lyautey's cultural qualifications for colonial rule, Wharton writes that "a keen feeling for beauty had prepared him to appreciate all that was most exquisite and venerable in the Arab art of Morocco, and even in the first struggle with political and military problems he found time to gather about him a group of archeologists and artists who were charged with the inspection and preservation of the national monuments and the revival of the languishing native art-industries" (221). Wharton does not deny France's colonial occupation so much as fold it into a curatorial role that is preoccupied with preserving national treasures that Moroccans themselves are unfit to protect. Lyautey is less a colonialist than a connoisseur. "Were the [colonial] experiment made on artistic grounds alone," Wharton writes, "it would yet be well worth making" (158).

"Artistic grounds," then, become for Wharton the Moroccan cultural territory that only select Westerners value and thus can rightfully possess. Wharton's travel book is a map of the same artistic geography, surveying the aesthetic grounds of enlightened French rule. Yet she also seems to know just how precarious these "grounds" are for a defense of colonialism. Her preface acknowledges that her own travel had been contingent upon military occupation ("the next best thing to a Djinn's carpet, a military motor, was at my disposal every morning" [viii]). At the same time, she attempts to distinguish her travel from a debased tourism sure to ruin Morocco through "the corruption of European bad taste." The preface recognizes that the uniqueness of Wharton's brand of travel lies in the fact that she visited in "the brief moment of transition between [Morocco's] virtually complete subjection to European authority, and the fast approaching hour when it is thrown open to all the banalities and promiscuities of modern travel" (viii). The preface sounds a note of melancholy that the rich "mystery" of Moroccan culture will "inevitably vanish" with the coming onslaught of Western travelers (ix). But the same wistfulness belies Wharton's own suppressed knowledge that the artistic grounds on which she justifies colonial subjection will culminate in little more than routinized sites for an army of tourists.

Kinship in Transit

In a peculiarly telling sentence from her memoir, Wharton writes that "at the end of the second winter in New York, I was married; and thenceforth my thirst for travel was to be gratified."[46] The sentence virtually erases her marriage from the account of her life. Any expected mention of a courtship, wedding, or honeymoon—not to mention a husband—has been swallowed up in the space marked by the terse semicolon. The first clause is passive ("I was married"), while the second joins the fact of her marriage not to the gratifications of love, sex, or companionship but to the excitement and satisfactions of travel. This rather curiously constructed sentence was no doubt Wharton's attempt to sidestep with proper discretion the misery that was her failed marriage to Theodore Wharton. But the sentence also tells a truth about Wharton, the truth that travel was for her a passion and a mobile institution, a kind of substitute for marriage that ordered her relations to people and places.

The grammar conjoining a marriage, an elided divorce, and a passion for travel in this sentence illustrates a central feature of Wharton's later fiction. In these novels the weave of departures and returns that make up her characters' perpetual traveling provides a striking picture of modern marriage and kinship. The institution of the family was changing as rapidly as any other social institution in this time. Giddens notes that modernity introduces a dynamism into human relationships, an instability that brings both ruptures and potentially freeing innovations.[47] Divorce, new kinds of sexual latitude, women's increasing autonomy from men, untraditional forms of family and association—all are instances of a "dynamism" as characteristic of the modern as is the speed of motorcars. Wharton's ambivalence about such dynamism is plain enough, both in her life and in her fiction. With caution and a marked anxiety, Wharton traded on the freedoms from traditional family and gender strictures that modernity was making available to women of wealth, and she finally divorced Theodore in 1913. Yet these dynamic features of modern sexuality and family in turn become the objects of a deft, funny, and often penetrating scrutiny in Wharton's novels. Behind her most pointed moments of satire we can read a disavowal, an attempt to indict a recklessness she wanted to distinguish from her own chosen life as a divorcée. Yet the disavowal itself is also an indirect acknowledgment that Wharton knew from the inside, as it were, the exhilaration as well as the damage that could come from ruptures in conventional family structures and more locally rooted ways of life.

Wharton found an ingenious way to capture this dynamism in fiction by severing the conventional marriage plot from local place and supplanting it with stories of divorces, remarriages, abandonments, and adoptions that transpire across time and space. Wharton's narratives of the affluent Americans who "inter-married, inter-loved and inter-divorced each other over the whole face of Europe" together distill one of her chief insights about modernity, her understanding that modern travel is a kind of index to the radical change within marriage and family. The ability in travel to rapidly exchange closeness for distance and to combine estrangement with intimacy reflects the mobile nature of modern kinship ties. Marriage and even blood relations are detachable, transplanted, improvised.

To this end, the travel plots of her later novels often deliberately induce a kind of disorientation in her readers as an initiation into the unsettled and often unsettling relations among the characters. Wharton's 1928 novel *The Children* opens on board an ocean liner bound for Italy. From his deck chair Martin Boyne observes a collection of children who defy his attempts to puzzle out their relation to one another and to the "little-girl-mother" who cares for them. Martin's confusion is our own, as children with differing accents, coloring, and last names behave as siblings. Their baffling presence on the steamship eventually becomes the most telling fact about their family identity. Crossing the Atlantic without any parent, the group of heterogeneous children is the product of myriad marriages, divorces, affairs, and remarriages among adults from at least three continents. The ocean liner is thus an appropriate host to children who owe their relation to siblings and "steps"—indeed, owe their own lives—to the couplings and breakups that are inseparable from their parents' incessant travel. Similarly, the striking absence of any mother or father on board reflects Wharton's emphasis on the losses and disruptions that can come with modern mobility. Where do these children belong, and to whom? These puzzles only deepen into more existential questions as the novel explains the complex "marital chessboard" that is the children's varied parentage.[48]

The novel also poses a further question: Are "the children" in fact children? Like Henry James in his *What Maisie Knew,* Wharton reconsiders what we understand as the nature of childhood. In the placeless context of travel, age and identity are no longer aligned. The oldest of the group, Judith Wheater, is variously "a playmate, mother, and governess all in one," and Martin has difficulty conjecturing her age. The more Martin saw of her, the narrator notes, "the more difficult he found it to situate her in time and space." Identity has become changeable and indistinct: "Whatever she was, she was only intermittingly."⁴⁹ This mutability of the otherwise certain identities of kinship and age becomes increasingly charged as the middle-aged Martin unwittingly falls in love with Judith. He acts on his unacknowledged desire by agreeing to guide and protect the children as a "father." As others force him to confront his sexual love for the teenage girl, Martin becomes enraged and then resigned, withdrawing from a world out of joint. In *The Children,* the vicissitudes of travel not only figure for us a new distance between parent and child but also forge new intimacies that shade into the taboo of incest.⁵⁰

Wharton's families and lovers supply fables of the "restructuring" of social relationships across the large-scale dimensions of time and space that Giddens identifies with modernity. In Wharton's world, kinship has become geography, a spatial reordering of the responsibilities and rights of the generations and the routes of intimacy and sexual access. Rather than offering a haven from a commercialized culture (as in domestic novels) or a resolution to class tensions (as in novels of manners), the family is a central site for the explosive forces unleashed during the "take-off period" of global modernization. Absorbing these forces, the family in Wharton's fiction is transformed by strains of vertigo, satirical farce, and an increasingly literalized vision of incest. These pressures culminate in characters' personal dislocations, through an individual "restructuring" of intimacy that is both compelling and frightening, and that eventually produces for certain characters the rupture of actual violence.

Modern dislocation has a specific site in *The Mother's Recompense.* Wharton both begins and ends the narrative in a French Mediterranean town that is a colony for "uprooted, drifting women." The unnamed Riviera resort is an archipelago for the social exile of women who had, as it were, traveled too much: in this "female world," an international collection of adulterers and divorcées do their time for having fled marriages or traveled as mistresses. Kate Clephane, Wharton's American protagonist, had escaped from the "thick atmosphere of [her husband's] self-approval and unperceivingness" by agreeing to set sail from New York for the West Indies on another man's yacht. As the gossips put it, Kate had "travelled" with "another man." It is clear that for Wharton, as for Kate herself, the real transgression was Kate's temporary abandonment of her young daughter, Anne. Soon after she fled her marriage, Kate had returned to reclaim her child from her husband's family but found that mobility was no longer on her side: upon arrival she was told that the Clephane family had left with little Anne "in a private car for the Rocky Mountains."⁵¹

With exile and abandonment as backdrop, however, *The Mother's Recompense* begins by holding out the possibility of their redemption. The novel opens with travel as a trope of homecoming: the ruling Clephane matriarch has died and Kate receives a telegram from her daughter asking her to sail back for New York. When an elated Kate descends on "the gangplank of the liner" in the New York port, she feels herself "born again."[52] She has been delivered, as it were, from a homelessness of geographical and family exile. What she discovers, however, is a terrible distortion of kinship rather than the redemption of a mother and her daughter. Kate learns that Chris, her former and much younger lover from her days in France, has been courting Anne in New York, unaware that Anne is Kate's own daughter. The prospect of a marriage between Anne and Chris is the horrific "recompense" awaiting Kate upon her return to New York society.

Kate's decision to flee her husband for Europe, then, eventually gives rise to a quasi-incestuous tangle with her daughter and former lover. Distance in space collapses into a damaging hyper-closeness in human relations. The secret that Kate's daughter might unwittingly marry Kate's onetime lover brings "instantaneous revulsion" to anyone who suspects it. Wharton conveys these distortions of kinship through a sense of the "physical nausea" of rapid transit: in one scene in which Kate rushes out of London by train, her state of alienation in time and space is so profound that it is literally sickening to her. From this vantage the world is nothing but "meaningless traffic."[53]

At the same time, Wharton's kinship stories are more than merely cautionary. That is, they measure risks and warn of dangers, but they also imagine a modern kinship that holds the possibility for altogether new forms of intimacy. When family relationships are chosen rather than merely inherited, Wharton suggests, they carry the promise of a reciprocity or pure affinity free from the petty tyrannies that mar traditional family relationships. Kate regains her status as a mother, for instance, only because Anne invites her to resume it, and as a result Kate conceives of their tie as a relation of "perfect companionship." She "could not picture having any rights over the girl."[54] The depth of her love finally compels Kate to relinquish even her cherished role as a mother and to return to her European exile. The freedom of modern kinship, its foundation in consent rather than in birthright, offers a tantalizing vision of unalloyed love. Only when relations are freely chosen can they have the affective depth that seems to stimulate Wharton's imagination. In contrast to her mockery of the adults who produce the motley "tribe" in *The Children*, for instance, Wharton reserves a profound if tenuous heroism for the children in their determination to assert the status of family against all other claims. It is precisely the absence of any clear legal or even blood relation that makes their choice to love and protect each other a poignant exception to the debased forms of kinship pervading the novel.

Wharton's portrait of family is fundamentally ironic: the radical instability of the modern family, its institutional fragility, is precisely what creates the possibility for believable bonds of love. In her *Glimpses of the Moon* (1928), for instance, it is only the pervasiveness of divorce that reintroduces the option of marrying for love. Nick and Susy Lansing, both without wealth of their own, undertake an "experiment" to marry for only as long as they can live on the wedding gifts and hospitality of their rich friends. By agreeing to relinquish the other when either of them has the opportunity of marrying for money, they rely on divorce to license their temporary marriage. In some respects Wharton holds out their bond as an attenuated form of love, a mere "bargain" to "stick to" when secure luxury beckoned. Yet the novel finally suggests that such an extraordinary if not perverse agreement is in fact the proof of an exceptional intimacy: the couple's "free-masonry of precocious tolerance and irony" is in the end the reader's only guarantor of authentic love in a world of dislocation.[55]

A proleptic agreement to divorce is the only way of contracting real love. Such ironies are permanent features of Wharton's modernity, where human relations and identities are rootless and mercurial. Nick and Susy's eventual renunciation of their special understanding is part of the novel's critique of the impermanence of modern marriage, but they really only escape this critique because they recognize in each other a superior adaptability to the ungrounded nature of modernity. Their finally confirmed marriage, in other words, is not a return to marital tradition but a glimpse of its uncertain future.

In *The Children* and *Glimpses of the Moon*, the improvised familial bonds in modernity can offer a "troubled glory," at least for the lucky few. Yet the Wharton novel most self-consciously about modernity also contains her darkest portrait of modern intimacy. In *Twilight Sleep*, the usual finesse of Wharton's social satire has been deliberately converted into blunt-edged narrative sarcasm. The modern adaptability of Mrs. Pauline Manford, for instance, is manifest in her reliance on a succession of debased fads, from the sham spiritualism of her guru the "Mahatma" to the "eurythmic exercises" she practices to reduce hip size. The norms assumed by domestic realism—the naturalness of the nuclear family, the pull of the marriage plot—

are so far removed from the Manfords' world as to be wholly strange if not forgotten. Indeed, the normative category of the family can be said to reappear in the metaphor of the freak show: Mrs. Manford "was used to such rapid adjustments [in her beliefs], and proud of the fact that whole categories of contradictory opinions lay down together in her mind as peacefully as the Happy Families exhibited by strolling circuses."[56]

Even more starkly than her other late novels, Wharton's *Twilight Sleep* presents modernity as distortion. The Manford drawing room looks "more like the waiting-room of a glorified railway station than the setting of an established way of life," and modern mobility has begun to appear limiting rather than freeing or seductively risky (31). The "breathless New York life" of ocean liners and motor travel has created a static world of mass-produced discontent.

> Today [Mrs. Manford] really felt it to be too much for her: she leaned back [in her car seat] and closed her lids with a sigh. But she was jerked back to consciousness by the traffic-control signal, which had immobilized the motor just when every moment was so precious. The result of every one's being in such a hurry to get everywhere was that nobody could get anywhere. She looked across the triple row of motors in line with hers, and saw each (as if in a vista of mirrors) an expensively dressed woman like herself, leaning forward in the same attitude of repressed impatience, the same nervous frown of hurry on her brow. (87–88)

Significantly, though, the affinities of kinship in this world still look like the best—perhaps the only—refuge for human feeling and fellowship. In the "oddly-assorted" Manford family, divorce and remarriage have actually produced a wider extension of mutual family sentiment. Pauline Manford and her two husbands "had been drawn into a kind of inarticulate understanding by their mutual tenderness for the progeny of the two marriages" (46). Indeed, one young woman's *refusal* to grant her husband a divorce is the novel's yardstick for measuring acts of cruelty. But, as if to exploit the reader's relief at finding "mutual tenderness" in the Manfords' checkered kinship, Wharton gradually undermines the shared affection of this "dual family" through a relationship of quasi-incest (141).

When Dexter Manford falls in love with his stepson Jim's wife, even the regenerative relations of family succumb to what one character calls the "slippery sliding modern world" (48). Dexter deceives himself that his feelings for Lita are brotherly. They share "the same free and friendly relation which existed, say, between Jim and Nona [Dexter's daughter]," he tells himself (216). The narrator glosses the thought as Dexter's "sense of having just grazed something dark and lurid," a metaphor of danger whose overtones reverberate with the fact that he is at this moment driving Lita at high speed in his private motorcar (216). With his hands on the steering wheel, he refrains from touching her. But pages later, the near miss becomes a "crash" when he throws off constraint and acknowledges his desire: "'Lita—' He put his hand over hers. Let the whole world crash, after this" (256).

In the novel's climactic scene, the violent trope of the "crash" is realized in the literal violence of a gunshot that shatters the family. During a stay at the Manfords' country house, Pauline's first husband, Arthur Wyant, attempts to kill Dexter for his betrayal of Jim, Wyant's son. But in the nighttime attack Wyant manages only to shoot and injure Nona Manford, Jim's half-sister. Prostrate and bleeding, Nona makes her radically ambiguous plea: "It was an accident. Father—an accident!" (299). But accidents are never merely the products of chance in Wharton's fiction. In a Wharton narrative, rather, the accident is a violent symptom of modern conditions, which few characters can see or understand but almost all can feel. With its power to distract, the spectacle of an accident can cover up those conditions at the same time it registers their force and potential for damage. Real or imagined, the accident is a sign of the velocities of change, the extraordinary power, and the resulting potential for destruction that accelerated in Wharton's era. In *Twilight Sleep*, Wharton makes the complexities of modern kinship into the scene of a wreck. Nona's hysterical claim that the shooting was an "accident" burdens her with the work of collective disavowal that frees the rest of the family for the "remedy of travel" prescribed "when rich people's nerves are out of gear" (306). While Nona lies immobile, the Wyants and Manfords scatter from Vancouver and the Rockies to Ceylon and Egypt.

The "possible crash" that animates Wharton's fiction combines the visual excitement of the popular spectacle with the sensations of risk in modern mobility. Much more than Weber's image of modernity as a static, restrictive "iron cage," Wharton's figure captures the cultural energies it also critiques, re-creating in art the speed and dread, the exhilaration and violence, that make up the phenomenology of modern culture.

Chapter 7
Neurological Modernity and American Social Thought

John Dewey believed that art offers access to the real, but he was not prepared to give pride of place to realism. In 1890, at the height of the debates on literary realism, he professed to be agnostic: "We hear much, on this side and that, of realism. Well, we may let realism go, but we cannot let go reality. The importance and endurance of poetry, as of all art, are in its hold upon reality." Dewey was persuaded that art had "outrun the slower step of reflective thought" in its ability to track the pace and intensity of modern experience. But even though he promoted the role of art in modern thought, Dewey was subtly reordering the tenets of a Howellsian brand of literary realism. Howells hoped that cultivating a literary system of reflective thought would allow the novel to recover a language of public reason from out of a chaotic domain of unreal fable and commercial mimesis. But for Dewey, the kinetic "movement of life, of experience," was giving ever-new shapes to reality, and rational reflection could only try to keep up: "We must, in the cold, reflective way of critical system, justify and organize the truth which poetry, with its quick, naïve contacts, has already felt and reported."[1]

Dewey traced his perspective back to Hegel, from whom he had drawn the lesson that there is "no special, apart faculty of thought belonging to and operated by a mind existing separate from the outer world."[2] But in giving priority to lived experience over systemic thought, he was also speaking to a new preoccupation with immediate, sensory life that was very much of his own time. For thinkers in a number of different disciplines, the textures of everyday experience and perception seemed to hold the secret to acquiring new knowledge. Ben Singer has dubbed this emphasis on everyday sensory life a "neurological conception of modernity."[3] Today we most often associate this neurological modernity with theorists such as Georg Simmel, Walter Benjamin, and Siegfried Kracauer, intellectuals who tried to analyze the physical and perceptual changes in ordinary experience that accompanied large-scale transformations in markets, communications, and technology. As Singer demonstrates, however, these social theorists were also tapping into a widespread sense already articulated by Simmel's contemporaries that modern life was bringing what he called an "intensification of nervous stimulation." Mass culture produced its own discourse of the neurological: in magazines, cartoons, tabloids, and popular novels, observers drew attention to a new phenomenal world marked by a range of perceived hazards, thrills, and novelties, from speeding trolleys to the "hyperstimulus" of posters and shouting street ads.[4]

Simmel's 1903 essay "The Metropolis and Mental Life" marks a turning point in this critical tradition for the way it relocates the site of thought. Instead of looking to the mental capacities of a certain kind of person, the "rational man," Simmel turns to the neurological operations of a certain kind of situated mind. The mental life of the city dweller, Simmel argues, reflects the environment of intense stimulation and sensory overload that increasingly shapes the everyday lives of modern subjects. "The rapid crowding of changing images, the sharp discontinuity of a single glance, and the unexpectedness of onrushing impressions"—these are the conditions or "sensory foundations" of new mental habits and modes of thought.[5] From this perspective, the sensationalism of commercial culture is largely an epiphenomenon; the kinetic spectacles and thrills that became the keynote of so many mass amusements and media were not the cause of a sensation-hungry mass audience but merely a profitable cultivation of a deeper structure of modern hyperstimulation—a commercialization of the shock of modernity.[6]

Dewey's comments on the active "movement of life" suggest the possibility that American thinkers were among the earliest theorists of a neurological modernity.[7] Genres of art exerted a strong influence on the way pragmatists developed their new styles of critical thought. As Dewey's comments suggest, pragmatists looked to literary forms for alternatives to what they perceived as the sterile speculations of traditional philosophy. George Herbert Mead argued that the novel provided important data for working out a "general theory of self-consciousness," for instance, and William James claimed that his close study of Goethe taught him the importance of surrender to the "literalness" of the material world. But even though the novel and other forms promised avenues of critical insight, for many writers immersed in questions of the materiality of consciousness, the specific techniques of literary realism no longer seemed the surest source of social discernment. Howells's wish to see literary sensibility enlisted as a searching means of social understanding would find ironic fulfillment in new genres—not in realist novels but in hybrid works of social theory, as the pragmatists and trained social thinkers such as Henry Adams and W. E. B. DuBois turned to literary perception and expression precisely at the point at which disciplinary systems of social thought seemed to them to fail.⁸

Henry Adams and the Aesthetics of Astonishment

In *The Education of Henry Adams* (1907), Adams calls his experience of the death of his sister "the sum and term of education."

> The first serious consciousness of Nature's gesture—her attitude toward life—took form then as a phantasm, a nightmare, an insanity of force. For the first time, the stage-scenery of the senses collapsed; the human mind felt itself stripped naked, vibrating in a void of shapeless energies, with resistless mass, colliding, crushing, wasting, and destroying what these same energies had created and labored from eternity to perfect. Society had become fantastic, a vision of pantomime with a mechanical motion; and its so-called thought merged in the mere sense of life.

Here education is not mental cultivation but its opposite: the mind's traumatic collapse into the materiality of "mere sense." The passage on his sister's death (she suffered the "terrors of jock jaw" as the result of a "miserable car-accident") represents only one of many moods in the book; Adams recovers from the blow to continue what he calls his "accidental education" as it went forward into the twentieth century. But the devastating lesson prefigures the final fruits of his education as embodied in the book's concluding laws of material entropy. To learn is to uncover the sheer materiality of shapeless mass and force in a world indifferent to human meaning: "Education went backward."⁹

In this dark moment, the revelation of a neurological modernity—mental life seen as determined by sensory life ("so-called thought merged in the mere sense of life")—looks like the end of the world. In truth, it is really only the end of Adams's world, something he realizes and makes clear in the larger context of the *Education*. Adams's narrative is a liberal apocalypse: his "accidental" lessons come in the form of a series of shocks that disassemble virtually every category of liberalism, from the autonomous mind and disinterested republican virtues to historical progress and national futurity. But although the apparatus of a liberal worldview collapses, the wreckage becomes the unlikely site for a "posthumous" literary analysis that issues from the consciousness that has survived the death of the liberal self. The compulsion to analyze endures. But what does it mean to think and write when "so-called thought" has discovered its own materiality?

Adams's achievement in forging a post-liberal narrative of U.S. culture and history has prompted many critics to see the *Education* as the first work of American modernism. But Adams's narrative, I contend, owes more to modernism's repressed other—mass culture—than to the poetics and ideologies that would eventually come to define the movement of literary modernism. The narrative voice of the *Education* is created from the literal disintegration of the bourgeois public sphere, the historical event that Habermas persuasively links to the advent of mass culture.[10] As Adams's analysis pushes past the limits of intelligibility that had structured his own thought, the result is a heterogeneity of psychic material and social signs that are characteristic of a "composite public sphere," an unsorted experiential horizon in which the energies and vocabularies from mass culture coexist and sometimes overlap with the critical-dialogic ideals of a traditional literary public.[11] Writing from within this experiential horizon, Adams fashions an acute style of literary analysis out of the felt shocks of discovering that his own thought has been constructed from "the stage-scenery of the senses."

The *Education* is a new genre: autobiography by default. Adams writes from the position of one who intended to offer the first truly scientific history of his age but can deliver only a record of his failure to do so. Adams is not being coy; his certainty about having failed is real enough. But he also presents his failure as a genuine discovery: Adams's education teaches him aright by revealing that the promise of historical intelligibility was wrong. The periods of Adams's life are thus the only means of ordering the broken remainders of a unified field theory of history that could not be written, and the progression of his ironized education presents fragments of Darwinist theory, medieval history, American diplomacy, far West travel and European tourism, Washington satire, pedagogy, thermodynamics, economic history, and poetic musings on women, Whitman, and sex. Several years before the *Education* was issued publicly Adams circulated the book among a group of friends, but many of these hyper-cultivated readers found it close to incomprehensible. Bernard Berenson, though captivated, called the style "over-Jamesian for my intelligence." The other James (William) offered what are among the most illuminating remarks when he pointed to the narrative's disjointed eclecticism: "There is a hodge-podge of world-fact, private fact, irony (with the word 'education' stirred in too much for my appreciation!)."[12]

Despite the note of irritation, William's description captures quite acutely Adams's primary methodological innovation. Once Adams no longer presupposes a supersensible rational mind that can order history from the outside, the intention to write a universal history turns into a disjunctive record of Adams's sense of historical displacement. Liberalism's structuring distinctions—the private and the public, the personal and the historical—give way, leaving world fact and private fact on the same plane. Rather than creating a unity of thought and events, this leveling only generates a fractured succession of experiences, historical images, and ironic reflections. Without a secure distance between thought and its objects, irony is no longer a trope of difference that can alter but also thereby reorient levels of meaning. Instead, it can only operate as a corrosive agent that disorients the reader with an excess of ironic reversals ("over-Jamesian") and thus performs Adams's own "backwards" education in the form of a reading experience.

Adams deliberately cultivates a readerly sense of vertigo. To read the *Education* is to feel a sense of mental disorientation; this would have been especially true for a liberally educated reader in 1907. Adams seeks to recreate in the reader the transformative mental shocks that are the basis of his new experiential vocabulary for understanding history and the historical mind. Few people could have felt as much in possession of history as Henry Adams, of course, which helps explain why almost no one renders with as much vividness the sensibility of historical displacement. Life as the great-grandson of one president and grandson of another meant that the town of Quincy, Massachusetts, the city of Washington, the U.S. State Department (where he served under his father in the British legation in London), and the White House were all at various times extensions of "home" in the most literal and intimate sense.

Because of this family history, Adams calls himself a "child of the seventeenth- and eighteenth-centuries" fated to "wake up to find himself required to play the game of the twentieth" (10). He enters the world, that is to say, expecting it to adhere to an "eighteenth-century fabric of a priori, or moral, principles," the regularities of fixed law that bind politics and virtue and promise to harmonize timeless nature and individual knowledge. Belief in those principles makes him an heir to the nineteenth century as well, or at least it appears that way to a boy who as yet "had no idea that Karl Marx was standing there waiting for him."

252   Chapter 7

> The boy naturally learned only one lesson from his saturation in such air. He took for granted that his sort of world, more or less the same that had always existed in Boston and Massachusetts Bay, was the world which he was to fit. Had he known Europe he would have learned no better. The Paris of Louis Phillippe, Guizot, and de Tocqueville, as well as the London of Robert Peel, Macaulay, and John Stuart Mill, were but varieties of the same upper-class bourgeoisie that felt instinctive cousinship with the Boston of Ticknor, Prescott, and Motley.... The system [was] the ideal of human progress. (36)

The young Adams makes the understandable assumption that the universal subject of human progress is "the boy," Henry Adams. He is right, which makes the assumption of universality wrong. That is, there was no one closer than Henry Adams—closer in sex, race, family position, education, and opportunity—to the standard individual assumed by classic liberalism unless it were Mill himself. Adams exploits his unique place in the history of transatlantic liberalism to argue that the human consciousness envisioned by classical liberal thought is in reality the mind-set of a particular social class, a transatlantic family of ideological kin. The most notable family trait, Adams confides, is the willful mistake of assuming that the thought of their clan is destined to be the mind of the whole world: "Boston had solved the universe; or had offered and realized the best solution yet tried. The problem was worked out" (37).

Adams learns otherwise, and the resulting sense of discontinuity and lapse is almost more physical than cognitive. Adams presents his early education as a series of lived shocks that are eventually fatal to his past self ("the boy") but that also give rise to the analytic power of the adult narrative voice that has survived. From an early age the puzzles of history are a provocation or spur, a disruption that is also a motive for thought. One such disruption comes at age twelve on a family journey to "the slave states" where Adams confronts the "moral problem that deduced George Washington from the sum of all wickedness" inherent in slavery (47). Another occurs in the Black District of Birmingham, England, where Adams experiences the "revelation of an unknown society" that existed among the industrial poor (73). These are among the primal scenes that will link his preoccupation with world history to his sense of possessing a torn or wounded material consciousness.

On one hand, the problems inherent in narrating history afford him a remarkable productivity. Adams capped a distinguished career as a historian with his nine-volume *History of the United States During the Administrations of Washington and Jefferson* (1889–91), and his immersion in twelfth- and thirteenth-century Europe became the basis of his *Mont Saint Michel and Chartres* (1904). On the other hand, in the retrospective view of the *Education* Adams's success as a historian seems only to deepen the problem of historical fact. One "must either teach history as a catalogue," he writes, "or as an evolution" with inherent moral meaning. Unfortunately, Adams "had no theory of evolution to teach, and could not make the facts fit one" (288). The dilemma is keenest for the teacher of history: "In essence incoherent and immoral, history had to be taught as such—or falsified." History now confronts him as a mere accumulation of painful and confounding episodes, perhaps all the more painful for his close proximity to the levers of power. Making sense of the "debacles" of the nineteenth century, and of the American past and future ("the nightmare of Cuban, Hawaiian, and Nicaraguan chaos"), comes to seem more urgent and yet more quixotic (339).

When the universal ideal of human progress turns out to be liberalism's local, insufficient "solution," history reappears before Adams as a broken succession of images and dark dreamscapes. But it is significant that Adams also recognizes a suspicious ethical ambiguity in casting himself as a hapless spectator to a panorama of historical debacles. In a letter to his close friend John Hay, Adams wrote of his impulse to watch the "circus" of modernity from the best seat in the house: "My lunacy scares me. I am seriously speculating whether I shall have a better view of the *fin-de-siècle* circus in England, Germany, France or India, and whether I should engage seats to view the debacle in London or Paris, Berlin or Calcutta."[13] Here and elsewhere, Adams expresses awareness of the risk he runs of falling into an attitude of ironic distance that shifts at will between intellectual engagement and inured detachment. In joining an image of a global cosmopolitan with the circus spectator, he recognizes a degree of literal derangement ("lunacy") in the idea of selecting a world capital from which to watch the world like a show. The incongruity of the trope conveys a sense of unease at his own social position and the analytic habits it has bred.

But there is still further significance to the circus allusion. Adams admitted to "haunt[ing] the lowest fakes of the Midway day and night" and had a fondness for exhibitions such as snake charmers and gladiatorial contests.[14] There is a streak of campy amusement in this confession, to be sure. But the remark also suggests there is more to Adams's allusions to entertainment like circuses and wax museums than an ironic patrician smile. The confession also helps locate an "aesthetics of astonishment" that is a crucial element in Adams's critical style. Tom Gunning has coined this phrase to describe the unique set of pleasures and shock effects that marked the new industry in commercial amusements flourishing at the end of the century. The illusion-based spectacles of dime museums and cinematographs, Gunning argues, are not evidence that mass audiences were easily duped or possessed childish tastes. Rather, they evince an eagerness for the "pleasurable vacillation between belief and doubt" that became possible only after the widespread decline of belief in miracles and marvels. Similarly, the "apparent miracles" performed by new mechanical amusements like the roller coaster were an exciting test of commonsense knowledge of physics at the same time that they channeled anxiety about modern technology into the electric sensation of the bodily thrill.[15] Non-narrative spectacles traded the logic of dramatic action and character psychology for the glamour that adhered to any successful act of display. In a world of crowded sights and signs, showmanship itself became a competitive field for the cultivation of skill and technique in producing astonishment.

It might strain the definition of aesthetics to count this collection of deliberately cultivated thrills and ruptures as a form of the beautiful; clearly the appeal to curiosity and sensory shock is at odds with the contemplation of beauty elicited by the calm rhythms of the pastoral or the grandeur of epic. But because an aesthetics of astonishment takes effect in an epistemological twilight, a heterogeneous zone in which systems of belief and logics of disenchantment clash and combine, Gunning argues that mass amusements make us aware of the "vertiginous experience of the frailty of our knowledge of the world."[16] A similar epistemological twilight, mixing the shadows of vanished eighteenth-century certainties with the dazzling science of the nineteenth, is the zone in which Adams tries to capture his own literary record of modernity. Here, too, sensory experience poses questions of epistemology and conducts a literary version of the "vacillation between belief and doubt." When the unraveling or "backwards" movement of his education leads him to locate the mind in the "stage-scenery of the senses," Adams draws on the disordered energies of mass culture to help create a new form of literary analysis. At one level, the simulations and discrepant styles of mass entertainment assist Adams's strategy of demystification, allowing him to recast a world that once seemed universal as an unreal or artificial construction ("lowest fakes of the Midway"). But in a more substantial way, Adams's cultivation of a literary aesthetics of astonishment allows him to articulate a new and starkly different kind of universality, a vision that recognizes a commonality in all sensate life while it still preserves different tracts of experience and distinct social minds as non-synchronous parts of the same reality.

Adams's literary version of showmanship is perhaps clearest in his quick-change staging of a dizzying array of selves. The *Education* refuses the obligation to trace a continuity of the autobiographical subject. Although he begins with a recognizable figure, "the boy," that subject disappears abruptly. In its place Adams offers a series of stand-ins for "Henry Adams" ranging from the whimsical to the bizarre. He is a "French poodle on a string" pulled from "one form of unity or centralization and another." He is a "worm." He "should have been a Marxist" but, no longer believing himself a universal subject, he recognizes that "some narrow trait of the New England nature" made him unable to convert. He is a "Conservative Christian anarchist," a "pilgrim of power," a circus "acrobat" on a high wire, a "posthumous person" who somehow still inhabits the world of the living, a kinsman of prehistoric "fish" and of modern-day "sharks." All are different incarnations of what he calls in his preface a "manikin" self, the tailor's dummy in a human shape and a passive model that exists to take the measure of someone else's suit of clothes.

The figure of the mannequin comes from *Sartor Resartus*, Thomas Carlyle's inventive exploration of a post-Romantic self that is no longer an organic and indivisible soul. But Adams's fondness for presenting and then rapidly changing such vivid models of self also suggests the department store mannequin that was already a familiar object behind plate-glass windows.[17] Even more than the experience of the shopper or the flaneur, however, Adams's transformation of Carlyle's literary figure suggests the experience of someone who has spent time "haunt[ing] the lowest fakes of the Midway" and other sites where poodles, acrobats, and wax mannequins might suggest effigies for a discontinuous self. By superimposing literary and commercial representations of subjectivity, Adams anticipates the new forms of perceptual identification that film theorists see as the foundation of cinematic experience. For the early cinematic viewer, going to the movies offered a discontinuous series of subjects, all of which solicit different forms of identification and attachment. As Kracauer argues, the filmgoer "lets himself be poly-morphously projected in a movie theater": "As a fake Chinaman he sits in a fake opium den, turns into a well-trained dog who performs ridiculously clear acts to please a female star, gathers himself into an alpine storm, gets to be a circus artist and lion at once."[18] Especially before the development of the more integrated, "classical" modes of cinematic narration, early film excelled at quick-change displacements of different subjects, scenes, and objects that invited desire and identification to travel wayward paths of experimental subjectivity.[19]

To identify the Midway and the cinema as sites of aesthetic culture, of course, dodges the question of the *commercial* nature of mass culture as a field of mediation. Can the market-driven experience available in mass genres really offer an opportunity for the kind of reflective thought or intersubjective dialogue we associate with public culture? Kracauer, even more than Benjamin, remained alert to the way commercial forms like the cinema stirred energies of subjective fantasy and identification with the aim of appropriating those energies for profit. Seen from this angle, the mobility and self-transformation encouraged in mass culture also signify a vulnerability to impersonal powers and capitalized interests. "One forgets oneself gazing," Kracauer writes of the cinema, "and the big dark hole is animated with the semblance of a life that belongs to no one and consumes everyone."[20] Similarly, Adams's mannequin self, for all its rapid mutations and reincarnations, is far from being a self-governing agent and is clearly outmatched by the modern universe of large-scale forces. As Adams saw it, modern conditions have made us "irritable, nervous, querulous, unreasonable, and afraid" (471), and with good reason. At the same time that it highlights human vulnerabilities, however, the horizon of mixed, discontinuous subjectivity evoked in mass culture sites also suggests that such genres can re-create *more* than fantasy only, that they can be open to accommodating conflicting attitudes and disparate needs that are otherwise excluded or reductively rationalized. And Adams's version of staging ludic images of quick-change subjectivity suggests a further possibility: a heterogeneous horizon of discontinuous experience has the potential to join fantasy and psychic projection with critical thought, for the purpose of seeking out what Adams will call "a new social mind" (470).

The social mind in the *Education* is material, divided, and dispersed, but for that very reason it is capable of recognizing its unexpected kinship with creatures as different as fish, war profiteers, and the dead. In his effort to uncover a new way to theorize the mind, Adams brought the aesthetics of astonishment to his lifelong study of science. Adams had hoped that science might supply the "ultimate Unity" he had never expected from religion and found fruitless to try to extract from history. Darwin's discoveries promise to offer the unity of a planetary history obedient to natural law. But Darwinism, too, turns out to look suspiciously like a god, worshiped as omniscient by supplicants looking to share its power. Adams's ironic, sometimes flippant-seeming treatment of scientific inquiry has led some critics to argue that he retreated from any belief in rationalism. Yet the literary turns that Adams brings to his meditations on science are not a disavowal of scientific thought but rather a means of placing the revelations of science together with the problems of human consciousness and history, a conjunction that scientists must refuse as the precondition of doing science but that the writer is capable of accommodating as a form of literary experimentation. This experiment is the larger reason for Adams's sustained grappling with Darwinism and other branches of science. Displacing his "troglodytic" origins in the Adams family, he restarts a family history from his "earliest ancestor and nearest relative the ganoid fish, whose name, according to Professor Huxley, was *Pterapsis*." This "oldest friend and cousin" will supply an "impersonal point for measure" with which to attempt to reconstruct a world of meaningful regularities (378).

Darwinism's effects on the imagination are the real interest for Adams: "For the young men whose lives were cast between 1867 and 1900, Law should be evolution from lower to higher, aggregation of the atom in the mass, concentration of multiplicity in unity, compulsion of anarchy in order" (224). Adams here is both confessing and mocking. He was certainly among the young men who learned to look to science for a new principle of unity. But as a radical ironist, Adams underscores the wholly human motives that made those men eager to believe in evolution's promise of order. History, in all its corrosiveness, extends to even the furthest reaches of speculative thought. For Adams's generation, the "seduction" of Darwinism lies not in its value as science but in its ideological appeal in the aftermath of the Civil War, a war that Adams had helped conduct as an aide to the Union delegation to England.

Unbroken Evolution under uniform conditions pleased everyone—except curates and bishops; it was the very best substitute for religion; a safe, conservative, practical, thoroughly Common-Law deity. Such a working system for the universe suited a young man who had just helped to waste five or ten thousand million dollars and a million lives, more or less, to enforce unity and uniformity on people who objected to it. (217)

The power of Adams's method, an avowedly anarchic power, lies in his insistence on linking even the most monumental natural phenomena with the finitudes of history, not to reconcile them but to pursue the implications of their disjunction. In nature, the implications of evolution are what they are; in human history, the implications of belief in evolution are of an altogether different order of meaning. And in that space of difference operate all the motives, aggressions, and ideals endemic to the conflicted sphere of human history. Adams's reference to the war dead, as casual as it is brutal, recalls us to the violence that cannot be sealed off from the meditations on far distant operations of natural law. Adams's "manikin," the disinherited human subject, has been pushed out of the center of the universe, just one more kinfolk of the Pterapsis fish. But so demoted, the human figure remains on the scene as the hapless subject of history in order to register the collusion, resistance, and denial that human subjects try to transact with an indifferent universe. The technique represents Adams's attempt to hold human actors accountable, even when the sphere of human action can no longer be judged by a transcendent moral law.

To look at the world this way is neither commonsensical nor comfortable. The historical consciousness in *The Education of Henry Adams* is committed to thinking analogically about incommensurable orders and thus to remaining suspended between terms that cannot otherwise meet. No one is more aware than Adams that it is a difficult posture to endure, not to mention an awkward and even risible one, and the image he selects for his own intellectual practice comes directly from commercial culture: "His artificial balance was acquired habit. He was an acrobat, with a dwarf on his back, crossing a chasm on a slack-rope, and commonly breaking his neck" (412). The image is self-deprecating, transforming a patrician's typical disdain for circus-style entertainment into a picture of his own analytic consciousness. But the image is also deadly serious. The same figure of a broken neck appears again when Adams describes his visit to the Paris World Exposition of 1900, the site he uses for the final lesson in education. With its heterogeneous collection of objects and images, the exposition presented "a new universe which had no common scale of measurement with the old." The facts of radium, radio waves, Daimler motors, kinetic gas, and giant electric dynamos declare a universe of "occult" energies that are literally unfathomable and distinctly threatening: "He found himself lying in the Gallery of Machines at the Great Exposition of 1900, with his historical neck broken by the sudden irruption of forces totally new" (363). The moment is a kind of death for the "Henry Adams" who has appeared throughout the book in his many guises. The magnitude of force he has encountered signifies the end to any consciousness that might articulate a principle of unity. Henceforth it will be "force," rather than consciousness, that is the true subject of history: "Continuity was broken" (351).

Adams's figure of "force" is both scientific and literary. His method of grasping historical disjunctions through an attempt at devising a literary "scale for the whole" allows him to compare different "lines of force that attract the mind" (300), from medieval Christian faith and erotic inspiration to the mechanical energies of the modern industrial age. As a literary figure, then, "force" is able to align and calibrate markedly different phenomena. But after the neck-breaking intellectual rupture in Paris, force becomes the principle that *defeats* literary intelligence and historical consciousness as it ascends to become the true subject of history. Force, clearly, is a non-human subject and obeys only what Adams calls a "law of acceleration," an internal logic that places it outside any scale for the whole. When, in his final chapters, Adams restarts his narrative to present a compressed history of force, human beings appear as the incidental figures that compose what might be called a race of mannequins: small objects of mass who await, all unconscious, for whatever will befall them in a world ruled by "bombs" (468).

Adams's analysis of a universe of force is derived from his study of science and world history, but force in the *Education* is also the power that saturates everyday life of the modern neurological subject. "Forces grasped his wrists and flung him about as though he had hold of a live wire or a runaway automobile," he writes of the modern subject. "Every day Nature violently revolted, causing so-called accidents with enormous destruction of property and life, while plainly laughing at man, who helplessly groaned and shrieked and shuddered, but never for a single instant could stop. The railways alone approached the carnage of war; automobiles and fire-arms ravaged society, until an earthquake became almost a nervous relaxation" (467). In passages such as these, Adams's "accidental education" becomes violently literal, riveted by an imagination of mechanical disasters and fatal accidents that had long been the preoccupation of tabloid papers, cartoons, and cinema.[21] A world governed by force seems dystopic to Adams's nineteenth-century mind: the education of the future "promised to be violently coercive" (470). His sister's death as the result of a "miserable car-accident" resonates with the sense infusing this passage that modern force is a capricious god who kills for sport. But precisely because of its aura of threat, for Adams force also becomes an indirect incitement to sympathetic identification: the violence of a mechanical accident or a bomb is a shock that brings the literary intellectual back to the "stage-scenery of the senses" he shares with all the other subjects of a mass society. The blind tyranny of force reminds Adams of the vulnerability of the body, a human commonality that becomes the basis of a new unity among modern strangers.

By articulating force, sensory experience, and literary analysis within the same textual horizon, the *Education* expands literary culture and complicates its implicit models of reason. With his "historical neck broken," Adams is able to explore social worlds that modern velocities of change have begun to articulate in spaces outside the literary public sphere, acknowledging the reality and complexity of experience that can be glimpsed in crowd life, Midway shows, and mechanical amusements. Adams's literary tropes and high-wire ironies bring the intellectual's talent for analysis to the complexities of modern neurological experience, even as it places before the view of the reader the picture of a vulnerable bodily creature, "an elderly and timid single gentleman in Paris, who never drove down the Champs Élysées without expecting an accident, and commonly witnessing one; or found himself in the neighborhood of an official without calculating the chances of a bomb" (467).

But, seen from another angle, Adams's literary evocation of the terrain of "force" is arguably *less* complex than those of mass entertainment, where evocations of terror and anxiety about modern force were combined with what John Dewey would call "enjoyments" and with the future-oriented practice of the "act of liking." The pleasure cultivated in mass culture suggests that "force" may have a future, not just an apocalyptic end, even if Henry Adams can only imagine a future that is "violently coercive." In theory, Adams can grasp the idea of a human future under the reign of force: "He was curious beyond all measure to see whether the conflict of forces would produce the new man, since no other energies seemed left on earth to breed" (472). When he reminds himself that human history will necessarily outlast his own life and mind, Adams's habit of self-obviation becomes an instrument of hope; the fact that history will produce a new kind of subject means it will bring a "new social mind" (470), one that may be able to see the continuity and futurity that Adams himself cannot. The "new social mind" was something Adams could anticipate but could not describe. But the pragmatist thinkers who were Adams's contemporaries turned to a foundation of sensory perception to try to describe and realize just such a mind by attending to the possibilities for pleasure in a world transformed by force.

Pragmatism and Neurological Modernity

Were the pragmatists the first philosophers of mass culture? Some of their detractors might agree, although for them such a title would signify only what is scandalous about the pragmatist project: its purported willingness to cater to ideas that are an easy sell. Bertrand Russell and G. E. Moore, for instance, saw pragmatism as an attempt to supplant the search for rational truth with a vulgar embrace of utility and expediency (an interpretation William James would renounce as "slander").[22] But if we approach mass culture in the way I have been addressing it in this study—as a formation of commercial publics able to recognize and articulate experience that exceeded what was intelligible to the bourgeois public sphere (modeled as it was after a middle-class reading public)—then it is possible to conceive of the classical pragmatists as theorists of mass culture, thinkers who hoped to discover the experiential truths of a neurological modernity.

The most distinctive claim of classical pragmatism was that the soundness of a particular idea could be evaluated more accurately in the world of action and behavior than by way of abstract systems of reasoning. C. S. Pierce argued that the validity of an idea lies in the conduct it dictates and inspires. Our concepts and beliefs are not abstract postulates we hold in our heads but implicit rules that direct our behavior. What counts most for pragmatists are the concrete effects of an idea, the extent to which it "works" in the world. The emphasis on a worldly verification of concepts meant that the pragmatists saw sites and artifacts of human thought where few other professional philosophers were likely to look. In a 1913 essay "The Social Self," for instance, George Herbert Mead wrote that "it is fair to say that the modern western world has lately done much of its thinking in the form of the novel."[23] The conduct depicted in a novel, and, indeed, the practice of writing or reading a novel, opens up a world of practical activity in which ordinary choices and everyday experience can count as forms of thinking.

Unlike Henry Adams, however, the pragmatists give few indications that they looked to forms of mass culture entertainment as direct aids to analysis. William James expressed the uneasiness about mass culture that was shared by many literary intellectuals when he worried that "excessive novel-reading and theatre-going" was eroding people's ability to channel mental stimulation into purposive action.[24] When the classical pragmatists speak directly to cultural forms, they tend to cite examples from literary culture (as with Mead's reference to the novel) or other high arts. James argued that the philosopher should immerse himself in works that are "suggestive rather than dogmatic," a syllabus that could include "novels and dramas of the deeper sort" along with speculative treatises in politics and economic reform, and Dewey invoked the examples of "listening to a symphony" and "viewing a picture gallery" as his touchstones for the pleasurable sense that comes from realizing that one has had a significant experience.[25] But even though the overt forms of mass culture tend to be either suspect or marginal within pragmatist analysis, by turning away from an a priori framework for inquiry, the pragmatists also redefine reason in a way that radically expands what can count as public meaning—not just the exchanges of the few (in rational-critical debate, contemplation of art, or published reflections and observations) but also the shared and sharable experience of the many. As a result, they were ultimately unwilling to pass judgment on what is unreal or fantastic as a prelude to eliminating it from the totality of meaningful experience, and they counted forms of desire and "acts of liking" as evidence for understanding human reason. The *amassed* data of the human world—expressive actions, feelings, and preferences—were the proper archive of inquiry for philosophy.

By theorizing the kinds of experience created in what James called a "pleasure-economy," the pragmatists give very different contours to their account of the real. James Livingston has argued that pragmatist thought is the first philosophical project to grapple with the profound cultural revolution that occurred at the end of the nineteenth century. At issue is a fundamental change in the social imaginary as it staged a "reconstruction of selfhood."[26] The epochal transition from industrial capitalism to the finance economy of corporate capitalism undercut the ability of the self-owning individual—exemplified in the freeholder or productive yeoman—to symbolize political and moral meaning through his productive labor. Under the new economic order, both the consumption of mass goods and the specialized mental labor of professionals became alternative sources of cultural status and authority, and the more ghostly or ungraspable stuff of a consumer society—desire and pleasure, cultural capital, knowledge work—became an unstable grammar of social value. In this dense new environment of goods, signs, and multiform abstractions like money and credit, neither the "solid citizen" (the productive male worker) nor the sturdy Yankee mind (the heir of Franklin) seemed particularly solid or sturdy as guides to the modern world.

As we have already seen in Adams, science had done its part to help erode a republican social imaginary as well. The extraordinary successes of nineteenth-century empirical study ended up displacing a model of the mind as an autonomous seat of reason.[27] Ever more rigorous empirical methods and instruments of measurement had produced a boomerang effect, doubling back on the thinking mind. Whereas scientists in the "classical regime" of the seventeenth and eighteenth centuries presumed that largely passive perceptual faculties merely channeled stimuli from an external reality, by the middle of the nineteenth century this unproblematic view of sensory perception was no longer tenable. Empirical advances kept turning up unexpected properties and problems in the sensory apparatus itself, from reflex action and reaction times to clinical pathologies. The result was a "generalized crisis in the status of the perceiving subject."[28] Perceptual experience was no longer just a conduit for delivering to the mind material for cognitive synthesis. Instead, the human sensorium became an object of scientific inquiry in its own right, leading to an "explosion" of research in the 1870s and 1880s into the makeup and functioning of the sensory apparatus.

William James was a key figure in this epistemological shift, a transition to what Jonathan Crary calls the "relocation of perception in the thickness of the body."[29] For James, moreover, this disciplinary shift was also a personal crisis. In a remarkable exchange of letters with his father, written in 1867 while William was studying in Berlin, James already pinpoints what will lead him to a decisive break with his father's metaphysical frame and its reliance on "some *a priori* logical necessity binding on the mind." Insisting that thought cannot be a force or facility that transcends nature and the body, William informed his father that he "cannot see at all in the way you seem to." Contrary to his father's metaphysical view, William had come to believe that "sensation, perception, and reason apparently have their roots in the nervous system, yet their form is entirely new and original." In Germany, James's turn to empiricism had engendered a troubling intellectual transformation (I am "drifting toward a sensationalism closed in by skepticism"), an episode that might be seen as a biographical version of the "generalized crisis" within the sciences that was undermining the classical model of the perceiving subject. Whatever the Oedipal dimensions of this crisis, for James (as for Adams) the scientific relocation of perceptual experience to the depths of the body was also a life event or lived experience—even, perhaps, a kind of somatic experience: James would later describe his "shattered frame" from this period as a form of physical sickness.[30]

Some of the overtones of panic can still be heard in James's famous chapters on consciousness in his *Principles of Psychology*. James begins the path of inquiry in the sensory data experienced in the individual mind. But unlike the British empiricists who held that sensation consists of discrete, atomistic building blocks, James insists that our senses confront a "teeming multiplicity of objects and relations" that lack any order, an "indistinguishable, swarming *continuum*, devoid of distinction." At times James's picture of the inner space of perception approaches the gothic; the evocation of a "black and jointless continuity of space and moving clouds of swarming atoms," for instance, hints at the state of near-madness recorded by Adams. In the larger context of the chapter, however, the notes of distress that animate such descriptions are merely a kind of trace or memory of a crisis now resolved. The teeming, swarming *that-ness* of materiality finally serves to make all the more impressive the agencies of attention and human will that create a coherent world out of the "inexpressive chaos" of material reality.[31] Because of its powers of selection, the individual mind carves out an orderly and inhabitable environment, and a beautiful one at that: it makes "a world full of contrasts, of sharp accents, of abrupt changes, of picturesque light and shade."[32] Thus, whereas Adams's gaze into the neurological mindscape threatens a frightening anarchy—"so-called thought merged in the mere sense of life"—James's portrait becomes not a gothic encounter with chaos but a neurological *Bildungsroman* that finds its logical fulfillment in the formed individual who possesses will, agency, and creativity.

The resemblance to a literary *Bildung* is not coincidental. For one thing, James's characterological figure for the mind turns out to be an artist ("the mind, in short, works on the data it receives very much as a sculptor works on his block of stone").[33] Even more significant, James's immersion in Goethe's works, and in *Wilhelm Meister's Apprenticeship* in particular, had been crucial to the resolution he found to his own sense of crisis.[34] Amid James's fear that his study of German experimental psychology was leading him into a purposeless sensationalism, Goethe provided him with the model of a mind that somehow seemed to derive its ability to create new forms precisely *from* its worldly, corporeal nature: "*everything* painted itself on [Goethe's] sensorium." What had confronted James as a troubling divide between thought and sense could be reconceived as a new unity, and the lesson he derived from Goethe—"a lesson of theoretical patience and respect toward the objective"—could cancel his father's warnings against "the bondage of sense" and allow him to understand the sensory apparatus as the very material of free and creative thought.[35]

The ontological unity of sense, action, and thought is of course the chief claim of pragmatism. Neurological research provided the point of departure for this new kind of philosophical inquiry that aimed to overcome the divide between mind and world, and James's *Psychology* became the foundation for the varieties of pragmatist thought pursued by Dewey and Mead, among others. The particular *way* James forges a unity between sensory life and human consciousness in the *Psychology,* however, requires closer examination if we want to understand how neurological modernity informed and challenged pragmatism. James's journey into the mind's sensory mazes arrives at a happy conclusion because human consciousness enjoys the powers of "selective attention" and "deliberative will." Because we possess these mental powers, the world of mass and force is "individualized by our mind's selective industry" (167). But if "selective attention" creates the world, what creates selective attention? If pragmatism is to refuse a priori or idealist categories, how can it account for the agency of selective attention itself? For the James of the *Psychology,* I contend, this notion of agency is derived from literature, from an inherited set of patterns—the *Bildungsroman* most decisively—that provides not only the images of a certain kind of person but also the practices for self-fashioning that James holds up for young readers, practices that can therefore realize the concepts of will and concentrated attention in concrete lives. But if this offers James something of a solution, by making a literary notion of the "heroic mind" (425) into verifiable idea, it also reintroduces the problem James is attempting to banish: the threat of limiting or distorting understanding that comes from imposing an a priori form at odds with widest range of human experience. This limitation will eventually prompt James to look outside high literary culture for alternative ways to understand states of human consciousness and what might issue from examining them.

At the heart of the challenge to James's reliance on the literary paradigm of *Bildung* is the problem of human attention, one of the most vexing topics for neurological study. Researchers like Wilhelm Wundt were at pains to pin down a precise cerebral location for an "attention center," and they looked to evolutionary thought to account for its origins. But Crary demonstrates the way experimentation tended to make attention an increasingly volatile and unstable concept: "Attention seemed to be about perceptual fixity and the apprehension of presence, but it was instead about duration and flux, within which objects and sensation had a mutating, provisional existence, and it was ultimately that which obliterated its objects."[36] Unlike a good many other researchers, James was candid and almost cheerful about admitting that attention and will themselves cannot be proven in neurological terms: "we do not know to what brain-processes they correspond." But there *is* physiological evidence: we have reason to think acts of will are material rather than "pure acts of spirit," James argues, because they are "subject to laws of habit," the repetitive neural activity through which the brain receives a material imprint of willed behavior and makes that will reflexive (150). Habits are the neurological record of willed individual choices, the contours of a life written in the neural paths of the brain. Like Rip Van Winkle, the drunkard tells himself that the latest drink won't count, but "down among his nerve-cells and fibres the molecules are counting it" (151).

The reference to Irving (or elsewhere to Goethe, Mill, and Rousseau, among others) is not the only feature that makes James's account of the mind an essentially literary account. Although will and attention are both indistinct categories, and might even be illusory according to the metrics of science, in the *Psychology* they are both real and foundational because of their powerful effects: will and attention inscribe in the body's organic matter a record of habits and choices, made manifest amid a succession of trials and opportunities and out of which an individual's ethical character is shaped, tested, and finally realized—a record, in short, identical to the novelist's blueprint for the human individual. Will and attention define the capacity to put forth "effort," and effort seems to be the "purpose of this human drama": "he who can make none is but a shadow; he who can make much is a hero" (425). What James ends by calling the "heroic mind" is an inherited trope or style for understanding human life that he derives more broadly from the liberal social imaginary but that has its most vivid archive in a canon of Anglo-European letters. When experimental science uncovered an overwhelming flood of sensations and fluid mental states, the story of a coherent and self-willed life—Wilhelm Meister's life, Goethe's own, or the life of the "strong-willed man" (419)—these models could supply the template for testing and confirming the reality of effective powers of "concentrated attention" and "energetic volition," despite the difficulty of placing them anywhere on a map of the brain.[37]

For James's critics, his emphasis on the will is a sign of what is most questionable about this brand of philosophy. Pragmatism is finally too *willful*: it licenses individual belief and expediency as the best measure of truth and bespeaks the wish of a crass society to identify truth with utility. Lewis Mumford remarked that pragmatism "smells of the Gilded Age."[38] But as with Henry Adams, James's emphatic, even obsessive concern with the individual is not at all a sentiment in harmony with a Gilded Age triumph of the will. On the contrary, it reflects his confrontation with evidence of the eclipse of the individual and a sense that his belief in autonomous reason and a self-willed mind may be unsustainable. Herein lies the significance of James's turn to literary paradigms. The James of the *Psychology* can be seen as attempting to rehabilitate the scene or topos of individual education that

Adams had found unsalvageable. To reground the capacity and dignity of a mind now seen as material—to avoid, as it were, the fate of Adams's "manikin"—James establishes a pedagogical space for the "heroic mind" within the truths of neurological science in order to keep faith with the possibility of unitary public reason.

In its emphasis on pedagogy, James's pragmatism can be classed with what I have analyzed as the museum movement. The *Psychology* is a cultural project to create a new institution—a neurological pedagogy—for meeting the crowded spaces of modern culture with their sensory assaults and hyperstimulation. Recognizing the *Psychology* as a form of civil pedagogy can help make sense of what is James's otherwise puzzling tendency to graft warnings and exhortations to the young onto his scientific anatomy of human brain function. In the chapter on habit, for instance, James's rich, detailed analysis of the involuntary, bodily operations of sense and habit modulates rather suddenly into an unlikely hymn to the power of choice, followed soon after by a compressed curriculum that recapitulates all of the branches of education as branches of individual choice: choice is the real principle behind logic ("reasoning is but a selective act of mind" [169]), behind aesthetics ("the artist notoriously selects" [171]), and at the root of ethics (on the "plane of Ethics . . . choice reigns supreme" [171]). The resolution of reason, art, and ethics into the act of choice returns the autonomous individual to the center of a "teeming" and indifferent sensory universe, and allows James to exhort young students to fashion their own identity through judicious choices.

By investing the selective capacity of the mind with the power to construct reality, James was not redefining truth as mere expediency. Against the claims of his detractors, James emphasizes that the long-term operation of human "verifying activities" places a great deal of restriction on what can pass for a valid idea. Pragmatist truth only emerges "in the long run and on the whole of course; for what meets expediently all the experience in sight won't necessarily meet all further experience equally satisfactorily. Experience . . . has a way of boiling over, and making us correct our present formulas." The key is to open the broadest possible "borders of experience."[39] In much of the early James, however, what I have called the literary paradigm of a fully realized individual life tends to operate as a regulative principle to rule out some kinds of activity as creditable experience. "Excessive novel-reading and theatre-going" (149)—a pathological symptom of a mass culture—is only one symptom of the dissolution of active selfhood that seems be enervating experience rather than expanding it. Similarly, in

The Will to Believe (1897), he invokes the "thousands of innocent magazine readers [who] lie paralyzed and terrified in the network of shallow negations" (538), the martyrs of mass print.[40] The thousands who thereby lose the firm outlines of character become something lesser or indistinct than individuals and congeal into a single mass body. In passages such as these, the regulative ideal of an all-knowing individual mind ("the perfectly wise man") serves to subtract certain kinds of data from what counts as the sum of human experience in which pragmatic verification can distinguish truth.

But experience, as James himself puts it, has a way of "boiling over." Even in the *Psychology*, James is already recording—albeit with a wary eye— forms of perception, attention, and experience that exceed the borders of his own high culture pedagogy. His description of the phenomenon of "dispersed attention" is an especially rich example inasmuch as James admits that this lapse from coherent selfhood is part of everyday experience. "Most of us probably fall several times a day into a fit somewhat like this":

The eyes are fixed on vacancy, the sounds of the world melt into confused unity, the attention is dispersed so that the whole body is felt, as it were, at once, and the foreground of consciousness is filled, if by anything, by a sort of solemn sense of surrender to the empty passing of time. . . . Every moment we expect the spell to break, for we know no reason why it should continue. But it does continue, pulse after pulse, and we float with it, until—also without reason that we can discover—an energy is given, something—we know not what—enables us to gather ourselves together, we wink our eyes, we shake our heads, the background-ideas become effective, and the wheels of life go round again. (211)

Because it wraps the subject in a "shell of lethargy," James finds this state of reverie vaguely troubling. At the same time, the very rhythm of his prose, the pauses and pulses of thought, the dreamy blurring that allows awareness of the body to emerge into the foreground, and the sensory experience of surrender all carry an unmistakable air of pleasure. James elsewhere acknowledges that the crucial faculty of selective attention is itself shaped by the pull of certain kinds of affective experience that he groups under the heading of "interest." As with the labile, floating sensations of a daydream, what counts in the category of the interesting is clearly a departure from the disciplined path of the will: " 'The interesting' is a title which covers not only the pleasant and the painful, but also the morbidly fascinating, the tediously haunting, and even the simply habitual" (415).

In moments such as these, James begins to recognize a wider range of sensory perceptions and modes of reflection as genuine forms of experience. Cognitive surrender, morbid fascination, and bodily pleasure may be among the human data that will aid "the growth of a mass of verification-experience."[41] The significance of this expansion of the parameters of experience became clearer in the years that followed the publication of the *Psychology*. In addition to publishing articles in scholarly journals, James began giving a series of talks aimed at reaching a broader public audience in order to expand the orbit of pragmatist analysis. As befits the mantle of a pragmatist, however, the experience of speaking in new public spaces also began to correct and enlarge his own ideas about what constitutes the public sphere itself.

His address titled "What Makes a Life Significant?" is especially instructive because it includes an autobiographical reflection on one of the occasions of public address. James tells of spending a week at the Chautauqua community in New York State, a "middle-class paradise" (863) devoted to learning and culture. But while the community was designed to cultivate every intellectual virtue that James extols, he was surprised to feel an immediate, involuntary sense of relief at the moment he was able to leave. He knows this relief represents a form of "self-contradiction"; as one of the invited lecturers recognized by this world as a cultural authority, his hostile reaction to the "atrocious harmlessness" (863) of the community is a puzzle. Upon reflection, he considers whether his unexpected dismay bespeaks a worried prognostication that modern society was elevating security and order at the expense of a "moral style" he calls "precipitousness": a close knowledge of risk, an awareness of death, a confrontation with emergencies that require intensity of effort and strength. Although there is more than a hint here of the anxiety about an erosion of civilized "manliness" that so alarmed men like Roosevelt, James's analysis ultimately takes another path. For, in a sudden moment of intellectual shock, he discovers that his whole diagnosis is based on a perspectival error: the "flatness" of the Chautauqua community represents not an enervation of the modern world but a blindness that mistakes middle-class cultivation for the whole of expressive modern society.

When this realization comes, the *way* he acquires the discovery is as notable as what he learns.

I was speeding with the train towards Buffalo, when, near that city, the sight of a workman doing something on the dizzy edge of a sky-scaling iron construction brought me to my senses very suddenly. And now I perceived, by a flash of insight, that I had been steeping myself in pure ancestral blindness, and looking at life with the eyes of a remote spectator. Wishing for heroism and the spectacle of life on the rack, . . . I had failed to see it present and alive. (865)

Ironworkers and firemen, peasant women in Vienna, and the Italian and Hungarian laborers constructing the Boston subway are all subjects who inhabit an "outside worldly wilderness" in which a pragmatic moral sense and discovery adhere in daily activity and risk. Millions of people around him live the "moral style" of "precipitousness." Suddenly the cultivated "city" represented by Chautauqua, a kind of public sphere utopia realized on earth, looks less like the space that will yield truth through critical discourse and contemplative art and more like a preserve of "ancestral blindness" (862).

Because a literary public is such an important resource for James's pragmatist pedagogy in the *Psychology*, it is all the more significant that his abrupt *exit* from a cultivated space like Chautauqua produces this new truth. What is more, the catalyst is not merely a change of location but the physical experience of transport: the sensation of speeding on a train, the kaleidoscopic effects of his moving vision, the sight of a worker out on the "dizzy edge" of a skyscraper at a vertiginous height above the earth. When he reports that the sight "brought me to my senses very quickly," we cannot fail to hear that the correction of his false idea is identical to his intense sensory experience.

In making a turn to the "laboring classes," James was not attempting to recover the figure of the productive worker as the standard for political and moral meaning. He takes the laborer's loss of the ability to substantiate social value through work as a vexing but accomplished fact. (In fact, he counters Tolstoy's "deification" of manual labor by describing at length the contemporary conditions that have made wage labor weak and easily exploited.) It is not manual work per se that matters here but rather the worlds that laborers create and inhabit, worlds that are "present and alive" with lived significance but that have been invisible *as* worlds to professors and other bookish folk. Literature is still James's touchstone for the ability to apprehend human worlds and communicate their operative ideas; the "higher forms of literature and fine art" (864) are for him the equivalent instruments to the scientist's microscope or spectrograph. But art, like science, can be held back by insufficient instruments, and James underscores the fact that few if any authors or genres seem to have apprehended the experience taking shape in the new worlds of industrial labor. He considers Howells a possible candidate but muses that this novelist may be "still too deep in the ancestral blindness, and not humane enough for the inner joy and meaning of the laborer's existence to be really revealed" (867). Tolstoy grasped the important matter of scale; the worlds inhabited by these subjects are "counted not by twos, or threes, tens, but by hundreds, thousands, millions" (869). But James is convinced that Tolstoy's unwillingness to grant existential importance to anything but the *inner* lives of the suffering populace leads the Russian novelist into the error of declaring "the whole phenomenal world and its facts and their distinctions to be a cunning fraud" (871).

Because the facts of the phenomenal world are precisely what hold the most significance for James, the "worldly wilderness" beyond the precincts of literary culture represents an expanded archive of experience. But are those "outside" worlds actually *public* worlds? That is, do they possess modes of expressive meaning that allow for collective self-discovery and communicable ideals? James himself seems undecided, in this essay anyway, about whether to count these worlds as truly public. "The significance of a human life for communicable and publicly recognizable purposes is . . . the offspring of two different parents," phenomenal reality and "ideal novelty," or a renewable set of ideas that can be revised through reflection and activity. James is convinced that the social worlds created outside bourgeois culture possess practical truths and intellectual ideals, but his default assumption still seems to make the sphere of literature the threshold for true publicness: "Must we wait for someone born and bred and living as a laborer himself, but who, by grace of Heaven, shall also find a literary voice?" (867).

Among the most intriguing experiments in this essay, however, is James's effort to represent a communicative act that occurs *across* the divide between literary culture and the worlds that exist in the "wilderness" beyond it. The "flash of insight" that reaches him while he is "speeding with the train towards Buffalo" is a sensory recognition. His own bodily perceptions seem to apprehend the meaningful "precipitousness" expressed by a man's dizzying physical activity before his mind does. Or, put another way, the bodily locale of James's experience of "coming to my senses" is the site of reason here; his corporeal self is the thinker who is able to grasp what was expressed on the skyscraper. Speed, movement, and spatial displacement have become a kind of language, a medium that translates and conducts a message. James recognizes the risk and physical hardships required of laborers; but the recognition experience itself—the "flash of insight"—is a kind of physical pleasure, an electric excitement that apprehends the ironworker's "dizzying" feat and the "moral" world it signifies, and that produces the sudden alteration in the way he understands the world. What has proven effective for communication in this moment is the excitement of a new truth or "ideal novelty," a pleasurable sense of significance that also defines and marks off a distinct experience as it communicates across different worlds.[42]

In a different essay from this period, "On a Certain Blindness in Human Beings," James asserts more overtly that the industrial-commercial worlds outside literary culture are indeed expressive, and that affective perception and pleasurable excitement can be the materials of a public language. He begins by spelling out the close connection between emotion and thought: "Our judgments concerning the worth of things, big or little, depend on the *feelings* the things arouse in us" (841). Feelings are thus a kind of index or representation of what is privately valued. But as James goes on to develop the communicative nature of feeling, it begins to emerge as a species of honest signal that is sharable and not simply a private index: "Wherever a process of life communicates an eagerness to him who lives it, there the life becomes genuinely significant." Although revulsion and distaste are no doubt pragmatic judgments as well, it is the pleasurable feeling of "eagerness"—a kind of desire or motive for seeking enjoyment—that seems to be the most expressive.

> Sometimes the eagerness is more knit up with the motor activities, sometimes with the perceptions, sometimes with the imagination, sometimes with reflective thought. But where it is found, there is the zest, the tingle, the excitement, of reality; and there is "importance" in the only real and positive sense in which importance ever anywhere can be. (843–44)

Here the expressivity of "eagerness" cuts across the full spectrum of human activity, from physical movement and sensory perception to the more symbolic operations of the imagination and thought. The sensation of "excitement" or a "tingle" might not be physiological (or it might be), but the pleasurable quickening denoted by these words is James's best description for the kind of significance—the meaning or pragmatic reason—that is articulated by the force of "eagerness."[43]

That which pleases and quickens begins to seem not just expressive and inherently communicable (and thus potentially public); it also begins to appear the most reliable guide to reality, a map to discerning "'importance' in the only real and positive sense." By shifting to an epistemology of neural and intellectual excitement, James articulates a philosophy for a society governed by what he called a "pleasure-economy." Like other intellectuals of the time, James borrowed the idea of a pleasure economy from Simon Patten, a University of Pennsylvania economist who analyzed the historical transition from a "pain economy" (indicative of an "age of deficits") to a "pleasure economy" that was emerging in the turn-of-the-century "age of surplus." James's use of this lexicon is not a sign that he approved of the economic status quo of monopoly capitalism or the existing distributions of wealth. But it does reflect that, as Livingston has argued, James was attempting to explore new ways of articulating the moral contours of selfhood after corporate capitalism had eclipsed the productive male worker as the standard by which to define and distribute value.[44] Within this lexicon, "pleasure" may be taken as a shorthand signifier for the new range of experiences, opportunities, and social spaces that multiply under the aegis of a consumer-driven economy. ("Leisure" is another umbrella term for this range of activities and spaces but to my mind a more restrictive one, inasmuch as, with the shift to valuing pleasure in a consumer culture, many kinds of practices—including "dizzying" acts of skillful labor—could become recognizable as pleasurably expressive.) What if we were to recognize value, James asks, in terms of enjoyment rather than productive work? What if doing and thinking were both different extensions of the same motive force of eagerness? If meaning were redefined by "feelings of excited significance" (850), it would by no means leave the field to leisure-class consumption or middle-class pursuits only (and would still include the arcane excitement of philosophy and other "strange indoor academic ways" [843]). And, although James never directly proposes it, such a paradigm might suggest further that mass culture attractions—laboratories for what can elicit "excited significance" from large numbers of people—represent a new species of public significance as well.

By taking sensory experience and pleasure as an index of pragmatic truth, James begins to exceed the boundaries of public reason as defined by traditional literary culture. The prophet of James's pleasure economy, however, is still a poet: James presents Walt Whitman as the scout and "contemporary prophet" of a world transformed by the critical and aesthetic possibilities of pleasure. Despite his intense interest in work and occupations of all kinds, Whitman is not a poet of labor because he himself is supremely unproductive: "considered either practically or academically" he is "a worthless unproductive being." Whitman the "ideal tramp" (851) dwells outside the world of work, but he writes from outside the world of literary culture as well, at least as defined by most contemporary literary standards. While Whitman is comparable to a poet like Wordsworth, who can turn a "worthless hour" (850) of reverie into beautiful verse, for Whitman the inherited canons of beauty or contemplative thought are all but irrelevant. Wordsworth's celebration of untouched nature seeks to return value to what has become worthless within an industrial economy, but Whitman looks to the phenomenological topography of a pleasure economy in which urban crowds, transport systems like ferryboats and omnibuses, strolling laborers, women's and men's fashions, shops with "great windows"—in short, any and all sites that afford "gayety and motion on every side" (853)—are sources of the pragmatic truths of "excitement" and thus carry a potential for public significance. For James, Whitman is the new pleasure economy worker, an "occupation" in which seeking corporeal feeling and immersion in human crowds count as "business sufficient and worthy to fill the days of a serious man" (851).

Writing from this position does not banish the differences between the separate worlds of manual labor, high culture, and a massed urban crowd; but it does reorient the value of all of those worlds around a different standard, the "excited significance" that they generate—or fail to generate—in Whitman's poetic mind. James has turned again to a literary author as the proof of the public nature of a certain sphere of experience, in this case, the sensory excitement in urban and commercial activity. But by selecting Whitman as his key example, he drastically redefines the parameters of publicness. For, once we include a Whitmanian regime of expressive value, a given idea or experience is public not only if it conforms to canons of rational argumentation, aesthetic refinement, or communicable ideals but also if it allows intelligible expression of the truths of "excited significance" in everyday commercial life and is open to renewal and transformation ("ideal novelty") through the experience of others. Expressing and exchanging these truths, James stresses, is crucial for a modern society: in an era where stricter divisions of labor tend to inculcate "our deadness toward all but one particular kind of joy," communicative exchange among social groups is needed to expand the public inventory of human "goods and joys" (857).

But could literature or philosophy fulfill this office of enlarging through exchange the range of publicly recognized goods? Whitman and James identify a wider domain of publicness, but their own writing and public addresses tend to reach only the more literate classes. Even Whitman's poetry, despite its radical openness to experience that lies outside the parameters of bourgeois literary culture, is likely to circulate only so far beyond a public of educated readers. Yet Whitman's own reflections on the mediation of experience point toward alternative modes of circulation and exchange, modes that begin to resemble the "composite publics" created by forms such as cinema. James reproduces a letter Whitman wrote to a friend about his habit of riding down Broadway atop a coach, a practice the poet presents as a confluence of "amusement" and "study." Although the letter is addressed to "Pete," Whitman also published it in his *Calamus* volume, merging an act of personal communication with the indirect address to strangers implicit in a published text.

In recording the process by which he opens himself to what James calls "significant presence," Whitman chooses language that anticipates the successful transmission of his experience to another mind: "*You know* it is a never ending amusement and study and recreation for me to ride a couple of hours of a pleasant afternoon on a Broadway stage in this way" (italics added). Agreement from "Pete," another stage driver, is more than likely; but as Whitman shifts into the pronominal second person to describe his experience, he is also able to anticipate and formally articulate a form of shared experience with an indefinite number of strangers, expressed through the grammatical structure of an intersubjective agreement among all who read his words.

You see everything as you pass, a sort of living, endless panorama—shops and splendid buildings and great windows; and on the broad sidewalks crowds of women richly dressed continually passing altogether different, superior in style and looks from any to be seen anywhere else—in fact a perfect stream of people—men too dressed in high style, and plenty of foreigners—and then in the streets the thick crowd of carriages, stages, carts, hotel and private coaches. (853)

Using the epistolary form to allow a nominally private address to reach an audience of unseen readers is a long-standing literary practice.[45] But *what* Whitman describes, the experience itself, differs significantly from the kind of communication that occurs in print. Whitman emphasizes a sensory experience that is at once a practice of enjoyment, a reflective "study," and a physical renewal or "recreation." It has little in the way of an idea or conceptual message, but it is still a transmission of meaning—by James's reckoning, the kind of meaning that matters most ("'importance' in the only real and positive sense"). This practice was originally undertaken in the company of another ("I . . . ride a trip with some driver friend on Broadway") but then widened into ever more inclusive acts of shared enjoyment, crossing over from the privacy of a letter to the publicity of a published book, and becoming finally a renewable practice that "you" can confirm by way of your own lived experience, when matching feelings of interest and the recollection of pleasure become a form of agreement: "*You will not wonder* how much attraction all this is on a fine day, to a great loafer like me, who enjoys so much seeing the busy world move by him, and exhibiting itself for his amusement."[46] Although watching the world exhibit itself might appear a form of passive spectatorship, for Whitman this practice is communicative, intersubjective, and finally public, a generative act that offers both images and techniques for recognizing "significant presence" in a commercial landscape. Just as significant, Whitman is not reluctant to compare the "attraction" of sitting side by side with a fellow observer and experiencing "gayety and motion" to a form of technological attraction, the panorama. Throughout the nineteenth century the panorama had been a popular machine that intensified the interactive seam between realism and illusion by adding motion to the display of painted and later photographic images and scenes. The panorama was also a clear precursor to the cinema, a medium that would realize Whitman's conceit of a "living" panorama in fantastic and unexpected ways.[47] Whitman wrote his description of the streaming life of Broadway in 1868; by 1900 filmgoers in small towns in Pennsylvania and Ohio could sit side by side to watch actuality films of busy Manhattan streets exhibited for their pleasure.

But does cinematic representation really count as a public medium? Or does the introduction of mechanical mediation make lived experience into an empty abstraction, a mere passive consumption? A cinematic audience, with no obvious means to interact with or "talk back" to a film, has seemed far removed from a reading public for many theorists. Whether a highly capitalized mass industry like film can allow for any element of critical reciprocity for a viewer remains one of the enduring debates in cultural theory. But Miriam Hansen's argument that early cinema offered a form of "composite" public, in which technologically mediated forms of publicity could coexist with local face-to-face relations, has an interesting resonance with Whitman's letter. For, in his private-but-published letter to Pete, Whitman had already superimposed a technological form of public mediation with a form of direct address to a personal friend without destroying or degrading the epistemology of shareable pleasure, and thereby enlarged the sites for new kinds of address and exchange Whitman invented in both his startling poetics and his public iconicity.[48]

Enlarging and extending the orbit of communicable experience was also the aim of William James. Taken far enough, in fact, his stated wish to achieve a "breadth of insight into the impersonal world of worths" on a "large objective scale" (851) might well *require* a mass medium like film. But while James's interest in "feelings of excited significance" drew him to the example of Whitman, as a public philosopher James's own angle of approach to such feelings was also distinct from that of either a poet like Whitman or an early filmgoer. Inasmuch as James wishes to test through critical reflection the implications of the idea that pleasurable quickening is a species of knowledge, he would fashion his own form for combing modes of public reason with a broad field of sensory experience.[49] The unusual areas of human experience that James explored, from psychic oddities and occult phenomena to animal behavior and religious belief in its multiple "varieties," can be seen as a blueprint for another species of composite public, aligning disparate fields of human experience with the critical practice he called "the sentiment of rationality" and allowing feeling to count as a binding element of reason. John Dewey would develop further this path of pragmatism by redefining the good as "enjoyments which are the consequence of intelligent action." The proper role of the philosopher, Dewey argued, was investigating the "real worth of likings" through methods of experimental empiricism.[50] Knowing and liking are different moments of a single dialectical activity, and inquiry of the sort that philosophers and scientists do is something like a laboratory of enjoyment. The pleasure economy is not merely for profit; it is also good to think with.

Indeed, the thinking self may *be* a pleasure economy. Mead's theory of the "social consciousness" holds that even our perception of individual selfhood is merely an effect of the active interplay between an "inner consciousness" and the images it has imported from an "outside world."[51] There is no content to our sense of self without interaction with the people and things that surround us, for we only grasp concrete impressions of an inner identity by imagining ourselves as others see us, much as we only know the features of our own face by looking in mirrors. As theorized by Mead, the self is a neurological Whitman, an ever-renewing "me" that exists by way of its emotion-driven responses to the innumerable "yous" it sees and reflexively incorporates as mirrors for the self. At the deepest levels of self-perception, consciousness itself is public, and a "social procedure" is the very stuff of subjectivity.

Mead, too, articulated his ideas largely in relation to literature. Drama, the novel, and the short story help supply images for emergent "types" and new "lines of thought," the new social realities and possibilities that as yet lack distinct names and concepts. Aesthetic forms are thus especially adept at articulating the newness of a perpetually changing reality and foster a concentrated version of the ongoing process by which the "inner consciousness" imports the "outer world."

> The great need is for imagery to present [others] to us. The drama and the novel do this, make people talk to us, as we to them. It carries on the mental process of thinking. Greek tragedy presented scenes . . . of distant social situations. Our realism reflects the new series of problems, which are not typical but novel. They require setting up types which had not been set up before, carrying out lines of thought which we had not carried out before.[52]

But it is not literature alone that can conduct our "processes of reflective thought." With its density of social images, Mead seems to count the novel as the first among equals; but other genres are also particularly promising vehicles for achieving "the introduction of values which were not recognized before": "Hence the short story, the photograph, the one-act play answer to the data in the science which cannot yet be fully organized or put into full relation with the rest of the field. Realism is helping us to develop imagery for social science."[53] By including a reproduced image, "the photograph," in the inventory of forms or images to think with, Mead's heuristic model for thought begins to look less like a reading public and more like the kind of expanded, heterogeneous "social horizon of experience" that characterizes the function of a cinematic public.

For Mead there is both a democratic and a scientific imperative to expand the "data" for social reflection beyond what has been known and transmitted from the past. Thus the archives of what counts as "realism" will necessarily include any expressive form that can be said to capture emergent experience. Dewey, too, acknowledges that both the data and the production of knowledge exceeds the bounds of higher culture: "knowing is a human undertaking, not an esthetic appreciation carried on by a refined class or a capitalistic possession of a few learned specialists, whether men of science or of philosophy."[54] What Mead was urging as a deliberate scientific project for scholars was occurring already at such sites as nickelodeons, where immigrants and women were able to "organize their experience on their own terms" by "creating a space for the actualization of involuntary memory, of disjunctive layers of time and subjectivity," at the same time as they absorbed images from unfamiliar social worlds, all of which permitted a "collective forum for the production of fantasy, the capability of envisioning a different future."[55] If mass forms present their own version of the danger of merging knowledge with "capitalistic possession" (hardly a danger for mass culture only, as Dewey notes), they also introduce their own conditions for what Dewey calls "active and alert commerce with the world." Indeed, some mass forms might well surpass the habits and conventions of high culture in encouraging awareness of the "complete interpenetration of self and the world of objects and events."[56]

Pragmatism experiments with the idea that pleasure can be a principle of openness, that desires and "acts of liking" do not necessarily lead us into enslavement by thoughtless appetites and asocial impulses (although the pleasure of sadism, as we will see, represents a problematic case). As with all experiments, this working premise is also a risk, especially in the context of a postliterary public. Given the asymmetries of economic power that characterize mass culture, there is a perpetual danger that mass forms will heighten rather than mitigate what James calls the "monstrously lopsided equation of the universe and its knower" (519). From the pragmatist perspective, the danger in mass culture is not its eagerness to cater to pleasure but the industry's economic incentives to homogenize tastes and practices and thus to reduce the total inventory of what James calls "goods and joys."[57] But there is also the possibility that openness to pleasure is also a path to a different function for the idea of publicness, a path to a redistribution of the daydreams, relations, objects, symbols, and images that are able to appear and circulate in unexpected ways among a theoretically unlimited number of strangers. Pragmatism is a wager on newness or "ideal novelty." If James's *Psychology* rescued consciousness from an "inexpressive chaos" through a literary paradigm of the mind, the pragmatic turns of James's own thought eventually brought him to value dizzying shifts and displacements among different social worlds that would necessarily exceed the boundaries of literary culture, a form of useful cultural anarchy in which "altered equilibriums" might bring "new ideals" (879).

Neurological modernity, then, becomes a fortunate fall, and James revises the trope of the accident to make it a figure for redemptive transformation: living with Whitman's openness to alterior experience will bring a moment of freeing transformation in which "the whole scheme of our customary values gets confounded [and] our whole self is riven, and its narrow interests fly to pieces, then a new centre and a new perspective must be found" (847). The promise of redemption lies not in the discipline of a "heroic mind" but in the possibilities of new ideals arising out of a riven, socially transformed self.

W. E. B. DuBois and the Publicity of the Wish

In *The Souls of Black Folk,* of course, the idea of a "riven self" has a far different meaning than the ecstatic transformation invoked by William James. Because DuBois was a student of William James's at Harvard, American pragmatism has a significant place in the variegated genealogy that scholars have uncovered for DuBois's philosophy of "double consciousness."[58] Among the pragmatist signatures most discernable in *Souls* is DuBois's decision to begin analysis at the level of lived experience, the "peculiar sensation" of being a black person in America. Whether the sentiment is spoken or unspoken, the white world endows the African American with the ascriptive status of a problem subject: "How does it feel to be a problem?" DuBois will try to express and analyze this species of feeling (which is inseparable from the "strange experience" of being publicly *addressed* as a species of problem).[59] The experience of African Americans represents a crucial test of the distribution of social value within the new pleasure economy. In *The Souls of Black Folk,* literary analysis is turned upon subjects, the black masses, who are not only on the margins of U.S. civil society, and largely invisible to the literary public, but whose place as objects of sadistic white pleasure represents a damning indictment of the dominant social imaginary. Including black experience within the "mass of verification-experience" is both the most stringent test and the most freighted possibility for pragmatist hope.

What does it mean when "acts of liking," as Dewey phrases it, include the pleasurable excitement of watching a lynching?[60] DuBois famously turned away from his career as a professor at Atlanta University in the aftermath of the lynching of Sam Hose. He had written a measured letter against the crime and left his university office with the intention of mailing it to the editor of the *Atlanta Constitution.* On his way through the streets, however, DuBois learned that Hose's charred and severed knuckles were on display in the shop window of a white proprietor. He turned back and never delivered the letter: "One could not be a calm, cool and detached scientist while Negroes were lynched."[61] The public spectacle of Hose's severed body parts bespeaks a set of historical and social conditions that traditional academic disciplines had no capacity to analyze. Like the pragmatists, DuBois believed that the sphere of desire and perceptual "eagerness" holds crucial information; by displaying what white Atlanta residents were eager or excited to see, shop windows displaying severed body parts were a grotesque source of social data.

Examining the data about what white Americans find pleasing reveals appalling patterns. Not only are lynchings staged and consumed as overt forms of amusement, images of lynched bodies are circulated as trading cards and mechanically reproduced in stereographs and "talking machines." A host of less vicious but still contemptuous images circulate in polite society.[62] DuBois recognizes that the white ability to *enjoy* black abjection is the affective force, both motive and reward, that animates public forms of "systemic humiliation." Varieties of white pleasure-taking include "amused contempt," "mockery" and "ridicule," "the distortion of fact and the wanton license of fancy," "the cynical ignoring of the better and the boisterous welcoming of the worse, the all-pervading desire to inculcate disdain for everything black, from Toussaint to the devil" (364, 369).

DuBois and the pragmatists are thus in agreement: critical attention to the sphere of feeling, and especially enjoyment, is needed to get at what a priori categories and ordinary modes of analysis ignore or dismiss. But in this and other ways, DuBois's confirmation of pragmatist tenets appears to undercut pragmatist optimism. If desires, affections, and enjoyments are the best guides to understanding human reality and even rationality, what excludes sadistic sentiments and anti-black enjoyments from counting as proper epistemological grounds for truth? In "The Construction of the Good," Dewey would address this question by identifying a class of "problematic goods," things that have been *desired* but have not yet proved to be *desirable*—not yet verified through reflection and intelligent action as things that are likely to remain an enjoyment in the future. For Dewey, the protocols of science and other disciplines of thought are necessary to rationally guide the process of predictive verification. But DuBois's report on black experience is discouraging here as well. For delight in black humiliation is not just limited to everyday life or violent mob outbreaks; it also operates within science itself. While the black man struggles, "sociologists *gleefully* count his bastards and his prostitutes" (368, italics added). White desire drives scientific knowledge of black life, leaving black subjects caught in the "fond imaginings of the other world which does not know and does not want to know our power" (369–70).[63]

DuBois also confirms the pragmatist idea of an embodied self. To be an African American in 1900 is to have already disproved Descartes and discovered that one's being has been relegated to the body rather than the mind: I think, therefore I know I am a body despised. This is the lived experience of the "men and women who had faced mobs and seen lynchings," experience that DuBois will add to the archive of recorded human perceptions and social facts.[64] Adams and James narrate their startled discovery of the notion that consciousness is unknowable apart from its embodiment in the world; but for black Americans this knowledge has a threatening immediacy that DuBois will insist on including in the record of experience necessary for any adequate theory of neurological modernity.

DuBois's description of African American double consciousness, created from the "sense of always looking at one's self through the eyes of others" (364), anticipates and vividly realizes Mead's model of a social self. But the difference of blackness in this context is instructive. If the black subject were identical to Mead's model of the self, if it existed only as a dynamic integration of the "memory images" of others' glances, attitudes, gestures, and verbal addresses, then the black self would have to live a kind of social death—one's consciousness would be identical to the "dead-weight of social degradation" (368) imposed through the "eyes of others." That this does *not* occur is the saving feature of African American "two-ness": because the black subject is divided she also possesses a consciousness *apart* from the "dead-weight" of social stigma. Doubleness is also a resource. Even Mead's normative self is subjected at certain junctures to what he calls the disintegrating moment when a "problem appears"—the moment when some form of dissonance disrupts the self's ability to harmonize the external "images" that make up consciousness. However distressing it might be, Mead argues, this moment of fracture is also a "forum of reflection," a space or occasion for a new critical understanding of both the surrounding social world and the internal processes that create self-consciousness.[65] As DuBois is reminded daily, the African American subject *dwells* in that moment of the disrupting "problem"; indeed, she must live its dissonance as a form of identity ("how does it feel to be a problem?"). But black American life, therefore, is also a unique forum of reflection, and the faculties of critical reflection that issue from being problematic produce the unique knowledge that DuBois calls "second sight."

By claiming a faculty of second sight for the African American masses, DuBois posits a critical and shareable knowledge produced outside the boundaries of the literary public—sometimes even outside the boundary of formal literacy itself, "the cabalistic letters of the white man" (367). But uncovering this knowledge also poses a puzzle: what kind of public can it actually *be* that is excluded from civil society? What sort of public life is possible in social conditions best likened to an "armed camp for intimidating Negroes?" (436). When forms of access, self-determination, and democratic interaction are as restricted as they are for the population of the Black

Belt, it may strain to the breaking point the very idea (and ideology) of the public sphere. As Houston Baker puts it, "How can black Americans, who like many others have traditionally been excluded from these domains of modernity, endorse Habermas's beautiful idea?"[66]

The history behind the question cannot but dim the beauty of the idea. But Baker goes on to argue that it is precisely this exclusion from the bourgeois public sphere that defines a different terrain of "associative and communicative norms" of a black public, or "counterpublic." In writing *Souls*, Baker argues, DuBois was less interested in condemning the segregation of black life per se than in transcribing the special institutions, psychosocial resources, and aesthetic codes for understanding and surviving modernity that were invented in the spaces of black associational life behind the veil. White publics in this modern pleasure economy, I have argued, were formed around norms of enjoyment; the black world, in contrast, had to generate a different kind of public norm that Baker calls the "publicity of the wish." Under Jim Crow, that is, black collectivities "had to fashion a voice, songs, articulations, conversions of wish into politics."[67] If anti-black sadism reveals troubling facts about what can be desired, black aspirations reveal what can be wished for, an expressive desire that confirms the public-sphere ideals of equality and self-making—confirms them, moreover, in the face of stark evidence that they are not (yet) real. With the birth of the black counterpublic, an associational world that is the *least* like a *Spectator* or *Tatler* public of propertied literate men conversing in coffeehouses becomes the world that rescues the idea of the public from being *merely* an ideological ruse or a wholesale fantasy.

The second-sight knowledge that comes from the black public sphere, however, is not a testament to Enlightenment ideals only. Black double consciousness also knows the darker truths of modernity. Those forced to be citizens without citizenship, those consigned to an "armed camp" of the state, also possess a lived knowledge about what is to be feared in modernity. DuBois articulates black folks' intimate understanding of the *modern* practice ("born of slavery and quickened to renewed life by the crazy imperialism of the day") of defining and treating human subjects "with an eye single to future dividends" (428). The pragmatist faith in experience here meets an especially severe test: how to find expressive forms to represent the experience of those least able to narrate Enlightenment stories of *Bildung* cultivation and self-sovereignty. This test, too, casts doubt on public sphere ideals. But DuBois anticipates Kracauer's claim that it is the experience of just such subjects that offers the epistemological ground for any historical knowledge worth having: "Cognition has to be grounded in the very sphere of experience in which historical change is most palpable and most destructive—in a sensual, perceptual, aesthetic discourse that allows for 'the self-representation of the masses subject to the process of mechanization.' "[68]

Kracauer is here speaking of the medium of film as the expressive mode most likely to convey the destructive historical experience of the masses. Like the Black Belt population that fashions a counterpublic for expressing the "publicity of the wish," the European masses that Kracauer has in mind turn to the materials of cinema as the "blueprint of an alternative public" that reflects yet-to-be-realized conditions of self-determination.[69] But Kracauer's invocation of the pleasure-driven medium of film, with its openness to fantasy, wish, and perceptual experience as the best markers of historical change, also suggests that film may be a particularly apt medium for thinking about the aesthetics of *Souls of Black Folk*. Strikingly, Baker describes *Souls* an "aesthetics of montage."[70] Neither a proper work of social science nor a recognizable literary genre, DuBois's "collection of fugitive essays," Baker argues, anticipates the techniques of Romare Bearden and other black artists who undertake experimental play with graphical, commercial, and media forms. Just as significant as any deliberate aspects of a "montaged style," however, is the fact that DuBois, the Berlin-educated intellectual and man of letters, could not write a literary work about the black masses *without* creating a fragmented and fissured text. That is, by taking up the materials of high literary culture for the purpose of representing the invisible public that exists behind the veil, he necessarily creates a record of the interruptions, ideological contradictions, and political willfulness that are the historical marks—the identifying scars—of the literary dream of human equality whenever it is tested against existing human history.[71]

To try to create a literary record of this sphere of experience, DuBois draws on memory wed to analysis and, like Adams, tries to place non-synchronized consciousness and historical fact together in a space that lies outside traditional historiography and philosophy. The aesthetic textures of image, sound, and fable do the work of representation and analysis. *Souls of Black Folk* attempts in this way a pragmatic test of the Deweyan "problematic goods" of American culture, submitting white sadistic pleasures, divided dreams of freedom, and nationalist promises to the pressures of reflective thought—and inviting white literary culture to join the work of thinking—in order to search this body of experience for the possibilities of new norms and values.

In the chapter "Of the Coming of John," DuBois conducts his most pointed experiment in bringing disparate cultural locations into a fractured montage image. In this drama of what William James would call "altered equilibriums," two young men and former childhood playmates—one black and one white—have both returned to their small Southern town after receiving education in the North. John Jones, the black man, struggles to endure the subordination of life behind the color line after awakening to new worlds of art and experience in the cosmopolitan milieu of New York City. The white John is merely bored, the confinement of the privileged. Then the fable's crisis: when he intercepts the white John attempting to rape his sister, Jones kills him. In this reversal of the lynching scenario, the white man becomes the lifeless body and "a thing apart." The racial order will right itself, of course, and the fable ends as Jones succumbs to a white lynch mob. But the poetic evocation of the lynching, presented from within Jones's consciousness, merges the destruction of the black man's body with his ecstatic memory of Wagner's opera *Lohengrin*, which he heard in a "great hall" in Manhattan. "Was it music, or the hurry and shouting of men?" The "last ethereal wail of the swan" from the aria is replayed in the "strange melody" (535)—perhaps the wail of his own cries—that accompanies the mob killing.

The composite form of a Wagnerian lynching gives the "peculiar sensation" of double consciousness a concrete and distressing texture, as if to stage such violence openly as the height of sublimity available within a white pleasure economy. Certainly this is not a documentary image of black experience; weaving Wagnerian opera and an inside view of Southern black life required knowledge that few Americans possessed, white or black. But DuBois is in fact relying on the perceived disparity between high aesthetic consciousness and the historical fact of violence against black bodies. For it is the shock of the unexpected conjunction that creates a meaningful effect and that allows the reader to experience a literary version of double consciousness. DuBois has superimposed the perceptual experience of the people "who have seen lynchings" (and suffered them) with the experience of those who carry Wagner's stormy melodies in their minds, in the hope, shared by Kracauer, of making his audience "confront the violence of difference and mortality rather than repress or aestheticize it" through totalizing monuments of a high culture.[72] Disjunction and fragmentation become virtues inasmuch as they refuse the elimination of facts and experience we find no pleasure in knowing. In turn, the shocking sounds and images of the story acquire their own form of beauty by opening a communicative pathway across social worlds and enacting a tragic transposition of William James's figure of the "riven self."

DuBois brings ethical and political urgency to the pragmatist project of coming to your senses. The final chapter of *Souls* focuses on the sorrow songs as an expressive form already internationally recognized as a world historical language (black diasporic culture, he reminds white Americans, has already gone public). The memories and wishes the songs transmit represent the best hope for waking up to what James would call new "sensible realities" that do not yet exist but could be realized in time. The closing scenario of *Souls* gives the literary intellectual a concrete location, at a distance from but in communication with the expressive forms of a black associative world. Seated near "these high windows of mine," DuBois speaks from the scholar's study that is the scene of his writing and the site from which he hears the song of "free" black voices "welling up to me from the caverns of brick and mortar below" (545–46). The figurative tableau, allowing the sound below to reach and move the writer above, gives a spatial expression to DuBois's wish to make the distance between high literary culture and black expressive culture into a veil that could be imaginatively rent. Partaking as it does of religious symbolism, the figure of the veil allows DuBois to imagine a future moment of "boundless justice" and the "redeeming of souls."

Despite these strains of prophetic revelation and redemption, DuBois's imagining of transformed social relations is not an exit from historical time. If and when change comes, it will be transmitted in human time and in worldly forms. This is a continuation of the "wishful publicity" that characterizes the black public sphere of the masses, now merged with the future-oriented ethos of pragmatist thought. Redemption dwells not at the end of the time but in the temporalities of the pending and the possible as they exist *in* time. Redemption arrives, according to James, in "knowledge of sensible realities [that come] to life inside the tissue of experience" (268).[73]

Or it does not arrive. The difference between a biblical prophecy and DuBois's investment in secular publicity can be seen in a scenario he wrote some four decades later, a tale that imagines a different version of the future historical possibilities that might be realized through sensory experience. In 1940, DuBois's autobiography *Dusk of Dawn* offers another fable of the veil, this time with the barrier figured as a wall of plate glass that traps a population of "prisoners." Although this black population is publicly visible to outside observers, the transparency of the modernized veil does nothing to facilitate recognition of or sympathy with those behind the glass. Black public speech, too, has become nothing more than senseless gestures.

> One talks on evenly and logically in this way [about civil rights and race relations], but notices that the passing throng does not even turn its head, or if it does, glances curiously and walks on. It gradually penetrates the mind of the prisoners that the people passing do not hear, that some thick sheet of invisible but horribly tangible plate glass is between them and the world. They get excited, they talk louder; they gesticulate. Some of the passing world stop in curiosity; these gesticulations seem so pointless; they laugh and pass on.

Instead hearing or recognizing the prisoners, observers who notice the people behind the glass reflexively become spectators who see objects of curiosity or entertainment only.

They remain spectators until the moment the glass is shattered, at which point they perceive only threat.

> Then the [imprisoned] people may become hysterical. They may scream and hurl themselves against the barriers, hardly realizing in their bewilderment that they are screaming in a vacuum unheard and that their antics may actually seem funny to those outside looking in. They may even, here and there, break through in blood and disfigurement, and find themselves faced by a horrified, implacable, and quite overwhelming mob of people frightened for their own very existence.

The religious metaphor of a veil has been replaced with a sleeker, more modern barrier of glass. Without the veil figure, the moment of breaking the barrier can only be an image of violent injury, not of revelation, and the intimation of a future that portends more violence still.

Neither the analytic resources of high literary culture nor the charismatic courage of mass culture or the vernacular seem to be available. Significantly, one of the terrors for the prisoners is the experience of a "vacuum" that leaves them voiceless and panicked. A fable of continuing racial stigma, the story is also a negative fable of the creative purchase that could be achieved through the interplay of high and low expression, evoked in a picture of the deadening, airless world where they have been lost.[74]

Conclusion
Literary Analysis and the Perception of Incongruities

In William Dean Howells's novel *A Hazard of New Fortunes* (1890), a literary editor and his wife leave the New York town house of a bright young woman and immediately witness a policeman grappling in the street with a female drunkard. The editor, stricken, asks how the two women can "really belong to the same system of things."[1] In a 1904 fictional film by the Biograph Company, *Photographing a Female Crook,* two policemen wrestle a woman into place for a mug shot. As the camera moves in for a closer view, the woman distorts her face into a grotesque expression to try to thwart the attempt at capturing an identifiable police photo. The matching scenes are an unlikely convergence, with a leading man of letters and a profit-seeking film company both choosing to represent the image of a female lawbreaker. But while the novel and the film present the same startling figure, the coincidence also highlights the difference in the way these two contrasting cultural languages take up what Henry James calls "incongruous phenomena." For Howells, the anomalous sight is a provocation, a spur to find a "system of things" that can make sense of a troubling image and turn incongruity into a higher order of understanding, whereas for the cultural system that is early cinema, the incongruity itself is a source of profit and a formal principle of production—the whole objective is to display the resistant face and body of a novelty, the "female crook."

Incongruity matters for Howells because of the value he invests in congruence. Howells defined realism as a literature of the commonplace and he thought of the realist project as a movement for "democracy in literature." But while his fiction features ordinary people and shared institutions—landladies and bookkeepers, courtrooms and flophouses—his notion of the common is closer to that of social scientists than of populists, a unit of analysis rather than a measure of democratic value. When Henry James remarked on Howells's "love of the common," he was speaking about the novelist's affinity for the truths of regularity. As James puts it, Howells "holds that in proportion as we move into the rare and the strange we become vague and arbitrary; that truth of representation, in a word, can be achieved only insofar as we can test and measure it."[2] Ordinary objects and familiar human types carry for Howells the virtues of frequency and probability, statistical regularities that managers and scientists value distinctly more than the populace. Methodologically, Howells's emphasis on the common resembles what Lorraine Daston and Peter Galison have described as the ethos of nineteenth-century scientists who sought to produce "reasoned images" by following stringent protocols for "weeding out atypical variations and extraneous details."[3] In James's words, Howells "looks askance at exceptions and perversities and superiorities, at surprising and incongruous phenomena in general."[4]

But as *Photographing a Female Crook* suggests, exceptions and perversities can carry their own order of regularity: rare and incongruous sights (more so than "reasoned images") are predictably interesting to large numbers of people. It is possible to see the birth of the film industry as a scatter-shot, profit-driven experiment to discover which images, visual effects, and cinematic plots could draw the interest of the largest number of people. The effort to maximize profit by drawing large audiences does not make cinema inherently democratic anymore than Howells's search for analytic regularities does so for realism. But it does dissolve the rationale for favoring "reasoned images" over incongruous ones. The first film companies followed the lead of the amusement industry and embraced the "aesthetics of disjunction" that flourished in such sectors as vaudeville, amusement parks, and dime museums.[5] Display, diversity, and shock trumped narrative coherence. Surprise and thrill were chosen over contemplative reflection. Miriam Hansen argues that because of early cinema's affinity for these disjunctive forms and pleasures, its advent is a symptom of "the disintegration of the bourgeois public sphere." As the norms of a bourgeois reading public lost sway, so too did the metrics of generality and abstractness, principles that were valued for their ability to uncover and circulate what was broadly representative of the interest of all. For Habermas, of course, the eclipse of these critical norms by mass culture and communication damaged the conditions necessary for meaningful public discourse. But Hansen argues for reading the disintegration of the bourgeois public sphere as part of a larger historical shift in conditions of public mediation, a second-wave transformation that saw "the emergence of qualitatively different types of publicity such as the cinema, with relations of representation and reception no longer predicated on the exclusionary hierarchies of literary culture."[6]

Hansen summarizes the paradox that has been widely noted (and often misinterpreted) about the symbology of the public sphere. The very commitment of public sphere thinking to the general over the partisan, to the inclusive and abstract over the local and the particular, also ended by excluding whole sectors and populations from counting as public. The principle of inclusiveness thus sanctioned "the exclusion of large areas of social reality in terms of participants (women, workers, social dependents) and subject matter (the material conditions of social production and reproduction, including sexuality and child-rearing)."[7] Even though film began as an unabashed commodity in the marketplace, filmmakers' eagerness in this period to solicit the largest possible audience, their willingness to supply any and all resonant images and effects, made cinema more responsive than high literary culture to the concrete desires and needs of marginal groups like women and immigrants.[8] Early cinema articulated "general" experience on a different basis than that of a reading public. It drew participants not primarily through an ideal of self-representation or a depiction of social reality for purposes of reflective thought, but by offering visibility to the unsorted material of everyday living. Rather than staging argumentation or opinion, cinema addressed a hunger for sensory pleasure (Edison, *The Kiss* and *The Eating Contest*); a wish for mobility and a memory of lost homelands (Pathé, travel shorts and urban "actuality" films); a consciousness of the body, clothing, and everyday self-presentation (Biograph, *Those Awful Hats;* Edison, *Sandow Flexing His Muscles*); a fascination with both mechanical wonders and physical demolition or undoing (Lumière, *The Arrival of a Train* and *Destruction of a Wall*); an interest in standard types as well as anomalous pariah figures like the female criminal (Biograph, *The Kleptomaniac* and *Photographing a Female Crook*); and even a delight in self-reflexive scenes of mass amusement (Edison, *Uncle Josh at the Moving Picture Show* and *Rube and Mandy at Coney Island;* Biograph, *From Showgirl to Burlesque Queen*).

But could such a mutable and fragmented medium really function as a form of publicness—as a site or matrix, that is, for articulating experience in conjunction with the experience of others? Was there anything like openness (access, reflexivity, intersubjectivity) possible in this broad horizon of disparate blocks of experience and unsorted images? If, following Hansen, we take early cinema as a paradigmatic example of a "postliterary" public, Howells's diagnosis of commercial culture as a vast terrain of disparate "shows and semblances" is remarkably close to Hansen's—with the important difference that Howells is unable to imagine anything public about such a sphere.[9] To take a heterogeneous collection of mimetic objects and experiences as a field of mediation alters radically the conception of public reason that had been fashioned after the model of a reading public.[10] Howells's impassioned campaign for realism, I have argued, is best understood as an attempt to allow a certain conception of the novel to restore and democratize a faculty of public reason that seemed to be under siege in an age of mass communication. Despite his alarm at "low" mass forms, it was actually Howells's fealty to an idea of a single, inclusive form of mediation—an intelligible "system of things" that could both explain and re-create social meaning among the broadest possible polity—that was behind his effort to institutionalize a hierarchy of literary value. This same commitment to a general, inclusive order of mediation made Howells not just an early theorist of publicity but also an eloquent witness to the transformation of the literary public sphere.

In *Hazard of New Fortunes,* Howells subjects the higher discernment of literary intellectuals to a trial by fire by testing them against a wildly disordered and disjunctive social field. The novel features a venture undertaken by a group of writers, artists, and their backers to launch a new literary magazine in New York. Howells was in this way hazarding his own literary precepts: was the analytic sensibility cultivated in high realism—nuanced critical reflections, a consciousness of close distinctions among social phenomena—adequate to discerning real civil relations from false semblances? In *Hazard* Howells shifts from his earlier preoccupation with mass media and entertainment to focus on mass society as a whole, its mutable, hard-to-grasp features, its hidden or absent causalities, its confused aggregation of civil spaces. But once he reconceived the social field in this way, it became harder to imagine the novel as a form that could articulate a set of intelligible civil relations through which one could find congruence for the whole—a "system of things."

Henry James saw in mass society a "collapse of all the forms," a loss of the consistency of conventions and shared assumptions that risks disabling altogether the metonymic architecture of the novel. Howells depicts a similar loss of grounding in his protagonist's confrontation with "the frantic panorama of New York" (158). Strange sights and novelties are not limited to places such as a dime museum, for fantastic objects and scenes are visible at every turn. The simplest city stroll holds "an uproar to the eye" (159). Cheap print seems as pervasive as air or bricks. When the editor, Basil

March, happens upon a vendor selling ballads stacked high on the pavement, he buys up a "pocketful." Human lives come into view as massed lives, visible in "swarming" populations in which even the members of the "vast prosperous commercial class" (262) look like replications of a single pattern.

In this decentralized world, literary culture is the closest thing to a center. Basil March absorbs the "huge disorder" of New York by viewing the city's scenes and inhabitants with an eye to their possible use as literary material. He is able to see "picturesque raggedness" (48) in otherwise distressing conditions. Riding on an elevated train, the gone-in-a-flash glimpses of family life he sees as he goes by tenement windows allow him to imagine domestic stories that could be told were a writer to linger in any one interior—although it is striking that, rather than imaginatively lingering in any domestic scene, Basil prefers the "infinite interest" he feels from the rapid succession of silenced visual images: "it was better than theater" (158), the narrator notes, and (one might add) a good deal like a silent movie. The magazine enterprise also provides the only point of contact among the novel's disparate characters, and literary circulation appears as one of the few remaining vehicles for shared reflection among Americans. The magazine's organizer, Fulkerson, characterizes the publication as "something in literature as radical as the American revolution in politics; it was the idea of self-government in the arts" (183). The pronouncement is close enough to Howells's own sentiments to recall his claims for realism as "democracy in literature." But Fulkerson, a slangy ad man and entrepreneur, hits upon his description in a pitch intended to advertise the magazine among literary celebrities and journalists, a context that gives "self-government in the arts" the air of a clever commercial slogan.

When it emerges as a piece of salesmanship, the idea that criticism and literary reflection could foster democratic governance ("self-government in the arts") begins to seem little more than a selling point, a sign that public relations are supplanting public reason. The resolution of Howells's plot does little to clarify things. Relations among the magazine staff members break down just as street violence erupts during a labor strike, a parallel that suggests that the association of realism with democracy may be either a faulty analogy (literature cannot be democratic nor democracy literary) or a logical error (literary culture does not foster self-government in politics). Howells's novel is explicit about looking to literary institutions as a space for cultivating public reason, but it is also increasingly doubtful about its own governing premise. Howells's *Hazard* thus seems to brood over the possibility of what Habermas calls a "refeudalization" of the public sphere, an erosion of the conditions that could permit shared deliberation among self-directed individuals, and their replacement by mass audiences that merely supply approval or acclaim for what is served up by powerful interests.

Henry James pointed out that Howells's analytic bent sometimes led him to include "factitious glosses" within the body of his novels.[11] If this tendency was a technical flaw (as James believed), it was also a clear index of the way Howells understood the public nature of the novel: as a reflective conversation among readers, ultimately predicated on the ideal of face-to-face relations. When Howells's intellectuals (lawyers, editors, ministers, artists) muse on the implications of their own story, they supply an instructive emblem of a certain idea of public reason. As they read, discuss, and argue (inducing the reader to do likewise as a virtual member of this circle), higher understanding emerges from the patient reflection and mutual intelligibility, if not agreement, among a community of minds. Precisely because this model for public reason is so ingrained in Howells's literary practice, however, it is all the more significant when, in *Hazard,* Howells's central literary intellectual attempts the task of finding some intelligible order or design in this field of apparent "disorder" and yet finds none.

Accident and then exigency seemed the forces at work to this extraordinary effect; the play of energies as free and planless as those that force the forest from the soil to the sky; and then the fierce struggle for survival, with the stronger life persisting over the deformity, the mutilation, the destruction, the decay of the weaker. The whole at moments seemed to him lawless, Godless; the absent of intelligent, comprehensive purpose in the huge disorder, and the violent struggle to subordinate the result to the greater good, penetrated with its dumb appeal [to Basil's] consciousness. (380)

Rather than a fabric of civil relations, society is now conceived as a field of outsized forces—energies, struggles, domination, and defeat. The intellectual's cultivated "consciousness," that key capacity for realism, is no longer able to calibrate cultural values but is rather an intelligence that can register all too keenly the disruptive forces of contingency and contest.

Howells's most ambitious effort to translate realist discernment into a synoptic museum of American modernity seems to end by eroding his own confidence in realist metonymy. Yet if this novel becomes a record of the limits of the literary public, it also records something else: the persistence of a mode of literary analysis that has been ejected from the bourgeois public sphere in which it was cultivated and is now operating, as it were, in exile. The liberal individual's powers of direct observation and reflection are no longer the sure origin and arbiter of positive knowledge. And yet realist observation, habituated to extracting meaning from the "modern instance," is still powerfully expressive for the way it articulates a shared social horizon that *includes* and displays the incongruities it cannot master—as Basil distills it, "this economic chance world in which we live and which we men seem to have created" (380).

In *Hazard of New Fortunes*, the perception of incongruities becomes a second-order realism of unanticipated eloquence. Much of its expressive power comes from the fact that literary reflection in fact *cannot* be a guarantor of a supersensible, autonomous mind, the linchpin of bourgeois public reason. To the contrary, in trying to represent a civil sphere of apparent "accident and exigency," the ordering habits of Basil's own analytic mind are themselves part of a "violent struggle to subordinate the result to the greater good." Thus even as he stands apart from the "uproar to the eye" he sees in the New York streets, Basil's own critical reflections cannot stay outside a phenomenology of struggle and contingency. Howells's realist methods begin to record a neurological modernity in which incongruous sights, atypical persons, unexpected speeds, and experiential textures are more likely to be signs of the real than any inventory of "reasoned images."

In dramatizing the breakdown of realist metonymy, *Hazard* registers discontinuities that would otherwise stay submerged or unnoticed. But what Basil understands as a failure of order or meaning is really the *emergence* into his view of tracts of experience that have been largely excluded from the representational spaces of public opinion and literary culture. A female alcoholic, "swarms" of children, unexpected violence in the streets: the discrepancies that Basil cannot reconcile through a discourse of "system" make for a negative or obverse picture of the eclecticism of experience avidly cultivated by expressive forms like cinema and vaudeville. The emerging medium of film can be seen as the mass culture counterpart to Howells's literary portrait of an "economic chance world," a terrain of disparate signs and images undergoing a material rearrangement, unable to be systematized by a master discourse, and opening up what Jacques Rancière calls a new "distribution of the sensible."[12] Precisely because *Hazard of New Fortunes* is something of an elegy for realist fiction, the rich, unstable register that Howells creates from the dissolution of the bourgeois public inadvertently becomes a literary form in which the strange and the incongruous begin to speak a new language of the real.

Or at least such incongruities can speak in theory—in Hansen's theory of a postliterary public like cinema, for instance. But can a *literary* work still qualify as a public language once literary culture is no longer taken as the exemplary public, once it is no longer the governing model for the way general human interests and worthy aesthetic tastes are tested and negotiated? Recent critics have argued that in the transition to literary modernism, novels essentially lose any claim or pretense to being public. Indeed, in Mark McGurl's version of this argument, novels lose any *wish* to be public, aspiring instead to become private art objects that belong to a restricted class of proprietary readers.[13] And novels become private objects, moreover, precisely by incorporating mass culture formally, taking in and refashioning the detritus of "low" social materials to produce a new hermetic language that refuses any affinity with other cultural discourses. No longer a public museum of the real, the "art-novel" becomes the elusive, gleaming possession of a new class of intellectual aristocrats. Although I take issue with aspects of this critical perspective, it does take us quite far toward explaining the social fate and formal shape of literary works in the postliterary milieu of the twentieth century, especially works we classify as high modernism. The estranging techniques and thematic obsessions that mark modernism might be seen as a reaction formation to the shock of realizing that literary culture is no longer identical with publicness, if indeed it ever was.

What remains to be seen, however, is whether literary culture's fall—which is also modernism's rise—from the status of a representative publicness leaves literary works with any capacity to reflect on the social. Because his fiction is intimately connected to the materials of commercial culture, Stephen Crane presents a significant test case for this question. Bill Brown has shown how Crane's writing emerges from a fractured, heterogeneous field in which mass culture materials are as important as literary conventions and institutions. In Brown's detailed analyses, Crane's innovations and critical obsessions become visible as "discursive redeployments of forms of mass amusements."[14] Images culled from the baseball field and the merry-go-round, the billiards hall and the freak show, enact odd metaphorical turns in the fabric of Crane's fiction. When an allusion to a football formation illuminates the terrain of war, when drowning men are likened to circus performers, Crane can be said to have seized upon the kinds of "incongruous phenomena" Howells strained to order within a single literary system, and made those same incongruities the basis of his vivid impressionism.

Like Whitman, Crane refuses to observe any inherited rules for the proper diction or attitude to bring to the social spaces he depicts, from a Bowery slum to a small-town barbershop. But unlike Whitman, Crane retains the fractures and misalliances that mark different patches of disjunctive experience brought together on the pages of his fiction. These fractures animate Crane's stories, setting off uncertain shifts between figure and ground and creating the sliding and flickering movement between registers that accounts for much of the uncanny effects of his writing. Especially when we consider the highly scenic or visual nature of his style, Crane's texts are less like the absorbing canvas of an impressionist painting and far closer to the movement of disjunctive images that would characterize early cinema. Indeed, Crane himself compared his fiction to "a series of sharply outlined pictures which pass before the reader like a panorama, leaving each its outlined impression."[15] And Joseph Conrad, a friend who had entertained the idea of collaborating with Crane on a play, would even write that "Crane and I must have been unconsciously penetrated by a prophetic sense of the technique and of the very spirit of the film-plays of which even the name was unknown to the world."[16]

Of course Crane would have resisted any suggestion that his fiction was *equivalent* to a mass genre like the early cinema, however prophetic it would have made him. McGurl is surely right to argue that Crane's superimposing of literary and mass materials was done with an eye to earning the symbolic capital that comes from inventing a new kind of "artistic purity."[17] In this sense Crane's use of mixed fragments and commercial novelties are more prophetic of Joyce than of the early film industry. McGurl's interpretation of *Maggie: A Girl of the Streets* makes a convincing case for reading this novel as a direct transformation of the New York materials of Howells's *Hazard* (and therefore as a besting of a literary mentor). Whereas Howells presents new materials of slums and crowds through the perspective of an external literary authority (Basil March), Crane eliminates that mediating social distance and writes, as it were, from within the space of the slum—thus in effect *removing* the space of literary culture altogether and collapsing the consciousness of the realist observer with the lived experience of the Bowery. If this bypasses the mediating space of literary culture, turning Howells's "sociological theme" into Crane's "famously ironic form," it also opens up a new order of the literary (modernism), one that exists beyond the social realities of the slum *and* the social reflections of an older literary culture, both of which now exist outside the atopia of Crane's spatialized style.[18] By this reading, the only *literary* interest Crane can have in the low, whether it is life in a slum, the low materials of mass culture, or indeed the now lowered values of Howellsian realism, lies in their use as materials for transposing into the higher values of modernist form.

While this account supplies a compelling social genealogy of modernist form, it also theorizes a species of literary form that has no capacity for social knowledge—no proximity to or reflective interest in the social realities it depicts. Bill Brown suggests something like this modernist privatization when he argues that the materials of mass amusement woven into the corpus of Crane's writing reappear in John Berryman's own incorporative use of Crane, where "obsolescent public pleasures resurface as private modernist techniques."[19] Brown's account of Crane's own writing, however, still holds to the idea that even when social materials are "buried" in the register he calls the "material unconscious" of the text, this rather uncommunicative space can still *think* (in some immanent fashion) about what it has absorbed: the social matter of modern work and play, war and material survival, the modern uses of pleasure and abjection. Novels, in other words, can still serve as a "a point of access to the knowledge that literature can energize."[20] Novels can go public—or at least Crane's novels can, and at least when their social meditations are unearthed through the right kind of critical reading. In McGurl's account, however, the literary work *uses up* the social by making it into the private forms of technique and career, and can offer neither social insight nor an altered social imaginary. Social to the core, the art novel is not public. As McGurl concedes, this way of reading also leaves literary critics without any real knowledge to offer, either: critics can merely "savor these intuitions of our own pointlessness."[21]

Taking literary form seriously often makes for critical dilemmas. But there is an alternative to the choice between a private art novel that acquires innovative form by sacrificing social knowledge and a public novel that acquires social insight only by excluding apparently extraliterary incongruities. Throughout this study I have put forth an alternative model of late-century literary analysis, an analytic art in which reflection on the social not only gives a formal shape to the body of the text but also grapples with extraliterary experience now visible *as* public in an age of mass culture. Crane describes the artist as a consciousness that moves "sideways," in transit across an unfixed horizon: "An artist . . . is nothing but a powerful memory that can move itself at will through certain experiences sideways."[22] No longer a fixed, supersensible mind, artistic consciousness moves through a field of social experience that may not be assimilable to any preexisting literary "system." If the figure of a powerful, sideways moving memory evokes an idea of a movie camera, it also describes a postliterary form of literary consciousness that has retained the capacity for critical reflection as a site of "memory" that encounters the new. It is therefore a vivid figure for the high literary consciousness I have argued emerged *out of* its analysis of a new set of agencies and publics, among them the imaginative appropriation of time and space available in such vehicles as mass fiction, cinema, and sensational amusements; the public solicitation of desire in department stores, theatrical posters, and advertisements; the risky but negotiable mass resonance of figures such as the public woman, the Indian celebrity-warrior, and the black entertainer; the unexpected solidarities among strangers that form around events like large-scale accidents and disasters.

Henry James, even more than Crane, affirms the idea that this postliterary form of analysis can be a conscious art and not just an unconscious textual object. Just as James's prefaces to the New York Edition theorize his fictional practice, his eccentric travel narrative *The American Scene* is the best account of James's theory of social observation, a practice that learns from and cultivates the "perception of incongruities."[23] He presents a picture of literary analysis that is neither the aesthete's detached contemplation nor the immersion in shock and sensation that marks the "aesthetics of astonishment" of mass amusement, but is rather a composite practice that emerges from the turbulent conjunction of both domains of experience. The perception of disjunctions has become an implicit epistemology: our best chance for social knowledge comes from thinking at the junctures and the ragged seams where consciousness confronts an experience of alterity, as observation and reflective thought move sideways across an unpredictable social horizon.

Like Howells's *Hazard of New Fortunes,* James's immersion in modern America prompts an elegiac reflection on the fall of a literary public sphere, even as his own prose bespeaks the rise of a more privatized literary modernism. The evidence is not just the decline in "literary desire" that he can detect, like a worried lover, even at places like Harvard. He also recognizes that forms and conventions bequeathed by literary culture have been outstripped by "the flood of the real." In New York, the city's "too defiant scale" defeats even the capacious resources of the nineteenth-century novel. The "multitudinous life" compressed into a skyscraper leads him to think of "the great wonder-working Emile Zola, and his love of the human aggregation." But the recollection of Zola finally serves to convince James that not even that novelist could master the "monstrous phenomena" that exceed any possibility of capture. That past order of literary meaning has "perished and lost all rights."[24]

Where literary culture has lost its "rights," James becomes in effect a foreign national, someone who belongs to another, distant sovereignty. James's sense of exile from the nineteenth-century republic of letters creates a feeling of disequilibrium even more than does his encounter with an unfamiliar American society. But James's "intimate surrender" (460) to the phenomena of this deterritorialized social field also teaches him what filmmakers and other mass culture producers already know, namely, that any object, person, or cultural mood can become public in a historical moment undergoing dramatic "reconfigurations of the shared sensible order."[25] Shoe sellers, the consumption of candy, and the superabundance of windows come into view as features on James's new map of the sensible. Nor are these features merely objects of perception and analysis arrayed before the vision of a remote spectator. The truly public nature of this scene, its ability to congeal collective interests and conduct shared meanings, is captured by James's oft-noted use of prosopopoeia, in which he hears and records the speech addressed *to him* by such subjects as a skyscraper, a New Jersey mansion, and by the air itself.[26] Literary consciousness is now public only by virtue of its surrender to the "vociferous" (445) strangeness of others' experience and sensibilities. James makes a place for phenomena that have been hitherto inassimilable to literary culture by opening the record of his own thought to a new order of publicness: the "acute demand for display" that had "pounced on the nation's understanding" (314) and offered up the bewildering array of persons, desires, and objects making up everyday life in the New York cityscape. Of necessity, the office of literature as James defined it—"the great extension, great beyond all others, of experience and of consciousness"—will require an open receptivity to extraliterary forms and spaces, the sites where new kinds of experience are being articulated and exchanged.[27]

If his "surrendered consciousness" has opened itself to the kind of wide-ranging materials available to a cinematic public, this is not to claim that James's writing is as accessible as a movie or an advertisement. He knows his sentences are most likely illegible to "eyes accustomed to the telegraphic brevity of the newspaper."[28] But neither are his fine discriminations and complexly nested observations merely the expression of tastes cultivated by an inherited literary culture. In writing as a serious interlocutor of the American "spectacle," James fashions a mode of expression that can best be called literary spectacle, drawing on and extending the strange, prodigious, misshapen, and deliberately sensational images and language of his late style. James may not be directly imitating the "sword-swallowing" (426) conspicuousness he experiences in everyday life in New York, but his prose reflects a tutelage in mass forms. Confronting disorienting scenes, he writes, calls for "great loops thrown out by the lasso of observation from the wonder-working motor-car" (395) (an image uncannily resonant with a famous Walter Ferguson photograph of Geronimo, in which he is seated at the wheel of a Cadillac alongside several fellow Indians in headdresses during a Wild West tour).[29] James's literary language is his backhanded homage to the freedom of mass culture to invent incautious, ad hoc forms to meet the exigencies of the age. He learns the lessons of its lack of deference, its alacrity in reading subcultures, the strategic virtues of its disproportionate and outsized dimension, its intensity of effect and rapidity of change, its ability to re-create and thus explore the somatic experience of modernity. James never embraces mass society and its forms uncritically; his openness to the new cultural forces and formations in New York is part of his effort to see and understand "'modernity,' with its terrible power of working its will" (484). James pledges to "go to the stake" (353) for literary discrimination with its commitment to analytic thought, but in *The American Scene*, literary thinking lives through a critical collaboration with the extravagant, impudent novelties of mass culture.

The strange and brilliant innovations of James's language are not simply the formal materials of a "war of position" among literary aspirants seeking prestige. Linguistic extravagance and formal disparities are also a sign of the epistemological and ethical demands to which James pays heed by dwelling for extended periods at the moment of the "inconceivable," the moment when he confronts a life or experience that seems inassimilable to his present frame of understanding. Alterity is an occasion for analysis, not simply for incorporation into the body of a Jamesian sentence. James's extended meditations on the "inconceivable alien" (426) are the best known—and most controversial—of these moments in *The American Scene*. Startled and absorbed by the "hotch-potch of racial ingredients" (456) everywhere visible in New York, he does not pretend the new immigrant populations are other than "alien," strangers to his own habits of thought and feeling. The "intensity of Jewish aspect" (465) of the new immigrant, or the rebuff he feels from an Italian laborer, triggers in James a sense of personal distance that he records in close detail. The emphasis on otherness in these passages can read like patrician recoil and in part may be just that. Yet preserving the immigrant's "inconceivable" aspect is also a strategic moment in his brand of literary analysis, as his thought opens itself to realities of difference that it cannot master but will not elide.

Among the most striking aspects of his analysis is the way James's sense of personal difference or distress is a sentiment that *disables* the affective structure of nationalism.[30] There is, he confesses, something that attracts him in the "close and sweet and *whole* national consciousness as that of the Switzer and the Scot" (428), but for an American no such consciousness is possible unless it seals itself against history and therefore proves itself a form of bad faith. If there is to be anything like an "American consciousness," it will mean a wholesale change in the very notion of a national collectivity: "the idea of the country itself underwent something of [a] profane overhauling" (427).

The puzzle devolves upon James, not the "alien." Refusing a facile assimilation of the foreigner into an assumed American identity and destiny means James is thrown back upon the limits of his own comprehension, and he records a "conscious need of mental adjustment."

He doesn't *know*, he can't *say*, before the facts. . . . It is as if the syllables were too numerous to make a legible word. The illegible word, accordingly, the great inscrutable answer to the questions, hangs in the vast American sky, to his imagination, as something fantastic and *abracadabrant*, belonging to no known language. (456)

The nonsensical adjective, creative yet opaque, is the modifier James would attach mentally to everything "American." Something unknown and unknowable hangs in the sky, an anti-symbol to the certainty of a transparent American destiny that had been the guiding sign from the time of the Puritans. To take in the "great 'ethnic' question" (455) is to admit the resistances and opacities of history, something inevitably corrosive to the transparency of national myth. For James, the matters of ethnicity and race are inscrutable signs that interrupt the otherwise unbroken prospect or "sky" that would figure a "sweet and whole" but falsified national future. If literature has any part in creating (or, alternatively, undoing) a nationalist structure of feeling, it will only do so in conjunction with the profane magic of collective conjuring—the mass culture *abracadabra*—that James observes everywhere in commercial culture.

A later episode that takes place at the site of monumental nationalist imagining confirms this insight in a strange and haunting way. Outside the Capitol building in Washington he encounters "a trio of Indian braves, braves dispossessed of forest and prairie, but as free of [the Capitol grounds] as they had ever been of these" (652). These Indians are also dispossessed—or, better, liberated—from the territories of U.S. literature, the fields in which they have been called upon to do so much labor for the national imaginary. Here Native Americans, too, are subjects of the pleasure economy, tourists in pursuit of their own tokens and impressions. In their bowler hats, and (as he imagines) with tobacco and photographs in their pockets, the modern appearance of these supposedly "vanished" Americans shatters the smoothed-over, monumental aura so deliberately cultivated at the Capitol. The strangeness of the sight—the men's ironic "freedom" to possess the grounds, their resemblance to "Japanese celebrities"—creates a rift that suddenly opens out to an unacknowledged history of violence, a cinematic flashback that had yet to appear on any screen.

They seemed just then and there . . . to project as in a flash an image in itself immense, but foreshortened and simplified—reducing to a single smooth stride the bloody footsteps of time. One rubbed one's eyes, but there, at its highest polish, shining in the beautiful day, was the brazen face of history, and there, all about one, immaculate, the printless pavements of the State. (652–53)

Originally conceived as an "agent of perception" for discerning civil relations from commercial distortions, high literary discernment will need to read inscrutable facts and "bloody" incivilities or it will read no more than what is already written on the "printless pavements of the State."

The shocks and disjunctions of James's language are not merely stylistic features of a literary object. They are also communicative features that reveal tectonic shifts in what is visible and invisible, and what is intelligible and what is opaque. James failed to provide what was expected of a book of travel impressions; critics complained that it did not give a "synthetic view of life seen from a certain centralizing point of view."[31] But James's abdication from this literary imperative allows *The American Scene* to remain open to unexpected social insight and incommensurable phenomena. There is for James a degree of "'lettered' anguish" (420) in knowing that the literary culture that has defined his own life and mind has been eclipsed. But through this same social transformation, James's literary sensibility has become an instrument of perception alert to the "various possibilities of the waiting spring of intelligence," the possibilities that are the "germ" for a new "resulting public" (420). "Literary desire" as James knows it is becoming the private modernist property of the few, but *The American Scene* also shows how a new inventory of experiences—pleasurable speed, involuntary memory, strange and profane sights—can be resources for critical reflection. The perception of incongruities reinvents the analytic possibilities of literature for a postliterary age.

Notes

Introduction

1. Allen Lee Hamilton, "Crash at Crush," *Handbook of Texas Online*, http://www.tshaonline.org/handbook/online/articles/CC/llc1.html; Mary G. Ramos, "The Crash at Crush," Texas Almanac Online, http://texasalmanac.com/history/highlights/crash; Lynn Kirby, *Parallel Tracks: The Railroad and Silent Cinema* (Durham, N.C.: Duke University Press, 1997), 59–60. Kirby notes that of the several hundred travel and scenic films produced between 1896 and 1902, most featured some aspect of train travel. When fiction films began to dominate cinema after 1902, the train remained a central figure, as both a subject and a site for panoramic camera work (19–20). In addition to producing films that featured railroad accidents, filmmakers deployed "the trope of train trauma" in diverse ways (70).

2. Planning began in 1898, and the first meeting of the National Institute of Arts and Letters took place in 1899. In 1904 a smaller, more select body chosen from the larger membership became the American Academy of Arts and Letters. John Updike, *A Century of Arts and Letters* (New York: Columbia University Press, 1998), ix, 1–3.

3. Tom Gunning discusses formal similarities between technologies of commercial entertainment at the turn of the century and the aesthetics of early film in "The Cinema of Attraction: Early Film, Its Spectator and the Avant-Garde," *Wide Angle* 8:3–4 (1986): 63–70, and "An Aesthetic of Astonishment: Early Film and the (In)credulous Spectator," *Art & Text* 34 (Spring 1989): 31–45.

4. Henry James, writing about the vastly expanded print market, gives a vivid description of a phenomenon for which he has no ready name: "our huge Anglo-Saxon array of producers and readers—and especially our vast cis-Atlantic multitude—presents production uncontrolled, production untouched by criticism, unguided, unlighted, uninstructed, unashamed, on a scale that is really a new thing in the world." H. James, "The Lesson of Balzac," in *Literary Criticism,* vol. 1, ed. Leon Edel (New York: Library of America, 1984), 116. Although the label "mass culture" was circulating widely by the 1940s, it has been used in conflicting ways and with different connotations. James Naremore and Patrick Brantlinger offer a useful overview in "Introduction: Six Artistic Cultures," in *Modernity and Mass Culture,* ed. James Naremore and Patrick Brantlinger (Bloomington: Indiana University Press, 1991), 1–23. Richard Ohmann discusses the reasons for using the term "mass culture" to describe commercial culture in the late nineteenth-century United States in *Selling Culture: Magazines, Markets, and Class at the Turn of the Century* (New York: Verso, 1996), 11–19. In this study, I use the term "mass culture" in a histori-

cally specific way to refer to the institutions and expressive forms that were able to generate a new scale of audience.

The emergence of mass culture in this period rested on the inauguration of new technologies and media (such as cinema and the mass press) and new forms of publicity (innovations in advertising and celebrity), as well as a profound restructuring of the U.S. economy (corporate capitalism and the changes it introduced into consumer culture). On the economic foundation for this "cultural revolution," see James Livingston, *Pragmatism and the Political Economy of Cultural Revolution, 1850–1940* (Chapel Hill: University of North Carolina Press, 1994), chapters 1–4. For a succinct overview of the scholarship on U.S. mass culture, see the bibliographic essay in Robert W. Rydell and Rob Kroes, *Buffalo Bill in Bologna: The Americanization of the World, 1869–1922* (Chicago: University of Chicago Press, 2005), 175–88. However, Rydell and Kroes do not discuss the scholarship on mass culture that has emerged in dialogue with Jürgen Habermas's study of the public sphere. See the works cited in note 21.

5. Like William Dean Howells's image of a "spectacular muse," drawn from a review he wrote about the new vogue for women's burlesque performance companies ("The New Taste in Theatricals," *Atlantic Monthly* 23 [1869]: 638), I borrow the phrase "frantic panorama" from Howells. *A Hazard of New Fortunes* (New York: Penguin, 2001), 158.

6. Hamilton, "Crash at Crush."

7. Henry James, *The Notebooks of Henry James,* ed. F. O. Matthiessen and Kenneth B. Murdock (Chicago: University of Chicago Press, 1947), 196.

8. Michael Warner, "The Mass Public and the Mass Subject," in *Publics and Counterpublics* (New York: Zone Books, 2002), 159–86.

9. Kirby, *Parallel Tracks,* 59–60.

10. Ibid., 60; Hamilton, "Crash at Crush."

11. In a document circulated in 1905 by Howells and poet Clarence Stedman, the academy defined its mission as rallying for standards of "dignity, moderation and purity of expression" and opposing "vulgarity, sensationalism, meretriciousness, lubricity" and "the tyranny of novelty." Updike, *Century of Arts and Letters,* 22.

12. Andreas Huyssen, *After the Great Divide: Modernism, Mass Culture and Postmodernism* (Bloomington: Indiana University Press, 1986), remains a central study on the divisions between high culture and mass culture. On the formation of this divide in the United States, see Lawrence Levine, *Highbrow/Lowbrow: The Emergence of Cultural Hierarchy in America* (Cambridge, Mass.: Harvard University Press, 1988). Amy Kaplan has made the most influential argument for the importance of a phobic opposition to mass culture by American literary realists in *The Social Construction of American Realism* (Chicago: University of Chicago Press, 1988). Bill Brown's far-ranging study of Stephen Crane marks a shift toward a more dialectical treatment of literary culture and mass culture. See *The Material Unconscious: American Amusement, Stephen Crane, and the Economies of Play* (Cambridge, Mass.: Harvard University Press, 1996).

13. The young protagonist in Howells's *The Minister's Charge* has to evacuate his apartment building when it goes up in flames and he is later hit by a trolley car.

A central character in *Annie Kilburn* is struck by a train and killed, his body badly mangled. I discuss Howells's reliance on sensational events (including a train accident) for the plot of *A Modern Instance* in Chapter 2. Henry James's claim to possess "the imagination of disaster," which appears in a letter, is quoted in Peter Brooks, *The Melodramatic Imagination: Balzac, Henry James, and the Mode of Excess* (New Haven, Conn.: Yale University Press, 1976), 153. Most critics, like Brooks, have associated this phrase with theatrical traditions of melodrama and tragedy, but precisely the melodramatic dimension of James's imagination, I argue, drew him to the energies of rupture in mass culture as an object of both fascination and alarm.

14. I discuss Wharton's use of the crash trope in Chapter 6. When Thomas Wentworth Higginson was approached to join the National Institute (the predecessor to the academy), he wrote that he had "one fatal objection, that it comprises one sex only," though his protest was ignored and he was enrolled in the membership list anyway. In 1906 Higginson nominated Julia Ward Howe, who was elected in 1908. Later that year, Higginson nominated Wharton and asked Mark Twain and editor Richard Watson Gilder to support the nomination, but the effort was defeated. Wharton was elected to the National Institute in 1926 and elevated to the academy in 1930. Updike, *Century of Arts and Letters*, 13. When Howe was elected, Henry Adams wrote to the leadership to note that "I do not see how we justify omitting Edith Wharton, for example, and I've no doubt that a dozen more would claim much higher literary credit than Mrs. Howe can claim" (100).

15. Henry Adams, *Novels, Mont Saint Michel, The Education*, ed. Ernest Samuels and Jayne N. Samuels (New York: Library of America, 1983), 1069. Adams was a founding member of the National Institute and was elected to the academy in 1905. Updike, *Century of Arts and Letters*, 298.

16. William James, *The Will to Believe* and "What Makes a Life Significant," in *Writings, 1878–1899*, ed. Gerald E. Myers (New York: Library of America, 1992), 510, 865. On William James's complicated affiliation with the academy, see Updike, *Century of Arts and Letters*, 20–22.

17. W. E. B. DuBois, *Dusk of Dawn*, in *Writings*, ed. Nathan Huggins (New York: Library of America, 1986), 573–74. According to R. W. B. Lewis, DuBois's *Souls of Black Folk* (1903) had "captured the attention" of members of the National Institute, and William James, his former teacher, admired the book. But there appears to be no record that he was considered for membership until the 1940s. Lewis, "1898–1907," in Updike, *Century of Arts and Letters*, 14. When DuBois's name was finally circulated for consideration, the ballot included the designation "Negro," causing a major controversy. Helen Keller, among others, protested, and Katherine Anne Porter submitted a letter of resignation (119–20).

18. See Jean-Christophe Agnew, "The Consuming Vision of Henry James," in *The Culture of Consumption: Critical Essays in American History, 1880–1980*, ed. Richard Wightman Fox and T. J. Jackson Lears (New York: Pantheon, 1983), 70–98. Another early example is Jennifer Wicke's treatment of James and other authors in *Advertising Fictions: Literature, Advertising, and Social Reading* (New York: Columbia University Press, 1988). In a different vein, Russ Castronovo's recent study examines "multiple subjects of democratic taste," from neo-Kantian scholars to residents of "slums." *Beautiful Democracy: Aesthetics and Anarchy in a Global Era*

(Chicago: University of Chicago Press, 2007), 1. But while Castronovo argues that aesthetic feeling can produce different, unpredictable modes of political agency, his critical framework largely dispenses with distinctions between high and low social locations in order to treat the aesthetic as a single rubric that extends across all sites, and thereby risks eliding the history of different publics that lies behind the question of democratic taste.

19. "In contrast to a political event," Hans Robert Jauss writes, "a literary event has no lasting results which succeeding generations cannot avoid. It can continue to have an effect only if future generations still respond to it or rediscover it." "Literary History as a Challenge to Literary Theory," *New Literary History* 2 (1970): 7–37, 11. For Pascale Casanova, "literary history is incarnated in the structure of the world of letters, which supplies its motive force," and "the events of the literary world take on meaning through the structure that produces them and gives them form and, in so doing, makes literature at once stake, resource, and belief." *The World Republic of Letters*, trans. M. B. DeBevoise (Cambridge, Mass.: Harvard University Press, 2004), 82. The impact of the mass culture industry on literary culture, I argue, was both a literary event—it shaped the history of literary production—as well as an event in social history, as is argued in the work of scholars like Jürgen Habermas and Arjun Appadurai.

20. Jürgen Habermas, *The Structural Transformation of the Public Sphere*, trans. Thomas Burger (Cambridge, Mass.: MIT Press, 1989), 175, 160, 161.

21. For Habermas, "the world fashioned by the mass media is a public sphere in appearance only." *Structural Transformation,* 171. While many of Habermas's interlocutors share his wariness about highly capitalized mass media and the asymmetrical power that structures the relationship between producers and consumers, a number of thinkers explore the possibilities for new kinds of publics in the postliterary era. See, for example, Oskar Negt and Alexander Kluge, *The Public Sphere and Experience*, trans. Peter Labanyi et al. (Minneapolis: University of Minnesota Press, 1993); Miriam Hansen, *Babel and Babylon: Spectatorship in American Silent Film* (Cambridge, Mass.: Harvard University Press, 1991); Warner, *Publics and Counterpublics;* and the scholars who contributed essays to *The Black Public Sphere: A Public Culture Book*, ed. Black Public Sphere Collective (Chicago: University of Chicago Press, 1995).

22. Howells is quoted in Edwin H. Cady, *W. D. Howells as Critic* (Boston: Routledge and Kegan Paul, 1973), 310–11.

23. The founding document for the academy is quoted in Updike, *Century of Arts and Letters*, 1.

24. The terms set forth by Pascale Casanova are useful for understanding the international basis for the nationalism of an institution like the American Academy. Although writers who are positioned outside of the world literary capitals (Paris and London in the nineteenth century) can make a bid for literary prestige in the name of an organic national culture, Casanova argues, the most secure literary value is earned only though an *international* economy of recognition—acceptance by the "world republic of letters." *World Republic of Letters,* 87. The founding of the American Academy, I would argue, marks a moment when U.S. national literary capital was "cashed in" for credit as modern world literature. Howells, for instance, pro-

moted American realism both as a form of national expression and as the debut of U.S. literary culture on the world stage as a contender for superior literary achievement. Casanova notes that Henry James saw American culture as deficient for supporting a world-class literary production and decamped for France and then England as a matter of "literary salvation" (83). But precisely because the academy was oriented toward an international "standard" of literary and high cultural value, James's identification with British culture was not inconsistent with his willingness to become a member of the American Academy of Arts and Letters. Although he could not attend meetings, James tried to stay active in voting for new members—although, tellingly, he confessed to the secretary in 1913 that often he had not heard of the names that appeared on his ballots. Updike, *Century of Arts and Letters*, 32–33.

25. Arjun Appadurai, *Modernity at Large: Cultural Dimensions of Globalization* (Minneapolis: University of Minnesota Press, 1996).

26. Ibid., 7, 5.

27. Ibid., 4.

28. Ibid., 5.

29. George Santayana's essays on "the genteel tradition" in the United States supplied a name for the post–Civil War generation of cultural authorities that was quickly adopted by subsequent critics who perceived the "revolt against gentility" by younger writers and thinkers (see Malcolm Cowley's essay of this title in *After the Genteel Tradition,* ed. Malcolm Cowley [New York: W. W. Norton, 1937]). For studies that make related but not identical arguments about the "sacralization" of high culture as a species of social control, see Alan Trachtenberg, *The Incorporation of America: Culture and Society in the Gilded Age* (New York: Hill and Wang, 1982); Neil Harris, *Cultural Excursions: Marketing Appetites and Cultural Tastes in Modern America* (Chicago: University of Chicago Press, 1990); Helen Lefkowitz Horowitz, *Culture and the City: Cultural Philanthropy in Chicago from the 1880s to 1917* (Lexington: University of Kentucky Press, 1989); and Levine, *Highbrow/Lowbrow*. For a recent attempt to revise the historical picture of post–Civil War liberal intellectuals as hidebound custodians of culture, see Leslie Butler, *Critical Americans: Victorian Intellectuals and Transatlantic Liberal Reform* (Chapel Hill: University of North Carolina Press, 2007).

30. On the turn to "antimodern" styles and spaces, see T. J. Jackson Lears, *No Place of Grace: Antimodernism and the Transformation of American Culture, 1880–1920* (Chicago: University of Chicago Press, 1981). James Livingston offers the contrasting view that interest in medieval art and history, for instance, can be seen not as escapist or therapeutic but as an effort to find a historical yardstick with which to gauge the "cultural revolution" of this period. *Pragmatism and the Political Economy,* 174–75.

31. Henry James, review of *Hours of Exercise in the Alps* by John Tyndall, *Atlantic Monthly* 28 (November 1871): 634.

32. Quoted in Edwin H. Cady, introduction to *A Modern Instance* (New York: Penguin, 1977), xxi. Howells refers to the "analytic school" in a letter to Mark Twain. *Mark Twain–Howells Letters: The Correspondence of Samuel L. Clemens and William Dean Howells, 1872–1910,* ed. Henry Nash Smith and William M. Gibson (Cambridge, Mass.: Harvard University Press, 1960), 535–36.

33. H. James, *Literary Criticism,* vol. 1, 229.

34. Phillip Barrish, *American Literary Realism, Critical Theory, and Intellectual Prestige, 1880–1995* (Cambridge: Cambridge University Press, 2001). Two other important studies that develop the idea of intellectual prestige as a formative element in American realism and modernism are Thomas Strychacz, *Modernism, Mass Culture, and Professionalism* (Cambridge: Cambridge University Press, 1993), and Mark McGurl, *The Novel Art: Elevations of American Fiction After Henry James* (Princeton, N.J.: Princeton University Press, 2001).

35. On the importance of a new social class of professionals in the formation of high literary culture, see Richard Brodhead, *Cultures of Letters: Scenes of Reading and Writing in Nineteenth-Century America* (Chicago: University of Chicago Press, 1993), and Strychacz, *Modernism, Mass Culture and Professionalism,* as well as Barrish, *American Literary Realism.* In this vein, McGurl argues that the professional's arch-value of intelligence displaces the bourgeois value of virtue as the master term of literary modernism. *Novel Art,* 10–19. But McGurl takes Howells's language about realism as a literature of "commonplace" virtue too literally (10). In fact, as Barrish shows—and as I argue from a different angle in Chapter 2—Howellsian realism was closely tied to the values of intellectual and cultural distinction, precisely as the critical power to discern the unitary civil order that the "great mass of American readers" seemed uninterested in discovering.

36. Steven Conn, *Museums and American Intellectual Life, 1876–1926* (Chicago: University of Chicago Press, 1998), 9. In his "incomplete" list, Conn mentions New York's Metropolitan Museum of Art and American Museum of Natural History; the Peabody Museum of Harvard; the University of Pennsylvania's Museum of Archaeology and Anthropology as well as the Philadelphia Museum of Art; Detroit's Institute of Arts; the Carnegie Museum of Pittsburgh; the Museum of Fine Arts in Boston; and Chicago's Art Institute and Field Museum. Cultural leaders in most of these cities also founded symphony orchestras, built concert halls, and established research universities during this period.

37. Gregory S. Jackson, *The Word and Its Witness: The Spiritualization of American Realism* (Chicago: University of Chicago Press, 2008).

38. Henry James, "The Lesson of Balzac," in *Literary Criticism,* vol. 2, ed. Leon Edel (New York: Library of America, 1984), 134.

39. On forms of rationality and cosmopolitanism in Victorian literature, see, for instance, Amanda Anderson, *The Powers of Distance: Cosmopolitanism and the Cultivation of Detachment* (Princeton, N.J.: Princeton University Press, 2001), and George Levine, *Dying to Know: Scientific Epistemology and Narrative in Nineteenth-Century England* (Chicago: University of Chicago Press, 2002). Among scholarly studies of nineteenth-century American literature in this vein, see Gregg Crane, *Race, Citizenship, and Law in American Literature* (Cambridge: Cambridge University Press, 2002); Mary Esteve, *The Aesthetics and Politics of the Crowd in American Literature* (Cambridge: Cambridge University Press, 2003); Jane Thrailkill, *Affecting Fictions: Mind, Body, and Emotion in American Literary Realism* (Cambridge, Mass.: Harvard University Press, 2007); and Martha Banta, *One True Theory and the Quest for an American Aesthetic* (New Haven, Conn.: Yale University Press, 2007).

40. Anderson, *Powers of Distance,* 3.

41. Bourdieu's studies of literary culture and aesthetic taste include *The Field of Cultural Production,* ed. Randal Johnson (New York: Columbia University Press, 1993), and *Distinction: A Social Critique of the Judgment of Taste,* trans. Richard Nice (Cambridge, Mass.: Harvard University Press, 1985).

42. Quoted in Joseph Horowitz, *Artists in Exile: How Refugees from Twentieth-Century War and Revolution Transformed American Performing Arts* (New York: Harper-Collins, 2008), 1–3.

43. Quoted in Joseph Horowitz, *Classical Music in America: A History of Its Rise and Fall* (New York: Norton, 2005), 8.

44. Miriam Hansen, for instance, discusses the ability of cinema to allow for "the transformation of seemingly fixed positions of social identity." *Babel and Babylon,* 112. However, Hansen also carefully traces the way new technologies of mass culture could sometimes serve to sustain and invent local ethnic customs and gendered forms of experience, even as they transformed perception and habits. On the bodily disorientations available at amusement parks, see John Kasson, *Amusing the Million: Coney Island at the Turn of the Century* (New York: Hill and Wang, 1978), and Brown, *Material Unconscious,* 46–56. In his essays collected in *Shadow and Act* (New York: Random House, 1964), Ralph Ellison led the way in analyzing the "physical complexity" of African American culture, complexity that was retained and transformed as local traditions were taken up in film, recording, and public performance venues (89).

45. W. James, "What Makes a Life Significant," 863.

46. Gorky's analysis appears in an appendix to Jay Leyda, *Kino: A History of the Russian and Soviet Film* (London: Allen and Unwin, 1960), 407–9. His account of Coney Island is in "Boredom," *Independent* 63 (August 8, 1907): 310–14.

47. Theodor Adorno, "Theses upon Art and Religion Today," in *Notes to Literature,* vol. 2, trans. Shierry Weber Nicholsen (New York: Columbia University Press, 1992), 296.

48. I am echoing Michael Warner's observation about the distinct and tenuous kind of agency that is organized by modern publics. Publics are the efficacious fictions that manage to function in a world where "our lives are minutely administered and recorded, to a degree unprecedented in history": "Without a faith, justified or not, in self-organized publics, organically linked to our activity in their very existence, capable of being addressed, and capable of action, we would be nothing but the peasants of capital—which, of course, we might be, and some of us more than others." *Publics and Counterpublics,* 69.

49. Georg Simmel, "The Metropolis and Mental Life," in *The Sociology of Georg Simmel,* trans. Kurt Wolff (New York: Free Press, 1950), 409–24; Stephen Kern, *The Culture of Time and Space, 1880–1920* (Cambridge, Mass.: Harvard University Press, 1983).

50. John Dewey's 1891 essay, "The Scholastic and the Speculator," appears in *The Early Works of John Dewey,* ed. Jo Ann Boydston (Carbondale: Southern Illinois University Press, 1969), 3:148–54. The quoted passage appears on page 151. James Livingston discusses this essay in *Pragmatism and the Political Economy,* 192–96.

51. W. James, "What Makes a Life Significant," and *Psychology: Briefer Course,* in *Writings, 1878–1899,* 876, 149.

52. Walter Benjamin, "Some Motifs in Baudelaire," in *Illuminations,* trans. Harry Zohn, ed. Hannah Arendt (New York: Schocken, 1968), 175.

53. Quoted in Cady, *W. D. Howells as Critic,* 311.

54. Henry James, "The Question of the Opportunities," in *Literary Criticism,* vol. 1, 652, 653, 652.

55. Hansen, *Babel and Babylon,* 12, 11. On the "politics of relationality," see chapter 3 of *Babel and Babylon,* 90–125, and Hansen, "Early Cinema, Late Cinema: Transformations of the Public Sphere," in *Viewing Positions: Ways of Seeing Film,* ed. Linda Williams (New Brunswick, N.J.: Rutgers University Press, 1995), 134–52.

56. W. James, "What Makes a Life Significant," 879.

57. The phrase "grope of wealth" is from Henry James, *The American Scene,* in *Collected Travel Writings: Great Britain and America,* ed. Richard Howard (New York: Library of America, 1993), 491. Given the attention that Simmel and others were beginning to give to the human sensorium, it is striking that here, as elsewhere in this work, James represents his encounter with the new displays of wealth in New York City as an aggressively tactile experience.

58. Edith Wharton, *The Custom of the Country* and *The House of Mirth,* in *Novels,* ed. R. W. B. Lewis (New York: Library of America, 1985), 754, 222.

59. H. James, *The American Scene,* 395.

Chapter 1

1. William Dean Howells, "Editor's Study," *Harper's Magazine* (October 1888), reprinted in *Editor's Study,* by William Dean Howells, ed. James W. Simpson (Troy, N.Y.: Whitston, 1983), 157.

2. George Brown Goode, "Museum-History and Museums of History," *Annual Report of the U.S. National Museum,* part 2 (Washington, D.C.: GPO, 1901), 65.

3. Henry James, *The Sacred Fount,* in *Novels, 1901–1902,* ed. Leo Bersani (New York: Library of America, 2006), 32.

4. Henry James, *Italian Hours,* in *Collected Travel Writings: The Continent,* ed. Richard Howard (New York: Library of America, 1993), 290, 315.

5. See David R. Shumway, *Creating American Civilization: A Genealogy of American Literature as an Academic Discipline* (Minneapolis: University of Minnesota Press, 1994), and Claudia Stokes, *Writers in Retrospect: The Rise of American Literary History, 1875–1910* (Chapel Hill: University of North Carolina Press, 2006).

6. William Dean Howells, *Criticism and Fiction, and Other Essays* (New York: New York University Press, 1959), 86, 53, 52, 54.

7. Ibid., 53, 73; William Dean Howells, "Henry James, Jr.," *Century* 25 (November 1882): 25–26.

8. Howells, *Criticism and Fiction,* 71.

9. Phineas T. Barnum, *Struggles and Triumphs; Or, Forty Years' Recollections of P. T. Barnum,* ed. Carl Bode (New York: Penguin, 1981), 103, 113. In his introduction Bode claims Barnum's autobiography become the second most widely read book after the Bible (23). Studies that examine Barnum in the context of cultural

history include Bluford Adams, *E Pluribus Barnum: The Great Showman and the Making of U.S. Popular Culture* (Minneapolis: University of Minnesota Press, 1997), and Benjamin Reiss, *The Showman and the Slave: Race, Death, and Memory in Barnum's America* (Cambridge, Mass.: Harvard University Press, 2001).

10. Henry James, *A Small Boy and Others* (New York: Scribner's, 1913), 154.

11. David Goodman, "Fear of Circuses: Founding the National Museum of Victoria," *Continuum* 3:1 (1990): 28.

12. B. Adams, *E Pluribus Barnum*, 115; A. H. Saxon, *P. T. Barnum* (New York: Columbia University Press, 1983), 112, 292–300.

13. Robert W. Rydell and Rob Kroes, *Buffalo Bill in Bologna: The Americanization of the World, 1869–1922* (Chicago: University of Chicago Press, 2005), 49.

14. Paul Starr, *The Creation of the Media: Political Origins of Modern Communications* (New York: Basic Books, 2004), 250–66, 251.

15. Rydell and Kroes, *Buffalo Bill in Bologna*, 78.

16. The critique appeared in the *British Quarterly Review* in 1871, but as I show later in this chapter, the same view of the American mass press was shared by intellectuals in the United States as well. Quoted in Starr, *Creation of the Media*, 255.

17. James, *A Small Boy*, 164, 162, 155, 165, 163.

18. Ibid., 170.

19. Ibid., 163.

20. W. E. B. DuBois, *The Souls of Black Folk*, in *Writings*, ed. Nathan Huggins (New York: Library of America, 1986), 545.

21. Richard Brodhead, *Cultures of Letters: Scenes of Reading and Writing in Nineteenth-Century America* (Chicago: University of Chicago Press, 1993), 133.

22. Scholars studying the links between mass culture and U.S. imperialism have recognized that mass genres are also able to foster an appropriative sensibility. Amy Kaplan, for instance, describes the way the "war film craze" conditioned viewers to see foreign territories like the Philippines as barbaric spaces in need of American rescue, an ideological achievement that in turn helped raise the low cultural status of early cinema. See chapter 5 of *The Anarchy of Empire in the Making of U.S. Culture* (Cambridge, Mass.: Harvard University Press, 2002), 146–70. But this body of scholarship also tends to overlook the possibility that imaginary appropriation of foreign spaces might also function in non-imperial projects such as the world building undertaken by immigrant and women viewers in the history of early cinema. See, for instance, Miriam Hansen, *Babel and Babylon: Spectatorship in American Silent Film* (Cambridge, Mass.: Harvard University Press, 1991).

23. Edith Wharton, *The House of Mirth*, in *Novels*, ed. R. W. B. Lewis (New York: Library of America, 1985), 225.

24. Scholars in the 1960s and 1970s tended to argue that the post–Civil War period featured a "hegemony of genteel culture" created through an "alliance between 'high' and 'middle' culture, between members of the cultural elite and commercial tastemakers," as John Kasson summarizes it. *Amusing the Million: Coney Island at the Turn of the Century* (New York: Hill and Wang, 1978), 5. More recent historians and critics, however, have directed attention to the way culture was also a site for internal competition, allowing for contests *among* members of the middle and upper-middle classes vying for social prestige. Richard Brodhead summarizes

"the formation of a translocally incorporated social elite in place of an older, locally based gentry order" in *Cultures of Letters*, 123.

25. Wharton, *Novels*, 71.

26. Jürgen Habermas describes this history in terms of a decisive shift in ideas about the public knowledge. Whereas bourgeois political theory of the eighteenth century posited the need for public discussion and debate of what had been formerly private matters of the state, in the nineteenth century the ideal of public knowledge was confronted with the openly market-driven imperatives of a regime of mass publicity. *The Structural Transformation of the Public Sphere*, trans. Thomas Burger (Cambridge, Mass.: MIT Press, 1989).

27. Charles Eliot Norton, "The Intellectual Life of America," *New Princeton Review* 6 (1888): 318.

28. William Dean Howells, "At a Dime Museum," in *Literature and Life* (Boston: Harper and Brothers, 1902), 199.

29. Starr, *Creation of the Media*, 252, 261.

30. Russel Nye, *The Unembarrassed Muse: The Popular Arts in America* (New York: Dial Press, 1970), 28–29, 39–40.

31. Habermas, *Structural Transformation*, 165–67.

32. Starr, *Creation of the Media*, 251–52.

33. Henry James, "The Question of the Opportunities," *Literary Criticism*, vol. 1, ed. Leon Edel (New York: Library of America, 1984), 651–62.

34. Starr, *Creation of the Media*, 252–53.

35. Anthony Giddens, *The Consequences of Modernity* (Palo Alto, Calif.: Stanford University Press, 1990), 21.

36. On the popularity of historical romance and its relation to the American realist movement, see Nancy Glazener, "The Romantic Revival," in *Reading for Realism: The History of a U.S. Literary Institution, 1850–1910* (Durham, N.C.: Duke University Press, 1997), 147–88.

37. William Dean Howells, "The New Taste in Theatricals," *Atlantic Monthly* 23 (May 1869): 638.

38. Howells, *Literature and Life*, 199, 194. Subsequent page references cited parenthetically in the text.

39. In addition to Kasson, *Amusing the Million*, see Donald G. Lowe, *History of Bourgeois Perception* (Chicago: University of Chicago Press, 1982); Stephen Kern, *The Culture of Time and Space, 1880–1918* (Cambridge, Mass.: Harvard University Press, 1983); Kathy Peiss, *Cheap Amusements: Working Women and Leisure in Turn-of-the-Century New York* (Philadelphia: Temple University Press, 1986); and Bill Brown, *The Material Unconscious: American Amusement, Stephen Crane, and the Economies of Play* (Chicago: University of Chicago Press, 1996).

40. Kasson, *Amusing the Million*, 86, 71, 70.

41. Ibid., 106–9.

42. James Livingston's analysis of the turn toward cultural history in U.S. historiography is relevant to this issue. By breaking with intellectual historians' emphasis on political discourse and written records, the social-cultural historians have been able to recover unarticulated experiences of excluded groups like women, immigrants, and African Americans. But cultural historians, Livingston argues, have

tended to assume these tracts of experience were largely sealed off from participation in dominant forms of mediation—symbols, shared language, mediated images and experiences. It is more fruitful, Livingston argues, to ask how forms of cultural mediation might have operated across different zones of experience, including the experience that emerges in consumer culture. See chapter 5 of *Pragmatism and the Political Economy of Cultural Revolution, 1850–1940* (Chapel Hill: University of North Carolina Press, 1994), 123–31. In addition to Livingston's own historical analysis, in *Material Unconscious* Bill Brown offers an example of literary analysis that uncovers cultural mediation operating *across* literary culture and consumer culture.

43. James, *Literary Criticism*, vol. 1, 100, 102, 100.

44. Amy Kaplan discusses Wharton's ambivalent relation to the "crowd" and to her own popularity among readers in chapters 2 and 3 of *The Social Construction of American Realism* (Chicago: University of Chicago Press, 1988).

45. Editor quoted in Nye, *The Unembarrassed Muse*, 43. Howells quoted in John W. Crowley, *The Black Heart's Truth: The Early Career of W. D. Howells* (Chapel Hill: University of North Carolina Press, 1985), 124.

46. See Shumway, *Creating American Civilization*, 25–60.

47. James, *Literary Criticism*, vol. 1, 101, 100, 102.

48. Henry James, *The Notebooks of Henry James*, ed. F. O. Matthiessen and Kenneth B. Murdock (New York: Oxford University Press, 1947), 111.

49. Wharton, *Novels*, 1072.

50. William Dean Howells, *The Minister's Charge*, in *Novels, 1886–1888*, ed. Don L. Cook (New York: Library of America, 1989), 16. Subsequent page references cited parenthetically in the text.

51. Thomas Sargeant Perry, "Ivan Turgenieff," *Atlantic Monthly* 33 (May 1874): 569.

52. On Edmund Yates's series, see Richard Salmon, *Henry James and the Culture of Publicity* (New York: Cambridge University Press, 1997), 109. Other examples of this genre include Jeannette Gilder, *Authors at Home* (New York: A. Wessels, 1889), and Francis Whiting Halsey, *American Authors and Their Homes* (New York: James Pott, 1901) and *Authors of Our Day in Their Homes* (New York: James Pott, 1902). In an essay on Howells in Gilder's *Authors at Home*, the journalist writes that "the most fitting place [for Howells] seems yonder desk, where the work awaits him over which but now his thoughtful brow was bending," and the study is presented as an incarnation of the "modern" nature of Howells's fiction. "There is nothing cobwebby, no dust of antiquity, nor medievalism, in this study" (201–2).

53. The titular novelist in "John Delavoy" is described as "the most unadvertised, unreported, uninterviewed, unphotographed, uncriticised of all originals." Henry James, *Complete Stories, 1898–1910*, ed. Denis Donoghue (New York: Library of America, 1996), 3.

54. Henry James, "The Death of the Lion," in *Complete Stories, 1892–1898*, ed. David Bromwich and John Hollander (New York: Library of America, 1996), 367–68.

55. James, *Literary Criticism*, vol. 1, 212. The best study of James's relation to modern forms of publicity is Salmon, *Henry James and the Culture of Publicity*.

56. A character in "Flickerbridge" argues that the "prodigious machinery" of

publicity will change the nature of a person's being. "You'll be exactly what you are," he tells a female companion, "but you'll be it all in a different way. We live in an age of prodigious machinery, all organized to a single end. That end is publicity—a publicity as ferocious as the appetite of a cannibal." James, *Complete Stories, 1898–1910*, 439.

57. James, *Notebooks*, 82.

58. James, *Complete Stories, 1892–1898*, 207.

59. James, *Complete Stories, 1898–1910*, 126.

60. James, *Notebooks*, 82.

61. James uses the phrase "perception of incongruities" to describe Fleda Vetch in the preface to *The Spoils of Poynton*, in *Literary Criticism*, vol. 2, ed. Leon Edel (New York: Library of America, 1984), 1149. The phrase also appears in *Washington Square*, in *Portrait of a Lady*, and in a review of George Eliot's *Felix Holt*, suggesting that that the ability to perceive incongruity is for James a signal critical faculty.

62. Eve Kosofsky Sedgwick, *The Epistemology of the Closet* (Berkeley: University of California Press, 1990).

63. James associates "the reader irreflective and uncritical" with a dominant "presence" of women and children in the mass reading audience. *Literary Criticism*, vol. 1, 103.

64. James speaks of "the insurmountable desire to know" in a long *Macmillan's* review of the published correspondence of Flaubert. "Flaubert's letters, indeed, bring up with singular intensity the whole question of the rights and duties, the decencies and discretions of the insurmountable desire to *know*." He raises this question, of course, even as he participates in the public circulation of Flaubert's letters and acknowledges that "to know is good, or to want to know, at any rate, supremely natural." *Literary Criticism*, vol. 2, 297.

65. Quoted in Lawrence Levine, *Highbrow/Lowbrow: The Emergence of Cultural Hierarchy in America* (Cambridge, Mass.: Harvard University Press, 1988), 219.

66. James, "The Lesson of the Master," *Complete Stories, 1884–1891*, ed. Edward Said (New York: Library of America, 1999), 583; James, "The Papers," *Complete Stories, 1898–1910*, 546.

67. Quoted in Neil Harris, "The Gilded Age Revisited: Boston and the Museum Movement," *American Quarterly* 14:4 (Winter 1962): 558.

68. Charles Chesnutt, *The Journals of Charles Chesnutt*, ed. Richard Brodhead (Durham, N.C.: Duke University Press, 1993), 172, 106, 111.

69. Edmund Clarence Stedman, *The Complete Pocket-Guide to Europe*, ed. Edmund C. Stedman and Thomas L. Stedman (New York: William R. Jenkins, 1898), x.

70. James Russell Lowell, "Critical Notices," *North American Review* 103 (1866): 612.

71. Howells quoted in Edwin H. Cady, *The Road to Realism* (Syracuse, N.Y.: Syracuse University Press, 1956), 158; William Dean Howells, *Their Wedding Journey*, quoted in Martin Jay, *Harvests of Change: American Literature, 1865–1914* (Englewood Cliffs, N.J.: Prentice-Hall, 1967), 38, 39.

72. James, *A Small Boy*, 34; James quoted in F. O. Matthiessen, *Henry James:*

The Major Phase (New York: Oxford University Press, 1944), 2. When Joseph Conrad described Henry James as the "historian of fine consciousness," he was echoing James's own critical vocabulary. Conrad is quoted in Pat Rogers, *Oxford Illustrated History of English Literature* (Oxford: Oxford University Press, 1987), 391.

73. "High-Brow," *Dial* 56 (April 1, 1914): 287–88.

74. Walt Whitman quoted in Levine, *Highbrow/Lowbrow*, 224.

75. Victoria Bissell Brown, *The Education of Jane Addams* (Philadelphia: University of Pennsylvania Press, 2007), 130.

76. Jane Addams, *Twenty Years at Hull-House* (New York: Macmillan, 1960), 72. Subsequent page references cited parenthetically in the text.

77. Jane Addams, *The Spirit of Youth and the City Streets* (New York: Macmillan, 1909), 69.

78. James, *Collected Travel Writings: The Continent*, 306.

79. Henry James, *The American*, in *Novels, 1871–1880*, ed. William T. Stafford (New York: Library of America, 1983), 515. Subsequent page references cited parenthetically in the text.

80. Kaplan, *Social Construction*; June Howard, *Form and History in American Literary Naturalism* (Chapel Hill: University of Carolina Press, 1985).

81. Henry James, *Letters*, vol. 1, ed. Leon Edel (Cambridge, Mass.: Harvard University Press, 1974), 137.

82. James, *Collected Travel Writings: The Continent*, 376, 378, 380.

83. Alistair MacIntyre, *After Virtue* (Notre Dame, Ind.: University of Notre Dame Press, 1981). MacIntyre analyzes Henry James as his representative of this social type.

84. Wharton, *Novels*, 570.

85. On the rise of transatlantic communication networks and their relation to economic developments, see Starr, *The Creation of the Media*, 153–230.

86. Edith Wharton, *The Touchstone* (New York: Harper Collins, 1991), 59, 120, 143, 142, 141, 57.

87. Henry James, *The Golden Bowl*, ed. Gore Vidal (Hammondsworth: Penguin, 1985), 143.

88. Bill Brown, *A Sense of Things: The Object Matter of American Literature* (Chicago: University of Chicago Press, 2003), 136–75.

89. Henry James, "Lady Barberina," in *Complete Stories, 1874–1884*, ed. William L. Vance (New York: Library of America, 1999), 761.

90. For an excellent study of James's use of the term "race" and contemporary racial discourses more broadly, see Sarah Blair, *Henry James and the Writing of Race and Nation* (New York: Cambridge University Press, 1996), especially 15–59. See also Kendall Johnson, *Henry James and the Visual* (New York: Cambridge University Press, 2007).

91. W. T. Stead, *The Americanisation of the World* (London: William Clowes, 1901), 7, 153. Stead writes that "no one who moves in journalistic circles can ignore the fact that many of the strongest Imperialists are heart and soul in favor of seeing the British Empire and the American Republic merged in the English-speaking United States of the World" (153). In "Lady Barberina," drawing-room discussions of "the intermarriage of the races" alternate with opinions on the question of

whether "English and American society ought to be but one—I mean the best of each—a great whole." *Complete Stories, 1874–1884*, 743, 739.

92. Spencer quoted in Blair, *Henry James and the Writing of Race*, 23. Dos Passos quoted in Thomas Gossett, *Race: The History of an Idea in America* (New York: Schocken Books, 1969), 326.

93. On the federation of industrialized cities, see Matthew Frye Jacobson, *Barbarian Virtues: The United States Encounters Foreign Peoples at Home and Abroad* (New York: Hill and Wang, 2000), 59–61. Also see Eric Hobsbawm, *The Age of Empire: 1875–1914* (New York: Vintage, 1989), 34–83. On the role of U.S. corporate policies in the "world contest" for markets, see Livingston, "Corporate Capitalism and Consumer Culture, 1890–1940," in *Pragmatism and the Political Economy*, 84–118.

94. Quoted in Blair, *Henry James and the Writing of Race*, 16. Although white Americans and Europeans were the largest clientele for leisure global tourism, recent scholarship has underscored the ways people of color participated in patterns of transcontinental travel in the nineteenth century and before. See, for instance, Farah Jasmine Griffin and Cheryl J. Fish, eds., *A Stranger in the Village: Two Centuries of African-American Travel Writing* (Boston: Beacon Press, 1998); Cheryl J. Fish, *Black and White Women's Travel Narratives: Antebellum Explorations* (Gainesville: University Press of Florida, 2004); and Sandra Gunning, *Moving Home: Travel and Self-Invention in the Nineteenth-Century African Diaspora* (Durham, N.C.: Duke University Press, forthcoming).

95. Quotations are from the constitution of the American Negro Academy. See Alfred A. Moss Jr., *The American Negro Academy: The Voice of the Talented Tenth* (Baton Rouge: Louisiana State University Press, 1981), 1.

96. Anna Julia Cooper, *A Voice from the South*, in *The Voice of Anna Julia Cooper: Including A Voice from the South and Other Important Essays, Papers, and Letters*, ed. Charles Lemert and Esme Bhan (Lanham, M.D.: Rowman and Littlefield, 1998), 176. There is uncertainty about Cooper's affiliation with the academy. Louise Hutchinson contends that Cooper was the "only woman ever elected a member." *Anna Julia Cooper: A Voice from the South* (Washington, D.C.: Smithsonian, 1981), 109. Mary Helen Washington, however, states that Cooper was never admitted as a member despite her presence at the first academy meeting. See Washington's introduction to the Schomberg edition of *A Voice from the South* (New York: Oxford University Press, 1988). Karen Baker-Fletcher asserts that "no formal documentation of her membership has been found." *A Singing Something: Womanist Reflections on Anna Julia Cooper* (New York: Crossroads, 1994), 48.

97. Alexander Crummell, *Destiny and Race: Selected Writings, 1840–1898*, ed. Wilson Jeremiah Moses (Amherst: University of Massachusetts Press, 1992), 285. Subsequent references cited parenthetically in the text. Also see *Civilization and Black Progress: Selected Writings of Alexander Crummell on the South*, ed. J. R. Oldfield (Charlottesville: University of Virginia Press, 1995).

98. William H. Ferris, *The African Abroad: or, His Evolution in Western Civilization*, 2 vols. (New Haven, Conn.: Tuttle, Morehouse and Taylor, 1913).

99. See, for instance, Kevin Gaines, *Uplifting the Race: Black Leadership, Politics, and Culture in the Twentieth Century* (Chapel Hill: University of North Carolina Press, 1996). Gaines uncovers the complexity that resulted from the "avowed

pursuit of a unified black middle-class subject predicated on historically static, and implicitly racialized, ideals of bourgeois morality," a project he calls ultimately "untenable" (154).

100. Vanessa R. Schwartz, "Cinematic Spectatorship Before the Apparatus," in *Cinema and the Invention of Modern Life*, ed. Leo Charney and Vanessa R. Schwartz (Berkeley: University of California Press, 1995), 314–15. More than 1.3 million visitors paid to experience this attraction, which cost only one franc. According to Schwartz, "reviewers remarked on the diversity of the crowd, which included peasants, workers (who had never seen the sea, the reviewer noted), bourgeois men and women, shopkeepers, and diplomats" (314).

101. On the "panoramic vision" of rail travel in relation to film, see Lynn Kirby, *Parallel Tracks: The Railroad and Silent Cinema* (Durham, N.C.: Duke University Press, 1997). On the Maerorama and the funicular car attraction, see Schwartz, "Cinematic Spectatorship," 314–15.

102. W. E. B. DuBois, "Criteria of Negro Art," *Writings*, 994. Subsequent page references cited parenthetically in the text.

Chapter 2

1. Henry James, "Matthew Arnold," in *Literary Criticism*, vol. 1, ed. Leon Edel (New York: Library of America, 1984), 730.

2. W. E. B. DuBois, *The Souls of Black Folk*, in *Writings*, ed. Nathan Huggins (New York: Library of America, 1986), 365.

3. Matthew Arnold, *Culture and Anarchy and Other Writings*, ed. Stephan Collini (New York: Cambridge University Press, 1993), 110.

4. Thomas Wentworth Higginson, "A Plea for Culture," *Atlantic Monthly* 20 (December 1867): 745–54.

5. John Sullivan Dwight, "Music as a Means of Culture," *Atlantic Monthly* 20 (September 1870): 321–31.

6. Choate and Olmstead quoted in Lawrence Levine, *Highbrow/Lowbrow: The Emergence of Cultural Hierarchy in America* (Cambridge, Mass.: Harvard University Press, 1988), 201, 202.

7. Michael Davitt Bell, *The Problem of American Realism: Studies in the Cultural History of a Literary Idea* (Chicago: University of Chicago Press, 1993). Bell's study of realism as a gender-anxious "masculine realism" overturned an earlier understanding of the realists as intellectuals at war with the dominant culture.

8. Phillip Barrish, *American Literary Realism: Critical Theory and Intellectual Prestige, 1880–1995* (New York: Cambridge University Press, 2001); Thomas Strychacz, *Modernism, Mass Culture, and Professionalism* (New York: Cambridge University Press, 1993); Mark McGurl, *The Novel Art: Elevations of American Fiction After Henry James* (Princeton, N.J.: Princeton University Press, 2001).

9. I am borrowing Mark McGurl's opposition between distinction and difference as "twin" critical terms that interpret the same body of literature in differing ways. *Novel Art*, 22.

10. Amy Kaplan, *The Social Construction of American Realism* (Chicago: University of Chicago Press, 1988); Kenneth Warren, *Black and White Strangers: Race and American Literary Realism* (Chicago: University of Chicago Press, 1995); Nancy Glazener, *Reading for Realism: The History of a U.S. Literary Institution, 1850–1910* (Durham, N.C.: Duke University Press, 1997).

11. Michel Foucault, *Discipline and Punish: The Birth of the Prison* (New York: Vintage, 1995), 11.

12. McGurl is citing John Guillory. *Novel Art*, 21.

13. McGurl, *Novel Art*, 20.

14. Bliss Perry, *The Life and Letters of Henry Lee Higginson* (Whitefish, Mont.: Kessinger, 2005), 328–29.

15. William F. Apthorp, "Music," *Atlantic Monthly* 35 (January 1875): 122–24.

16. Bryant quoted in Levine, *Highbrow/Lowbrow*, 201.

17. William Dean Howells, *Criticism and Fiction, and Other Essays*, ed. Clara Marburg Kirk and Rudolf Kirk (New York: New York University Press, 1959), 15. Subsequent page references cited parenthetically in the text after the abbreviation *CF*.

18. *Scribner's Monthly* 14 (September 1877): 716; Edith Wharton, *Old New York*, in *Novellas and Other Writings*, ed. Cynthia Griffin Wolff (New York: Library of America, 1990), 344.

19. W. J. Henderson, "Music," *New York Times—Illustrated Magazine*, October 25, 1898, 4.

20. Quoted in Tony Bennett, "The Multiplication of Culture's Utility," *Critical Inquiry* 21 (1995): 878. The language belongs to a British administrator, Anthony King, but is echoed by numerous American authorities, as documented elsewhere in this chapter. In the monograph in which Bennett expands these claims, *The Birth of the Museum: History, Theory, Politics* (New York: Routledge, 1995), he discusses a number of Anglo-American exchanges regarding art administration. On the joint Anglo-American development of high literary culture in the period after the Civil War, see Leslie Butler, *Critical Americans: Victorian Intellectuals and Transatlantic Liberal Reform* (Chapel Hill: University of North Carolina Press, 1997).

21. "Certain Dangerous Tendencies in American Life," *Atlantic Monthly* 42 (October 1878): 385–402.

22. In addition to Habermas, see Bennett, *Birth of the Museum*, 26–27. David Lloyd and Paul Thomas demonstrate a convergence between theories of the modern state and theories of culture in nineteenth-century Britain in *Culture and the State* (New York: Routledge, 1997). Like Bennett, however, Lloyd and Thomas's astute Foucauldian analysis of liberal theories of culture tends to accept theoretical discourse as a description of historical reality. While it is clear that those theories had a dominant influence on government policy and practice, in the United States as well as the United Kingdom, we cannot assume those practices completely reshaped culture in their image. I argue that many sectors of commercial culture, for instance, were unable to be brought under the influence of state and civic policies. And the intimate if hostile relations between high culture and commercial culture meant that liberal theory did not completely govern those domains either.

23. See Paul DiMaggio's influential two-part study, "Cultural Entrepreneur-

ship in Nineteenth-Century Boston," *Media, Culture and Society* 4 (1982): 33–50, and part 2, 303–22. Also see the museum essays collected in Neil Harris, *Cultural Excursions: Marketing Appetites and Cultural Tastes in Modern America* (Chicago: University of Chicago Press, 1990). For a more recent study, see Steven Conn, *Museums and American Intellectual Life, 1876–1926* (Chicago: University of Chicago Press, 1998).

24. George Brown Goode, "Museum-History and Museums of History," *Annual Report of the U.S. National Museum* (Washington, D.C.: U.S. GPO, 1898), 70.

25. George Brown Goode, "The Museums of the Future," *Annual Report*, 243; Goode, "Museum-History," 72.

26. Quoted in Bennett, *Birth of the Museum*, 885.

27. Bennett, "Multiplication of Culture's Utility," 881.

28. DuBois, *The Souls of Black Folk*, in *Writings*, ed. Huggins, 489.

29. "Certain Dangerous Tendencies," 385–402.

30. Bennett, *Birth of the Museum*, 62.

31. For a detailed study of the institutional development of American literary realism in the context of competing literary movements, see Glazener, *Reading for Realism*.

32. Wharton, *Novellas*, 360.

33. Goode, "Museum-History," 73, 72.

34. On private libraries and rare books, see Martin Jay, *Harvests of Change: American Literature, 1865–1914* (Englewood Cliffs, N.J.: Prentice-Hall, 1967).

35. William Dean Howells, *A Modern Instance*, in *Novels, 1875–1886*, ed. Edwin H. Cady (New York: Library of America, 1982), 327. Subsequent page references cited parenthetically in the text. Howells complained of the "distempered imitations" and "exaggerated emotions" of popular romance in one of his "Editor's Study" columns in 1887, reprinted in *Editor's Study*, by William Dean Howells, ed. James W. Simpson (Troy, N.Y.: Whitson, 1983), 86.

36. On the transatlantic history of burlesque troupes, see Robert C. Allen, *Horrible Prettiness: Burlesque and American Culture* (Chapel Hill: University of North Carolina Press, 1991).

37. William Dean Howells, "The New Taste in Theatricals," *Atlantic Monthly* 23 (May 1869): 635–44.

38. Quoted in Edwin H. Cady, introduction to *A Modern Instance* (New York: Penguin, 1887), viii–ix.

39. Quoted in Allen, *Horrible Prettiness*, 136–37. Allen discusses the burlesque *Ixion* and the performer Lydia Thompson in several places in his study.

40. Michael Anesko, *Letters, Fiction, Lives: Henry James and William Dean Howells* (New York: Oxford University Press, 1997), 24.

41. Quoted in Cady, introduction, xxi.

42. Quoted in Glazener, *Reading for Realism*, 113.

43. Goode, "Museum-History," 72.

44. Levine, *Highbrow/Lowbrow*, 149.

45. Quoted in Bennett, *Birth of the Museum*, 2.

46. Howells quoted in Glazener, *Reading for Realism*, 112. On the increased cultural value for the realm of fact, see Miles Orvell, *The Real Thing: Imitation and*

Authenticity in American Culture, 1880–1940 (Chapel Hill: University of North Carolina Press, 1989), 198–239, and Shi, *Facing Facts*, 66–78.

47. Bill Brown, *The Material Unconscious: American Amusement, Stephen Crane, and the Economies of Play* (Chicago: University of Chicago Press, 1996), 239. On Repplier and other critics of Howells's realism, see Glazener, *Reading for Realism*, 147–88.

48. Lowell quoted in Glazener, *Reading for Realism*, 46.

49. William Dean Howells, *The Rise of Silas Lapham*, in *Novels, 1875–1866*, 877. Subsequent page references cited parenthetically in the text.

50. Phineas T. Barnum, *Struggles and Triumphs: Or, Forty Years' Recollections of P. T. Barnum*, ed. Carl Bode (New York: Penguin, 1981), 47. Subsequent page references cited parenthetically in the text.

51. For an especially astute analysis of Penelope's affection for Lapham's habits of speech and the importance of vernacular in general for Howells's realism, see Barrish, *American Literary Realism*, 16–47. My interpretation of the novel is also indebted to Donald E. Pease, "Introduction," and James M. Cox, "*The Rise of Silas Lapham*: The Business of Morals and Manners," both in *New Essays on the Rise of Silas Lapham*, ed. Donald Pease (New York: Cambridge University Press, 1991).

52. Howells's letter to James quoted in Anesko, *Letters, Fiction, Lives*, 272.

53. McGurl, *Novel Art*, 34.

54. Henry James, review *Hours of Exercise in the Alps* by John Tyndall, *Atlantic Monthly* 28 (November 1871): 634.

55. McGurl, *Novel Art*, 20.

56. Henry James, *The Prefaces to the New York Edition*, in *Literary Criticism*, vol. 2, ed. Leon Edel (New York: Library of America, 1984), 1230.

57. Ibid.

58. Jonathan Arac, *Huckleberry Finn as Idol and Target: The Functions of Criticism in Our Time* (Madison: University of Wisconsin Press, 1997).

59. Cady, introduction, xvi.

60. Twain quoted in Bell, *Problem of American Realism*, 43.

61. Ibid., 44. Howells wrote back that he appreciated Twain's ability to see Howells's fiction in this light ("I analyze as little as possible"), although he acknowledges that most critics and readers classify his work with "the analytic school" (214).

62. Mark Twain, "What Paul Bourget Thinks of Us," in *Collected Tales, Sketches, Speeches, and Essays*, ed. Louis J. Budd (New York: Library of America, 1992), 167, 164, 165.

63. Brooks quoted in Levine, *Highbrow/Lowbrow*, 212.

64. Randall Knoper, *Acting Naturally: Mark Twain in the Culture of Performance* (Berkeley: University of California Press, 1995), 4. Also see Susan Gillman, *Dark Twins: Imposture and Identity in Mark Twain's America* (Chicago: University of Chicago Press, 1989).

65. Levine, *Highbrow/Lowbrow*, 212.

66. On Twain's career as "America's first coast-to-coast writer" and his adaptations of mass genres, see Philip Fisher, "Mark Twain," *The Columbia Literary History of the United States*, ed. Emory Elliott (New York: Columbia University Press, 1988), 633, 635.

67. Jane Thrailkill, *Affecting Fictions: Mind, Body, and Emotion in American Literary Realism* (Cambridge, Mass.: Harvard University Press, 2007), 48.

68. Sacvan Bercovitch, "Deadpan Huck: Or, What's Funny About Interpretation," *Kenyon Review* 24 (2002): 97.

69. Where Thrailkill tends to integrate the physiological effects of Twain's humor with an interpretive "wisdom" the reader acquires at the end of the process, Bercovitch views the humorous shocks as working against the "comforts" of literary interpretation. Thrailkill, *Affecting Fictions*, 48.

70. Bercovitch, "Deadpan Huck," 121. To support this argument, Bercovitch points to a consistent set of discrepancies between "the text before us," read "literally," and "the meaning we assign it, spiritually" (103).

71. Ibid., 119. On the shifting cultural conflicts manifest in the reception of *Huckleberry Finn*, see Arac, *Huckleberry Finn as Idol*, and Gerald Graff and James Phelan, *The Adventures of Huckleberry Finn: A Case Study in Critical Controversy* (New York: St. Martin's Press, 1995).

72. James, *Literary Criticism*, vol. 2, 1230.

73. Henry James, "The Question of the Opportunities," in *Literary Criticism*, vol. 1, ed. Leon Edel (New York: Library of America, 1984), 651. Subsequent page references cited parenthetically in the text.

74. He wrote to his brother William that behind the U.S. press coverage of the Spanish-American War of 1898 he could perceive "nothing but the madness, the passion, the hideous clumsiness of rage, the mechanical reverberation; and I echo with all my heart your denouncement of the foul criminality of the screeching newspapers. They have long since become, for me, the danger that overtops all others." *The Letters of Henry James*, ed. Percy Lubbock (New York: Scribner's, 1920), 280–81.

75. Henry James, "The Lesson of Balzac," in *Literary Criticism*, vol. 2, 119. Subsequent page references cited parenthetically in the text.

Chapter 3

1. William Dean Howells, "The New Taste in Theatricals," *Atlantic Monthly* 23 (May 1869): 642–43. Subsequent page references cited parenthetically in the text.

2. Charles Dudley Warner, "Editor's Drawer," *Harper's Monthly* 80 (May 1890): 972–73.

3. Quoted in David E. Shi, *Facing Facts: Realism in American Thought and Culture, 1850–1920* (New York: Oxford University Press, 1995), 87, 94.

4. James Weir, Jr., "The Effect of Female Suffrage on Posterity," *American Naturalist* 29 (1895): 825.

5. Sedgwick quoted in Mary Kelly, *Private Woman, Public Stage: Literary Domesticity in Nineteenth-Century America* (Chapel Hill: University of North Carolina Press, 1984), 130. Kelly's study is among the first generation of scholarship on the significance of private and public domains for women. For a more recent example, see Elizabeth Dillon, *The Gender of Freedom: Fictions of Liberalism and the Literary Public Sphere* (Palo Alto, Calif.: Stanford University Press, 2004).

6. See Meredith McGill, *American Literature and the Culture of Reprinting, 1834–1853* (Philadelphia: University of Pennsylvania Press, 2003), and Melissa Homestead, *American Women Authors and Literary Property* (New York: Cambridge University Press, 2005).

7. Francis Lieber, *Manual of Political Ethics*, vol. 2 (Philadelphia: Lippincott, 1876), 125.

8. Henry James, *The Bostonians*, in *Novels, 1881–1886*, ed. William T. Stafford (New York: Library of America, 1985), 858. Subsequent page references cited parenthetically in the text.

9. Hjalmar Hjorth Boyeson quoted in Francesca Sawaya, *Modern Women, Modern Work: Domesticity, Professionalism, and American Writing, 1890–1950* (Philadelphia: University of Pennsylvania Press, 2003), 62.

10. See Michael Davitt Bell, *The Problem of American Realism: Studies in the Cultural History of a Literary Idea* (Chicago: University of Chicago Press, 1993), and Alfred Habegger, *Gender, Fantasy, and Realism in American Literature* (New York: Columbia University Press, 1982).

11. After the initial version of this chapter was written for the *Cambridge History of American Literature*, Jennifer Fleissner's excellent study of American naturalism offered a parallel argument regarding women and naturalism. Because women's lives (more than men's) were assumed to be governed by corporeality, Fleissner contends, women became the paradigmatic subjects of literary naturalism. See *Women, Compulsion, Modernity: The Moment of American Naturalism* (Chicago: University of Chicago Press, 2004). Because Fleissner includes Henry James and Edith Wharton among her roster of naturalists, however, it is clear that the categories of naturalism and realism have a good deal of overlap in her study (as in most literary histories). However, what seems distinctive about the importance of women to the Howellsian mode of realism, I argue, is the crisis their corporeality posed for an older model of a literary public sphere. Jean Lutes demonstrates the way the unavoidable corporeality of women journalists posed a similar crisis for the ideals of public sphere discourse. See *Front Page Girls: Women Journalists in American Culture and Fiction, 1880–1930* (Ithaca, N.Y.: Cornell University Press, 2007). As I argue in this chapter, scientific discourse (so crucial to the naturalist project) helped resolve or at least evade the crisis of the disintegration of the literary public sphere by accepting a corporeal human subject as a normative object of analysis.

12. Charles Knowles Bolton, *The Reign of the Poster* (Boston: Winthrop B. Jones, 1895), [1]. Also see Arsene Alexandre et al., *The Modern Poster* (New York: Scribner's, 1895).

13. Nathaniel Parker Willis quotes this phrase from a report in the *Weekly Herald* in his *Memoranda of the Life of Jenny Lind* (Philadelphia: Robert E. Parker, 1851), 95.

14. Henry James, *The Notebooks of Henry James*, ed. F. O. Matthiessen and Kenneth B. Murdock (New York: Oxford University Press, 1947), 47.

15. James's relation to European realist fiction is examined in Richard Brodhead, *The School of Hawthorne* (New York: Oxford University Press, 1986). On James's time in Paris, see Peter Brooks, *Henry James Goes to Paris* (Princeton, N.J.: Princeton University Press, 2007).

16. Quoted in Marcus Verhagen, "The Poster in Fin-de-Siècle Paris: 'That Mobile and Degenerate Art,'" in *Cinema and the Invention of Modern Life*, ed. Leo Charney and Vanessa R. Schwartz (Berkeley: University of California Press, 1995), 115.

17. Ibid., 122.

18. Ibid.; Henry James, *Literary Criticism*, vol. 2, ed. Leon Edel (New York: Library of America, 1984), 229.

19. James discusses the "power to guess the unseen from the seen, to trace the implication of things, to judge the whole by the pattern" in his essay "The Art of Fiction," in *Literary Criticism*, vol. 1, ed. Leon Edel (New York: Library of America, 1984), 53.

20. Ibid.

21. Harriet Spofford quoted in Nancy Glazener, *Reading for Realism: The History of a U.S. Literary Institution, 1850–1910* (Durham, N.C.: Duke University Press, 1997), 23.

22. Constance Fenimore Woolson, "Miss Grief," in *Stories by American Authors*, vol. 4 (New York: Scribner's, 1899), 33. Subsequent page references cited parenthetically in the text.

23. James, *Literary Criticism*, vol. 1, 640.

24. Woolson quoted in Anne E. Boyd, *Writing for Immortality: Women and the Emergence of High Literary Culture* (Baltimore: Johns Hopkins University Press, 2004), 153, 174. Also see Cheryl Torsney, *Constance Fenimore Woolson: The Grief of Artistry* (Athens: University of Georgia Press, 1989).

25. William Dean Howells writes that "the whole field of human experience was never so nearly covered by imaginative literature in any age as this; and American life especially is getting represented with unexampled fullness." *Criticism and Fiction, and Other Essays* (New York: New York University Press, 1959), 68.

26. Henry Adams, *The Letters of Henry Adams*, vol. 5, ed. J. C. Levenson et al. (Cambridge, Mass.: Belknap Press, 1988), 497.

27. Chopin quoted in Per Seyersted, *Kate Chopin: A Critical Biography* (Baton Rouge: Louisiana State University Press, 1980), 84–85.

28. Edith Wharton, *The Letters of Edith Wharton*, ed. R. W. B. Lewis and Nancy Lewis (New York: Scribner, 1988), 99.

29. Edith Wharton, *The House of Mirth*, in *Novels*, ed. R. W. B. Lewis (New York: Library of America, 1985), 336, 337.

30. Ibid., 121; Edith Wharton, *The Uncollected Critical Writings*, ed. Frederick Wegener (Princeton, N.J.: Princeton University Press, 1998), 15–16.

31. *Book Review Digest* (New York: H. W. Wilson Co., 1907), 470.

32. Paul Broca, "Broca on Anthropology," *Anthropological Review* 6 (1868): 46.

33. Elsie Clews Parsons, *The Old-Fashioned Woman*, ed. Carl N. Degler (New York: Harper and Row, 1966), 49.

34. Cynthia Eagle Russett, *Sexual Science: The Victorian Construction of Womanhood* (Cambridge, Mass.: Harvard University Press, 1989), 104, 120, 122–23.

35. Robert W. Rydell, *All the World's a Fair: Visions of Empire at American*

International Expositions, 1876–1916 (Chicago: University of Chicago Press, 1987), 100.

36. Russett, *Sexual Science*, 35.

37. Johann Jakob Bachofen, *Myth, Religion, and Mother Right: Selected Writings of J. J. Bachofen*, trans. Ralph Manheim (Princeton, N.J.: Princeton University Press, 1992), 100.

38. Quoted in Randall Knoper, *Acting Naturally: Mark Twain in the Culture of Performance* (Berkeley: University of California Press, 1995), 49. For a good introduction to Menken's remarkable transatlantic career as a poet, an actress, and a celebrity, see *Infelicia and Other Writings,* ed. Gregory Eiselein (Orchard Park, N.Y.: Broadview Press, 2002).

39. Henry James, *The Portrait of a Lady*, in *Novels, 1881–1886,* 231. My discussion of Jamesian observation is drawn in part from my analysis of Jane Campion's cinematic interpretation of *Portrait of a Lady*, "Conscious Observation: Jane Campion's *Portrait of a Lady*," in *Henry James Goes to the Movies,* ed. Susan M. Griffin (Lexington: University Press of Kentucky, 2002), 127–46.

40. Quoted in James Gargano, *Critical Essays on Henry James: The Late Novels* (New York: G. K. Hall, 1987), 40.

41. Henry James, preface to the New York edition of *Portrait of a Lady*, in *Literary Criticism,* vol. 2, 1075.

42. Henry Adams, *Democracy,* in *Novels,* ed. Jayne N. Samuels (New York: Library of America, 1983), 7, 43.

43. Ibid., 108.

44. James, *Literary Criticism,* vol. 2, 1084. In his preface James speaks of Isabel "motionlessly seeing" during her "meditative vigil."

45. Jonathan Crary, "Unbinding Vision: Manet and the Attentive Observer in the Late Nineteenth Century," in *Cinema and the Invention of Modern Life,* 47.

46. William James, *Psychology: Briefer Course,* in *Writings, 1878–1899,* ed. Gerald E. Myers (New York: Library of America, 1992), 211. The text is James's own abridgment of his *Principles of Psychology.*

47. See Russett, *Sexual Science,* and Ludmilla Jordanova, *Sexual Visions: Images of Gender in Science and Medicine Between the Eighteenth and Twentieth Centuries* (Madison: University of Wisconsin Press, 1993). J. M. Charcot and Pierre Janet's studies of female hysteria and hypnotism are among the best-known researches in this vein. See Janet Beizer, *Ventriloquized Bodies: Narratives of Hysteria in Nineteenth-Century France* (Ithaca, N.Y.: Cornell University Press, 1994).

48. Crary, "Unbinding Vision," 58. Crary associates research in perception with aesthetic projects like Manet's "faciality" (57), Mallarmé's "sublime disavowal of the immediate" (63), and Muybridge's research in visual sensation (65) as related explorations of the mental binding and unbinding of perceptual elements, explorations that emerge after the model of the "anchored" classical observer has been eclipsed.

49. Charlotte Perkins Gilman, "The Yellow Wallpaper," in *The Yellow Wallpaper: A Sourcebook and Critical Edition,* ed. Catherine J. Golden (New Brunswick, N.J.: Rutgers University Press, 2004), 131, 142, 132.

50. Jane Thrailkill, *Affecting Fictions: Mind, Body, and Emotion in American*

Literary Realism (Cambridge, Mass.: Harvard University Press, 2007), 119. Thrailkill recognizes that Gilman understood the "assaultive" possibility of aesthetic expression, but she concludes that "The Yellow Wallpaper" finally affirms a calming or therapeutic function of aesthetic adaptation. But if readers were able to experience a degree of reflective detachment that the narrator is not, accounting for the particular and changing nature of readers' responses (the gothic "chill" reported by contemporary readers as opposed to the politically inflected frisson experienced by feminist readers who returned the story to public prominence, for instance) depends on attending to the social dimension of Gilman's literally shocking story. By closely analyzing women's corporeal lives, both Gilman and neurological scientists were in part addressing the social sensation of female publicity.

51. Ibid., 132, 144, 83. Here my interpretation concurs with Fleissner's analysis of Gilman's story. Fleissner argues that the story's incomplete, non-linear form reflects a conviction (characteristic of literary naturalism) that women's corporeal lives can still represent creative and transformative possibilities. *Women, Compulsion, Modernity*, 52–74.

52. Kate Chopin, *The Awakening*, in *Complete Novels and Stories*, ed. Sandra M. Gilbert (New York: Library of America, 2002), 562. Subsequent page references cited parenthetically in the text.

53. Harold Bloom, ed., *Kate Chopin* (New York: Chelsea House, 2007), 2; Lynda Sue Boren and Sara deSaussure Davis, *Kate Chopin Reconsidered: Beyond the Bayou* (Baton Rouge: Louisiana State University Press, 1999), 183.

54. Kate Chopin, "At the 'Cadian Ball," *Complete Novels*, 306.

55. See, for instance, Richard Brodhead, *Cultures of Letters: Scenes of Reading and Writing in Nineteenth-Century America* (Chicago: University of Chicago Press, 1993), 107–41. Many critics have challenged this view of regionalism. For a summary of dissenting arguments, see Karen L. Kilcup and Thomas S. Edwards, introduction to *Jewett and Her Contemporaries: Reshaping the Canon* (Gainesville: University Press of Florida, 1999), 1–30.

56. See Grace Elizabeth Hale, *Making Whiteness: The Culture of Segregation in the South, 1890–1940* (New York: Vintage, 1999).

57. Kate Chopin, "Nég Créol" and "Lilacs," *Complete Novels*, 426, 759.

58. Kate Chopin, "A Pair of Silk Stockings," *Complete Novels*, 816. Subsequent page references cited parenthetically in the text.

59. Erika D. Rappaport, "'A New Era of Shopping': The Promotion of Women's Pleasure in London's West End, 1909–1914," in *Cinema and the Invention of Modern Life*, 145.

60. Ibid., 148.

61. Kate Chopin, "An Egyptian Cigarette," *Complete Novels*, 895.

62. In addition to Crary, see the magisterial study of the scientific pursuit of uncontaminated knowledge in Lorraine Daston and Peter Galison, *Objectivity* (New York: Zone Books, 2007). Also see George Levine, *Dying to Know: Scientific Epistemology and Narrative in Victorian England* (Chicago: University of Chicago Press, 2002).

63. Margaret Cohen, "Panoramic Literature and the Invention of Everyday Genres," in *Cinema and the Invention of Modern Life*, 234.

64. James Livingston goes so far as to argue that twentieth-century feminism would not have been possible without the transition to corporate capitalism and its consumer-driven economy, a shift that eventually terminated the authority of the male freeholder as the paradigm of political identity. See *Pragmatism, Feminism, and Democracy: Rethinking the Politics of American History* (New York: Routledge, 2001). Also see Miriam Hansen's discussion of the contradictions in turn-of-the-century consumerism and its relation to female desire in *Babel and Babylon: Spectatorship in American Silent Film* (Cambridge, Mass.: Harvard University Press, 1991), 85–86, 114–25. Kathy Peiss offers a case study of the way immigrant women used amusements like cinema as sites for collective reception and entry into spaces outside the home. *Cheap Amusements: Working Women and Leisure in Turn-of-the-Century New York* (Philadelphia: Temple University Press, 1986).

65. Miriam Hansen argues that "virginal stars" like Lillian Gish and Mary Pickford and women directors such as Alice Guy Blancé, Ida May Park, and Lois Weber relied on the conventions and rhetoric of domesticity and female virtue at the same time that early cinema began importing "images of female competence, courage, and physical movement" and inviting sympathy and even identification with sexually powerful women. As a result, the early film industry, and even individual films, often "blurred the distinction" between virtuous, dependent women and active, sexual agents. *Babel and Babylon*, 119–21. The same kinds of contradictions were at play in the design of department stores, where appeals to maternal duty and self-sacrifice existed in tandem with affirmations of female self-indulgence. See Rappaport, "'A New Era of Shopping,'" 145–46.

66. See the contemporary reviews collected in the Norton critical edition of the novel. *The Awakening*, ed. Margo Culley (New York: W. W. Norton, 1994), 164, 170, 166.

67. Heather Kirk Thomas, "'What Are the Prospects for the Book?': Rewriting a Woman's Life," in Boren and Davis, *Kate Chopin Reconsidered*, 36–57.

Chapter 4

1. For a useful overview of the key arguments about the ideological implications of American mass culture, see Robert W. Rydell and Rob Kroes, *Buffalo Bill in Bologna: The Americanization of the World, 1869–1922* (Chicago: University of Chicago Press, 2005). Alexander Saxton, in *The Rise and Fall of the White Republic: Class Politics and Mass Culture in Nineteenth-Century America* (New York: Verso, 1997), argues that early forms of mass culture allowed Jacksonian Democrats to widely disseminate a combination of economic populism and white supremacist sentiments. Rydell and Kroes argue that post–Civil War mass culture forms such as the circus, dime novels, and world's fairs drew upon "America's most durable ideological cement, white racism," to subdue class conflicts, mend sectional hostilities, and pursue imperial projects abroad (27).

2. Chauncey Yellow Robe, "The Menace of the Wild West Show," *Quarterly Journal* 2 (1914): 224–25, reprinted in *Talking Back to Civilization: Indian Voices from*

the Progressive Era, ed. Frederick E. Hoxie (Boston: Bedford/St. Martin's Press, 2001), 115–18.

3. Phineas T. Barnum, *Struggles and Triumphs; Or, Forty Years' Recollections of P.T. Barnum*, ed. Carl Bode (New York: Penguin, 1981), 286–87. Subsequent page references cited parenthetically in the text.

4. The names of these chiefs are recorded by Barnum in *Struggles and Triumphs*, 286. The account of the Washington summit in Lincoln's *Collected Works* does not mention any individual leaders by name. *The Collected Works of Abraham Lincoln*, vol. 6, ed. Roy P. Basler et al. (New Brunswick, N.J.: Rutgers University Press, 1953), 151–52. See David A. Nichols, *Lincoln and the Indians: Civil War Policy and Politics* (Urbana: University of Illinois Press, 1978), 186–87.

5. Charging that "the Indian Department was the most corrupt in our government," Bishop Henry Whipple of Minnesota denounced the "falsehood" of addressing Indians as independent nations in treaties while in reality destroying tribal governments by making chiefs "the pliant tools of traders and agents powerful for mischief, but powerless for good." Quoted in Nichols, *Lincoln and the Indians*, 6–7.

6. Stan Hoig, *The Sand Creek Massacre* (Norman: University of Oklahoma Press, 1961). Historians have been unable to fix an exact number, but most estimate the death toll at between two hundred and five hundred, and concur that women and children were probably two-thirds of the dead.

7. Chivington quoted in "New Perspectives on the West," PBS, available at http://www.pbs.org/weta/thewest/people/a_c/chivington.htm. Also see Bruce E. Johansen, *The Native Peoples of North America: A History* (New Brunswick, N.J.: Rutgers University Press, 2006), 365–66.

8. Bluford Adams, *E Pluribus Barnum: The Great Showman and the Making of U.S. Popular Culture* (Minneapolis: University of Minnesota Press, 1997), 182–92.

9. Rydell and Kroes, *Buffalo Bill in Bologna*, 31–32; Joy S. Kasson, *Buffalo Bill's Wild West: Celebrity, Memory, and Popular History* (New York: Hill and Wang, 2000), 93–121.

10. Pokagon's composition has a murky publication history, and it is not clear whether the published pamphlet is the same text Pokagon delivered at the fair ceremony. Frederick Hoxie reprints "The Red Man's Greeting" from a text published in Hartford, Michigan, in 1893, with C. H. Engle listed as the publisher; Hoxie presents the text as the speech Pokagon delivered at the fair. *Talking Back to Civilization*, 29–35. This text, printed on birch bark, was also distributed by Pokagon and Engle at his public appearances. I have drawn from the text reprinted in Bernd C. Peyer, *American Indian Nonfiction: An Anthology of Writings* (Norman: University of Oklahoma Press, 2007), 233–39, where it is titled "The Red Man's Rebuke." Peyer asserts that Pokagon wrote the "Rebuke" before he delivered his speech on "Chicago Day." Also see the account in Cheryl Walker, *Indian Nation: Native American Literature and Nineteenth-Century Nationalisms* (Durham, N.C.: Duke University Press, 1997), 209–10, where Walker asserts that the "Rebuke" is distinct from the address Pokagon delivered at the fair.

11. Simon Pokagon, "The Red Man's Rebuke" (later changed to "The Red Man's Greeting"), in Peyer, *American Indian Nonfiction*, 233. Subsequent page references cited parenthetically in the text.

12. Peyer, "Biography," in *American Indian Nonfiction*, 241.

13. Walker, *Indian Nation*, 209–11.

14. On the diplomacy of Penn and the area Native nations, see James M. Merrell, *Into the American Woods: Negotiations on the Pennsylvania Frontier* (New York: Norton, 2000).

15. If scholars by and large have been slow to address Native-European relations expressly as a history of imperialism, the imperialist nature of European nation building was not lost on Native Americans. As Nathaniel Thayer Strong, a Seneca, put it plainly in 1841, "The aborigines of this continent, from their first intercourse with the nations of Europe, have been the victims of that most unjust principle of colonization upon which the government of each nation first discovering any particular portion of this vast country, assumed over it unqualified dominion, both as to its soil and its inhabitants." Strong quoted in David J. Carlson, *Sovereign Selves: American Indian Autobiography and the Law* (Urbana: University of Illinois Press, 2006), 53. But this historical pattern does not negate the possibility of diplomacy that Native peoples could and did attempt as an exercise of their sovereignty. On Native views of treaties and sovereignty, see Joanne Barker, *Sovereignty Matters: Locations of Contestation and Possibility in Indigenous Struggles for Self-Determination* (Lincoln: University of Nebraska Press, 2005), and Vine Deloria Jr. and Clifford Lytle, *The Nations Within: The Past and Future of American Indian Sovereignty* (Austin: University of Texas Press, 1998).

16. William P. Dole, in Francis Paul Prucha, *Documents of United States Indian Policy*, 3rd ed. (Lincoln: University of Nebraska Press, 2000), 95. Although Dole was suggesting that Native peoples were largely dependent on if not helpless before the strength of the U.S. military, it is notable that the Plains tribes were able to negotiate the most favorable treaties—the Fort Laramie Treaty of 1868, for instance—after they had successfully resisted or defeated U.S. forces through armed warfare. On the treaty and its context in Red Cloud's War, see Jennifer Viegas, *The Fort Laramie Treaty, 1868: A Primary Source Examination of the Treaty* (New York: Rosen, 2005).

17. Carlson, *Sovereign Selves*, 37.

18. On modes of "forest diplomacy," see Robert Williams, *Linking Arms Together: American Indian Treaty Visions of Law and Peace, 1600–1800* (New York: Routledge, 1999), and the essays in *The History and Culture of Iroquois Diplomacy*, ed. Francis Jennings (Syracuse, N.Y.: Syracuse University Press, 1985). Also see Daniel K. Richter, *The Ordeal of the Long-House: The People of the Iroquois League in the Era of European Colonization* (Chapel Hill: University of North Carolina Press, 1992), and Dennis Matthew, *Cultivating a Landscape of Peace: Iroquois-European Encounters in Seventeenth-Century America* (Ithaca, N.Y.: Cornell University Press, 1993).

19. Constance Rourke, "The Indian Background of American Theatricals," in *Literature of the American Indians: Views and Interpretations*, ed. Abraham Chapman (New York: New American Library, 1975), 256–65, 259. Also see Lawrence C. Wroth, "The Indian Treaty as Literature," in *Literature of the American Indians*, 324–37.

20. Eric Cheyfitz, "The (Post)Colonial Construction of Indian Country," in

The Columbia Guide to American Indian Literatures of the United States Since 1945, ed. Eric Cheyfitz (New York: Columbia University Press, 2005), 8. Carlson also discusses the aesthetic or performative dimension of treaties to make a similar point about the pervasive influence of law in the genre of Native autobiography. *Sovereign Selves*, 34–55.

21. Invoking treaty making as a site of possible transcultural meaning does not mean excluding the history of coercion that is bound up with the history of white-red treaties. Cheyfitz argues that attention to the colonial context of Native American literature "keeps the meaning of the term 'collaboration' oscillating between notions of coercion and cooperation" and allows us to recognize the intercultural nature of the literature without erasing the imperial conditions behind its collaborative production. "The (Post)Colonial Construction of Indian Country," 85–86. Recent studies that explore the complexity of the history of European-Native treaties include Bruce Johansen, ed., *Enduring Legacies: Native American Treaties and Contemporary Controversies* (New York: Praeger, 2004), and Charles Wilkinson, *Blood Struggle: The Rise of American Indian Nations* (New York: Norton, 2006). For an approach to the question of treaties in relation to narrative, see Mark Rifkin, "The Territoriality of Tradition: Treaties, Hunting Grounds, and Prophecy in Black Hawk's *Narrative*," *American Literature*, forthcoming.

22. See Jürgen Habermas, *The Structural Transformation of the Public Sphere*, trans. Thomas Burger (Cambridge, Mass.: MIT Press), 141–235.

23. Joseph Roach, *Cities of the Dead: Circum-Atlantic Performance* (New York: Columbia University Press, 1996), 87.

24. Ibid., 88.

25. Roach describes "orature" as a category that "goes beyond a schematized opposition of literacy and orality as transcendent categories; rather, it acknowledges that these modes of communication have produced one another interactively over time." *Cities of the Dead*, 11.

26. On the Mohawk embassy, see "Feathered People," in Roach, *Cities of the Dead*, 119–78, and Richard P. Bond, *Queen Anne's American Kings* (Oxford: Clarendon Press, 1952). The London reception of the Mohawk embassy shows the "British willingness to adopt the protocols of Forest Diplomacy, which they had learned from a new generation of skilled translators, colonials who had lived among the Iroquois and who understood their language and culture." *Cities of the Dead*, 161. Roach discusses the "pen and ink work" incorporated into the performative protocols of the Iroquois Condolence Council (138).

27. Roach, *Cities of the Dead*, 121.

28. See Michael Warner, *Publics and Counterpublics* (New York: Zone Books, 2002), 123–24.

29. As Robert Allen Warrior points out, unlike the intellectuals who organized a pan-Indian public, leaders who favored a "nationalist, noncooperationist" mode of resistance turned to religious movements such as the Ghost Dance movement, peyotism, and the emergent Native American Church, responses that did not rely on published literature or produce a written ideology. *Tribal Secrets: Recovering American Indian Intellectual Traditions* (Minneapolis: University of Minnesota Press, 1995), 9–14.

30. Ibid., 5–14. Lucy Maddox discusses the Society of American Indians and the writings of several of its leading figures in *Citizen Indians: Native American Intellectuals, Race, and Reform* (Ithaca, N.Y.: Cornell University Press, 2005). The first full history of the society appears in Hazel Hertzberg, *The Search for an American Indian Identity: Modern Pan-Indian Movements* (Syracuse, N.Y.: Syracuse University Press, 1972).

31. Arthur C. Parker, "Certain Important Elements of the Indian Problem," *Quarterly Journal* 3 (1915): 24–38, reprinted in Hoxie, *Talking Back to Civilization*, 99. See also Joy Porter, *To Be an Indian: The Life of Iroquois-Seneca Arthur Caswell Parker* (Norman: University of Oklahoma Press, 2001).

32. Warner, *Publics and Counterpublics*, 51.

33. Charles A. Eastman, *From the Deep Woods to Civilization: Chapters in the Autobiography of an Indian* (1916; repr., Lincoln: University of Nebraska Press, 1977), 150.

34. Charles A. Eastman, *The Soul of the Indian: An Interpretation* (1911; repr., Lincoln, Neb.: Bison Books, 1980), x.

35. Eastman, *From the Deep Woods*, 150.

36. Roach, *Cities of the Dead*, 34.

37. Warrior, *Tribal Secrets*, 13.

38. Ibid., 2.

39. For a discussion of contemporary and recent evaluations of the society's successes and failures, see Maddox, *Citizen Indians*, 121–25.

40. Gerald Vizenor makes a similar point about the writing of the "postindian" author: "Natives have always been on one road of resistance or another, creating postindian myths and tricky stories in the very ruins of representation and modernity." Gerald Vizenor and A. Robert Lee, *Postindian Conversations* (Lincoln: University of Nebraska Press, 2003), 21. In addition to Vizenor's extensive work on Native expressivity, recent work on strategies of literary nationalism also address the question of the generative mediation that can result from heterogeneous conditions of oral and written expression. See, for instance, Jace Weaver, Craig S. Womack, and Robert Warrior, *American Indian Literary Nationalism* (Albuquerque: University of New Mexico Press, 2005).

41. Zitkala-Sa (Gertrude Bonnin), *American Indian Stories* (Lincoln: University of Nebraska Press, 1985), 49. Subsequent page references cited parenthetically in the text.

42. P. Jane Hafen, introduction to Zitkala-Sa, *Dreams and Thunder: Stories, Poems, and "The Sun Dance Opera,"* ed. P. Jane Hafen (Lincoln: University of Nebraska Press, 2001), xx. This important collection contains many of Bonnin's previously unpublished writings.

43. Chauncey Yellow Robe refers to the "Indian show craze" in "The Menace of the Wild West Show," 118. On Indian shows, see L. G. Moses, *Wild West Shows and the Images of American Indians, 1183–1933* (Albuquerque: University of New Mexico Press, 1996). Moses notes that within two years of Cody's first tour, almost fifty rival companies were staging Indian shows and often copying many of Cody's features (23).

44. See Moses, *Wild West Shows*, 29–41. The period beginning with the Pow-

der River battles of the late 1860s to the Battle of Little Big Horn in 1876 gave national and international prominence to Sioux leaders and fighters. As a result, the Sioux were the most heavily recruited by show managers and the most prominently advertised. Moses calls Sitting Bull "the first great show Indian" (30). For more on the paradoxical ways that Sioux victories and defeats have long mediated forms of collective consciousness, national and otherwise, see Michael A. Elliott, "Indian Patriots on Last Stand Hill," *American Quarterly* 58:4 (2006): 987–1015.

45. See Philip J. Deloria's discussion of Indian shows, in which he argues that actors like Rocky Bear and Red Shirt performed "not simply as wild Indians but as visiting dignitaries involved in cultural and political exchange." *Indians in Unexpected Places* (Lawrence: University of Kansas Press, 2004), 70. But while the performers might have been received as "dignitaries" in Britain and Europe, in the United States their status was tied to the popularity of their role as warriors.

46. Roach notes that when Cody's company visited New Orleans in 1884, the performers paraded through the streets: "It is important to imagine the spectacle of costumed and armed Plains warriors, some of them recent victors over Custer, striding proudly through the streets of New Orleans" and moving freely outside the designated space of the performance arena. He also discusses the "double nature" of Cody's shows, "falling somewhere between a folklore procession, with its gala emphasis on crafts and special skills, and a military parade, with its emphasis on the display of national power and national will." *Cities of the Dead,* 202–3. Alan Trachtenberg discusses the interest of figures like the publicist Joseph Dixon in associating Indians as a "warrior race" with a militarily strong American nationalism. *Shades of Hiawatha: Staging Indians, Making Americans, 1880–1930* (New York: Hill and Wang, 2004), 211–77.

47. Roosevelt quoted in Angie Debo, *Geronimo: The Man, His Time, His Place* (Norman: University of Oklahoma Press, 1976), 419.

48. Luther Standing Bear, *My People the Sioux,* ed. E. A. Brininstool (Boston: Houghton Mifflin, 1928), 128. Sitting Bull would later appear with Cody's company. When the enthusiasm for the Ghost Dance religion swept through the Great Plains in 1890, Cody sought to mediate the crisis by meeting with Sitting Bull, but panicked authorities refused to permit it. Sitting Bull was killed when he resisted arrest in the ensuing massacre. See Dee Brown, *Bury My Heart at Wounded Knee* (New York: Henry Holt, 1970), 436.

49. Pratt's criticisms of Wild West shows appear in Carlisle publications such as *The Indian Helper, The Morning Star,* and *The Red Man and Helper.* Issues are housed in the Beinecke Rare Book and Manuscript Library, Yale University.

50. Yellow Robe, "The Menace of the Wild West Show," in Hoxie, *Talking Back to Civilization,* 117–18.

51. Ibid., 118. Standing Bear's father had performed for one season in a production called "Doc Carver's Wild America Show," and his brother Henry helped organize and recruit performers for a show in New York, which Standing Bear joined for a time. On his show business career, see Richard Ellis, "Luther Standing Bear: 'I Would Raise Him to Be an Indian,'" in *Indian Lives: Essays on Nineteenth and Twentieth Century Native Americans,* ed. L. G. Moses and Raymond Wilson (Albuquerque: University of New Mexico Press, 1985).

52. Commissioner of Indian Affairs Thomas J. Morgan, quoted in *Americanizing the Indians: Writings by "Friends of the Indian," 1880–1900*, ed. Francis Paul Prucha (Cambridge, Mass.: Harvard University Press, 1973), 311.

53. From the *Eighteenth Annual Report of the Executive Committee of the Indian Rights Association* (1900), quoted in Prucha, *Americanizing the Indians*, 316.

54. Ibid., 311.

55. Ibid., 314, 315.

56. Ely Parker, quoted in Carlson, *Sovereign Selves*, 59.

57. Luther Standing Bear, *Land of the Spotted Eagle* (Boston: Houghton Mifflin, 1933), xv. In this work—published later in his career—Standing Bear underscores that "lurid fiction, cheap magazines, motion pictures, and newspapers" often presented distorted pictures of Native life, but he doesn't include Wild West shows (228).

58. Ibid., 245.

59. Ibid., 27–28. Trachtenberg discusses Standing Bear's self-construction as "An Official Sioux Authority" and links this California persona to his authority as Oglala "chief," which Standing Bear shapes during the same period. *Shades of Hiawatha*, 296–99.

60. Trachtenberg discusses Standing Bear's angry response to the reader's report for *Land of the Spotted Eagle* that the ethnologist Frederick Webb Hodge wrote for Houghton Mifflin. *Shades of Hiawatha*, 304–5. Standing Bear's preface acknowledges the "inestimable" help supplied by white ethnologist Melvin Gilmore, while the book as a whole is his attempt to correct and displace ethnographic "explanations that are more often than not erroneous." *Land of the Spotted Eagle*, xv.

61. Lucy Maddox argues that "engaging in forms of performance was seen by these earlier intellectuals as a political necessity" and that writers "were, to a large extent, responding to the American public's insistence in placing Indian people, individually and collectively, in performative roles." *Citizen Indians*, 5, 7. While Maddox offers many persuasive analyses of the modes of performance taken up by Native intellectuals, by arguing that they adopted performative expressivity as a matter of political necessity she implies that they would have preferred to speak and write in the same discursive modes as white intellectuals. I argue, rather, that performative roles had the potential to be just as congruent as print publication—if not more so—with their aims of communicating a Native "thought world" or constructing the context for a pan-Indian public sphere. Modern intellectuals may rely on print media, but not all modern thought identifies reason with the rationality of print discourse.

62. Charles A. Eastman, *The Indian Today: The Past and Future of the First American* (New York: Doubleday, 1915), 159; Eastman, *From the Deep Woods*, 187–88.

63. Eastman, *The Indian Today*, 159.

64. Geronimo, *Geronimo: His Own Story*, ed. Frederick Turner (1906; repr., New York: Penguin, 1996), 37–46. Subsequent page numbers cited parenthetically in the text.

65. Debo, *Geronimo*, 423–24.

66. Ibid., 419.

67. John Clum, "The Apaches," *New Mexico Historical Review* 4 (April 1929): 115.

68. Roach, *Cities of the Dead*, 76, 78.

69. Geronimo was billed in shows as the "tiger of the human race" and "the Apache terror." Debo, *Geronimo*, 423.

70. Blaine Kent quoted in Debo, *Geronimo*, 424–25. In his introduction, Barrett quotes Lieutenant Purington's view that Geronimo "deserved to be hanged." *Geronimo: His Own Story*, 40.

71. Debo, for instance, calls Geronimo a "wily bargainer." *Geronimo*, 410. Another scholar says he became a "tireless promoter of himself." Quoted in Carter Revard, *Family Matters, Tribal Affairs* (Tucson: University of Arizona Press, 1998), 128.

72. For instance, it appears that Geronimo could have refused to go to St. Louis, as he initially threatened to do. But when he grew "tired of the crowds" in St. Louis and asked permission to go back to Fort Sill, the War Department would not let him leave. Debo, *Geronimo*, 410–14.

73. Debo, *Geronimo*, 421. Some Chiricahua Apaches were imprisoned with Geronimo at Fort Sill. It isn't clear if he is referring to those Apaches, to the "remnant" of the tribe in the Southwest, or to the Apache nation as a whole.

74. On Barrett's difficulties in acquiring permission and the anxious documentation he included in the first edition, see David Murray, *Forked Tongues: Speech, Writing, and Representation in North American Indian Texts* (Bloomington: Indiana University Press, 1991), 69–71. For other discussions of the production of *Geronimo: His Own Story*, see Arnold Krupat, *For Those Who Came After: A Study of Native American Autobiography* (Berkeley: University of California Press, 1988), 61–62; Revard, *Family Matters*, 126–28; and Eric Gary Anderson, *American Indian Literature and the Southwest: Contexts and Dispositions* (Austin: University of Texas Press, 1999), 51–54.

75. Debo, *Geronimo*, 419.

76. Ibid., 420.

77. In the 1860s, Senator William Pitt Fessenden of Maine was one of the few lawmakers to ask why the federal government was not deploying military power against white settlers who encroached on reserved Indian lands. "There is no difficulty, I take it, in Kansas or Oregon in keeping men off the lands that are owned by white men," Fessenden noted. "But when the possessor happens to be an Indian, the question is changed altogether; the law of God, the higher law . . . requires that the white man should steal from the Indian; and if he cannot do it in any other way, he is to cut his throat; and if he is not strong enough to do this, the Government of the United States is to help him!" Quoted in Nichols, *Lincoln and the Indians*, 190.

78. Silko incorporates the instability of Geronimo's photographic image and warrior publicity in her novel *The Almanac of the Dead* (New York: Simon and Schuster, 1991). Anderson argues for reading Geronimo's book as addressing not just the U.S. authorities of his age but present and future "general readers," making the book a textual form of "council." *American Indian Literature*, 56–57. Also see Anderson's discussion of Silko's incorporation of the figure of Geronimo on pp. 63–76.

79. *Geronimo, His Own Story,* dedication page. See Deloria's discussion of the relation between the "cultural politics" of Indian performers in popular culture and the "Native-centered assertions of sovereignty." *Indians in Unexpected Places,* 235. Deloria views the Indian politics of popular performance as a cultural politics that ultimately failed once its "window of opportunity" closed (233–40). But I am arguing that, with its historical affiliations to a Native literary public, the domain of Indian mass performance can be seen as continuous with a literary counterpublic that has an indefinite temporal horizon.

Chapter 5

1. "Leo Gowongo," *Colored American Magazine* 1 (1900): 37.
2. For a summary of the discourse of the "New Negro," see Henry Louis Gates Jr. and Gene Andrew Jarrett, introduction to *The New Negro: Readings on Race, Representation, and African American Culture, 1892–1938* (Princeton, N.J.: Princeton University Press, 2007).
3. On the "Blackville Gallery" series in *Leslie's Weekly,* see Caroline Gebhard, "Inventing a 'Negro Literature': Race, Dialect, and Gender in the Early Work of Paul Laurence Dunbar, James Weldon Johnson, and Alice Dunbar-Nelson," in *Post-Bellum, Pre-Harlem: African American Literature and Culture, 1877–1919,* ed. Barbara McCaskill and Caroline Gebhard (New York: New York University Press, 2006), 167.
4. Langston Hughes, "The Negro Artist and the Racial Mountain," in *Voices from the Harlem Renaissance,* ed. Nathan Huggins (New York: Oxford University Press, 1995), 307.
5. Charles Chesnutt, *The Journals of Charles W. Chesnutt,* ed. Richard Brodhead (Durham, N.C.: Duke University Press, 1993), 125.
6. Thomas Wentworth Higginson, "Negro Spirituals," *Atlantic Monthly* 19 (June 1867): 685.
7. Chesnutt, *Journals,* 125.
8. Gebhard, "Inventing a 'Negro Literature,'" 162–66. On black dialect, also see Gavin Jones, *Strange Talk: The Politics of Dialect Literature in Gilded Age America* (Berkeley: University of California Press, 1999); Elsa Nettels, *Language, Race and Social Class in Howells's America* (Lexington: University Press of Kentucky, 1988); and Henry Louis Gates, "Dis and Dat: Dialect and the Descent," *Figures in Black: Words, Signs, and the "Racial" Self* (New York: Oxford University Press, 1987), 167–89.
9. Charles Chesnutt, *The Conjure Woman,* in *Stories, Novels, and Essays,* ed. Werner Sollors (New York: Library of America, 2002), 25.
10. Charles Chesnutt, quoted in William L. Andrews, *The Literary Career of Charles W. Chesnutt* (Baton Rouge: Louisiana State University Press, 1980), 21.
11. Chesnutt, *Journals,* 140.
12. Charles Chesnutt, quoted in Nancy Bentley and Sandra Gunning, eds., Bedford Edition of *The Marrow of Tradition* (New York: Macmillan, 2002), 6.

13. Charles Chesnutt, *The Marrow of Tradition*, in *Stories, Novels, and Essays*, 555. Subsequent page references cited parenthetically in the text. My interpretation of *Marrow of Tradition* and Chesnutt's career more generally has been influenced by Richard Brodhead, *Cultures of Letters: Scenes of Reading and Writing in Nineteenth-Century America* (Chicago: University of Chicago Press, 1995), and Eric Sundquist, *To Wake the Nations: Race in the Making of American Literature* (Cambridge, Mass.: Harvard University Press, 1994).

14. Miles Orvell, *The Real Thing: Imitation and Authenticity in American Culture, 1880–1940* (Chapel Hill: University of North Carolina Press, 1898), 35; Vanessa Schwartz, "Cinematic Spectatorship Before the Apparatus: The Public Taste for Reality in *Fin-de-Siècle* Paris," in *Cinema and the Invention of Modern Life*, ed. Leo Charney and Vanessa R. Schwartz (Berkeley: University of California Press, 1995), 297–319, 297.

15. See Grace Elizabeth Hale, *Making Whiteness: The Culture of Segregation in the South, 1890–1940* (New York: Vintage, 1998).

16. William Dean Howells, "A Psychological Counter-Current in Recent Fiction," *North American Review* 85 (December 1901): 699–701, reprinted in Bentley and Gunning, *The Marrow of Tradition*, 456.

17. See Bryan Wagner's fascinating analysis of the way white control of public space produced the threat of violence and the stigma of criminality for African Americans in the historical Wilmington and in Chesnutt's novel. "Charles Chesnutt and the Epistemology of Racial Violence," *American Literature* 73 (2001): 311–37.

18. Howells, "A Psychological Counter-Current," 456.

19. Ibid.

20. For a broad analysis of the social and political backdrop to the racial implications of realism, see Kenneth W. Warren, *Black and White Strangers: Race and American Literary Realism* (Chicago: University of Chicago Press, 1995).

21. Charles Parkhurst, quoted in Kevin K. Gaines, *Uplifting the Race: Black Leadership, Politics, and Culture in the Twentieth Century* (Chapel Hill: University of North Carolina Press, 1996), 70.

22. Charles Chesnutt, "The Future American," in *Stories, Novels, and Essays*, 850, 846, 847.

23. For a theoretical elaboration of this critical perspective, see Susan Willis, "Memory and Mass Culture," in *History and Memory in African American Culture*, ed. Genevieve Fabre and Robert O'Meally (New York: Oxford University Press, 1994), 182.

24. James Weldon Johnson, *Along This Way* and *The Autobiography of an Ex-Colored Man*, in *Writings*, ed. William L. Andrews (New York: Library of America, 2004), 324, 65.

25. Paul Laurence Dunbar, *The Sport of the Gods* (New York: Signet, 1999), 1. Subsequent page references cited parenthetically in the text.

26. Johnson, *Along This Way*, in *Writings*, 308.

27. For instance, Gebhard argues that Johnson's recollection of Dunbar's remarks on dialect are colored by his own growing unease with literary uses of black dialect. Other evidence, including letters the poet wrote to Alice Dunbar-Nelson,

suggest that Dunbar in fact did not disavow his dialect poetry. "Inventing a 'Negro Literature,'" 169–74.

28. For a recent study of Dunbar's career in musical theater and black American theater generally, see Karen Sotiropoulos, *Staging Race: Black Performers in Turn of the Century America* (Cambridge, Mass.: Harvard University Press, 2006). Recent studies in African American performance traditions also include Daphne A. Brooks, *Bodies in Dissent: Spectacular Performances of Race and Freedom, 1850–1910* (Durham, N.C.: Duke University Press, 2006), and Susan Curtis, *The First Black Actors on the Great White Way* (Columbia: University of Missouri Press, 1998).

29. Alan Dale, quoted in Sotiropoulos, *Staging Race*, 159.

30. Paul Laurence Dunbar, "The Negroes of the Tenderloin," *New York Sun*, quoted in Gaines, *Uplifting the Race*, 181.

31. *Variety* 36 (October 17, 1914): 13.

32. Aida Overton Walker, "Colored Men and Women on the American Stage," *Colored American Magazine* 9 (October 1905): 571, 575.

33. Aida Overton Walker, quoted in David Krasner, "Rewriting the Body: Aida Overton Walker and Cakewalking," *Theater Survey* 37:2 (November 1996): 81.

34. "Aida Overton Walker," *Pittsburgh Leader*, May 11, 1906.

35. Ibid.

36. Johnson, *The Autobiography of an Ex-Colored Man*, in *Writings*, 56. Subsequent page references cited parenthetically in the text.

37. Johnson, *Along This Way*, in *Writings*, 299.

38. Carla Peterson, "Commemorative Ceremonies and Invented Traditions: History, Memory, and Modernity in the 'New Negro' Novel of the Nadir," in *Post-Bellum, Pre-Harlem*, 38, 39.

39. Albion Tourgée, *Pactolos Prime* (Upper Saddle River, N.J.: Gregg Press, 1968), 303, 320.

40. Toni Morrison, "Rootedness: The Ancestor as Foundation," in *Black Women Writers (1950–1980): A Critical Examination*, ed. Mari Evans (Garden City, N.Y.: Anchor Press, 1984), 339.

41. W. E. B. DuBois, "A Vacation Unique," in Shamoon Zamir, *Dark Voices: W. E. B. DuBois and American Thought, 1888–1903* (Chicago: University of Chicago Press, 1995), 221. Subsequent page references cited parenthetically in the text.

42. See Kevin Gaines's discussion of Corrothers in *Uplifting the Race*, 193–208.

43. Pauline Hopkins, *Of One Blood: Or, the Hidden Self* (New York: Washington Square Press, 2004). Subsequent page references cited parenthetically in the text.

Chapter 6

1. Edith Wharton, *The Custom of the Country*, in *Novels*, ed. R. W. B. Lewis (New York: Library of America, 1985), 754. Subsequent page references to Wharton novels from this volume cited parenthetically in the text.

2. Quoted in Claire Preston, *Edith Wharton's Social Register* (New York: Macmillan, 2000), 136, 137.

3. Dale Bauer, *Edith Wharton's Brave New Politics* (Madison: University of Wisconsin Press, 1994), 5; R. W. B. Lewis, *Edith Wharton: A Biography* (New York: Fromm International, 1975), 247.

4. On Wharton's analysis of spectacles produced by the rich, see Amy Kaplan, *The Social Construction of American Realism* (Chicago: University of Chicago Press, 1988), 88–103.

5. Edith Wharton, *Edith Wharton: The Uncollected Critical Writings*, ed. Frederick Wegener (Princeton, N.J.: Princeton University Press, 1996), 156.

6. Arjun Appadurai, *Modernity at Large: Cultural Dimensions of Globalization* (Minneapolis: University of Minnesota Press, 1996), 2.

7. Editorial in *Outlook*, September 15, 1900. The editorial is quoted in Ben Singer, "Modernity, Hyperstimulus, and the Rise of Popular Sensationalism," in *Cinema and the Invention of Modern Life*, ed. Leo Charney and Vanessa R. Schwartz (Berkeley: University of California Press, 1995), 83.

8. Roland Robertson, *Globalization* (London: Sage, 1992), 25–31; Anthony Giddens, *The Consequences of Modernity* (Palo Alto, Calif.: Stanford University Press, 1990), 21.

9. Quotations appear in Wolfgang Schivelbusch, *The Railway Journey: the Industrialization of Time and Space in the Nineteenth Century* (Berkeley: University of California Press, 1977), 143, 130, 129, 145.

10. Ibid., 159, 138.

11. Emile Zola, *La Bête Humaine*, trans. Leonard W. Tancock (New York: Penguin, 1977), 74.

12. Andrea Stulman Dennett and Nina Warnke, "Disaster Spectacles at the Turn of the Century," *Film History* 4 (1990): 103, 104.

13. Bill Brown, *The Material Unconscious: American Amusement, Stephen Crane, and the Economies of Play* (Cambridge, Mass.: Harvard University Press, 1996), 116–17.

14. Bill Brown discusses commentary that writer Theodore Waters published in *Harper's Weekly* on whether the next advance in disaster spectacle for jaded New Yorkers might not require putting patrons on a burning steamboat and only rescuing them "at the last moment." *Material Unconscious*, 117. Gorky's comments on Coney Island appear in "Boredom," *Independent* 63 (August 8, 1907): 310–14.

15. Michael Warner, *Publics and Counterpublics* (New York: Zone Books, 2002), 176–86.

16. Brown, *Material Unconscious*, 118.

17. William Dean Howells, *Criticism and Fiction, and Other Essays* (New York: New York University Press, 1959), 52.

18. Edith Wharton, "A Little Girl's New York," *Harper's* 176 (1937): 362. Even though a number of Wharton novels were made into movies during her lifetime, like most inside as well as outside the industry she viewed cinema as a low cultural form. See Brigitte Peucker, *The Material Image: Art and the Real in Film* (Palo Alto, Calif.: Stanford University Press, 2006), 19–20.

19. In *The Ethnography of Manners* (New York: Cambridge University Press, 1995), I theorized this reflexive dimension of Wharton's literary practice in terms of professional anthropology. Wharton established the analytic function of her fiction,

its ability to view social manners from a second-order social position, in part by borrowing critical techniques from social science.

20. Philip Sidney Bagwell, *The Transport Revolution from 1770* (London: Batsford, 1974), 107; Michael J. Freeman and Derek H. Aldcroft, eds., *Transport in Victorian Britain* (New York: Manchester University Press, 1988), 232.

21. Tom Gunning, "Tracing the Individual Body: Photography, Detectives, and Early Cinema," in *Cinema and the Invention of Modern Life*, 16.

22. Quoted in William Henry Flayhart, *The American Line, 1871–1902* (New York: Norton, 2000), 109.

23. Ibid., 259–80.

24. Ibid., 289–93.

25. F. Lawrence Babcock, *Spanning the Atlantic* (New York: Knopf, 1931), 189; Flayhart, *American Line*, 132, 226–39.

26. See Jennie Kassanoff's discussion of the effect of the *Titanic* disaster on literary intellectuals and other cultural observers. Kassanoff's compelling interpretation of Wharton's novel *The Reef* further confirms how deeply an imagination of transport disaster could animate Wharton's analysis of manners. *Edith Wharton and the Politics of Race* (New York: Cambridge University Press, 2004), 83–111.

27. See the works of Ulrich Beck for a leading example of the sociological theorizing of a "risk society." On specific "strategies of containment" in Victorian writing that operated to manage the emergent sense of modern risk, see Elaine Freedgood, *Victorian Writing About Risk: Imagining a Safe England in a Dangerous World* (New York: Cambridge University Press, 2000).

28. See the essay collectively authored by the Seminar for Hypertheory and Heterology (SHaH), "How It Feels," in *Crash Cultures: Modernity, Mediation and the Material*, ed. Jane Arthurs and Iain Grant (Bristol: Intellect Books, 2003), 24.

29. See, for instance, the range of essays in Arthurs and Grant, *Crash Cultures*.

30. John Eric Erichsen, quoted in Schivelbusch, *Railway Journey*, 140.

31. I have drawn on Jane Thrailkill's astute discussion of Erichsen in *Affecting Fictions: Mind, Body, and Emotion in American Literary Realism* (Cambridge, Mass.: Harvard University Press, 2007), 99–104. See Thrailkill's analysis of the role of the "terror-stricken man" in the way medical and literary authors worked through problems in conceiving an embodied and dependent personhood.

32. Edith Wharton, *The Mother's Recompense*, in *Novellas and Other Writings*, ed. Cynthia Griffin Wolff (New York: Library of America, 1990), 623, 670, 710.

33. Edith Wharton, "The Great American Novel," in *Uncollected Critical Writings*, 156.

34. Edith Wharton, *A Backward Glance*, in *Novellas*, 897, 817.

35. Edith Wharton, *Life and I*, in *Novellas*, 1080–81.

36. Wharton, *Novellas*, 780–81.

37. Wharton, *Uncollected Critical Writings*, 156–57.

38. Wharton, *Novellas*, 827.

39. Walter Benjamin, *The Arcades Project* (Cambridge, Mass.: Harvard University Press, 1999), 77–78.

40. Wharton, *Novellas*, 1058–59.

41. Preston, *Edith Wharton's Social Register*, 136–37.

42. Wharton, *Novellas*, 978, 980.

43. Frederick Wegener, "'Rabid Imperialist': Edith Wharton and the Obligations of Empire in Modern American Fiction," *American Literature* 72 (2000): 788.

44. Quoted in ibid., 786–87.

45. Edith Wharton, *In Morocco* (New York: Scribner's, 1920), 182, 22. Subsequent page references cited parenthetically in the text.

46. Wharton, *Novellas*, 853.

47. See chapters 1 and 4 in Giddens, *Consequences of Modernity*. Giddens also discusses the relationship between modernity and kinship in *The Transformation of Intimacy: Sexuality, Love, and Eroticism in Modern Societies* (Palo Alto, Calif.: Stanford University Press, 1992).

48. Edith Wharton, *The Children* (New York: Simon and Schuster, 1997), 40, 18.

49. Ibid., 39, 38, 39.

50. Philip Barrish discusses the centrality of incest in Wharton's later work and offers an incisive reading of Wharton's use of the theme in *Twilight Sleep*. *American Literary Realism, Critical Theory, and Intellectual Prestige, 1880–1995* (New York: Cambridge University Press, 2001), 97–127.

51. Wharton, *Novellas*, 570, 553, 562, 583, 563.

52. Ibid., 596.

53. Ibid., 717, 652, 650.

54. Ibid., 606, 607.

55. Edith Wharton, *The Glimpses of the Moon* (New York: D. Appleton, 1922), 1, 327, 17.

56. Edith Wharton, *Twilight Sleep* (New York: Simon and Schuster, 1997), 23, 22. Subsequent page numbers cited parenthetically in the text.

Chapter 7

1. John Dewey, "The Scholastic and the Speculator," *Early Works, Volume 3, 1882–1898*, ed. Jo Ann Boydston (Carbondale: Southern Illinois University, 1975), 148–50.

2. John Dewey quoted in James Livingston, *Pragmatism and the Political Economy of Cultural Revolution, 1850–1940* (Chapel Hill: University of North Carolina Press, 1994), 191.

3. Ben Singer, "Modernity, Hyperstimulus, and the Rise of Popular Sensationalism," in *Cinema and the Invention of Modern Life*, ed. Leo Charney and Vanessa R. Schwartz (Berkeley: University of California Press, 1995), 72. Singer extends his study of neurological modernity and cinema in *Melodrama and Modernity: Early Sensational Cinema and Its Contexts* (New York: Columbia University Press, 2001).

4. Georg Simmel, "The Metropolis and Mental Life," in *The Sociology of Georg Simmel*, ed. Kurt H. Wolff (New York: Free Press, 1950), 410.

5. Ibid.

6. Singer offers a detailed overview of the claims for and critique of the "modernity thesis" in studies of early film and mass culture. *Melodrama and Modernity*, 101–30.

7. In part because Theodor Adorno and Max Horkheimer criticized James and Dewey, intellectual historians have tended to see pragmatism as having little in common with European Critical Theory and its interest in mass culture. See Martin Jay, *The Dialectical Imagination: A History of the Frankfurt School and the Institute of Social Research, 1923–1950* (Boston: Little, Brown, 1973). But renewed interest in pragmatism among intellectual historians has produced new claims (and counterclaims) about the place of pragmatist thought in genealogies of Continental philosophy and social theory. See the essays in *The Revival of Pragmatism: New Essays on Social Thought, Law, and Culture*, ed. Morris Dickstein (Durham, N.C.: Duke University Press, 1998). The work of German scholar Hans Joas has helped recover the influence of the pragmatists on European social thought. See especially *Pragmatism and Social Theory* (Chicago: University of Chicago Press, 1993). James Livingston stakes out one of the stronger claims by arguing that James and Dewey in particular established the foundation for what would become poststructuralist theories of the subject. See *Pragmatism, Feminism, and Democracy: Rethinking the Politics of American History* (New York: Routledge, 2001), 57–76. Mead's influence on Habermas and other European theorists is explored in Mitchell Aboulafia, *The Cosmopolitan Self: G. H. Mead and Continental Philosophy* (Urbana: University of Illinois Press, 2006).

8. For a broader perspective on the "textual margin between literature and sociology" (15), see Susan Mizruchi's excellent study, *The Science of Sacrifice: American Literature and Modern Social Theory* (Princeton, N.J.: Princeton University Press, 1998).

9. Henry Adams, *The Education of Henry Adams* (New York: Penguin, 1995), 276, 354. Subsequent page references cited parenthetically in the text.

10. Jürgen Habermas, *The Structural Transformation of the Public Sphere*, trans. Thomas Burger (Cambridge, Mass.: MIT Press, 1989), 141–235.

11. I draw the idea of a "composite public sphere" from Miriam Hansen, "Early Cinema, Late Cinema: Transformations of the Public Sphere," in *Viewing Positions: Ways of Seeing Film*, ed. Linda Williams (New Brunswick, N.J.: Rutgers University Press, 1995), 147.

12. Bernard Berenson quoted in Bernhard Minninger, *Henry Adams: The Education of Henry Adams: Selbstanalyse, heuristisches Experiment und Autobiographische Formtradition* (Berlin: P. Lang, 1994), 222. William James quoted in Jean Gooder, introduction to *The Education*, xl.

13. Henry Adams, *Henry Adams and His Friends: A Collection of His Unpublished Letters*, ed. Harold Dean Carter (Boston: Houghton Mifflin, 1947), 260. Inasmuch as Adams's close friend Hay was secretary of state with a central role in shaping U.S. expansionist policies, Adams was intimately acquainted with the details of American imperialism. On Adams's relation to Hay and foreign policy, see John Carlos Rowe, "Henry Adams's Education in the Age of Imperialism," in *New Essays on The Education of Henry Adams*, ed. John Carlos Rowe (New York: Cambridge University Press, 1996), 87–114.

14. *The Letters of Henry Adams,* vol. 4 (1892–99), ed. J. C. Levenson et al. (Cambridge, Mass.: Harvard University Press, 1982–88), 132.

15. Tom Gunning, "An Aesthetics of Astonishment: Early Film and the (In)-Credulous Spectator," in *Viewing Positions,* 117.

16. Ibid., 122.

17. See Cindy Weinstein's discussion of the resonance of Adams's mannequin with a department store mannequin and with economic and labor conditions more generally in *The Literature of Labor and the Labors of Literature: Allegory in Nineteenth-Century American Fiction* (Cambridge: Cambridge University Press, 1995), 173–206.

18. Siegfried Kracauer, "Boredom," in *The Mass Ornament: Weimar Essays,* trans. Thomas Y. Levin (Cambridge, Mass.: Harvard University Press, 1995), 332.

19. On the formation of the classical mode of cinematic narration that emerged out of the more eclectic style of early film, see Kristin Thompson, "The Foundation of the Classical Style, 1909–28," in *The Classical Hollywood Cinema: Film Style and Mode of Production to 1960,* ed. David Bordwell, Janet Staiger, and Kristin Thompson (New York: Columbia University Press, 1985), 155–240.

20. Kracauer, "Boredom," 332.

21. Singer, *Melodrama and Modernity,* 59–99.

22. For a summary of critiques of pragmatism, see John Patrick Diggins, *The Promise of Pragmatism: Modernism and the Crisis of Knowledge and Authority* (Chicago: University of Chicago Press, 1994).

23. George Herbert Mead, "The Social Self," *Journal of Philosophy* 10 (1913): 378. Mead offered an expanded version of this idea in his lectures of 1914, published in *The Individual and the Social Self,* ed. David L. Miller (Chicago: University of Chicago Press, 1982), 100–105.

24. William James, *Psychology: Briefer Course,* in *Writings, 1878–1899,* ed. Gerald E. Myers (New York: Library of America, 1992), 149.

25. William James, "The Moral Philosopher," in *Writings, 1878–1899,* 614; John Dewey, "The Psychology of Effort," in *Early Works,* vol. 5, *1882–1898,* 155.

26. Livingston, *Pragmatism and the Political Economy,* 84.

27. In Richard Rorty's synthetic description, the common-denominator assumption about the subject in Western thought (a "picture of the self common to Greek metaphysics, Christian theology, and Enlightenment rationalism") was "the idea that the human self has a center (a divine spark, or a truth-tracking faculty called 'reason') and that argumentation will, given time and patience, penetrate to this center." *Objectivity, Relativism, and Truth: Philosophical Papers, Volume I* (New York: Cambridge University Press, 1991), 176. Rorty argues that this "picture" began to be seriously challenged in the 1890s. Challenges to his model of the self also had large implications for debates on the status of women, although I do not discuss them in this chapter. See, for instance, Charlene Haddock Seigfried, *Pragmatism and Feminism: Reweaving the Social Fabric* (Chicago: University of Chicago Press, 1996).

28. Jonathan Crary, "Unbinding Vision: Manet and the Attentive Observer in the Late Nineteenth Century," in *Cinema and the Invention of Modern Life,* 50.

29. Ibid., 47.

30. James Livingston quotes from and discusses the exchange of letters between William James and his father in *Pragmatism, Feminism, and Democracy*, 125–29.

31. William James, *Principles of Psychology* (Boston: H. Holt, 1890), 224, 284, 288–89.

32. James, *Psychology: Briefer Course*, in *Writings, 1878–1899*, 169. *Psychology: Briefer Course* is a shortened version of the original *Principles of Psychology*. Subsequent page references cited parenthetically in the text.

33. This passage appears in the longer *Principles of Psychology*, 288.

34. On the central importance of Goethe to the resolution of James's intellectual crisis, see Ralph Barton Perry, *The Thought and Character of William James* (Cambridge, Mass.: Harvard University Press, 1948).

35. William James, quoted in Livingston, *Pragmatism, Feminism, and Democracy*, 127, 126.

36. Crary, "Unbinding Vision," 51.

37. See the history offered by Lorraine Daston and Peter Galison by which "well-educated bourgeois males were wholly persuaded that they were in possession of a monolithic self, defined by an indomitable will." *Objectivity* (New York: Zone Books, 2007), 228. Daston and Galison locate William James at one end of a spectrum of the "scientific self" for the way he theorizes a "bustling, willful self" that meets and presides over "the clamor of perception" like an "energetic executive" (201). While they accurately describes James's portrait of the self in the *Psychology*, I argue that James later revised this "willful" self to acknowledge a more desiring and divided model of selfhood.

38. Lewis Mumford, quoted in Livingston, *Pragmatism and Political Economy*, 200.

39. William James, "The Meaning of Truth," in *Writings, 1902–1910*, ed. Bruce Kuklick (New York: Library of America, 1988), 834.

40. William James, *The Will to Believe*, in *Writings, 1878–1899*, 538.

41. Ibid., 584.

42. For a close analysis of the way non-linguistic experience becomes communicable significance for James and Dewey, see James T. Kloppenberg, "Pragmatism: An Old Name for Some New Ways of Thinking?" in Dickstein, *Revival of Pragmatism*, 83–127. Surveying contemporary versions of pragmatism, Kloppenberg sees a key division between those who reject or minimize the Jamesian valuation of experience in favor of the linguistic (Richard Rorty and Richard Poirier, for instance) and those who value the centrality of experience for the way it confirms "the intersection between the conscious self and the world" (pragmatist historians like Kloppenberg who require "the possibility of connecting the arguments we construct to the lives we write about" [93]).

43. Jane Thrailkill discusses William James's linkage between somatic experience and consciousness in *Affecting Fictions: Mind, Body, and Emotion in American Literary Realism* (Cambridge, Mass.: Harvard University Press, 2007), 36–43. Thrailkill draws from the work of James and Dewey to underscore the affective and bodily dimensions of aesthetic experience in general and "experience-based" (21) realism in particular. Although I agree with Thrailkill that both pragmatists and realists

were responding to the physical "commotion of modernity" (36), what is largely missing from her rich analysis is any sense of the institutional anxieties that made intellectuals worry about the possibility that a neurological modernity was eroding the conditions necessary for public reason. The starkest target of that anxiety, I have argued, was the new forms of mass culture, forms that directly cultivated the "tingle" of bodily experience for profit. I argue that pragmatism and realism should both be seen as cautious and conflicted efforts to discover whether modes of thought and literary analysis inherited from the literary public sphere can survive and adapt to a postliterary culture dominated by commercial media.

Mary Esteve closely attends to the anxieties that Thrailkill largely elides, emphasizing the fears about whether public deliberation and "abstract reason," seen as necessary for sound political action, could survive in an age of "crowds." *The Aesthetics and Politics of the Crowd in American Literature* (New York: Cambridge University Press, 2003). But where Esteve is concerned to demarcate practices of public reason from aesthetic experience available in mass forms, I am interested in how the superimposing of these domains created a potentially efficacious "composite public."

44. Patten began to describe the "pleasure economy" in the 1890s. His 1907 book, *The New Basis of Civilization* (New York, Macmillan), became a popular work and spread his ideas about this "economic revolution" widely. See Livingston, *Pragmatism and Political Economy*, 67–70. Bill Brown discusses this shift to a "pleasure economy" in *The Material Unconscious: American Amusement, Stephen Crane, and the Economies of Play* (Cambridge, Mass.: Harvard University Press, 1996), especially 1–26.

45. On the public or civil "orientation" of the private subjectivity conveyed in a letter, see Habermas, *Structural Transformation*, 43–51. A large body of scholarship has studied the dialectical relation between private subjectivity and public expressive forms. For a recent study that, like Habermas, locates the origins of this dialectic in eighteenth-century European culture, see Michael McKeon, *The Secret History of Domesticity: Public, Private, and the Division of Knowledge* (Princeton, N.J.: Princeton University Press, 2005).

46. Whitman, quoted in James, *Writings, 1878–1899*, 853–54, italics added.

47. On the panorama, see Richard Atlick, *The Shows of London* (Cambridge, Mass.: Harvard University Press, 1978). Daphne Brooks discusses the history of the panorama in the United States, especially in its relation to racial spectacle. *Bodies in Dissent: Spectacular Performances of Race and Freedom, 1850–1910* (Durham, N.C.: Duke University Press, 2006). On the relation of the panorama to early cinema, see Vanessa R. Schwartz, "Cinematic Spectatorship Before the Apparatus: The Public Taste for Reality in *Fin-de-Siècle* Paris," in *Cinema and the Invention of Modern Life*, 311–16.

48. Whitman himself might be said to have insisted on his poetry as postliterary expressivity: "No one will get at my verses who insists on viewing them as a literary performance, or attempt at such performance, or as aiming mainly toward art or aestheticism." "A Backward Glance O'er Travel'd Roads," in *Poetry and Prose*, ed. Justin Kaplan (New York: Library of America, 1982), 671. For a sense of the remarkable and varied ways that Whitman's life and person became the materials of

both private adoration and public association, see Michael Robertson, *Worshipping Walt: The Whitman Disciples* (Princeton, N.J.: Princeton University Press, 2008).

49. James does not argue that either experience or a sensation like pleasure constitutes knowledge, only that feeling is a vital component in the process of knowing. For a closer breakdown of the role of feeling and sentiment, see "The Stream of Consciousness" in *Psychology* (especially "'Substantive' and 'Transitive' States of Mind," in *Writings, 1878–1899*, 159–62), and "The Sentiment of Rationality," *Writings, 1878–1899*, 950–85.

50. John Dewey, "The Construction of the Good," in *Pragmatism, Old and New*, ed. Susan Haack (Amherst, N.Y.: Prometheus, 2006), 400.

51. George Herbert Mead, "The Mechanism of Social Consciousness," in *Journal of Philosophy, Psychology, and Scientific Methods* 9 (1912): 406.

52. George Herbert Mead, "1914 Lectures in Social Psychology," in *The Individual and the Self: Unpublished Work of George Herbert Mead*, ed. David L. Miller (Chicago: University of Chicago Press, 1982), 101.

53. Ibid., 98, 101.

54. John Dewey, "The Need for a Recovery of Philosophy," in *Creative Intelligence: Essays in the Pragmatic Attitude* (Boston: H. Holt, 1917), 64.

55. Miriam Hansen, *Babel and Babylon: Spectatorship in American Silent Film* (Cambridge, Mass.: Harvard University Press, 1991), 111–12.

56. John Dewey, *Art and Experience*, in *The Essential Dewey, Volume 1: Pragmatism, Education, Democracy* (Bloomington: Indiana University Press, 1998), 400.

57. Clearly the consolidation of cultural industries in the twentieth century has shown that this wariness about homogenization was not unfounded. In addition to Habermas's discussion of "refeudalization" in *Structural Transformation*, see Pascale Casanova's comments on literary production in *The World Republic of Letters*, trans. M. B. DeBevoise (Cambridge, Mass.: Harvard University Press, 2004), 164–72. But as I argued in chapter 1, the same economic and infrastructural conditions that were the basis for mass culture industries were also the foundation for a new order of media, genres, and publics that were more local and diversified rather than homogenized. Sociological studies have made the same argument for twentieth-century culture. See, for instance, Tyler Cowen, *In Praise of Commercial Culture* (Cambridge, Mass.: Harvard University Press, 1998).

58. Arnold Rampersad observes that different conceptualizations of the idea of "double consciousness" were in the air during the period DuBois wrote *Souls*, including the psychology William James was teaching at Harvard when DuBois was his student. *The Art and Imagination of W. E. B. Du Bois* (Cambridge, Mass.: Harvard University Press, 1976), 74. Also see Adolph L. Reed, *W. E. B. Du Bois and American Political Thought: Fabianism and the Color Line* (New York: Oxford University Press, 1997), 93–126. A number of studies have argued that DuBois's critical thought should be understood as a form of pragmatism; see, for instance, Cornel West, *The Evasion of American Philosophy: A Genealogy of Pragmatism* (Madison: University of Wisconsin Press, 1989); Ross Posnock, *Color and Culture: Black Writers and the Making of the Modern Intellectual* (Cambridge, Mass.: Harvard University Press, 1998); and Richard Cullen Rath, "Echo and Narcissus: The Afrocentric Pragmatism of W. E. B. Du Bois," *Journal of American History* 84 (1997): 461–95.

DuBois's place within the pragmatist tradition is also discussed in essays by Paul Taylor and James Kloppenberg, both of which appear in *The Range of Pragmatism and the Limits of Philosophy*, ed. Richard Shusterman (Oxford: Blackwell, 2004). But also see the closely argued claim by Shamoon Zamir that the model of consciousness that DuBois develops in *Souls* and other early writings is grounded in a Hegelian historicism that is sharply at odds with William James's pragmatism. *Dark Voices: W. E. B. Du Bois and American Thought, 1888–1903* (Chicago: University of Chicago Press, 1995), 113–68. My thanks to Hannah Wells for information and discussions on this body of scholarship.

My own interest in DuBois's model of consciousness is not whether it should be classed with pragmatism but how its insistence on including African American experience and white American sadism changes the prospects and possibilities of public expressivity in an age of mass culture.

59. W. E. B. DuBois, *The Souls of Black Folk*, in *Writings*, ed. Nathan Huggins (New York: Library of America, 1986), 363. Subsequent page references cited parenthetically in the text.

60. It is notable that William James identified lynching in terms of white pleasure in a letter he wrote to an Illinois newspaper, claiming that lynchers were "feeding their imaginations" in a drive for "more drastic excitement." But significantly, James describes those who lynch as "illiterate whites," as if to cordon off sadistic pleasure from any relation to literary understanding. James is quoted in Russ Castronovo, *Beautiful Democracy: Aesthetics and Anarchy in a Global Era* (Chicago: University of Chicago Press, 2007), 20. See Castronovo's wide-ranging discussion of the complex relations between aesthetic feeling and racial violence in his chapter, "Beauty Along the Color Line: Lynching, Form, and Aesthetics," 106–35.

61. W. E. B. DuBois, *Dusk of Dawn*, in *Writings*, 603.

62. In *Making Whiteness: The Culture of Segregation in the South, 1890–1940* (New York: Vintage, 1998), Grace Elizabeth Hale describes the new array of racist consumer products and public amusements, including the sound recording of a lynching on Edison's "talking machine" (227).

63. On the topic of DuBois's relation to social science, see the special issue of *boundary 2*, 27:3 (Fall 2000), titled *Sociology Hesitant: Thinking with W. E. B. Du Bois* and edited by Ronald A. T. Judy. Of particular relevance are Judy's introduction, 1–35; the reprinted DuBois essay, "Sociology Hesitant," 37–44; and Tommy Lott, "Du Bois and Locke on the Scientific Study of the Negro," 135–52. Also see Mizruchi, *Science of Sacrifice*, 269–366.

64. W. E. B. DuBois, *The Autobiography of W. E. B. DuBois: A Soliloquy on Viewing My Life from the Last Decade of Its First Century* (Geneva: International Publishers, 1968).

65. Mead, "The Social Self," 378.

66. Houston A. Baker Jr., "Critical Memory and the Black Public Sphere," in *The Black Public Sphere* (Chicago: University of Chicago Press, 1995), 13.

67. Ibid., 20, 16.

68. Siegfried Kracauer, quoted in Miriam Hansen, "America, Paris, the Alps: Kracauer (and Benjamin) on Cinema and Modernity," in *Cinema and the Invention of Modern Life*, 377. Hansen comments that "the cinema is a signature of modernity

for Kracauer not simply because it attracts and represents the masses, but because it constitutes the most advanced cultural institution in which the masses, as a relatively heterogeneous, undefined, and known form of collectivity, can represent themselves as a public." For a historical version of this argument, with empirical analysis of women's and working-class cinematic audiences in turn-of-the-century United States, see Hansen, *Babel and Babylon*.

69. Hansen, "America, Paris, the Alps," 377.

70. Baker, "Critical Memory," 22.

71. DuBois's own view of cinema was ambivalent at best. Attuned as he was to the myriad ways that white people found to enjoy black humiliation, he regarded the growing popularity of black vaudeville and the proliferation of segregated venues like movie houses and dance halls with wariness. But Karen Sotiropoulos argues that the bricolage styles that characterize the creativity of the "Bohemian Tenth" of African American entertainers are actually parallel with DuBois's effort at imagining a black kingdom of culture. *Staging Race: Black Performers in Turn of the Century America* (Cambridge, Mass.: Harvard University Press, 2006), 197–236. On DuBois's account of attending nickelodeon, see Castronovo, *Beautiful Democracy*. For a study of black "reconstructive spectatorship" of cinema, see Jacqueline Stewart, *Migrating to the Movies: Cinema and Black Urban Modernity* (Berkeley: University of California Press, 2005).

72. Hansen, "America, Paris, the Alps," 389.

73. For a developed analysis of the temporalities of black diasporic experience, especially as explored in the writing of C. L. R. James, see David Scott, *Conscripts of Modernity: The Tragedy of Colonial Enlightenment* (Durham, N.C.: Duke University Press, 2004).

74. DuBois, *Dusk of Dawn*, in *Writings*, 650.

Conclusion

1. William Dean Howells, *A Hazard of New Fortunes* (New York: Penguin, 2001), 216. Subsequent page references cited parenthetically in the text.

2. Henry James, *Literary Criticism*, vol. 1, ed. Leon Edel (New York: Library of America, 1984), 502–3.

3. Lorraine Daston and Peter Galison, *Objectivity* (New York: Zone Books, 2007), 42, 44.

4. James, *Literary Criticism*, vol. 1, 503.

5. Miriam Hansen, *Babel and Babylon: Spectatorship in American Silent Film* (Cambridge, Mass.: Harvard University Press, 1991), 108.

6. Ibid., 11.

7. Ibid. Critics have charged Habermas with adopting the same exclusionary criteria for publicness as the bourgeois sphere he has analyzed historically, and it is true that he says little about gender, sexuality, or race in *The Structural Transformation of the Public Sphere*, trans. Thomas Burger (Cambridge, Mass.: MIT Press, 1989). But see Michael Warner's discussion of the diverse kinds of public discourse

Habermas recognizes in his historical account. A unitary public opinion, Habermas acknowledges, is a "fiction." *Publics and Counterpublics* (New York: Zone Books, 2002), 55–56. According to Warner, "there is no necessary conflict between the public sphere and the idea of multiple publics" (56). Indeed, social movements like feminism and queer politics rely on the governing concepts and practices that become available only through a public sphere environment (50). Also see Hansen's discussion of both the critical tools and "heuristic limitation" that are implicit in Habermas's modeling of the public sphere after a reading public. *Babel and Babylon,* 8–16.

8. To cite only one example, Hansen quotes a writer for the *Jewish Daily Forward* who observed, "our Jews feel very much at home with the detectives, oceans, horses, dogs, and cars that run about on the screen.'" *Babel and Babylon,* 108.

9. Hansen recognizes that a cinematic public lacks the characteristics of familiar interactive participation that govern the normative idea of a public. But, in an argument she develops at length, Hansen contends that early cinema "helped immigrants organize their experience on their own terms, . . . not only by creating a space for the actualization of involuntary memory, of disjunctive layers of time and subjectivity, it also offered a collective form for the production of fantasy, the capability of envisioning a different future. More than any entertainment of the period, the cinema figured as the site of magical transformations—of things, people, settings, and situations" that promise "the transformation of seemingly fixed positions of social identity." *Babel and Babylon,* 111–12.

10. As the film industry developed, it consciously began to fashion itself after a literary public by turning to such forms as film libraries and museums. Intellectuals like Vachel Lindsay in effect repeated Howells's strategy of borrowing the prestige and pedagogical authority of the museum to certify a lower form—cinema, in this case—as a high art form with public significance. For an excellent history of this institutional development, see Peter Decherney, *Hollywood and the Cultural Elite: How the Movies Became American* (New York: Columbia University Press, 2005). But while these institutional collaborations invoked and thus extended the authority of an older bourgeois literary culture, the ability of a visual, mass medium to acquire and in some respects supplant literature's role as a site of public reason is one of the strong indicators of a postliterary moment.

11. James, *Literary Criticism,* vol. 1, 502.

12. Jacques Rancière, *The Politics of Aesthetics,* trans. Gabriel Rockhill (New York: Continuum, 2004), 39.

13. Mark McGurl, *The Novel Art: Elevations of American Fiction After Henry James* (Princeton, N.J.: Princeton University Press, 2001).

14. Bill Brown, *The Material Unconscious: American Amusement, Stephen Crane, and the Economies of Play* (Cambridge, Mass.: Harvard University Press, 1996), 55.

15. Stephen Crane quoted in Martin Jay, *Harvests of Change: American Literature, 1865–1914* (Englewood Cliffs, N.J.: Prentice-Hall, 1967), 69–70.

16. Joseph Conrad quoted in Brown, *Material Unconscious,* 109.

17. McGurl, *Novel Art,* 92.

18. Ibid., 103.

19. Brown, *Material Unconscious*, 26.
20. Ibid., 5.
21. McGurl, *NovelArt*, 22.
22. Stephen Crane, quoted in Jay, *Harvests of Change*, 62–63.
23. Henry James, *Literary Criticism*, vol. 2, ed. Leon Edel (New York: Library of America, 1984), 1149.
24. Henry James, *The American Scene*, in *Travel Writing: Great Britain and America*, ed. Richard Howard (New York: Library of America, 1993), 413, 412, 456, 424. Subsequent page references cited parenthetically in the text.
25. Rancière, *Politics of Aesthetics*, 40.
26. Bill Brown's analysis of the audible voice that things and buildings acquire in *The American Scene* suggests that even the non-human can partake of public consciousness and may be as crucial to the distribution of the sensible world as are human subjects. *A Sense of Things: The Object Matter of American Literature* (Chicago: University of Chicago Press, 2003). My interpretation of *The American Scene* has also been informed by Ross Posnock, *The Trial of Curiosity: Henry James, William James, and the Challenge of Modernity* (New York: Oxford University Press, 1991); Sarah Blair, *Henry James and the Writing of Race and Nation* (Cambridge: Cambridge University Press, 1996); and Kendall Johnson, *Henry James and the Visual* (Cambridge: Cambridge University Press, 2007).
27. James, *Literary Criticism*, vol. 2, 1061.
28. A contemporary critic, H. G. Dwight, made this observation about James's style in a retrospective essay published in the wake of James's visit to the United States. Dwight is quoted in Posnock, *Trial of Curiosity*, 143.
29. For critical discussions of Ferguson's 1904 Geronimo photograph, see Jimmie Durham, "Geronimo!" in *Partial Recall: Photographs of Native North Americans*, ed. Lucy R. Lippard (New York: Norton, 1992), 55–58, and Philip J. Deloria, *Indians in Unexpected Places* (Lawrence: University of Kansas Press, 2004), 168–69.
30. It is worth noting in this context that major forms of mass culture—cinema, the mass press, amusement parks—functioned from the first as international industries, even though they often became the vehicles of nationalist and imperial sentiment. It took a highly organized, funded campaign by U.S. companies, for instance, to "Americanize" the early movie industry. See Richard Abel, "The Perils of Pathé, or the Americanization of Early American Cinema," in *Cinema and the Invention of Modern Life*, ed. Leo Charney and Vanessa R. Schwartz (Berkeley: University of California Press, 1995), 183–223, and Decherney, *Hollywood and the Cultural Elite*. Robert W. Rydell and Rob Kroes document the transnational reach of mass culture forms, although they emphasize a context of economic and cultural "Americanization" in which supposedly national industries are exported to other nations, thus downplaying the non-national technologies and innovations that were the basis for cinema, circuses, world's fairs, and cartoons. *Buffalo Bill in Bologna: The Americanization of the World, 1869–1922* (Chicago: University of Chicago Press, 2005).
31. Quoted in Roger Gant, *Henry James: The Critical Heritage* (New York: Routledge, 1997), 444.

Index

Abbot, Edwin A., *Flatland*, 214
aborigines, exhibition of, 36–37
actresses: cross-dressing, 16, 83, 109, 114–16, 132; sexual power of, 117; social agency of, 138–39
Adams, Henry, 7; and American imperialism, 340 n.13; as autobiographical subject, 255, 256; historical consciousness of, 250, 251, 253, 257–58; William James on, 250–51; knowledge of poverty, 252; literary aesthetics of, 254; literary analyses by, 19, 100; mannequin tropes of, 255, 256, 258, 259, 267, 341 n.17; in National Institute, 305 n.15; at Paris World Exhibition, 258, 259; on slavery, 252; study of science, 256; on women in modernity, 128. Works: *Democracy*, 134–35; *The Education of Henry Adams*, 249–53, 255, 256–60; *Esther*, 23, 128; *History of the United States During the Administrations of Washington and Jefferson*, 252; *Mont Saint Michel and Chartres*, 253
Addams, Jane: crisis of consciousness, 53; on search for culture, 52–53
Adorno, Theodor, 340 n.7; on mass culture, 17
adultery, in *A Modern Instance*, 82
aesthetics: of astonishment, 253–54, 256; culture and, 72–73, 76–77, 86; of disaster, 220, 225; of disjunction, 289; of distraction, 17, 18; of European imperialism, 234–35; of industrialization, 11; "low," 206; of museums, 22; politics and, 69–70, 72, 306n. 18; of posters, 119–20; of realism, 91; spectacle and, 29; therapeutic function of, 325 n.50; Whitman on, 52, 55; women's pleasure in, 144
Africa, in transatlantic literature, 61
African Americans: in cinema, 309 n.44; civil society and, 189, 199, 206; commercial culture and, 189–90, 211; dance of, 195, 207–8; diasporic experience of, 286, 346 n.73; folk-art of, 211; inner life of, 214; labor exploitation of, 64; modernity and, 283; Northern interest in, 190–97; participation in American culture, 69, 77; public sphere and, 188, 283; racist depiction of, 202; social recognition for, 193; sorrow songs of, 286; as spectacle, 195; urban culture of, 6, 203, 204–6, 209–10; violence against, 194, 196, 198, 199, 280–81, 335 n.17, 345 n.60. *See also* fiction, African American; intellectuals, African American; performers, African American
agents, Indian: carceral power of, 177; and Wild West shows, 177, 178
American Academy of Arts and Letters, 2, 303 n.2, 304 n.11; on high culture, 9; international standards of, 307 n.24; and mass culture, 3–4; nationalism of, 306 n.24
American Museum of Natural History (New York), 26
American Negro Academy, 14; black bourgeoisie of, 63; goals of, 60–61
amusement parks, 2, 39–41; Gorky on, 17, 224; museums and, 26; sensation at, 39–40; staged disasters at, 224; as unifying force, 27
amusements: mass, 53, 163, 254, 260; mechanical, 254, 276; racist, 345 n.62; urban, 53
antimodernism, 10, 307 n.30
Apaches: Barnum's exploitation of, 153; captivity of, 184, 185, 333 n.73; Geronimo's advocacy for, 184; sovereignty for, 186, 187
Appadurai, Arjun, 219; on mass culture, 7–9
Arac, Jonathan, 101
Arnold, Matthew: cultural theories of, 28, 51–52; *Culture and Anarchy*, 69
The Arrival of a Train (Lumière), 17, 290
art: autonomy of, 46; collectors of, 56–58; and consciousness, 52–53; dissent in, 9; and mass-mediated society, 73; moral

art (continued)
   meaning of, 78; postmodern, 37; rationality in, 13; social power of, 8, 70
art, analytic, 11–14; critical practice of, 13; transformations within, 19
art, European: American acquisition of, 56–58; French, 119; Henry James's experience of, 28–29
art, high: Howells on, 36–37; and mass forms, 6–7; and nationalism, 70–71, 73; social power of, 91
art novels, 72, 295, 297
astonishment, aesthetics of, 253–54, 256
attention, human: William James on, 268; scientific study of, 136; selective, 265
Austen, Jane, 122, 231
authority: cultural, 27, 80, 100; state, 177
authors: cultural mission of, 78–79; virility of, 113–14
authors, African American, 212–17; historical romances by, 212; on mass culture, 189–90
authors, women: celebrity of, 117; on condition of women, 129; as public figures, 112, 114; realist, 122–28, 139–40, 148, 149; regionalist, 127–28, 140–43; use of science, 129–30, 138–39
authors' studies, private: DuBois's, 286; glamour of, 44, 45; intrusions into, 47; versus mass media, 42; of realists, 42–43; spectacle and, 35–39, 44–46; symbolism of, 42, 44

Bachofen, Johann, *Das Mütterecht*, 132
Baker, Houston, 283, 284
Ballard, J. G., 230; *Crash*, 222, 223
Balzac, Honoré, 125; educative practice of, 107–8
Barnum, P. T., 2; American Museum of, 25–26, 28, 88; business acumen of, 94, 95; exploitation of Native Americans, 152–54, 163–66; Great Traveling Museum of, 155; influence in France, 119; mansion of, 95–96; readers of, 98; *Struggles and Triumphs*, 25–26, 94, 97, 152, 310 n.9
Barrett, S. M., 180, 182, 183, 184, 333 n.74
Barrish, Phillip, 71
Bauer, Dale, 218, 219
Bearden, Romare, 284
beauty: DuBois on, 68; female, 117–18; Kantian laws of, 5. *See also* aesthetics

Bell, Michael Davitt, 71
Benjamin, Walter, 18–19, 236, 247, 256
Bennett, Tony, 76, 77
Bercovitch, Sacan, 104, 321 n.70
Berenson, Bernard, 250
Berryman, John, 297
Bildung, literary paradigm of, 264, 265, 283
Birmingham school (of criticism), 73
Black Kettle (Cheyenne leader), 154
boarding schools, Native American, 172–74
Boas, Franz, 168
Bolton, Charles Knowles, *The Reign of the Poster*, 117
Bonnin, Gertrude, 7; autobiographical stories of, 172–74; lettered persona of, 174; periodical fiction of, 172; public role of, 175; use of irony, 173; white audience of, 174
Booth, John Wilkes, 121
Boston: burlesque in, 83; cultural discernment in, 95; cultural institutions of, 85; Gallery of Fine Arts, 88; Museum of Fine Art, 76–77, 85; Symphony Orchestra, 77
"Boston marriages," 116–17
Bourdieu, Pierre, 14, 309 n.41; on habitus, 15, 16
bourgeoisie: black, 317 n.9; and male self, 342 n.37; public sphere of, 5, 20, 76, 168–70, 261, 289, 294, 346 n.7; thought world of, 169; travel by, 236
Bourget, Paul, 102
Broca, Paul, 131
Brodhead, Richard, 29–30, 53, 311 n.24, 335 n.13
Brooks, Van Wyck, 102, 305 n.13
Brown, Bill, 58, 225–26, 295, 337 n.14; on Crane, 297, 304 n.12; on cultural mediation, 313 n.42; on Henry James, 348 n.26; on realism, 224
Brown, William Wells, *Clotel*, 212
Bryant, William Cullen, 74
burlesque, 83–84, 109, 114–16, 122; transatlantic, 319 n.36
Burnand, F. C., *Ixion; or the Man at the Wheel*, 83–84

Cable, George Washington, 101
capitalism: consumer, 7; corporate, 273, 326 n.64; cultural dimensions of, 17–18, 20, 98–99; destructive capacity of, 56; of Gilded Age, 97; global, 8; role of feminism

in, 326 n.64; role of manners in, 97; in transatlantic travel, 56–57; transformations to, 262
Carlson, David J., 161
Carlyle, Thomas, *Sartor Resartus*, 255
Carnegie, Andrew, 56–57
Casanova, Pascale, 5, 119, 306 n.19, 344 n.57
"Certain Dangerous Tendencies in American Life" (*Atlantic*), 77–78
Chaucer, Geoffrey, 42
Chéret, Jules, 119
Chesnutt, Charles, 6, 12; dialect stories of, 192; literary autonomy of, 49–50; national recognition of, 50; Northern audience of, 190–97; plantation fiction of, 191; race in works of, 202; social portraits of, 99; stenography business of, 200–201; travel by, 50, 67; on uplift of white race, 193–94; use of realism, 195, 196, 197, 200, 201. Works: "The Future American," 202; *The Marrow of Tradition*, 194–201, 203; "Po' Sandy," 192–93
Cheyenne tribe, Barnum's exploitation of, 153
Cheyfitz, Eric, 161
Chivington, Colonel John, 154, 165
Choate, Joseph, 70
Chopin, Kate, 6–7, 129; critical reception of, 149–50; European influences on, 140; feminist champions of, 148, 150; local color fiction of, 140–43; realism of, 139, 140, 145, 148, 149. Works: "At the 'Cadian Ball," 141–42; *The Awakening*, 139–40, 145–50; *Bayou Folk*, 140, 142; "An Egyptian Cigarette," 145; "Lilacs," 142; "Nég Créol," 142; "A Pair of Silk Stockings," 143–44, 145
cinema: aesthetic culture of, 256; African Americans in, 309 n.44; Americanization of, 348 n.30; of attractions, 7; aural protocols for, 2; expressive mode of, 284; influence on social identity, 309 n.44; modernity of, 340 n.6, 345 n.68; neurological modernity and, 339 n.3; postliterary nature of, 295, 347 n.10; shock in, 18–19; as site of public reason, 347 n.10; visual excess in, 17; visual protocols for, 2; war, 311 n.22; Western, 178, 179
cinema, early, 255–56; disjunction in, 289; DuBois on, 346 n.71; eclectic style of, 341 n.18; staged crashes in, 1, 3; types of experience in, 290; Wharton on, 337n. 18; women in, 326 n.65
civilization: divisions within, 157–58; Victorian, 61, 62
civil society: African Americans and, 189, 199, 206; commercial culture in, 118; postbellum, 200; Southern, 193; unity in, 99. *See also* public sphere
Cobb, Sylvanus T., 33
Cody, Buffalo Bill, 2, 14, 175, 330 n.43; New Orleans visit of, 331 n.46; Sitting Bull and, 331 n.48
Cohen, Margaret, 147
colonialism, French, Wharton on, 238–39
Columbian Exposition (Chicago, 1893), 91; Native Americans at, 156–59, 166–67
Columbus and the Discovery of America (Barnum production), 155
commerce: African American intellectuals on, 67; global, 234; transatlantic, 56–58; in urban public sphere, 31. *See also* culture, commercial
communication: of experience, 276–77; intercultural, 177; non-print, 275; oral, 170; among social groups, 274
communication systems: consolidation of, 27; effect on mass culture, 48; revolution in, 73; transatlantic, 57, 315 n.85; transformations in, 25; Wharton on, 219
Coney Island: amusement parks of, 39; disaster spectacles at, 224; Gorky at, 17, 224; hotels of, 89
Conn, Steven, 10–12, 308 n.36
Connolly, "Head-On" Joe, 3
Conrad, Joseph, 296, 315 n.72
consciousness: of alterity, 298; black, 280, 282, 283; cultivation through travel, 52–53, 54, 56–58, 60–61, 66; disruptions to, 293; effect of mass culture on, 90; historical, 250, 251, 253, 257–58; in Henry James's works, 134, 135, 136; William James on, 136, 268, 342 n.43; literary, 49, 223, 298–99; materiality of, 248; national, 301; postliterary forms of, 297–98; racial, 60; role of social class in, 252; and sensory experience, 277; in *Souls of Black Folk*, 284, 285; women's, 135–40, 144, 146, 324 n.44
consumerism: in Chopin's fiction, 143; disruption of social order, 16; mass, 262; in public sphere, 148. *See also* culture, commercial

352   Index

Coolidge, Archibald, 238
Cooper, Anna Julia, 316 n.96; *A Voice from the South*, 61
corpses, beautiful, topos of, 132–33, 134, 137
Corrothers, James, "A Man They Didn't Know," 215
Crane, Stephen, 295–97; on artistic consciousness, 297; *Maggie: A Girl of the Streets*, 296
Crary, Jonathan, 263, 265; *In the Conservatory*, 136–37
crashes: in modernist fiction, 222; staged, 1, 2–3; in Wharton's writings, 21, 221–22, 226, 229–33, 246, 305 n.14
Crawford, Francis Marion, 34
criticism, literary, 73; realist principles of, 87–88
Crummell, Alexander: and high culture, 62–64; transatlanticism of, 64; travel writing of, 67. Works: *America and Africa*, 61; "The Attitude of the American Mind Toward Negro Intellect," 64, 65; "The Destined Superiority of the Negro," 62; *The Future of Africa*, 61, 62
Crush, William George, 1, 2
Crystal Palace (New York), 28
cultural institutions: in *A Modern Instance*, 88–89; social hierarchies in, 15–16
culture: analytic, 10–12; and anarchy, 69; black urban, 6, 203–6, 209–10; European, 29, 51; experiencing subjects of, 20; liberal theories of, 318 n.22; of money, 98; Native American, 14; role of race in, 69; and social justice, 69–70; and the state, 76–78; value of facts in, 1, 319 n.45. *See also* mass culture
culture, aesthetic, 72–73; civic promotion of, 76–77; Howells on, 86
culture, American: African American participation in, 69, 77; class competition in, 311 n.24; commercial values in, 235, 236; feminization of, 120; global influence of, 7–8; improvement campaigns in, 73–75; Henry James on, 307 n.24; postbellum, 30–31, 71, 311 n.24; post-Custer, 152; post-liberal, 250; stratification of, 71; unity in, 105; Wharton's view of, 235–36
culture, commercial: African Americans and, 189–90, 211; American preference for, 101; amusement parks in, 40; capitalism in, 17; in civil society, 118; competition with literary realism, 79–81, 84–85, 89–90, 94; desire in, 147, 148, 326 n.64; disparities in, 290–91; icons of, 128; as knowledge site, 17; of late nineteenth century, 303 n.4; in *A Modern Instance*, 82; opportunity in, 19–20; power of, 4; sensationalism of, 248; shaping of reality, 25, 196; spectacle in, 37–38; state control of, 318 n.22; Twain on, 101; in the United States, 235, 236; Wharton on, 219; women's appreciation of, 144–45. *See also* mass culture
culture, high: acquisition habits in, 29–30, 63; African American intellectuals and, 62–64; agencies of, 76–78, 79; analytic instinct in, 13; Anglo-American, 318 n.20; appropriation of, 53; autonomy of, 25; capitalism in, 20; class power through, 10; consciousness in, 52–54, 56–58; Dewey on, 278; diffusion of, 76; European influence on, 29, 51; experience outside of, 269–72; institutionalization of, 9; inwardness of, 80; labor and, 270–71, 274; mass culture and, 8–9, 12–13, 26–29, 111, 279, 304 n.12; in *A Modern Instance*, 85–86; postmodern art in, 37; in public sphere, 169; race and, 60–61, 66; as social control, 9–10, 75, 307 n.29; transatlantic, 63, 64, 65; working class view of, 78
culture, literary: analysis in, 20–21; dissemination through periodicals, 78, 79; emergence of, 24; kinetic experience in, 21; mass culture and, 5, 48, 99, 306n. 19; models of reason in, 260; in *A Modern Instance*, 88; nationalist, 284; pedagogical projects of, 105; role in public reason, 5, 168–69; social agency and, 104

Daklugie, Asa, 180
dance, African American, 207–8; cakewalk, 195, 205, 207
danger: in modernity, 227, 245; in Wharton's fiction, 230–31. *See also* disasters
Darwinism, 256–57
Daston, Lorraine, 289
Dawes Act, 167
DeLillo, Don, 230
department stores: design innovations in, 7; desire in, 298; displays in, 26, 89; phantasmagoric environment of, 147; theatricality of, 109; women's consciousness and, 144
desire: in commercial culture, 147, 148, 326

n.64; in department stores, 298; Dewey on, 281; expressiveness of, 272
Dewey, John, 7, 18; on amusements, 260; William James's influence on, 264; on pleasurable sensation, 261–62; on realism, 247; *Thought News* project, 19
Dickens, Charles, train accident of, 223, 224
difference: discouragement of, 74–75; in realism, 71–72, 99, 317 n.9
diplomacy: European, 161; kinesthetic medium of, 161–62; Native American, 152, 153, 158–66, 172, 177, 327 n.5, 328 nn. 15–16, 18; in public sphere, 162, 164–65; sensory experience of, 164, 166
disasters: aesthetics of, 220, 225; in American literature, 4–5; fictional, 230; literary pleasure in, 225, 226; mass mediation of, 3, 225–26; poetics of, 221; psychological effects of, 222–26, 232–33; staged, 1, 2–3, 38, 220, 224, 337 n.14; Wharton's tropes of, 226, 232–33; in Zola's fiction, 223–24
discernment, 82; of incongruities, 302; in realism, 82, 133, 249, 293
distinction, realist, 99, 317 n.9; versus conspicuousness, 30–31; discernment in, 82, 133, 249, 293; in Howells's fiction, 86, 98; understanding of marriage, 90
divorce, in Wharton's fiction, 241, 244, 245
Dole, William, 160, 328 n.16
Douglass, Frederick, 209
DuBois, W. E. B., 7; on aesthetic apprehension, 66–67, 68; on American economic empire, 29; on color line, 59–60; disaster fables of, 4; on double consciousness, 280, 282, 283, 344 n.58; exile in Africa, 50; and William James, 280; literary analyses by, 19; on lynching, 280, 285; montage images of, 284, 285; museum tropes of, 23; pragmatism of, 281, 344 n.57; prisoner metaphor of, 287; scholar's study of, 286; and social science, 345 n.63; transatlantic travel of, 66–67. Works: "Criteria of Negro Art," 66; *Dusk of Dawn*, 286–87; *The Souls of Black Folk*, 69, 77, 280, 284–86, 305 n.17; "A Vacation Unique," 213–15
Dunbar, Paul Laurence, 6, 61; dialect verse of, 189, 203, 205; musical theater career of, 205–6, 336 n.28; travel by, 65; use of "low" aesthetic, 206. Works: *Clorindy*, 205–7; *The Sport of the Gods*, 203–6, 217

Dunbar-Nelson, Alice, 206
Dvorak, Antonin, 15
Dwight, John Sullivan, 70

eagerness, expressivity of, 272, 273
Eakins, Thomas, 11
Eastman, Charles Alexander, 7; *From the Deep Woods to Civilization*, 169–70; on Indian shows, 180; local color fiction of, 170
Eastman, Elaine Goodale, 170
Engle, C. H., 156
Enlightenment: human understanding in, 51; public sphere of, 76; social surveillance in, 13
Ethnological Congress of the Barnum and London Circus (1884), 155
Europe: aesthetics of imperialism in, 234–35; art of, 28–29, 56–58; culture of, 29, 51; diplomacy of, 161; imperialism of, 234–35, 238–39, 328 n.15; influence on Chopin, 140; literary realism of, 122, 322 n.15; museums of, 26, 52–55
evangelization, Christian, 61
exhibitions, commercial, 25–26. *See also* museums
expansionism, American, 234, 238, 340 n.13
expatriates, American, in Paris, 237–38

femininity: and publicity on, 115, 118; spiritualized, 112, 113, 114
feminism: and capitalism, 326n. 64; championing of Chopin, 148, 150
Ferris, William, 66; *The African Abroad*, 63
fiction: autonomy of, 46; Howells's understanding of, 85; William James on, 261; as museum exhibit, 22. *See also* realism, literary
fiction, African American, 6; counterfactual worlds in, 213–17; dialect in, 191–92; genres of, 213; occult in, 192, 193; romances, 212; science in, 213–17. *See also* literature, African American
fiction, American: cultural pedagogy in, 12–13; domestic, 117, 123, 213, 242; expert representations in, 24; local color, 140–43, 146, 170; marriage in, 82, 84, 90; museum tropes in, 23; plantation, 142, 191; reform, 33; regional, 127–28, 140–43, 146; transatlantic marriage in, 58–59; urban exposés in, 34. *See also* realism, literary

354   Index

fiction, commercial: distribution of, 34; historical, 34–35; Henry James on, 12, 107, 108; of late nineteenth century, 32–35; romances, 34, 35, 212, 312 n.36, 319 n.35; social engagement in, 33; technology in, 34; Twain's use of, 103, 105, 320 n.66; working-girl, 33. *See also* mass print media
Field, Cyrus, 57
Flaubert, Gustave, 122, 140; James on, 314 n.64
force: Henry Adams's topos of, 258–60; in mass entertainment, 260
fourth dimension, 214; of world history, 217
Frankfurt school (of criticism), 73
Frick, Henry Clay, 56–57
Fullerton, Morton, 238

Galison, Peter, 289
Gebhard, Caroline, 192, 335 n.27
gender: in literary realism, 110–11, 112, 123; in representation of subjectivity, 128–29; scientific study of, 131; shifts in norms, 114–15
Geronimo, 14; appeal to Roosevelt, 183–85, 186; "book-making" by, 180, 182, 186; captivity of, 180–83, 186; celebrity of, 176, 179–87; charisma of, 7; entrepreneurial skill of, 182; knowledge of public culture, 180; performance by, 185–86; photographs of, 181, 333 n.77, 348 n.2; religious conversion of, 183; at St. Louis World's Fair, 182, 183, 185, 333 n.72
Ghost Dance movement, 329 n.2, 331 n.48
Giddens, Anthony, 220, 240
Gilded Age: capitalism of, 97; materialism of, 20; pragmatism of, 266; success stories of, 93
Gilman, Charlotte Perkins: study of science, 138–39; "The Yellow Wallpaper," 137–39, 325 nn.50–51
Glazener, Nancy, 71, 72
Goethe, Johann Wolfgang von, William James's study of, 248, 264, 266
Goode, George Brown, 22, 77, 80; "museum idea" of, 87
Gorky, Maxim, on kinetic experience, 17, 224
Gowongo, Leo, 6, 188–89, 202
Great Britain, "race union" with United States, 59
Griggs, Sutton, *Imperium in Imperio*, 215
Gunning, Tom, 253–54, 303 n.3

Habermas, Jürgen: on bourgeois sphere, 346 n.7; on Enlightenment, 76; on mass culture, 5–6, 20, 33, 289–90; on mass media, 306 n.21; on postliterary era, 9; on print culture, 168–69; on public knowledge, 312 n.26; on public sphere, 293, 304 n.4, 347 n.7
Hafen, Jane, 175
Haggard, Rider, 35
Hansen, Miriam, 20, 276, 295, 309 n.44, 326 nn.64–65; on cinematic public, 347 n.9; on disjunction, 289
Hay, John, 253, 340 n.13
Haymarket riot (1887), 99
Hegel, Georg Wilhelm Friedrich, 247
Higginson, Henry Lee, 73
Higginson, Thomas Wentworth, 305 n.14; folk songs of, 190, 191; "A Plea for Culture," 70
Hinton, C. H., "What Is the Fourth Dimension?" 214
homosexuality, cultural prohibitions on, 48
Hopkins, Pauline, 6; *Of One Blood*, 216–17; *A Primer of Facts Pertaining to the Early Greatness of the African Race*, 216
Howard, June, 55
Howells, William Dean: analytic school of, 11, 86, 291, 293, 307 n.32, 320 n.61; on Chesnutt, 197, 200–201; class anxieties in, 97–98; on cultural elevation, 78–79; on cultural knowledge, 81; cultural pedagogy of, 12–13; depiction of class anxieties, 97–98; literary authority of, 42; on mass journalism, 41; museum tropes of, 22; outsider status of, 92–93; realism of, 11, 19, 24, 44, 87, 125, 247, 288, 306 n.24, 308 n.35; on sensation, 24, 25; social vision of, 93; on spectacle, 2, 197, 226; transatlantic travel of, 50; on Twain, 102; on "The Yellow Wallpaper," 138. Works: *Annie Kilburn*, 128, 305 n.13; "At a Dime Museum," 35–39; *Criticism and Fiction*, 80; "Editor's Study" column, 42, 43; *A Hazard of New Fortune*, 99, 288, 291–96, 298; *The Minister's Charge*, 43, 89, 304 n.13; *A Modern Instance*, 82–93, 305 n.13; "The New Taste in Theatricals," 109; *The Rise of Silas Lapham*, 93–99, 320 n.51; *Their Wedding Journey*, 51; *The World of Chance*, 99
How It Feels to Be Run Over (film), 1, 5
hyperstimulation, modern, 248, 267

identity: black, 198, 202, 207, 209, 211, 213, 215–17, 282; cinematic influence on, 309 n.44; civil, 189; collective, 181; family, 241; gender, 109, 112–13, 115, 131; inner, 277; William James on, 267; novelists', 108; political, 326 n.64; public, 178; social, 140, 309 n.44, 347 n.9; spiritual, 216; in travel, 241; in Twain's fiction, 102

identity, national, 27; Henry James on, 301; race and, 202; in realism, 55–56; transatlantic travel and, 50, 55–56

Iggorrotes (Philippine tribe), 185

imaginaries, mass-mediated, 8, 9

imperialism, European, 234–35, 238–39; Native Americans under, 328 n.15

incest, Wharton's tropes of, 242, 245, 339 n.50

incongruity: discernment of, 48, 302, 314 n.61; Henry James on, 288, 298, 300, 302; in postliterary age, 302; understanding of, 288–89, 294

Indian shows. *See* Wild West shows

industrialization: aesthetics of, 11; federations in, 59, 316 n.93

intellectuals, African American: on American commerce, 67; high culture and, 62–64, 66; on mass culture, 189–90; racism and, 60–61

intellectuals, Native American, 7, 14, 166–67; and bourgeois public sphere, 169–70; on mass culture, 175; on performance, 332 n.61; of SAI, 171

irony, Henry Adams's use of, 251, 253, 257, 260

Iroquois Confederacy, 164

Jackson, Gregory, 12

James, Henry: authors' studies on, 45, 46; on collapse of forms, 3, 4, 291; on commercial culture, 19–20, 21, 301; on commercial fiction, 12, 33–34; cultural criticism of, 7; imagination of, 305 n.13; on incongruity, 288, 298, 300, 302; kinetic experience in, 6; on mass print media, 40–41, 45–46, 303 n.4, 314 n.63; on Matthew Arnold, 69; moral dramas of, 100; museum tropes of, 23; naturalism of, 322 n.11; on New Woman, 110, 115; periodical publications of, 22; on publicity, 45, 46, 48–49, 105, 118, 314 n.56; realism of, 54; sensational images of, 299–300; sense of exile, 299; sexuality of, 48; on Spanish-American War, 321 n.74; on spectacle, 27–28; Twain on, 102; use of analysis, 24, 100; on Wharton, 218. Works: *The American*, 23, 54–56; *The American Scene*, 298–302, 348 n.26; "The Art of Fiction," 323 n.19; "The Aspern Papers," 47; *The Bostonians*, 113, 116–18, 120–22, 128; *Daisy Miller*, 128, 133, 134; "The Death of the Lion," 45; *The Golden Bowl*, 57–58; *Italian Hours*, 56; "John Delavoy," 313 n.53; "Lady Barberina," 58–59, 315 n.91; "The Lesson of Balzac," 107; "The Lesson of the Master," 48; "The Passionate Pilgrim," 57; *Portrait of a Lady*, 57, 133–35; *The Princess Cassimassima*, 128; "The Question of the Opportunities," 19, 105; "The Right Real Thing," 46, 47; "The Siege of London," 58; *Small Boys and Others*, 28; *Transatlantic Sketches*, 50–51; *What Maisie Knew*, 241

James, William, 7; on Henry Adams, 250–51; on commercial culture, 16; empiricism of, 263; on human agency, 264; literary references of, 266, 270; on mass culture, 18, 267; pedagogy of, 267, 270; on perceptual experience, 263, 277; pragmatism of, 261, 269; "riven self" trope of, 286; on social redistributions, 20; and *Souls of Black Folk*, 305 n.17; study of Goethe, 248, 264, 266; on wonder-sickness, 4. Works: "On a Certain Blindness in Human Being," 272–75; *Principles of Psychology*, 136, 263–68, 279, 342 n.37; "What Makes a Life Significant?", 269–71; *The Will to Believe*, 268

Jarry, Alfred, 119

Jauss, Hans Robert, 5, 306 n.19

Jim Crow era, 16, 63, 65, 201, 283

Johnson, James Weldon, 203, 205; and black dialect, 335 n.27; law studies of, 210. Works: *Along the Way*, 210; *The Autobiography of an Ex-Colored Man*, 209–12; *Toloso*, 210

Johnson, Rosamond, 210

Joplin, Scott, "Great Crush Collision," 3

Kaplan, Amy, 55, 71, 311 n.22, 313 n.44

Kasson, John, 40, 311 n.24

Kent, Blaine, 181, 182

Kern, Stephen, 18

kinetic experience, 2, 3; Dewey on, 247; high literary culture and, 6, 21; mass appeal of,

kinetic experience (*continued*)
  17; in mass print media, 41; urban, 40. See also sensation; velocity
kinship: destructive, 231; in modernity, 240, 244, 339 n.47; and travel, 241; in Wharton's fiction, 241–46
knowledge: cultural, 81; and pleasure, 277, 344 n.49; public, 312 n.26; scientific pursuit of, 325 n.62
Kracauer, Siegfried, 247, 283; on film, 255, 284, 346 n.68
Kroes, Rob, 27

labor: African American, 64; and high culture, 270–71, 274; unrest, 98
language, historical change in, 31
Leslie's Weekly, "The Blackville Gallery," 189
Levine, Lawrence, 103
Libbey, Laura Jean, 33
liberalism: cultural theories of, 318 n.2; in public sphere, 14; structuring distinctions of, 251; transatlantic, 252
libraries, public and private, 80–81
Lieber, Francis, 113
Lind, Jenny, 112, 117
literature: cultural criticism through, 200; in public culture, 163; social control through, 72; sociology and, 340 n.8; travel and, 49–50
literature, African American, 14, 212–17; dialect, 189, 191–92, 203, 205, 335 n.27; mass culture in, 189–80; role of travel in, 62–64, 66. See also fiction, African American
literature, American: disasters in, 4–5; emerging forms of, 106; multiple values in, 106–7; Native American, 14; shock in, 19; velocity in, 19. See also fiction, American; realism, literary
literature, travel, 50–51, 53–68; African American writers of, 62–64, 66; cultivation of consciousness in, 52–53, 54, 56, 57–58, 60–61, 66; West Africa in, 61–62. See also travel, transatlantic
Little Big Horn, reenactment of, 175–76
Livingston, James, 16, 262, 307 n.30; on cultural history, 312 n.42; on feminism, 326 n.64
Lloyd, David, 77, 318 n.22
Lowell, James Russell, 92; on Howells, 50; *My Study Window*, 42, 43
Luna Park (amusement park), 39

Lyautey, Hubert, 238–39
lynching: in Chesnutt's fiction, 195, 198; DuBois on, 280, 285; William James on, 345 n.60; pleasure in, 280–81; as spectacle, 199

MacIntyre, Alistair, 56, 315 n.83
Manet, Édouard, portraits of women, 136
mannequins, Henry Adams's trope of, 255, 256, 258, 259, 267, 341 n.17
manners: and capitalism, 97; novels of, 35, 230, 231, 242; of transatlantic travel, 66–67
mansions: Barnum's, 95–96; in *The Rise of Silas Lapham*, 96–97
marriage: in mass culture, 90; in *A Modern Instance*, 84, 90; transatlantic, 58–59, 315 n.91; in Wharton's fiction, 241, 243–44
Marx, Karl, 251
mass culture: African American authors on, 189–90; African imagery in, 217; Barnum's influence on, 119; capitalism in, 17–18; censorship of, 75–76; commercial matrix for, 7; in Crane's fiction, 295–96; Dewey on, 279; disasters in, 3, 225–26; economic power of, 279; in *The Education of Henry Adams*, 250; "effectists" of, 81, 103; effect of communications systems on, 48; effect on consciousness, 90; effect on public sphere, 162; effect on women, 113–14; emergence of, 304 n.4; and high culture, 8–9, 12–13, 26–29, 111, 279, 304 n.12; ideological implications of, 326 n.1; imaginative appropriation in, 29–30; and imperialism, 311 n.22; interest in blackness, 203; William James on, 261, 267; versus interior sensibility, 44–45; international industries of, 348 n.30; in Jacksonian democracy, 326 n.1; kinetic experience in, 2, 3; literary analysis of, 6, 7, 37–38; literary culture and, 5, 48, 99, 306 n.19; local color and, 140–41; market for, 33; marriage in, 90; mobility in, 256; Native Americans and, 14, 151, 175; neurological discourse on, 248; power of, 94; pragmatists on, 18, 260–62, 279; profit motive in, 3; publicity in, 47–48, 226; racism in, 326n. 1; realism and, 48, 99; religion in, 12; self-determination in, 20; sensation in, 3, 15, 169; shared perceptions in, 27; socialized identities in, 15–16, 92; social power of, 91; transnational, 118; Twain on, 103; as unifying force, 27; Wharton on, 218;

women in, 110–11. *See also* culture, commercial
mass entertainment, 254; as artifact, 53; and with commerce, 163; force in, 260
mass print media, 7; acculturation through, 85; versus authors' studies, 42; disorientation in, 41; intellectuals on, 311 n.16; Henry James on, 40–41, 45–46, 303 n.4, 314 n.63; William James on, 268; kinetic experience in, 41; mediated intimacy in, 48; modernity in, 35; of nineteenth century, 32–35; proliferation of, 27; quantity of, 105–6, 108; sensationalism in, 32; social relations and, 34–35; success stories in, 97. *See also* fiction, commercial
Mazeppa; or, The Wild Horse of Tartary, 132–33, 138
McGurl, Mark, 71, 72, 295; on difference, 317 n.9; on literary prestige, 100, 308 n.35
Mead, George Herbert: William James's influence on, 264; model of self, 282; on the novel, 248; "The Social Self," 261
Melville, Herman, *Moby Dick*, 89
memory: involuntary, 7, 278, 302, 347 n.9; of pre-industrial world, 142; textual sites of, 212
Menken, Adah Isaacs, 132–33, 138
mental life, sensory determination of, 249–50
Metropolitan Museum of Art (New York), 76
middle class, improvement of, 72, 75–76. *See also* bourgeoisie; women, middle-class
Mill, John Stuart, 252
Miller, Kelly, 61
millionaires: boasting by, 95–96; journalistic portraits of, 93; in *The Rise of Silas Lapham*, 94
minstrelsy, 199; Chesnutt's depiction of, 195, 196, 198; racism of, 206
mobility: literary autonomy and, 49–50; in mass culture, 256
modernism: Henry Adams's, 250; in Crane's fiction, 296–97; estrangement in, 295; high, 9; readerly intellection in, 72
modernity: in Henry Adams's works, 254; African Americans in, 283; in amusement parks, 40; collapse of forms in, 3, 4; danger in, 227, 245, 337 n.27; kinship in, 240, 244, 339 n.47; in mass print media, 35; in *A Modern Instance*, 87; Native American engagement with, 178–79; neurological, 247–49, 260–79, 282, 294, 339 n.3, 343 n.43; publicity in, 46; sensation in, 4, 16, 247, 248; sexuality in, 240; travel in, 231, 237; urban, 196; velocity in, 219; in Wharton's fiction, 244–45; women's status in, 128
Mohawk embassy (London, 1710), 163–64, 329 n.26
Montezuma, Carlos, 170–71
Moore, G. E., 261
morality: in art, 78; in realism, 92
Morocco, under French rule, 238–39
Morrison, Toni, 213
Mumford, Louis, 266
museum idea, 87; Barnum and, 25; as literary idea, 22–24
museums: aesthetic purity of, 22; amusement parks and, 26; circulating collections of, 77; curiosities in, 88–89; dime, 35–39, 254, 291; early, 88; representative specimens in, 87, 88; as secular temples, 23–24; theatricality of, 25
museums, European, 26, 52–53, 55; Henry James's depiction of, 54
museums, metropolitan, 26, 76–77; and analytic culture, 12; mimetic aspects of, 29

National Institute of Arts and Letters, 303 n.1
nationalism: black, 60–61, 62–63; high art and, 70–71, 73; in Indian shows, 331 n.46; Henry James on, 301; literary, 70, 92, 330 n.40; literary meaning in, 54–55
Native Americans: amnesty for, 154; Barnum's exploitation of, 152–55, 163–64; communication with Anglo-Americans, 170, 171; deculturation of, 172; diplomatic efforts of, 152, 153, 158–66, 172, 177, 327 n.5, 328 nn. 15–16, 18; education of, 167, 170, 172–75; encroachment on land of, 333 n.77; engagement with modernity, 178–79; under European imperialism, 328 n.15; experience of public culture, 165; freedom of, 301–2; intellectual rights of, 168; justice for, 160, 162; media representation of, 151; national symbolism of, 156–57; performative expression of, 178–80, 185, 332 n.61, 334 n.7; primitivist depictions of, 171, 180; public agency of, 180; sensory reception of, 160–61; thought worlds of, 169–70; as visual objects, 174. *See also* intellectuals, Native American; Wild West shows

naturalism: in American realism, 55; women and, 322 n.11
nervous system, effect of velocity on, 222–23. See also modernity, neurological
New Negro, 188, 334 n.2
newspapers: as burlesque, 83, 84; cost of, 34; of late nineteenth century, 32–33; sensationalism in, 82, 83, 84. See also mass print media
Norton, Charles Eliot, "The Intellectual Life of America," 32, 33

Olmstead, Frederick Law, 70
orature, Native American, 163, 164, 170, 175, 329 n.25; Geronimo's, 185; instability of forms, 171–72
Orvell, Miles, 196

"Panorama of the Fleet of the Compagnie Générale Transatlantique," 65, 317 n.100
panoramas, 276, 343 n.47; in Crane's fiction, 296; mechanical, 65–66; of Old South, 196
Paris (luxury liner), 228
Paris World Exhibition (1900), 258, 259
Parker, Arthur C., 7, 14, 167–68; Iroquois legend publications of, 172
Parker, Ely, 178
Parkhurst, Charles H., 202
Parsons, Elsie Clews, *The Family*, 131
Patten, Simon, 273, 343 n.44
Penn, William, 158, 328 n.14
performance: culture of, 120–21, 162–63; human agency and, 121; Native American, 178–80, 185–86, 332 n.61, 334 n.7; in public culture, 163; Twain's use of, 101, 102, 103; by women, 112
performers, African American, 188, 202, 203, 209; innovations of, 208, 346 n.71; respectability of, 207; typecasting of, 210
periodicals: dissemination of literary culture, 78, 79; promotion of realism, 81; women regionalists in, 127–28
Perry, Thomas Sergeant, 74
Phelps, Elizabeth Stuart, *The Story of Avis*, 123–24
Philadelphia Centennial fair (1876), 60
philanthropy, social control through, 73, 75–76
Photographing a Female Crook (film), 288, 289, 290
Pierce, C. S., 261

plantation fiction, 142, 191
pleasure: economies of, 273, 274, 277, 283, 302, 343 n.44; multiple levels of, 37; racist, 281, 283, 284, 346 n.71; relationship to knowledge, 277, 344 n.49
Plessy v. Ferguson (1896), 199
Pokagon, Simon: on civilization, 157–58; Columbian Exhibition speech, 156–59, 166–67, 327 n.10; death of, 166
posters, lithographic, 117–18; aesthetic of, 119–20
Potawatomi tribe, Christianity of, 156
pragmatism, 14, 18, 248, 249; attention in, 265; choice in, 267; classical, 261; European critical theory and, 340 n.7; of Gilded Age, 266; human will in, 265–66; neurological modernity and, 260–79; role of experience in, 342 n.42; self in, 281; sensory perception in, 260
Pratt, Richard Henry, 177, 331 n.49
professionals, nineteenth-century: literary culture and, 308 n.35; prestige of, 79; travel by, 50
progress, human, universality of, 252, 253
public discourse, poetics of, 166
publicity: commercial forms of, 20; in elite society, 30–31; female, 325 n.50; and femininity, 115, 118; Henry James on, 45, 46, 48–49, 105, 118, 314 n.56; in mass culture, 47–48, 226; in *A Modern Instance*, 82; in modernity, 46; and state power, 177; technologically mediated, 276; transformations in, 290; of the wish, 284; for women authors, 112, 114
public reason, 31, 163; expansion of boundaries, 273; films as site of, 347 n.10; neurological modernity and, 343 n.43; public relations and, 292; role in literary culture, 5, 168–69, 292
publics: academic, 171; agency of, 309 n.48; cinematic, 347 n.9; disparate, 103; emergent, 5; pan-Indian, 151, 166, 171, 180, 329 n.29, 332 n.91; postliterary, 290, 295. See also reading publics
public sphere: African Americans and, 188, 283; anarchy in, 72–73; black, 64–65; bourgeois, 5, 20, 76, 168–70, 261, 289, 294, 346 n.7; commercial publicity in, 20; communicative modes in, 6; composite, 250, 275, 277, 340 n.11; consensus in, 90; consumer-

ism in, 148; diplomacy in, 164–65; effect of mass culture on, 162; ejection of analysis from, 293–94; of Enlightenment, 76; exclusions from, 290; Geronimo in, 182–83; high culture in, 169; incongruities in, 294; liberal, 14; middle-class women in, 109–13, 116–18, 122, 138, 322 n.11; Native Americans in, 151, 169–70, 176; print culture of, 168–69; private sphere and, 48, 58; race politics in, 63; reason in, 5, 163, 168–69; refeudalization of, 293, 344 n.57; social imaginary in, 65; transcultural, 159; urban, 31
Putnam, Frank, 168

race: high culture and, 60–61, 66; Henry James on, 59, 301, 315 n.90; politics of, 63; role in culture, 69, 326 n.1; role in national identity, 202; transatlantic travel and, 59–68; Victorian idea of, 62
racism: African American intellectuals and, 60–61; in amusements, 345 n.62; in depiction of African Americans, 202; in mass culture, 326 n.1; in minstrelsy, 206; pleasure in, 281, 283, 284, 346 n.71
railroad travel: in early films, 303 n.1; in postbellum United States, 141–42; velocity in, 227. *See also* train wrecks
Rancière, Jacques, 294
rationality: Enlightenment, 31; William James on, 277; in Victorian literature, 308 n.39
reading publics: bourgeois, 289; communication among, 107; expansion of, 105; middle-class, 261; public reason of, 293; shared significance among, 108; women in, 111
realism, literary, 14; aesthetics of, 91; African American alternatives to, 215–16; analytic, 10–14, 24, 86, 120–21, 218, 293; anxiety in, 91, 97–98; versus burlesque, 83; Chesnutt's use of, 195, 196, 197, 200, 201; competing literary movements and, 319 n.31; competition with commercial culture, 79–80, 81, 84–85, 89–90, 94; contradictions in, 71; cultural authority of, 100; cultural knowledge in, 81; democratic nature of, 11, 292; Dewey on, 247; difference in, 71–72, 99; European, 122, 322 n.15; Foucaultian critics on, 72; gender in, 110–11, 112, 123; historical measurement in, 87; Howells's, 11, 19, 24, 44, 87, 125, 247, 288, 306 n.24, 308 n.35; intellectual prestige of, 308 n.34; marriage in, 82, 84, 90; masculine, 317 n.7; and mass culture, 48, 99; morality in, 92; naturalism in, 55; observers in, 55; portrayal of United States in, 323 n.25; poster art and, 119; promotion by periodicals, 81; psychological depth in, 120, 121; race in, 335 n.20; readers and, 54, 92; science and, 87, 91; self-determination in, 121; social questions in, 71, 72, 92; social science imagery in, 277; spectacle and, 81–82, 89–90; Twain's engagement with, 101, 102; women authors of, 122–28, 139–40, 148, 149. *See also* fiction
regionalism, in American fiction, 126–28, 140–43, 146
Repplier, Agnes, 74, 91
Roach, Joseph, 152, 181, 329 n.25; on Buffalo Bill, 331 n.46; *Cities of the Dead*, 162–63; on Native American diplomacy, 164
Robertson, Roland, 220
romances, fictional, 34, 35, 312 n.36, 319 n.35; by African Americans, 212
Roosevelt, Theodore (president), 269; Geronimo's appeal to, 183–85, 186; inauguration of, 176, 179–80, 184; use of spectacle, 176
Roosevelt, Theodore, Sr., 26
Roscoe, William, 91
Rourke, Constance, 161
Russell, Bertrand, 261
Rydell, Robert, 27

Samuel Coleridge-Taylor Society, 15
Sand Creek massacre, 154; death toll at, 327 n.6
Schivelbusch, Wolfgang, 223, 227
science: in African American fiction, 213–17; and literary realism, 87, 91; role in social imaginary, 262–63; women authors' use of, 129–30, 138–39
sea, in Chopin's fiction, 146
Sedgwick, Eve, 48
self: William James on, 286; male bourgeoisie, 342 n.37; Mead's model of, 282; in pragmatism, 281
self-determination: in mass culture, 20; in realism, 121
self-reflection, women's, 137, 140. *See also* consciousness, women's
Selfridge, Harry Gordon, 144

sensation: at amusement parks, 39–40; communicative nature of, 272; Howells on, 24, 25; in mass amusements, 254; in mass culture, 3, 15, 169; in modernity, 4, 16, 247, 248; pleasurable, 261–62; scientific study of, 263; unity with thought, 264; urban, 248; of velocity, 269, 270, 271; visual, 324 n.48; wealth in, 310 n.57

sensationalism: of commercial culture, 248; in mass print, 32; in museums, 25; in newspapers, 82, 83, 84

Silko, Leslie Marmon, 187, 333 n.78

Simmel, Georg, 236, 247, 310 n.57; "The Metropolis and Mental Life," 248

Singer, Ben, 247, 248, 340 n.6

Sitting Bull: death of, 331 n.48; false interpreters of, 176–77; in Wild West shows, 178, 331 n.48

Society of American Indians (SAI), 167, 330 n.39; intellectuals of, 171

South, the: in Chopin's fiction, 142; civil relations of, 193; Northern interest in, 190–97; in plantation fiction, 142, 191

spectacle: Henry Adams's enjoyment of, 253, 254; Chesnutt's depiction of, 198; in commercial culture, 28–37; effect on aesthetics, 29; Howells on, 2, 197, 226; in journalism, 199; non-narrative, 254; poetics of, 44; private studies and, 35–39, 44–46; versus reading, 38, 39; realist fiction and, 81–82, 89–90; riots as, 199–200; urban, 89; Wharton on, 219, 337 n.4. *See also* mass entertainment; Wild West shows

Spencer, Herbert, 59

Spofford, Harriet Prescott, 123

Standing Bear, Henry, 178, 331 n.51

Standing Bear, Luther, 176; authority as chief, 332 n.59; on citizenship, 179; on mass print, 332 n.57; *My People the Sioux*, 177; view of Indian shows, 178, 179

Starr, Paul, 27

Stead, W. T., 59, 315 n.91

Stedman, Edmund Clarence, 50, 127, 304 n.11

stereographs, 35, 65

St. Louis World's Fair, Geronimo at, 182, 183, 185, 333 n.72

Strychacz, Thomas, 71

subjectivity: African American, 212, 282; civil orientation of, 343 n.45; mass, 3, 225, 230; in mass culture, 256; neurological, 259, 260; postliterary, 225; in Western thought, 341 n.27

Tanner, Henry, *The Raising of Lazarus*, 65

theater, black, 205–6, 336 n.28; commercial nature of, 207–8

Thomas, Paul, 77, 318 n.22

Thompson, Lydia, 83

Thrailkill, Jane, 138, 338 n.31, 342 n.43; on Twain, 103, 321 n.69

Titanic disaster, cultural effect of, 338 n.26

Tolstoy, Leo, 270, 271

Trachtenberg, Alan, 26–27, 332 n.60

train wrecks: psychology of, 222–23, 231; staged, 1, 2–3, 38

travel: colonized people and, 233; disaster in, 221, 233; fashion and, 236; literature and, 49–50; military ventures and, 228; in modernity, 231, 237; by professional classes, 50

travel, transatlantic, 50–51; acquisitive mind in, 54, 63; aesthetic disavowal in, 56; African American literature and, 62–64, 66; capitalism in, 56–57; DuBois's, 66–67; high literature and, 50; increase in, 227–28; in Henry James, 56; kinship and, 241; manners of, 66–67; marriage and, 58–59; national identity and, 55–56; pursuit of cultivation through, 52–53; race and, 59–68; shared experience of, 50; wealth powering, 228, 229; in Wharton's works, 219, 220–22, 229, 236–38, 241–43, 246

treaties: as intellectual forms, 161; intercultural nature of, 329 n.21; with Native Americans, 151, 158, 159, 161, 164, 175, 327 n.5, 328 n.16; performative dimensions of, 329 n.20

Twain, Mark: comic techniques of, 101–2; engagement with realism, 101, 102; Howells and, 24; *Huckleberry Finn*, 103, 104, 105; literary analysis by, 19, 102, 320 n.61; newspaper career of, 103; psychological humor of, 321 n.69; reversals of meaning in, 104–5; use of performance culture, 101, 102, 103

United States: crowd civilization in, 75; economic empire of, 29; global influence of, 7–8, 59, 234, 235, 238, 311 n.22; Native American policy of, 153–54, 158–61, 167, 175, 176; "race union" with Britain, 59

universalism, 13

urban culture, black, 6, 203, 204–6, 209–10

velocity: conveyance of meaning, 271; William James's sensation of, 269, 270, 271; in modernity, 219; and nervous system, 222–23; in transatlantic travel, 228; Wharton's tropes of, 218, 219, 221, 226, 228, 230, 243, 246

Wagner, Richard, DuBois on, 280, 285
Walker, Aida Overton, 6, 202, 205, 207, 211; dance of, 208; on racial prejudice, 208
Walker, George, 205
Wallace, Lew, 34
Warner, Michael, 3, 225, 346 n.7; on public agency, 309 n.48; on public discourse, 166
Warren, Kenneth, 71
Warrior, Robert Allen, 171, 329 n.29
Washington, D.C., Native American delegation to, 153
Weber, Max, 8
Weekly Museum (periodical), 22
Weir, James, 110, 113
Wharton, Edith, 7; analytical fiction of, 337 n.1; aversion to crowds, 41, 313 n.44; childhood of, 234–35; disaster tropes of, 226, 232–33; divorce in works of, 241, 244, 245; incest tropes of, 242, 245, 339 n.50; love of speed, 218, 219; marriage of, 240; on mass publicity, 226; on mechanical power, 233–34; on modernity, 244–45; motorcar of, 237; naturalism of, 322 n.11; residence in France, 237–38; social portraits of, 99; study of social relations, 130; use of science, 129; velocity tropes of, 218, 219, 221, 226, 228, 230, 243, 246; view of American culture, 235–36. Works: *The Age of Innocence*, 42–43; *A Backward Glance*, 234–35; *The Children*, 241, 243, 244; *The Custom of the Country*, 56, 128, 218, 236; "False Dawn," 74, 79; *Glimpses of the Moon*, 244; *The House of Mirth*, 30–32, 129, 220–22, 226, 228–30, 231–33; *Life and I*, 235, 236; *The Mother's Recompense*, 233, 242–44; *Summer*, 231; *The Touchstone*, 57; *Travel in Morocco*, 238–39; *Twilight Sleep*, 244–46, 339 n.50; *The Writing of Fiction*, 130
Wharton, Theodore, 240
White, Richard Grant, 84
white supremacy, 199, 200, 215, 326 n.1
Whitman, Walt: on aesthetic understanding, 52, 55; literary culture and, 273–74; nature in, 146–47, 148; postliterary expressivity of, 343 n.48; readership of, 274–75; on sensory experience, 275; transmission of experience, 275–76
Wild West shows, 7, 14, 21, 175–80, 179, 330 nn.43–44, 331 nn. 46, 48–49, 51; allegory in, 175–76; diplomacy in, 162; Indian agents and, 177, 178; nationalism in, 27, 331 n.46; Native American critique of, 177–78; Sioux in, 175, 331 n.44; Sitting Bull in, 178, 331 n.48; state power and, 177, 178, 180
Williams, Bert, 205
Wilmington, N.C., racial violence in, 194, 196, 335 n.17
Woman Question, 71, 110
women: aesthetic pleasures of, 144; agency of, 136, 149; in antebellum era, 112; autonomy of, 240; and commercial culture, 144–45; consciousness of, 135–40, 144, 146, 324 n.44; corpse topos of, 132–33, 134, 137; desire of, 147, 148; empirical representation of, 132; erotic agency of, 148–49; ethnography of, 131–32; hysterical, 137–38, 324 n.47; lecturers, 112; and naturalism, 322 n.11; poster beauties, 117–18; representations of, 111; as scientific object, 130–32; self-reflection by, 137, 140; status in modernity, 128; suffering of, 124–25; taxonomy of, 131. *See also* authors, women
women, middle-class: agency of, 149; mass culture and, 113–14; in public sphere, 109–13, 116–18, 122, 138, 322 n.11; in Wharton's works, 231
Woolson, Constance Fenimore, 135; literary success of, 126–27; realism of, 124, 125, 127. Works: *Anne*, 127; "At the Chateau of Corinne," 127; "Miss Grief," 124–27; "The Street of the Hyacinth," 127
Wordsworth, William, 274; author's study of, 42
Wounded Knee massacre, 167; film re-creations of, 177–78

Yates, Edmund, 313 n.52; *Celebrities at Home*, 44
Yellow Robe, Chauncey, 151; "The Menace of the Wild West Show," 177–78

Zola, Emile, 298; *La Bête Humaine*, 223–24

Acknowledgments

I have received vital help at all stages of the unusual genealogy of this book. Its origins lie in Sacvan Bercovitch's invitation to contribute to *The Cambridge History of American Literature.* Saki's ability to uncover relations between the literary and the historical remains the gold standard; aspiring to meet that standard was a challenge and an inspiration. I also received encouragement at important junctures from Susan Mizruchi and Richard Brodhead. I am grateful to Cambridge University Press for permission to draw on my contribution to the *History,* which, with the addition of four new chapters and the thorough revision of what remains, is now a work much changed from the earlier study in both substance and argument.

It has been a delight to work with the University of Pennsylvania Press in producing *Frantic Panoramas.* Jerry Singerman, my editor, has been astute and unfailingly generous. He has also been exceptionally patient as this study grew and was transformed beyond what either of us had anticipated. Erica Ginsburg and Jennifer Backer supplied editorial acuity that was much appreciated. Detailed reader's reports from Phillip Barrish and Mary Esteve offered critical insight as well as practical suggestions; I availed myself of the wisdom of both.

I am grateful for the support I received from the University of Pennsylvania while working on this book. Past and present graduate students played a crucial role in deepening my account of the generative relations between literary writing and mass culture. A special debt is owed Justine Murison and Mark Sample, whose research in the archives of turn-of-the-century mass culture introduced me to two of the figures I examine here. Martha Schoolman was and is an astute reader who has earned her reputation for improving others' drafts. Kendall Johnson and Mark Rifkin were intrepid guides to several questions in Native American studies. Hannah Wells was an especially helpful interlocutor on the topic of pragmatism, and Amina Gautier was always ready and willing to talk about Chesnutt.

Many colleagues at Penn have given direct and indirect support to this study. Amy Kaplan, Max Cavitch, Jim English, and Peter Decherney gave me their books, shared their ideas, and supplied sage advice. Comments from Heather Love and Josephine Park helped me discover solutions to lingering critical problems. Tim Powell offered a thoughtful response to an early version of my chapter on the Native public sphere. I owe much to colleagues and friends in other institutions who extended invitations to present my work or who helped me feel intellectually recharged in ways large and small: Chris Looby (original lunch companion), Bethany Schneider, Julia Stern, Chris Castiglia, Hester Blum, Mark Eaton, Paul Gilmore, Bill Brown, Jonathan Auerbach, Robert Levine, Sandra Gunning, Gordon Hutner, Dale Bauer, Greg Pingree, Jeffory Clymer, Wai Chee Dimock, and Michael Warner. In addition to his good offices as a reader, Greg Jackson engineered more than one visit to places that featured a warm climate and delightfully smart people. Elaine Freedgood asked pivotal questions that made walking in Scottish hills or Paris gardens that much more enjoyable.

By making life a happy passage, my family has made work more rewarding and a lot less taxing. My parents, Barbara and Joseph Bentley, and my sisters and their families continue to offer much valued support. The Ulrich family is unmatched in the ranks of in-laws. Jamie Bentley Ulrich and Nathan Ulrich have brought joy and a great deal of fun. I owe the most to Karl Ulrich, to whom I have dedicated this book with deepest gratitude.